A History of the English Church

Edited by the late Very Rev. W. R. W. STEPHENS, D.D., F.S.A.,
Dean of Winchester,
and the Rev. WILLIAM HUNT, M.A.

VI

THE ENGLISH CHURCH

FROM THE ACCESSION OF CHARLES I.
TO THE DEATH OF ANNE

THE ENGLISH CHURCH

FROM THE ACCESSION OF CHARLES I.
TO THE DEATH OF ANNE
(1625-1714)

BY THE

REV. WILLIAM HOLDEN HUTTON, B.D.

FELLOW TUTOR AND PRECENTOR OF ST. JOHN'S COLLEGE, OXFORD:
EXAMINING CHAPLAIN TO THE BISHOP OF ELY

London

MACMILLAN AND CO., LIMITED

NEW YORK: THE MACMILLAN COMPANY

1903

PREFACE

THE writer of this book is conscious of the many defects which must needs occur in such an attempt to describe in any detail, and yet in a brief space, so important and critical a period in the history of the English Church; but to avoid misconception he begs that it may be observed that he has studiously restricted his work to the defined limits of the series of which it forms part. He has not written of the history, extremely important though it is during the years here dealt with, of other religious bodies: the history of the historical Church in England, with its continuity of ministry and doctrine, has alone been directly considered. Such a restriction the author believes to have been absolutely necessary in order to present at all truly the history of the English Church as the English Church saw it. And for a similar reason this book has not dealt with Ireland or Scotland, closely though they were connected with England. Nor is it a history of literature, or philosophy, or theology, or music, in relation to the Church.

No one can feel more deeply than the author both his indebtedness to the work of the great historian of the early Stewarts who has recently passed away, and the difficulty of presenting at all an original treatment of a period which has in its earlier years been so fully covered by Dr. Gardiner, and in its later has been treated by Dr. Overton, Dr. Stoughton, and others. That he has omitted much that they have told so well, and that he has tried at different points of the history to direct attention to other views or other aspects, may, he hopes, in the circumstances, be excused. He will not be surprised to learn that he has omitted, in so large a field, much that some readers may think should have found place in his pages. He can only say that he has tried to read the tangled history of the times anew for himself, and to present a true picture of it.

Some pages here and there in the book have previously appeared in *The Guardian* and *The Pilot*, or have been delivered among the lectures at the Laud Commemoration 1895. Parts of Chaps. VIII. IX. and XVIII. have recently been published (during a delay in the publication of this book for which the author is not responsible) in the *Church Quarterly Review*. Due thanks are tendered to the proprietors for their courtesy in allowing the speedy reprint of what was originally designed for this book.

His friend and former pupil, the Rev. S. Leslie Ollard, Vice-Principal of St. Edmund Hall, has most kindly helped the author by looking through the proofs.

CONTENTS

CHAPTER I

THE ACCESSION OF CHARLES I.

THE seventeenth century was a time of crisis, as serious as the Reformation, in the history of the English Church. The masterful and moderating hand of Elizabeth once removed, men began to look out more freely over a wide expanse of thought and life, and to carry the principles which they had adopted into vigorous action. The Thirty Years' War, the suppression of the political and ecclesiastical separation of the Huguenots, and the establishment of Protestant supremacy in the United Provinces, appealed to Englishmen as great religious questions. And in the freedom which they had won for themselves the sharp divisions of opinion in England tended to stand out more clearly. With the reign of Charles I. began the decisive struggle which was to fix the limits of the Reformation, and to determine whether the English Church should maintain the principles of doctrine and order enunciated in the Preface to her Book of Common Prayer and her Ordinal. The divergence between historic, traditional Christianity, with its creeds and its Episcopal system, and the new dogmas and disciplines which had been elaborated in Germany and Switzerland, and which were echoed from many English pulpits, was one which must eventually lead to open conflict. The years from 1625 to 1662 mark the duration of that conflict, and hardly before 1714 had its echoes died away.

In the period of which this book is to treat there is an

S

extraordinary wealth of interest—doctrinal, disciplinary, constitutional, personal.   Much of it must here be passed by with but slight notice, and attention will chiefly be directed to the important principles and the important characters as they are viewed from the standing-point of the Church as a continuous historic body.   The interesting and fruitful history of the societies which now definitely separated from the Church must be put aside ; and, for the same reason, the period of the Church's disestablishment will receive but scant notice. We must be content to trace how events moved, and why, to human view, they moved in the direction which they took.

On March 27, 1625, King James I. passed away at Theobalds.   He made a pious end, spending all his last days in prayer, and receiving absolution and the Holy Communion. His only surviving son watched by him assiduously, and with him the friend for whom the dying king had done so much— George Villiers, Duke of Buckingham.

Clarendon, looking back forty years afterwards, records that Charles, Prince of Wales, succeeded to the crown with as universal a joy in the people as can be imagined,
The accession of Charles I. and in a conjuncture when all the other parts of Christendom were very solicitous of his friendship ; and he refused to look back into the past for the causes of the discontents which were soon to overthrow the monarchy. But the very days of mourning showed the disturbance of popular feeling ; it was whispered that the late king had been poisoned by Buckingham, and eventually his physician, Sir William Paddy, was examined on the matter.   The accusation was, of course, ridiculous, but it showed how popular feeling went.   It was of ill omen for the young king that he so greatly trusted his father's favourite, the object of almost universal distrust and dislike.

On May 1, 1625, the king was married by proxy at Paris to Henrietta Maria, daughter of Henry IV. of France.   On May 7 he attended the solemn funeral of his father in Westminster Abbey, an act of filial piety which was contrary to precedent.   Williams, Bishop of Lincoln and Lord Keeper, preached a sermon on " Great Britain's Solomon."   It was a time of national mourning, for the plague was rife, and a day of public fasting was held on July 2.   When the plague abated it was at last possible for the coronation to take place, and, after a day of thanksgiving on January 29, 1626, the king was crowned on the Feast of the Purification of the Blessed Virgin.

Considerable interest attaches to the coronation of Charles I.   At the crowning of his father the form had been drawn up in haste, and the new king desired that a special revision of the office should be made.   He issued a commission to Abbot, the archbishop, and other prelates, to act in the matter.   His coronation, Feb. 2, 1626.   Of this committee an energetic member was William Laud, Bishop of St. David's, who, from the beginning of the reign, through the influence of the Duke of Buckingham, rose steadily in the king's favour.   Laud also acted a special part in the coronation itself, being appointed to act as deputy for the Dean of Westminster—Williams, Bishop of Lincoln, who was already in disgrace.   The most minute care was taken in the preparation of the form, and the manuscript notes of Laud on the printed text, which are extant, show with how scrupulous an exactness he prepared every detail.   From the consecration of the oil to the ordering of the procession, from the warning of the king on the previous evening to spend his time in contemplation and prayer, down to the provision for his position at every point of the ceremony, all was settled with reference to ancient precedents.   Question was made many years later as to the form of coronation oath which the king took, but it was proved to have been the same that was taken by his father—the form, in fact, which had continued with scarce an alteration of phrase since the days of the old English kings.

In the new king Englishmen saw a man who differed in notable particulars from his father.   Charles had been trained in the doctrine and discipline of the English Church. He was devout, temperate, chaste, serious—they are the very words of a Puritan lady—but reserved. Said a clerical critic, " our sovereign had not the art to please." " A mild and gracious prince, who knew not how to be or to be made great," wrote Laud years later, in the bitterness of his grief at " the murder of Strafford."   Sir Henry Wotton, diplomatist, ecclesiastic, and poet, wrote in 1633 a " panegyrick " of his master, which happily expresses what churchmen thought and courtiers knew about their young king eight years before. "When you had assumed the crown, before all other things there was resplendent in you a religious mind, the support of kingdoms, the joy of good men. The Chapel Royal was never more in order. The number of eminent divines daily increased. Sermons in no age more frequented; in none more learned; and the examples of the prince more effectual than the sermons. No execrations rashly proceeded from your mouth. Your ears abhorring not only any wanton but even the least sordid word." Such Charles seemed to his friends. Difficulties were to disclose weaknesses in his character, adversities to develop its genuine piety. But from first to last the king remained a devoted son of the Church.

He came to the throne with two attachments close to his heart and his mind. The first was the friendship that had begun with his boyhood for George Villiers, Duke of Buckingham, the fascinating "Steenie" of his father, King James. Buckingham's was a charming personality, spoilt by success. He was a man of vicious life but not of vicious heart, one who sinned and repented and sinned again, till he came to his sudden tragic end by the assassin's knife. Those who knew him saw how much good was in him. Laud, to whom he had confessed his sins, prayed constantly that he might be devout in God's truth and Church. He had listened seriously to the controversy held in the presence of his mother between English and Roman divines, and he had formed his opinions on those of the school of Andrewes. It was through him, there can be no doubt, that the new king was led to form the second great attachment of his life, an attachment rather of the mind than of the heart, but one durable in the principles which its influence instilled. On the night before the coronation it was the duty of Laud, as deputy for the Dean of Westminster, to advise the king of his duties and of how to prepare for them. Perhaps it was then that the bishop became the king's confessor. Certainly from that hour they worked hand in hand for Church and State. The great ecclesiastical figure of Charles's reign, overpowering all others by the breadth of his aims and the firmness of his determination, was Laud.

William Laud was born at Reading on October 7, 1573,

His interests and attachments.

" a man of ordinary but very honest birth." He had risen slowly, and not without lapses and disappointments, and through many interesting experiences. As a child he must have been stirred by the national enthusiasm in the days of the Armada. As a boy at St. John's College, Oxford, he had for chamber-fellow a bright lad with strong leanings towards Romanism, who afterwards became a Benedictine, and for tutor one who became a good parish priest and a good bishop, and who taught him to found his studies on " the noble foundations of the Fathers, councils, and the ecclesiastical historians." As a man he had first an academic, then a wider training. In the university he was first scholar, then fellow, of St. John's College, Oxford, and later tutor and proctor. In the world he was chaplain to Charles Blount, Lord Mountjoy, succeeding in the office a brother-fellow of his college. In this post it was that he committed the error which all his life he never ceased to bewail. He married his master to the unhappy lady who had long been his mistress, Penelope, Lady Rich, the " Stella " of Philip Sidney's romantic verse, a divorced woman, whom the law of the Church would not suffer to wed. " Serving my ambition and the sins of others," was his own sad comment on the act. Yet it is significant that he studied ancient authorities on the subject of divorce, both before and after his act ; and when he concluded that he was wrong he honestly expressed it. " The authority of the canon law, true, to putting away his wife, but neither silent nor unexpressed to marrying again," he wrote in his comment on the Earl of Devonshire's tract, written after Lord Mountjoy had been raised in the peerage. Thus Laud's first contact with the world was unfortunate. In the university, too, he was not at his ease. He had become a definite and active opponent of the Calvinistic teaching, and he had suffered, as the restorers of old paths so often suffer. In dissertations and in sermons he championed the position, familiar to the leaders of the English Reformation, and emphatically asserted by Andrewes and Buckeridge, that the English Church had departed from Rome only as regards her errors, and that the right of reform, so long as the foundation was untouched, belonged to every national church. No less did he depart from the extreme Protestants by his asser-

Early career of William Laud.

tion of the Divine right of Episcopacy. He was attacked by the Calvinists, and was convented before the Vice-Chancellor, but he was saved from condemnation by the intervention of more liberal thinkers from outside, and of the Chancellor of the University himself.

In August 1608 Laud became chaplain to Bishop Neile of Rochester, "a man"—so wrote Heylin in later days— "who very well understood the constitution of the Church of England, though otherwise not so eminent in all parts of learning as some other bishops of his time; but what he wanted in himself he made good in the choice of his servants, having more able men about him from time to time than any other of that age." Neile introduced his chaplain to King James, who soon appreciated his talents, but seems always to have doubted his wisdom. In 1611 Laud was elected president of his college after a hot contest, which even went, on appeal, to the visitor, and at last to the king. For eleven years he "governed the college in peace, without so much as the show of a faction." His good work was recognised. He lived down the Calvinist opposition, was made a royal chaplain, and in 1616 became Dean of Gloucester, with the king's special command to "reform and set in order what he found there to be amiss." He carried out Queen Elizabeth's injunctions as to the position of the altar, having it moved to the east end. Beyond this he did nothing of note. In 1621 he became Bishop of St. David's. From that time he began gradually to be employed in affairs of State, became acquainted in some degree of intimacy with Prince Charles, and was the close friend of Buckingham. He was preaching at Whitehall on March 27, 1625, when the news came that the king was dead.

Laud and the State.

For the late king Laud had a sincere respect as "the most learned prince that this kingdom hath ever had for matters of religion," with "an assured confidence in Christ." For his son he had a genuine affection. Within a week of the old king's death his successor chose Laud to preach at the opening of Parliament. The sermon, owing to the plague, which caused all ceremony to be laid aside, was not preached till June 19. It very clearly set out the lines of the

alliance between Church and king as they appeared to
the sovereign and to his chief ecclesiastical adviser. His
Two significant passages may be quoted, for they announce-
serve as clues to much that came after. If there political
was to be a settled and flourishing State and a principles.
a Church without "dissolution," then "the king must trust
and endear his people ; the people must honour, obey, and
support their king ; both king and peers and people must
religiously serve and honour God. Shut out all superstition
in God's name, the farther the better ; but let in no profaneness therewhile. If this be not done, take what care you can,
God is above all human wisdom, and in some degree or other
there will be *liquefactio terræ*, a 'melting,' or a waste, both
in Church and State." And again, with a reminiscence of
Hooker, he said, " It is not possible in any Christian commonwealth that the Church should 'melt' and the State stand
firm ; for there can be no firmness without law, and no laws
can be binding if there be no conscience to obey them ;
penalty alone could never, can never, do it. And no school
can teach conscience but the Church of Christ." With such
opinions Charles was in thorough sympathy.

AUTHORITIES.—Clarendon, *History of the Great Civil War ;* Heylin,
Cyprianus Anglicus. For the coronation of Charles I. see the volume with
that title, edited by the Rev. Christopher Wordsworth for the *Henry Brad-
shaw Society ;* Laud's *Works* (Library of Anglo-Catholic Theology).

CHAPTER II

THE CONTROVERSY WITH ROME AND ITS CONSEQUENCES

CHARLES at once showed that he placed the utmost confidence in Laud. Within a fortnight of his father's death
he requested a list of the most eminent divines
to be prepared for him that he might from among
them select his chaplains and those whom he should
consider worthy of promotion. Laud drew up the list and
Buckingham gave it to Charles. Each name was marked
with the letter O or P. Of Puritans Charles had a very clear
opinion. He looked upon them, says Clarendon, "as a very
dangerous and seditious people, who would, under pretence of
conscience, which kept them from submitting to the spiritual
jurisdiction, take the first opportunity they could find, or
make, to withdraw themselves from his temporal jurisdiction,
and therefore his Majesty caused these people to be watched,
and provided against with the utmost vigilance." It was not
likely that he would promote any of the clergy who held their
views. He would clearly give his favour to the Orthodox.

This was soon put to the test. The Roman controversy
advanced a stage in the first year of Charles's reign. It
passed from the study of theologians into the arena
of public life. The earlier contentions between
English and Romanist writers have been dealt with
in Volume V. of this history, and the names with which we
have now to deal have already been referred to. But the
details belong so definitely to the reign of Charles I. and are
so closely connected with his chief ecclesiastical adviser that
they must be spoken of more fully here.

Charles and the Puritans.

The Roman controversy.

The fame of Laud himself had largely been won by a contest with a Romanist, while King James was still on the throne,
in May 1622.

Laud's conference with Fisher was, like many of the
controversies of the time, caused by a pressing personal case
of conscience.   The Countess of Buckingham,   Laud's con-
mother of the brilliant George Villiers, had prob- ference with
ably already been converted to Romanism, by one   Fisher.
Percy, or Fisher, a very notable Jesuit ; she had been followed
by her son's wife, and the duke himself seemed very likely to
be lost to the English Church.   Conferences at first took
place, by Buckingham's wish or the king's command, between Dr. Francis White, Rector of St. Peter's, Cornhill,
and Fisher.   After two meetings had been held, the king
desired Laud, then Bishop of St. David's, to take part in the
discussion.   Fisher printed his account of the conference—
and White also : and Laud at last was compelled to do the
same.   Reply and retort followed, and eventually in 1639—
seventeen years after the conference had taken place—Laud
found it necessary to publish a complete record of the proceedings.   The form of the book makes it irksome reading
nowadays.   Sentence by sentence Fisher's book is taken,
and dissected, and answered.   Such a method has the
advantage of completeness, but it can hardly fail to be
extremely tedious.   It is difficult to collect and marshal the
arguments : it is hard to see the wood for the trees.

Some account of the contents of this famous book must
be given before the principles upon which Laud conducted
this, his most important controversy, are stated,
as a necessary introduction to the special contests Points of the
which followed.   controversy.

The points round which the battle was fought were
chiefly :

   (1) The Apostolic succession as the guarantee of the in-
        fallibility of the Faith in the Church : the Jesuit
        claimed that this guarantee could be found only in
        Rome.
   (2) The Roman claim that "the Roman Church only,
        and such others as agree with it in faith, hath
        true Divine, infallible faith, necessary to salvation."

(3) The Roman statement that the faith had never been
changed by the Roman Church.

The chief point was what was meant by the infallibility of
the Church. The ground was very different from that of the
Puritan contention. It was admitted by both sides that
there is a continual and visible Church : but the meaning of
its infallibility was in question.

First, there was the familiar Roman claim that the Fathers
recognised the Roman Church as infallible. Here it is little
more than a question of translation. St. Cyprian and St.
Jerome and St. Gregory Nazianzen, St. Cyril and Rufinus—
what did they mean in some passages quoted? Laud had
no difficulty, we should say, in showing that none of them
thought of any permanent infallibility in the Roman Church
or bishops. And to that point he returns when the arguments
are summed up at the end of the controversy. There is no
Scriptural or primitive warrant for an infallible pope. A
Jesuit attacking Laud's book some years later appears to have
conceded this point, for he says, " Catholic faith (in this
particular) only obliges us to maintain that the pope is infallible when he defines with a general council."

From a general denial of the pope's infallibility Laud
passed to a particular assertion of the errors of the Roman
Church and bishops in special points—in the
"worship of images, and in altering Christ's institution in the Blessed Sacrament, by taking away
the cup from the people, and divers other particulars." But
first he examined the position of the Greek Church as a permanent witness against the exclusive claim of Rome. " They
[the Greeks] continue a true Church in the main substance to
and at this day." The *Filioque* controversy is discussed with a
clearness and accuracy that is none too common. " That
divers learned men were of opinion that a *Filio et per Filium*,
in the sense of the Greek Church, was but a question *in
modo loquendi,* "in manner of speech, and therefore not
fundamental, is evident." "You," he says, turning to his
Jesuit antagonist, "You may make them no Church (as
Bellarmine doth), and so deny them salvation, which cannot
be had out of the true Church ; but I for my part dare not do
so. And Rome in this particular should be more moderate,

The errors
of Rome.

if it be but because this article, *Filioque*, was added to the
Creed by herself.   And it is hard to add and anathematise
too.   It ought to be no easy thing to condemn a man in
foundation of faith ; much less a Church ; least of all so
ample and large a Church as the Greek, especially so as to
make them no Church.   Heaven's gates were not so easily
shut against multitudes, when St. Peter wore the keys at his
own girdle."   Here again Laud showed his keen insight into
really vital points : the permanence of the Orthodox Eastern
Church is a standing refutation of the exclusive claim of Rome.

From this arose a discussion as to what were fundamentals
of the faith : Laud said "the Articles of the Creed."   Here
occurs the curious passage in which Laud appears   The funda-
to maintain the actual descent of our Blessed Lord   mentals of
into "the lowest pit of hell and place of the damned,"   the faith.
and not merely into the *limbus patrum*, or into Hades—
appears only, for it cannot be said that he clearly states the
opinion, since he declares that "the Church of England takes
the words as they are in the Creed, and believes them without
further dispute, and in that sense which the ancient primitive
Fathers of the Church agreed in."   And this leads naturally
to the discussion of the liberty which the Church allows.
Here England, says Laud, stands boldly free and tolerant,
where Rome is rigid and bitter.

"She comes far short of the Church of Rome's severity,
whose anathemas are not only for Thirty-nine Articles but for
very many more—above one hundred in matter of doctrine—
and that in many points as far remote from the foundation ;
though to the far greater rack of men's consciences, they must
be all made fundamental, if that Church have once determined
them : whereas the Church of England never declared that
every one of her Articles are fundamental in the faith.   For it
is one thing to say, No one of them is superstitious or
erroneous ; and quite another to say, Every one of them is
fundamental, and that in every part of it, to all men's belief.
Besides, the Church of England prescribes only to her own
children, and by those Articles provides but for her own
peaceable consent in those doctrines of truth.   But the
Church of Rome severely imposes her doctrine upon the
whole world, under pain of damnation."

The positive Articles of the English Church claim all to be founded on Holy Scripture—the negative to be refutations of doctrines not so founded. But how, says the Jesuit, do you know Scripture to be Scripture? Laud will not answer "solely by the tradition of the Church," but rather—(1) the unanimous and constant witness of the Church; (2) the internal light and testimony which Scripture gives to itself; (3) the testimony of the Holy Ghost in the souls of men; (4) natural reason considering the books. These together give evidence which may commend itself to any thoughtful and earnest inquirer. Reason, indeed, is the bulwark not the slave of religion. "For though I set the mysteries of faith above reason, which is their proper place, yet I would have no man think they contradict reason or the principles thereof. No, sure : for reason by her own light can discover how firmly the principles of religion are true ; but all the light she hath will never be able to find them false."

The position of Holy Scripture.

This question of evidence for the Scripture is argued at great length ; Hooker is cited and defended, tradition is weighed, and the Roman claims for it all examined : yet Laud maintains his position, that the supremacy of the Bible rests upon cumulative not particular proof. "The key that lets men into the Scriptures, even to this knowledge of them, that they are the Word of God, is the tradition of the Church : but when they are in, they hear Christ Himself immediately speaking in Scripture to the faithful ; and 'His sheep' do not only 'hear' but know 'His voice.'" Perhaps in few parts of his treatise is Laud more clear and trenchant and rational than he is here, or more strictly theological. Faith and reason have never perhaps more clearly had their claims vindicated and their limits admitted. The terseness of the language is the fit symbol of the accuracy and condensation of the thought.

Evidence and faith.

"Though the evidence of these supernatural truths, which Divinity teaches, appears not so manifest as that of the natural ; yet they are in themselves much more sure and infallible than they. For they proceed immediately from God Himself, that Heavenly Wisdom, which being the foundation of ours, must needs infinitely precede ours, both in nature and excellence. ' He that teacheth man knowledge shall not He know?' And therefore, though we reach not the order of their deductions, nor can in this life come to the vision of them, yet we yield as full and firm assent, not only to the articles, but to all the things rightly deduced from them, as we do to the most evident principles of natural reason. This assent is called faith; and 'faith being of things not seen,' would quite lose its honour, nay itself, if it met with sufficient grounds in natural reason whereon to stay itself. For faith is a mixed act of the will and the understanding; and the will inclines the understanding to yield full approbation to that whereof it sees not full proof. Not but that there is most full proof of them, but because the main grounds which prove them are concealed from our view and folded up in the unrevealed counsel of God; God in Christ resolving to bring mankind to their last happiness by faith and not by knowledge, that so the weakest among men may have their way to blessedness open."

Miracles, he very clearly asserts, even our Lord's and the Apostles' miracles, are not in themselves and by themselves "evident and convincing proofs."

And so the argument went on, till the Countess of Buckingham herself broached the question upon which all depended—Would the bishop grant the Roman Church to be the right Church?

On this his answer develops the chief points on which his own position as an English churchman was based, and which he repeated in his history written in the Tower, as the only grounds on which the English Church can justify her separation from Rome.

The true Church.

There were errors in faith into which Rome had fallen which made it necessary for the Church of England to reform herself. This she did without departing from the Catholic faith once for all delivered to the saints. And she did not depart from the essential unity of which that faith is the bond, or from the Apostolic discipline and ministry which preserve it. Thus Rome is a true Church, though erring—yet not *the* true Church. England also is a true Church. Errors there were in the reformers, as there were in the popes: and the work of reformation is admittedly a most difficult one. And yet, through it all, the essence has been preserved, and the English protest against nothing but the errors of the Roman Communion.

The Jesuit on the other side repeats the claim to infallibility based on the Rock of Peter : and Laud denies that the rock was Peter's person, and asserts that it was his faith.   So the English separation is not from the "General The Roman Church," but from the Church of Rome—and claim. "even here the Protestants have not left the Church of Rome in her essence but in her errors ; not in the things that constitute a church, but only in such abuses and corruptions as work toward the dissolution of a church."

And who is to be the judge ?   A general council : it is Laud's appeal, and that of the whole English Church since the Reformation.   And where that cannot be had How to be we fall back on the Holy Scriptures ; for the Council decided. of Trent had no general assent of the Catholic Church, and the claim of the pope to continuous supremacy is contrary to historical fact.   The Church in general cannot err in a fundamental point, having the perpetual presence of Christ.   A particular Church can err, and particular Churches have erred.   General councils may err, as that of Constance erred when it ordered that the Holy Eucharist should be received by laymen only under one kind, and made this rule "a law which may not be refused."   Such judgments, being contrary to the command of Christ, may be reversed.   So again the debate turns back upon the pope's infallibility ; and Laud declares that the doctrine of intention alone, as defined by the Council of Trent, refutes the claim. For he cannot be infallible unless he be pope, and the intention of conferring the Sacraments by which he has received his spiritual powers and privileges cannot be proved.

From this he comes to the errors that he saw in the practice of the Roman Church of his own day in the common teaching of transubstantiation, of communion in one kind, of invocation of saints, of adoration of images—errors all of them practical, but not all to be found in the avowed teaching of the Roman Church.

As the debate narrows, the Jesuit turns from particulars, which are hard to defend, to a general assertion which appeals powerfully to the timid. "You admit," he says in effect, "that we may be saved; are you not safer therefore with us, as we deny there is salvation in your Church?"

"This will not hold," replies Laud: "on this ground, indeed, you should accept the Anglican doctrine of the Eucharist, for you only add the 'manner' of that Presence which we admit to be real. For we admit the salvation of Romanists, as individuals, not as members of the Roman communion—that is, as they believe the Creed and hold the foundation Christ Himself, not as they associate themselves willingly and knowingly to the gross superstitions of the Romish Church." Thus obstinate teachers of false doctrine are without excuse, though their sincere and simple followers may be in a state of salvation.

The claims of the English Church.

And so finally we return to the confidence which may be reposed in the English Church.

"To believe the Scripture and the Creeds, to believe these in the sense of the ancient primitive Church, to receive the four great General Councils, to believe all points of doctrine generally received as fundamental in the Church of Christ, is a faith in which to live and die cannot but give salvation."

This book went to the root of the matter; and it was on the lines which it developed that Charles desired to uphold the teaching and the position of the English Church. Of its Eucharistic doctrine something may be said later. It is time now to turn to the controversies which became public within a few years of the time when Laud met Fisher and before the results of their conference were given to the world.

The case of the Countess of Buckingham had been but one example, in high place, of persistent Roman propagandism. The country was visited by many Roman agents, who used the Calvinist teaching that was so common to discredit the claim of the national Church to represent the faith once for all delivered to the saints. The case of Dr. Richard Mountague was a notable one. It showed both the importance of the Calvinist position among the laity of England and the strength of the reaction which was to restore the balance of theological teaching.

Mountague and the Romanists.

Richard Mountague, rector of Stanford Rivers, in Essex, was already a notable man. A scholar of King's College,

Cambridge, he had returned to Eton to join in the literary work of the great Sir Henry Savile, for whom he edited several orations of St. Gregory Nazianzen, and began to edit St. Basil the Great. Savile was, he noted, in later years, "the first means of his advancement"; and by his influence no doubt it was that Mountague was enabled, after his appointment as Dean of Hereford in 1616, to return, by exchange, to Windsor as a canon. He held several other preferments, and he soon attracted the attention of James I., by whom he was requested to undertake an answer, at first in conjunction with Casaubon, and after his death alone, to the *Ecclesiastical History* of Baronius. He published the first part of his work in 1622, which, says Fuller, "had he finished it, might be balanced with that of Baronius, and which would have swayed with it for learning and weighed it down for truth"; and he wrote also against Selden's book on tithes; so that when he again appeared in print, in 1624, he was a practised, as well as a learned, controversialist.

Certain "Romish rangers" had been vexing his parish; and a pamphlet, entitled "A Gag for the New Gospel," had been circulated, which identified the teaching of the English Church with Calvinism. Mountague set himself to reply, and published "A Gag for the New Gospel? No! A New Gag for an Old Goose, who would needs undertake to stop all Protestants' mouths for ever with 276 places out of their own English Bible." He wrote in easy, familiar language, and he took up the position of the school of Andrewes, that though the Church of Rome was corrupt she was not apostate, and that England differed from her only in her errors. Denying transubstantiation, he asserted the real presence of Christ in the Sacrament of the Altar. He asserted the power of absolution, but denied the necessity of confession in all cases. And for outward adornment of churches he wrote: "Not the making of images is misliked, but the profaning of them to unlawful uses in worshipping and adoring them." The style of the pamphlet was intentionally such as to catch the popular ear. Writing to his friend Cosin, the author admitted that he had written bitterly and tartly, "which I did purposely, because the ass deserved to be so rubbed." It was a style in

A New Gag for an Old Goose.

which he excelled.   As Fuller quaintly puts it, " his great parts
were attended with a tartness of writing ; very sharp the nib
of his pen, and much gall mingled in his ink, against such as
opposed him.   However, such the equability of the sharpness
of his style, he was impartial therein ; be he ancient or
modern writer, Papist or Protestant, that stood in his way, they
shared all equally taste thereof."   He set himself, indeed, in
his own words, " to stand in the gap against Puritanism and
Popery, the Scylla and Charybdis of Ancient Piety."   And
such men were, indeed, like Shakespeare's *Adam*, " not for
the fashion of those times."   The House of Commons was
always eager to enter the arena of theological controversy, and
when it was addressed on the iniquity of Mountague's
pamphlet, it at once applied to the Archbishop of Canterbury.

Abbot was himself a Calvinist, and old age and misfortune
had taught him caution.   He advised Mountague to revise his
opinions.   Instead he applied to the king in person.   It was
in the last days of James's life, yet the king's keen scent for
theological discussion was not abated, and when he had heard
the matter he exclaimed, " If that is to be a papist, so am
I a papist."   Mountague indeed was, as Laud saw, "a very
good scholar and a right honest man, a man every way able
to do God, his Majesty, and the Church of England great
service," and James was in no mind to discredit a
student.   To James, then, Mountague submitted a The *Appello Cæsarem.*
new pamphlet, which was only published after the
king's death—" Appello Cæsarem : A Just Appeal from two
Unjust Informers."   It was a bold vindication.   As to
Calvinists and their doctrine of free-will he wrote plainly, " I
am none, I profess, of that fraternity—no Calvinist, no
Lutheran, but a Christian."   His aim was to vindicate his
interpretation of the English formularies as being the natural
one, and his interpretation of the Bible as being that of the
English Church.   He refused to be bound by the Synod of
Dort or by any private opinions.   The Church of Rome, he
asserted, is not a sound, yet a true, Church.   All that papists
say is not Popery.   " Particular churches have and may err ;
the Catholic, Universal Church hath not, cannot, err."

Mountague was singularly free from the popular delusions
of his day.   There was no reason to believe the pope to be

anti-Christ, he said. "That the pope is *magnus ille anti-Christus* is neither determined by the public doctrine of the Church nor proved by any good argument of private men. . . . The matter of the great anti-Christ fits the Turkish tyranny every way as well as the papacy." As to images, we reject the popish doctrine and practice both, concerning adoration; but the Church of England does not condemn the historical use of images. We hold a doctrine of Absolution and of the Real Presence. "The difference between us and popish writers is only about the *modus*, the manner of Christ's presence in the Blessed Sacrament." It was not likely that these sentiments would commend themselves to a Puritan House of Commons, though a modern writer, of whose impartiality there can be no doubt, considers that Mountague was one who gave "a temperate exposition of the reasons which were leading an increasing body of scholars to reject the doctrines of Rome and of Geneva alike." Nor was the matter improved, in the eyes of Calvinists, by the fact that Mountague had also published a treatise on the Invocation of Saints, called "Immediate Address unto God alone," in which he asserted that it might be reasonable, though not necessary, to ask the angel-keeper ever by each man's side to "pray for me," and concluded with a prayer that God, "Glorious in His Holy saints now and ever, grant us of His grace, through their intercession for His Church in Christ, that we may so pass through things temporal that finally we lose not things eternal, but together with all the saints departed may rise again to immortal life."

Its teaching and its reception.

Such doctrines as these were more than a Puritan House of Commons could endure. A committee reported strongly against Mountague on July 7, 1625, and it was decided to proceed against him, not on directly theological grounds, but for dishonouring the late king, for disturbing Church and State, and for treating the rights and privileges of Parliament with contempt. He was committed to the custody of the serjeant-at-arms. The House of Commons thus entered on the extra-legal course which was to be carried so far by both parties in the struggle that was to come. Charles was equally determined and at least as injudicious.

Intervention of the House of Commons.

While Mountague was still in prison he made him his chaplain, and on July 9 intimated to the House of Commons that "what had been there said and resolved without consulting him in the case was not pleasing to him." On the 11th Parliament was prorogued. The action of the king seemed more magnanimous than safe, for, says Heylin, "There was much magnaminity in preferring the man whom he beheld as well in his personal sufferings as in his great abilities, yet was it not held safe for the king, as his case then stood, to give such matter of exasperation to the House of Commons." On August 2, when the Parliament was sitting at Oxford, Mountague was too ill to attend, and after a hot discussion, in which Coke and Heath spoke with great bitterness, proceedings were laid aside for the moment, though with a threat of impeachment.

Shortly afterwards conferences were held on the doctrinal questions involved. Early in the year the Bishops of London (Mountain or Montaigne), Durham (Neile), Winchester (Andrewes), Rochester (Buckeridge), and St. David's (Laud) were consulted by the king's command and reported in Mountague's favour. Already three of the bishops, while the House of Commons was sitting, had written to Buckingham in support of the opinions Mountague had expressed. The Church of England, they maintained, was in her Reformation never "busy with every particular school-point. The cause why she held this moderation was, because she could not be able to preserve any unity amongst Christians, if men were forced to subscribe to curious particulars disputed in schools." The points with which Mountague dealt, they declared, were partly the "resolved doctrine of the Church of England," partly those "fit only for schools, and to be left at more liberty for learned men to expound in their own sense, so they keep themselves peaceable and distract not the Church." To this plea for tolerance the three bishops added a dignified protest of constitutional rights. The clergy's submission under Henry VIII. was not in any matter to Parliament, but that "if any difference, doctrine or other, fell in the Church, the king and the bishops were to be judges of it in a National Synod or Convocation; the king first giving leave, under his broad seal, to handle the points in difference. But the Church never submitted to any other judge, neither, indeed,

The opinion of the bishops.

can she, though she would." To do other would be to "depart from the ordinances of Christ, and the continual course and practice of the Church." A shrewd hint was added that the opinions which Mountague had attacked were subversive also of the government, and that the countenance of the Synod of Dort to such teaching was of no avail—"and our hope is that the Church of England will be well advised, and more than once over, before she admit a foreign synod, especially of such a church as condemneth her discipline and manner of government, to say no more." This was on August 2, 1625, and the hands subscribed were those of Buckeridge and Howson as well as of him whose mind spoke most clearly in the words, Laud, Bishop of St. David's

The later report was signed on January 16, 1626. Its important words were these : "We have met and considered, and for our particulars do think that Mr. Mountague,

Their certificate of Mountague's orthodoxy. in his book, hath not affirmed anything to be the doctrine of the Church of England but that which in our opinion is the doctrine of the Church of England, or agreeable thereunto. And for the preservation of the peace of the Church we in humility do conceive that his Majesty shall do most graciously to prohibit all parties, members of the Church of England, any further controverting of these questions by public preaching or writing, or any other way, for the disturbance of the peace of this Church for the time to come."

The advice was followed. Already Charles was in a position of grave political distress. The Commons were high in opposition, Eliot was rousing enthusiasm as the leader of a constitutional party, foreign relations were in disorder to the point of disgrace, and Buckingham was dismissed. By the summer of 1626 the king seemed face to face with war at home and abroad. In the Church only he hoped to find peace.

But the Church was no more quiet than the State. Pamphlets against Mountague still poured from the press.

The pamphlet warfare. "A Dangerous Plot Discovered : by a discourse wherein is proved that Mr. Richard Mountague in his two books, the one called A New Gag, the other A Just Appeal, laboureth to bring in the faith of Rome and

Arminius under the name and pretence of the doctrine and
faith of the Church of England" (London, printed for Nicholas
Bourne at the Exchange, 1626), was addressed "to the High
and Honourable Court of Parliament, praying that you will
(1) take this cause into your consideration; (2) preserve
the faith of our Church in the purity it hath had hitherto;
(3) endeavour to prevent the corrupting of it in time to
come." A good example of the feeling which was now readily
finding expression, it protested against all the points on which
Mountague had controverted the Puritan view, as on the
authority of the Church, the efficacy of baptism, and the real
presence. A "second parallel" tried to convict Mountague
of Arminianism, and "Pelagius Redivivus" compared "the
new to the old error." Charles determined to silence the
disputants. Parliament was dissolved on June 15. On the
following day was issued a proclamation to enforce silence
on controverted points. Who was the gainer by Declaration
these disputes but only the Church of Rome? of the
Let men be silent on the deep points which had king.
"given much offence to the sober and well grounded readers
and hearers of these late written books on both sides."

Did men think then that Reason would suggest articles
of peace? If they did they must have known little of the
history of mankind. It was no day in which the
voice of wise moderation could be heard. "The The two
bishops were more liberal than the House of parties.
Commons," says a great modern authority. Students understood their subject as amateurs could not; and with the
students was the knowledge and the temper which alone, and
in the future, should make settlement possible. Charles, with
real delicacy of insight, looked beyond the petty disputes to
larger and more statesmanlike issues for the Church. At his
back stood a man of clear vision and determined will, who
would not palter with his conscience. Unity was the passion
of their lives, and for nothing was the age, in England or
abroad, less prepared. The king's declaration, and many a
wise saying of wise men, fell on empty ears.

AUTHORITIES. — Besides those given for Chap. I., Hacket, *Scrinia
Reserata;* Fuller, *Church History;* the works of the chief divines, most of
which are reprinted in the Library of Anglo-Catholic Theology. The pamph-

let literature is voluminous and important.   There are many contemporary diaries, the most notable of which is Laud's.   The State Papers, Domestic, are full of details of importance.   Among modern writers, S. R. Gardiner, *History of England;* G. G. Perry, *History of the Church of England;* and the lives of the prominent persons of the day in the *Dictionary of National Biography.*   An excellent new edition of Laud's *Controversy with Fisher*, by C. H. Simpkinson, 1901.

CHAPTER III

THE RISE OF LAUD

WITH the dissolution of Parliament and the issue of the king's proclamation it seemed perhaps for a moment as if there might be peace. Two years passed. Buckingham's murder removed one great danger from the king. The news came to Laud as he was with the Arch- The beginning of Laud's power. bishop at Croydon, consecrating Mountague to the see of Chichester, on August 24, 1628. Whatever the king might say in proclamations, it was clear that he had his own opinions in Church matters, and that they were those of Mountague and Laud. Such promotion indeed was "more magnanimous than safe." But Buckingham's place must be filled, and, though not outwardly, Laud filled it.

Since 1626 much had happened, of which we have first to tell. The one competitor had already, by Buckingham himself, been swept from Laud's path. On October 25, 1626, John Williams, Bishop of Lincoln, The rivalry of Bishop Williams. Dean of Westminster, and Lord Keeper of the Great Seal of England, was required to give up the ensign of his high legal office. It seemed the end of a great career. A subtle Welshman, of ancient family and ready learning, he had been brought forward by Lord Chancellor Ellesmere. "The chaplain," says his friend and eulogist, Bishop Hacket, "understood the soil on which he had set his foot, that it was rich and fertile, able with good tendance to yield a crop after the largest dimensions of his desires." Preferments came rapidly to him. As a parish priest he "walked as a Burning Light before his brethren," a

23

constant and ready preacher, "he lived like a magnifico at home," full of hospitality and charity. Buckingham became his patron, and it was he who brought over the young duchess to the English Church. When he became Dean of Westminster, he was generous in the restoration of the abbey and the further endowment of the school. King James took a fancy to the astute, capable, supple ecclesiastic, and made him Lord Keeper and Bishop of Lincoln, so "he reaped no less than two harvests in one month." He won the reputation of a clever lawyer, and to the last he held the confidence of the old king. Charles looked upon him with another eye. On the day after the king's accession Williams "commended two out of his own family to be preferred," and the king coldly made no answer. Buckingham had already begun to distrust him. He was indeed not one whom men learnt to rely upon. Laud felt that he was his enemy. In the discharge of his duty as bishop he was shamefully lax. He had never, it seems, resided in his diocese; and to the king this was intolerable. From the very beginning of the reign he was in disgrace, and when the great seal was taken from him, he at last retired to the manor of Buckden, where he built a great house, laid out fine gardens and lived in stately fashion. There he waited, ready, if need be, to throw the weight of his ability on to the side of the opposition to the king's ministers.

From the date of Williams' retirement the advancement of Laud was unchallenged. He was indeed the only great man among the bishops. On September 25, 1626, Lancelot Andrewes, Bishop of Winchester, "*lumen orbis Christiani*," as Laud calls him in his diary, passed away. Abbot the Archbishop of Canterbury spent the last years of his life in insignificance, removed from all royal favour through his political opposition to the king's measures, and, as he thought, by the influence of Laud. Of this we shall hear more shortly. Bishop Morton of Lichfield, Bishop Field of Llandaff, Bishop Harsnet of Norwich, Bishop Howson of Oxford, Bishop Davenant of Salisbury, Bishop Mountaigne of London, Bishop Buckeridge of Rochester, Bishop Neile of Durham, were all men of eminence but not of power. Each had characteristic merits,

The insignificance of the bishops.

none was without learning, and perhaps none was above criticism. Certainly Bishop Mountaigne is remembered now chiefly as the "swan-eating and canary-sucking" prelate of Milton's attack. One at least of the Elizabethan bishops lingered on, Toby Matthew, Archbishop of York, a doughty champion in the past of the English Church against Edmund Campion, a sturdy ruler of the North, and a man of humour also. He was near his end. Of the new bishops none was especially notable, save perhaps Goodman of Gloucester, whose Lenten sermon before the king in 1626 called attention to his approximation towards Roman doctrine, and who, though some of the most learned of the bishops decided that he spoke rather incautiously than falsely, was never sincere in his attachment to the Reformation. The bishops were not men, as the king felt, to guide the Church in difficult ways. He "chid" them all, Laud tells, in the spring of 1626, "that in this time of Parliament we were silent in the cause of the Church, and did not make known to him what might be useful, or was prejudicial, to the Church, professing himself ready to promote the cause of the Church." There was in truth no leader till Laud came forward to fill the place. On August 26, 1626, he was elected Bishop of Bath and Wells. When Andrewes died he succeeded him as Dean of the Chapel Royal. On July 15, 1628, he was translated to London. By this time the Puritans looked on him as the head and front of all offence against them. "Laud, look to thyself. Thy life is sought. As thou art the fountain of all wickedness, repent thee of thy monstrous sins, before thou be taken out of the world," were the words of a paper in St. Paul's churchyard, the beginning of a long series of bitter libels.

On the political side of Laud's career it would be foreign to the purpose of this book to dwell. But his political position must be briefly noted, for it was an important cause of the unpopularity which was shown by the lampoons. Laud's political career.

The employment of ecclesiastics in offices of State was universal throughout Europe, and Laud, though he certainly did not seek office, was ready to undertake any work which the confidence of the king might thrust upon him. The State

Papers of the early years of Charles I. show him gradually more and more busied in secular matters, in affairs of trade and finance, in the committee on Foreign Affairs, and on the commission of the Admiralty. His impatience of mere officialism is revealed in many of his letters to Thomas Wentworth, Earl of Strafford, whom politics and religion alike made his friend. An energetic man in all he undertook, his work, and his theory of work, were "thorough." But he was much less of a politician than the people fancied, and his political platform was the platform of his masters, of Hooker, and Bodin, and Aristotle.

The doctrine of the Divine right of kings was not developed by Laud but was full-blown when he came into power. It was the answer of English controversialists to the advocates of the papal claims. Its completest expression may be found in words, probably in Laud's own writing, written at the culmination of his power, in 1640. "The most high and sacred order of kings is of Divine right, being the ordinance of God Himself, founded in the laws of nature, and clearly established by express texts both of the Old and New Testaments." That this Divine right was a right to govern wrong was a view which Laud would have been the first to reject; but to take up arms against even tyranny was as clearly in his eyes unlawful. He denied that there was "an absolute power" in the king; and he declared to the last that he "was never yet such a fool as to embrace arbitrary government." All this seems confusion to the modern thinker: but the truth is that clear definitions, except in the hands of the lawyers, whose definitions were almost invariably favourable to an exalted royal prerogative, were not often, in the early seventeenth century, either concise or consistent. And Laud was no master of phrase, but a plain, blunt man, and he "could not conceive that the judges would put that under their hands to be law which should afterwards be found unlawful." It is not difficult for any reader of his works to understand how natural was his attitude towards the monarchy, or how far removed from any assertion of arbitrary principles.

But, none the less, "*noscitur a sociis.*" That the conse-

The Divine right of kings.

quences of the doctrine of Divine right were pressed to
an extremity is shown clearly enough by the
instance of Dr. Robert Sibthorpe, a Northampton   Its chief
exponents:
clergyman, who preached in the church of St.   Sibthorpe,
Sepulchre in that town on February 22, 1627, a sermon
on Romans xiii. 5, warmly recommending a loyal response
to the king's demand for a general loan.   The loan had
aroused much discussion, and a royal commission had inquired at Northampton in the previous month the opinion of
the country clergy as to its lawfulness.   Sibthorpe argued
strongly in favour of the loan, and he printed his sermon and
sent it to the king.   It contained a statement that "if princes
command anything which subjects may not perform, because
it is against the laws of God or of nature, or impossible, yet
subjects are bound to undergo the punishment without either
resistance or railing and reviling; and so to yield a passive
obedience where they cannot exhibit an active one."   The
phrase was one that was to have a famous history.

The sermon did not pass unchallenged.   The king sent it
to Archbishop Abbot for his license, and personally answered
some of the objections which the primate made to it.   Still
Abbot refused to license it, and it was only on the intervention of Laud that it was licensed by Mountaigne, Bishop of
London, after four other bishops had signified their assent.
The king, wrote Laud, conceived the sermon to be "for his
special service."   No sooner was it published than it was
vehemently denounced.   The king took its author under his
protection, made him one of his chaplains in ordinary, and
gave him (January 24, 1629) his special pardon.   He was
soon forgotten, in the Parliament's zest for higher game.
He joined the king's garrison at Oxford in 1643, was ejected
from his livings in 1647, but recovered them at the Restoration, and he died shortly after.

The case of Sibthorpe served to show the strong divergence in opinion on constitutional matters between the king
and the archbishop.   Abbot resisted Charles to the face;
and Charles ordered him to withdraw to Canterbury.   He protested because of his disagreement with the citizens.   He was
required to reside within his diocese, and he regarded this,
no doubt rightly, as disgrace.   He was clearly in opposi-

tion to the king's political views, and he was strongly hostile
to Laud. Finally on excuse, not without ground, of his
illness, the archbishop's jurisdiction was put in commission, to
be exercised by the Bishops of London, Durham, Rochester,
Oxford, and Bath and Wells, October 19, 1627.

More important than that of Sibthorpe was the case of
Roger Manwaring. Both were notorious, at a time when

Manwaring. churchmen would have been wise to keep their
political views from notoriety. Both reflected on
the chief churchman, innocent though he was of offence.
The case of Dr. Roger Manwaring is in some respects parallel
to that of Sibthorpe. In July 1627 he preached before the
king two sermons in which he strongly asserted the duty of
subjects to pay taxes demanded by kings on special occasions,
" if upon necessity extreme and urgent," declaring that if the
demand were not excessive, it would be very hard for a subject " to defend his conscience from that heavy prejudice of
resisting the ordinance of God, and receiving to himself
damnation " if he refused it. The sermons were published
immediately and were fiercely resented. In March 1628
they were severely attacked in the House of Commons, and on
June 9 Pym impeached Manwaring before the Lords. He was
condemned to a fine of £1000, to imprisonment during
pleasure of the House, to be suspended from preaching any-
where for three years, and before the court for ever; and he
was required to acknowledge his offence. The punishment
was undoubtedly illegal, as well as absurdly severe for
what was at most the maintenance of an unconstitutional
theory of government. Manwaring submitted and was imprisoned. " He that will preach more than he can prove, let
him suffer for it," said Charles; " I give him no thanks for
giving me my due ": but he gave him a formal pardon, and
presented him to the living of Stanford Rivers. In 1633
he was made Dean of Worcester; in 1635 he succeeded
Laud's successor as Bishop of St. David's. The rest of his
history may be told here. The Short Parliament revived the
attack upon him, being greatly disturbed at his promotion in
spite of the earlier sentence. The king personally intervened
to prevent the Lords depriving him of his bishopric, Laud
rightly explaining that they had no such power apart from the

king. He escaped for the time, but was imprisoned by the Long Parliament, and died in great poverty in 1653.

These cases, if they show that neither Charles nor Laud was as vehement in assertion of royal prerogative as is sometimes supposed, sufficiently illustrate the indiscretion of the master, for which the servant often suffered.

Charles was by no means interested only in the political aspect of religion. The State Papers of his reign show him still more interested in moral reform, and most of all in seeing that the bishops and clergy did their duty. He was incurably Erastian. His eye everywhere followed the investigations of Laud. It lighted in 1630 even on the good Bishop Bayly of Bangor, whose *Practice of Piety* was the devotional guide of three generations. Bayly had been Vicar of Evesham, where he had preached the sermons which were afterwards adapted for his book. Afterwards in London as chaplain to Henry Prince of Wales he had won wider fame, and in 1616 he was consecrated to Bangor, where he worked assiduously till 1631. In the year before his death he had to defend himself from the charge of admitting to holy orders persons who had not subscribed to the Prayer-book and Articles. He vindicated his action, and declared that he had everywhere provided " preaching ministers," and preached every Sunday himself; that he had taken care that catechising was duly observed, and that he was assiduous in visiting, in confirming, and in holding synods of his clergy. Charles was ever on the watch. He was determined to see that every bishop did his duty as he thought it ought to be done; and he was impatient of interference. To the end of his life he was hopelessly obstinate and incautious. His treatment of Manwaring and Sibthorpe was foolish : the later history of Mountague is an instance still more significant of the king's want of wisdom.

Charles's activity in Church matters.

We have seen the nature of the dispute which arose over the works of that eager controversialist, and the hopes that it would die down after the king's declaration in favour of peace. But the hopes were disappointed ; and indeed Charles was, in his early years at least, no friend to half measures. Parliamentary opposition made

The promotion of Mountague.

him the more determined to support his friends. Before the controversy about the *Appello Cæsarem* had had time to abate, Bishop Carleton of Chichester, one of Mountague's bitterest opponents, died. Charles, by the advice of the hot-headed Buckingham, nominated to the vacant bishopric the man who lay under the censure of Parliament. On July 14, 1628, Richard Mountague was elected Bishop of Chichester. When the election came to be confirmed in Bow Church nine articles were presented against him, charging him with Popery. A contemporary pamphlet, " The Appeal of the Orthodox Ministers of the Church of England against Richard Mountague," thus describes the scene. " The judge aforenamed [Dr. Neve], taking the paper of objections, first seemed to read them over silently to himself ; and then delivered them to the said elect Bishop Mountague, who seemed also to read them over silently to himself, and then with an untoward look and trembling hand gave them back again to the judge, who called to him one Dr. Samms of the Arches, advising with him what to do with the business ; and he told him he would run into a præmunire if he did not proceed : who thereupon gave the objector, Mr. Jones, an answer to this effect : My good friend, you have given here objections against this my lord of Chichester, but your objections are not in due form of law, because they have not a Doctor's hand unto them, neither have you an advocate to plead your objections. Therefore, nevertheless, by virtue of his Majesty's commission under the great seal I proceed to confirm him." Mountague himself then spoke. He had subscribed, he said, the Articles and Homilies, and given all the pledges of his loyalty to the Church that it was possible to give. If any one would, privately or publicly, confute his books, himself would be the first to burn them. The controversialist would not budge an inch.

By such men, whom he was to some extent obliged to support, the cause which Laud had at heart was certainly not advanced. It was his misfortune that he could not rely upon the discretion as well as the good intentions of his agents; and he was not always discreet himself. Many stories of his sharpness of retort are told, in which, if they are exaggerated, there is a clear foundation of

Weakness of Laud's position.

truth. Many people " spoke extreme ill of him, as the cause of all that was amiss,"

> pernicious protector, dangerous peer,
> That smooth'st it so with King and commonweal.

As the years went on it became clearer and clearer that he was without any strong personal support, a minister, like Richelieu in France, who depended wholly on the king. " But then I have nothing but the king's word to me ; and should he forget or deny it, where is my remedy ? " So he wrote to Strafford in 1636. It was all along the weakness of his position.

But, none the less, in spite of his own personal defects of manner and the mistakes of his indiscreet supporters, Laud won his way to the achievement of his great aim. This was simply to restore to the Church of England a dignified simplicity of worship and a loyal obedience to the formularies which had come to her from the past through the age of her Reformation.

Laud was prepared for the great work which he was to undertake by experience of every branch of clerical labour. At Oxford he had been a fellow, a lecturer, and the head of his college. He knew academic life and its weaknesses intimately, and when he came to be *His preparation for his work.* Chancellor of the University of Oxford he instituted a thorough reformation of the statutes, which provided a code destined to endure for more than two hundred years. As a parish priest, too, he had considerable experience of country life. If he did not reside long on any of his benefices he visited them regularly and preached often. As Dean of Gloucester he had the king's instructions to restore the dignity of the Cathedral worship, and he succeeded, though he was "much pestered with the Puritan faction." As Bishop of St. David's he paid only two visits to his diocese, but he left distinct marks of his activity and munificence, and he kept a close watch upon his see from London. He was Bishop of Bath and Wells for only two years, and cannot be said to have left much impression there.

But when he came to London, on July 15, 1628, he was able personally to direct the work of what was already a great diocese.

His clergy urged him to the suppression of nonconformity;
and he set about the task, as letters sent to him show,
with discretion. "Prudent, moderate, courteous,"
the clergy found him, "patiently forbearing them,
giving them time to consult conformable ministers, and vouch-
safing to confer with them himself." So a letter describes him.
Not only in London was he busy in the duties of his office,
and in social work such as the suppression of play-houses that
tended to vice, but outside he had much work to do. As
superintendent of the English congregations on the continent
of Europe it was his duty to see that they conformed to the
established use of the English Church. He was
concerned in the conversion of Mohammedan visitors
to England and the restoration of "renegados." He
was responsible, too, for a serious reminder of the obligations
of the episcopal office addressed by the king to Archbishop
Abbot. Seeing that divers bishops live in and about London,
wrote Charles to the primate, to the ill example of the
inferior clergymen and the hindrance of God's service and
the king's, the archbishop is required to command all bishops
to their sees, those only excepted whose attendance at court
is necessarily required. And further, none were to be permitted to reside upon their own lands or on benefices held *in
commendam*, but only in their episcopal houses. The order
was certainly needed, as the bitter wailing of Bishop Williams
when he was ordered to leave London for his diocese well
evidenced.

Again, he was active in the restoration of St. Paul's
Cathedral church, a work which was to win again the most
solemn associations for what should be the great
centre of London worship, but had for long been used
almost as an alley on 'Change. Under his guidance
eminent preachers began to attract crowds to the
services, and the fabric was repaired to be a worthy setting
for the Divine offices celebrated within. The quiet dignity
of Cathedral worship had always a great attraction for Laud.
His visitation inquiries show how careful he was in requiring
an exact obedience to the statutes of the different chapters
from those who were bound to them. He took great interest
in the disturbance which occurred at Durham, when Peter

Laud as Bishop of London.

His wide interests.

His care for the public services of the Church.

Smart, one of the prebendaries, protested against the use of the canonical vestments and against the Cathedral service, and was in consequence of his contumacy deprived of his prebend.   In 1630 Bishop Howson, who had been translated from Oxford to Durham, wrote to Laud, then Bishop of London, giving an historical narrative of the "innovations" in the service in his cathedral church.   They began, he said, with the omission of the prayers at six in the morning, intended especially for householders and servants, and usual in other cathedral churches.   This alteration gave great offence, and at the request of Justice Hutton and many others the six o'clock prayers were restored, whereupon "the innovating part ordered the customary morning service so, by reading more than is usually read and by a great variety of music, that they wearied the congregation with extraordinary long service, beginning after eight of the clock and continuing till after eleven."   To remedy this, Bishop Howson directed that the Nicene creed should occasionally be said instead of sung, as also the responses after the commandments.   "These alterations gave general content, the people, after their own parochial services, which were early, coming by troops to the cathedral, there being no set sermon in the morning in the whole city."

Letters such as these show both Laud's interest in the detailed arrangements of cathedral services and the important position which he had already assumed before the death of Abbot.   He was consulted indeed on every subject of interest to the Church, by all classes, from the king and the lords of the council down to parish priests in difficulties "among false brethren."

Of Laud's relations with the parochial clergy, a characteristic example is to be found in the letter of one Dr. Samuel Brooke, written to the Bishop of London on December 15, 1630.   With a postscript skilfully eulo- Puritan activity. gising Laud's tractate against Fisher as one of the most novel, pure, lively and yet substantial, judicious and learned pieces he ever read in his life, and with the commendation of a little tract of his own to such sober judgment as that of the author whose work he was commending, he concludes an acute summary of the situation with which the Episcopate

D

had to deal. " Predestination," he writes, " is the root of Puritanism, and Puritanism the root of all rebellion and disobedient intractableness, and all schism and sauciness in the country, nay, in the Church itself." It was this false doctrine which had made so many thousands of the people, and so great a part of the gentry of the land, opponents of the ancient Church teaching. These it was who began to speak as if their teaching was that of the Church, "they will have the Church of England to be theirs," and they wounded her " at the very heart, with her own name." There was a deeper cause of alienation too : " where nothing is done, the weeds will grow, as they do." All the while the activity of antagonism, which Dr. Brooke rightly observed was growing, and Parliamentary action was becoming in Laud's view distinctly dangerous. There is among the State Papers of the year 1628 an account of the purport of eight Bills, which, it is said, in the indorsement by Bishop Laud, "should have passed in the Commons against the Church in that session." They were against citations without a previous presentation by churchwardens : to take away the prohibited times for matrimony ; to subject scandalous ministers to trial by temporal judges ; to allow any man to leave his own parish church on Sundays if there be no sermons ; that no clergyman shall be justice of peace ; that no man shall be urged to subscribe but only to the articles of 1562 ; to deprive clergymen who teach contrary to the said articles ; to limit the major excommunication to cases of heresy.

It is clear that Laud was watching the proceedings of Parliament with the keenest interest and with grave dissatisfaction. He made elaborate notes of what was done, collected precedents for royal action in view of further difficulties, and was prepared to resist all interference of the Commons in matters belonging properly to the Church. But still it was his chief aim to suggest "articles of peace." There can be no doubt that it was with this purpose that the king, under his advice, issued in November, 1628, the famous declaration now prefixed to the Thirty-nine Articles. Thus it runs :

Charles's endeavours to make peace.

" For the present, though some differences have been ill raised, yet we take comfort in this, that all clergymen within our realm have always most willingly subscribed to the Articles established; which is an argument that they all agree in the true, usual, literal meaning of the said Articles; and that even in those curious points, in which the present differences lie, men of all sorts take the Articles of the Church of England to be for them; which is an argument again, that none of them intend any desertion of the Articles established. That therefore in these both curious and unhappy differences, which have for so many hundred years, in different times and places, exercised the Church of Christ, We will, that all further curious search be laid aside, and these disputes shut up in God's promises, as they be generally set forth to us in the Holy Scriptures, and the general meaning of the Articles of the Church of England according to them. And that no man hereafter shall either print, or preach, to draw the Article aside any way, but shall submit to it in the plain and full meaning thereof: and shall not put his own sense or comment to be the meaning of the Article, but shall take it in the literal and grammatical sense."

"Predestination is the root of all Puritanism, and Puritanism the root of all rebellion and disobedient intractableness." Only in the plain teaching of the English Church, apart from Rome's hyperdefinite decisions, and Calvin's desperate ventures of distorted logic, did Laud look to find "articles of peace." It was in this hope that in September, 1633, he took up the work of Primate of All England, when Charles called him to Canterbury on the death of Abbot.

AUTHORITIES.—Hacket, *Scrinia Reserata;* Laud, *Works;* and the State Papers, Domestic, are the chief authorities for this chapter. Archbishop Abbot wrote a vindication of his action, which was published in Rushworth's *Historical Collections*, i. 435 *sqq.* (ed. 1659). The works of Sibthorpe and Mountague give their views: Laud's Letters to Wentworth, in *Strafford Papers*, 1739, give occasional illustrations: and the lives of Sibthorpe, Manwaring, and Mountague, in the *Dictionary of National Biography*, add details and references.

CHAPTER IV

OPPOSITION, PURITAN AND ROMANIST

LAUD as archbishop was confronted by two obvious dangers, the opposition of Puritans and the opposition of Romanists. When these have been considered, it will be well to sketch the work which he actually accomplished and the position of the Church of England during his primacy.

Puritanism in 1633 was practically an organised party, though it had somewhat indefinite limits. It traced all its "schism and sauciness" back to the days when Cartwright was confronted by Hooker, and when the Martin Marprelate tracts made vulgar mock of Church institutions. To destroy the episcopal constitution of the Church, as it had been destroyed under John Knox in Scotland, was the aim of the leaders of English Puritanism in 1633, as of their predecessors eighty years earlier. In the eyes of the State the position had little changed.

Puritanism as a party.

The policy of the Stewarts in the treatment of the Puritans was simply a continuance of that of Elizabeth. James had an almost insane dread of political plotters and anarchists, and he had a very deep-seated belief in the wisdom of his mighty predecessor. His terrors too were encouraged by the creatures of the court; and he fell readily into the policy, which commended itself also to his theological sympathies, of setting a watch on the nonconformists' agencies by the State. It was not the Church that was anxious to persecute. There is proof that every stir of episcopal activity had its origin in the court. It was James, not the bishops, who originated the maxim,

The policy of the Stewarts in relation to theirs.

"No Bishop no King," and proceeded to draw from it a very definite course of action which was intended to defend the monarchy through an assertion of inquisitorial powers on behalf of the Church. Charles held the same opinions on the politics of Puritanism as his father, and he showed from the beginning of his reign that he was in favour of no tolerance.

Perhaps the best example that can be given of the views of the majority of the Puritans and of their consequent divergence from the National Church is to be found in the history of those who left England for conscience sake, and after settling temporarily in Amsterdam and Leiden eventually sailed for Virginia. With the action of these men may be compared the speeches of Lord Saye and Sele, concerning the Liturgy of the Church and upon the bishops' power in civil affairs, both of which were answered by Laud.

With regard to the "Pilgrim fathers" it is not very easy to speak. They have been dealt with in their place in an earlier volume of this history of the English Church. Of the theological opinions of the more distinguished **The Pilgrim fathers.** members two very different views might be obtained. We might hold that their objection to the Church was, like that of the Millenary Petitioners, a sincere and earnest repulsion from all that belonged to the historic and continuous Christian society. Bastwick blames their moderation. He writes in 1646 : " The extremist extent of their desires reached but to the removal of all the Ceremonies and Innovations ; the taking away of the service book [*Book of Common Prayer*] : and the pulling down of the High Commission Court (which was called the Court Christian, though it was rather Pagan), and the removal of the Hierarchy, root and branch ; and the setting up and establishing of a godly Presbytery throughout the kingdom." And with this may be compared the declaration written at Leiden early in 1618, that " we do wholly and in all points agree with the French Reformed churches, according to their public 'Confession of Faith.'"

But, on the other hand, we may form a very different conclusion, when we find a declaration from the same conscientious men that they assent wholly to the Thirty-nine Articles, and that they acknowledge the Episcopal authority.

There is a significant addition to each clause of this document which shows that the real danger to the pilgrims, and the real opposition which they were anxious to deprecate, came from the king and the State. It is indeed difficult to arrive at a clear conclusion from the evidence afforded of the somewhat elastic consciences of these good folk. We may, however, admit that they had a rooted aversion to lawn sleeves ; for they were very angry with Master Blackwell because he obtained the Puritan Archbishop Abbot's blessing on his voyage.

Another aspect of the controversy with the Puritans is vividly represented by two of Laud's answers to the speeches of one of their prominent champions.

Lord Saye and Sele was an obstinate and eccentric noble-man with that curious and unwarranted confidence in his
Laud's con troversies with Lord Saye and Sele. own judgment, and that ignorant contempt for the opinions and the birth of other people, which sit so characteristically upon some reforming peers. Both the speeches of his to which Laud thought fit to write answers were made after the archbishop was imprisoned, and when he was unable to answer for himself in debate in the House of Lords ; and there was a special meanness in such an attack as Lord Saye's, when the object of it was standing trial for his life.

The first speech " touching the Liturgy " was divided into three parts: (1) a contemptuous account of Laud's origin and career ; (2) a plea for extemporary rather than written forms of public worship ; (3) a vindication of himself and his friends from the charge of separatism. To the first point the arch-bishop had a very dignified reply ; and indeed the matter does not concern us. The birth of an archbishop neither justifies nor condemns his theology. To the two other points there was more need to reply, and it is not without interest to-day, when we have been told that there could have been no dissent but for Laud, to observe the form the reply took. First, there was a vindication of the right of the Church to ordain set forms of prayer. The apostles certainly had power, and exercised it, to enjoin doctrine, and used a form of ordination by imposition of hands, and a " form of whole-some words." And, indeed, " no question can be made but

that the Church of Christ had and hath still as much power
to ordain a set form of prayer as any of these things." Lord
Saye and Sele said that the use of fixed forms of prayer made
men preach but poorly. There have been at different times
many reasons given for bad sermons : this of Lord Saye's was
a strange one in a church of great preachers and of fixed
forms, and Laud had no difficulty in showing its absurdity.
Again, would not learned bishops be better employed in
making prayers of their own than in repeating those
of other people ? Laud answers this too, and sums
up by saying, " The question is not whether a
negligent set form of prayer, or a good form of set prayer
negligently and without devotion offered up to God (as too
often they are, God help us), be better than other prayers,
carefully composed and devoutly uttered ; but simply whether
a good set form of prayer (such as the Liturgy of the Church
of England is) be made so evil, only by the enjoining of it, as
that therefore the service itself ought to be refused." It was,
indeed, a strange contention to which Lord Saye had brought
himself—that because forms, lawful in themselves, had been
enjoined by public authority, they must be rejected by the
individual conscience.

(1) In its
religious
aspect.

The question of separatism brings us still more clearly into
the region of modern controversy. Lord Saye and Sele
assumed the position that by adherence to the Universal or
Catholic Church was meant nothing more than the holding of
the chief articles of the Christian faith, that there was no
schism but in rejecting them, and that every particular church
and congregation might do as it pleased in the matters of order,
of liturgy, of worship. Two lines of argument may be taken
up in answer to this : (1) The lawful demand of authority
upon the individual conscience ; (2) the practical impos-
sibility of differing in order and worship from the Church
without also departing from the faith. Both these Laud em-
phasises. It is absurd to deny that you separate when history
and the evidences of men's eyes and ears are against you.
" I humbly conceive that it is certain that he, whoever he be,
that will not communicate in public prayer with a National
Church which serves God as she ought, is a separatist. But
the Church of England, as it stands established by law, serves

God as she ought ; therefore, my lord, by his general absent-
ing himself from her commands in prayer, is a separatist."

This is a logical and complete answer. You must allow
those who have adhered to a continuous historic religious
body to define what they mean by separation from
it ; and churchmen considered Lord Saye and his
school to be separatists. It was as easy to show that Brownists
and Independents had in many cases departed from the
faith—and indeed, that all Anabaptists and Brownists "agree
that the Church of England is unchristian " ; and it was a
good occasion for a stern condemnation of Calvinism.
"Almost all of them say that God from all eternity reprobates
by far the greater part of mankind to eternal fire, without any
eye at all to their sin. Which opinion my very soul abomin-
ates. For it makes God, the God of all mercies, to be the
most fierce and unreasonable tyrant in the world. For the
question is not here, what God may do by an absolute act of
power, would He so use it upon the creature which He made
of nothing ; but what He hath done, and what stands with
His wisdom, justice, and goodness to do." Laud knew at
least how to go to the root of the matter, and in this answer
he puts it very clearly that the Puritan position was nothing
else than this—that the Church government of the day was
unchristian and the Church wrong in fundamentals.

Separatism.

The second speech of Lord Saye's which Laud answered
was his oration against the bishops on the Bill for taking
away their votes in the House of Lords. The
archbishop's answer was a defence of the historic
ministry. (1) He sketched the history of the
priesthood in the Old Testament, showing its Divine sanction
and its continuous succession, and the place of the priesthood
in temporal affairs. " Nothing of like antiquity can well be
more clear than that four thousand years before, and under
the Law, the priests, especially the chief priests, did meddle
in and help manage the greatest temporal affairs." (2) He
discussed the bearing of the Old Testament on Christian
usage. (3) He defended the historic order of Episcopacy—
" It is the constant and universal tradition of the whole
Church of Christ, which is of greatest authority next to
Scripture itself, that bishops are successors of the apostles

(2) In its political aspect.

and presbyters made in resemblance of the seventy disciples."
(4) He explained, and justified by history and the advantage
of the nation, the right of bishops to sit in the House of
Lords.   Some shrewd sayings must have gone   Constitutional
home.   "The bishops of England have been ac-   position of
counted, and truly been, grave and experienced   the bishops.
men, and far fitter to have votes in Parliaments for the
making of laws than many young youths that are in either
House. . . . If they spend their younger studies, before they
meddle with divinity, as they may and ought, sure there is
some great defect in them, if they be not as knowing men in
the rules of government as most noblemen.   Others there are
who spend all their younger time in hawking and hunting,
and somewhat else."   From this he passes to a general justification of clergymen's mingling in civil affairs—a sensible and
temperate assertion of the wisdom of admitting their share in
the common life.   In history, indeed, Laud was more than a
match for his opponents.   The constitution recognises, for a
longer time than it recognises any other power but that of the
crown, the right of the bishops to sit in the chief council of
the nation.

All this may to-day seem very tedious.   The important
point to observe is that,—with all the wearisome emphasis on
detail which makes the seventeenth century controversies so
intolerable to modern taste—Laud always contrives to seize
the true point at issue, and to raise the discussion to the
highest level.   Lord Saye's two speeches against the Liturgy
and against the possession by the clergy of any political power
afford the archbishop the occasion of showing in clear but
temperate language that a fixed form of worship is more
reasonable, more historical, and more reverent than extemporary effusions, and that reason, history, and common sense
allow to the clergy (who owe their spiritual power nevertheless
to God alone) the right to act equally with their brethren, justly,
honourably, and not as partisans, in the politics of their country.

The controversy in which Laud was engaged with the
Puritans was doubtless keenest in practical life ; but his
printed works show as clearly what the real point of contention was.   Should the English Church depart from her history
and undergo a new reformation after the model of the foreign

Protestants ?   To this Laud by his writings, as by his deeds,
helped her to answer decisively No.

These two pamphlets, in which his reply to the Puritan
attack is summarised, have a pathetic interest. They were
written by the old man in the Tower, weak and ailing, and
standing in deadly peril of his life. They were his protest for
what he believed to be the right, uttered when others were
silent who might with much less danger to themselves have
spoken. They showed, if nothing else, the indomitable
courage of the man and his deep sincerity. The Church
system was to him no accretion upon a primitive faith but its
true and eloquent expression ; and what he held for truth,
that no terrors could induce him to suppress. Such was
the position assumed by Laud in opposition to Puritan
controversialists.

His theory of Anglicanism, in answer to Roman claims,
has already been summarised. It may be well in this place
Laud's
Anglican
principles. to note that it involved an assertion that the English Church truly holds the Catholic doctrines
of Baptism, and of the real presence and the sacrifice in the Eucharist : but the whole contention all returns
to the same climax. Rome is not infallible, and England
holds to the firm faith of Christ. Laud's *Controversy with
Fisher*, published fully in 1639, is indeed a remarkable
and courageous assertion, extraordinarily bold, clear, uncompromising and vital in its treatment of the real questions at
issue between England and Rome. Laud, whatever may be
said about details of his book, did unquestionably go to the
root of the matter : and it is upon the lines on which he
treated it that the controversy, so long as it continues, must
be pursued.

Remarkable as is the evidence which his book affords to
the clearness and the prescience of Laud's mind, there is in
it, perhaps, a still greater claim on the respect and gratitude
of Christians. And this it is important to note in any general
consideration of his policy. It contains a plea, large and
liberal indeed for the times, for toleration and mercy and an
avoidance of that " cursing spirit " which Hammond, Laud's
true disciple, so strongly condemned. " The Church of
England never declared that every one of her Articles is

fundamental," and " I will never take it upon me to express
that tenet or opinion, the denial of the foundation only excepted, which may shut any Christian, even the meanest, out
of heaven."   Laud in this, as in his Catholicism, expressed,
according to the views of the noblest of his contemporaries,
the true mind of the English Church.

This, strictly speaking, is all we can say of Laud in controversy against the Puritans and against Rome.   In these
speeches and in these arguments alone was he concerned.
He entered into controversy swiftly and decisively, but rarely.
He was not a controversialist, though he left memorials of his
work in that field of which any controversialist might be proud.

He was not a controversialist, but he was certainly an
ecclesiastical statesman.   As such the position of the
Romanists in England was constantly brought   Laud
before him.   How were they to be dealt with ?   and the
What was the attitude of the Church of England   Romanists.
to these schismatics from her fold ?   The first question was
one which the law of England answered with relentless
severity.   So long as the Roman Catholics in England were
in a position in which ecclesiastical obligation seemed to
compel them to be traitors, it was not unnatural that a State,
by no means sure in the foundation of its claims, should
retain in its Statute book the most stringent penalties against
recusancy.   And these a very strong body of public opinion,
reinforced both by a knowledge of the struggles of continental
Protestants and by the bitterness of Calvinistic prejudice, was
eager in urging the king to inflict.   In the year of
his accession Charles issued letters to Archbishop   The penal
Abbot requiring that no good means be neglected   laws.
for discovering " Jesuits, seminary priests, and other seducers
of our people to the Romish religion, or for repressing
Recusants and delinquents of that sort, against whom
you are to proceed by excommunication and other
censures of the Church, not omitting any other lawful
means to bring them to public justice."   Three   Laud's views
months before this the council had ordered that   on the
recusants should not be allowed to retain their   question.
arms.   Charles, on the other hand, had married a Roman
Catholic wife, with some suggestion at least of toleration for

those of her religion in England, and he was not himself at all of a persecuting temper.

Laud, as best he could, tried to carry out the principles of toleration which he himself held, while studiously obeying the law. He would himself have preferred to leave these religious questions to the Church to deal with, but the State tied down the Church at every point. So he wrote to Strafford on September 9, 1633, just after the announcement of his translation to Canterbury: "As for the Church, it is so bound up in the forms of the Common Law that it is not possible for me, or for any man, to do that good which he would do or is bound to do. For your Lordship sees, no man clearer, that they which have gotten so much power over the Church will not let go their hold: they have indeed, fangs with a witness, whatsoever I was once said in passion to have." In Ireland his letters to Strafford show that he strongly advised the tolerant execution of the recusancy laws, the non-exacting of the fines, and the like. In England his direct influence on the policy of the State in this matter was not great. The king was dragged whither he would not by the Puritans, and the House of Commons was certainly unwilling to listen to Laud's wishes on such a point. It has been asserted that the appointment of Windebanke as Secretary of State was designed to further a *rapprochement* with Rome : but there is no evidence for such a view.

Religiously, there were two aspects of the Roman question which affected Laud. There were the negotiations with the pope which Panzani, Con, and Rossetti, papal agents at the English court, were eager to set on foot : and there was the matter of individual conversions. It seems at one time that Windebanke, Secretary of State, entertained the idea that reunion was not impossible, and approached Charles on the subject ; but Laud warned the king that if he wished to go to Rome the pope would not stir a step to meet him. Bishop Mountague met Panzani several times, adhering always strenuously to the security of his own orders. The interviews probably became known, for when he sent his son in 1635 to Rome it was suspected that there was some secret business. But probably the two matters were in no way connected. More important was the mission of Dom Leander of St.

Negotiations with Rome.

Martin (a Welshman, whose name was John Jones) in 1634.
He had been at Merchant Taylors' School and at
St. John's College, Oxford, and was well acquainted   The mission
with Laud.   Windebanke said to Panzani, "if we   of Dom
had neither Jesuits nor Puritans in England I   Leander,
am confident a reunion might easily be effected"; and   1634.
a Benedictine was thought both at Rome and at the
English court to be a much less dangerous person than either.
Dom Leander came to inspect the English Romanists and to report on such matters as the oath of   Dom
allegiance.   It seems that a curious offer had already   Leander's
been made to Laud of a cardinal's hat: but Laud   England.
had naturally refused "till Rome should be other than she is."
None the less it was not difficult for Leander to see that there
were points of approximation.   In his report he emphasised the
fact that the English Churchmen with whom he had to deal
considered "as schismatics those other Protestant churches
scattered throughout Europe who have repudiated and turned
away from the ancient ecclesiastical hierarchy."   His interviews with important persons came to nothing, for the English
Episcopate was firm in its adherence to Reformation standards.
He got so far as to draw up instructions for an agent who was
to be sent from Rome to report on the question of reunion,
advocating an assembly of moderate men to discuss points
of difference, and he advised for concessions on the part of
the pope that communion in both kinds might be granted,
and the marriage of the clergy and the liturgy in English be
allowed, "also the admittance of the English clergy (coming
to agree in points of faith) in their prelatures, dignities, and
benefices, either by re-ordination *sub conditione*, since their
orders here be invalid or dubious, or by way of *commendam*,
as many princes ecclesiastical and other beneficiated persons
are admitted."   Nothing came of the suggestion.   It is
unlikely that it ever came to the ears of Laud.   It was revived under Charles II., but at this time the death of Dom
Leander caused the business to fall into other and less
sympathetic hands, and no progress was made.   The later
Roman agents, notably Panzani, were ignorant of English life:
and even if Laud had been willing to go a step to meet them
the project of reunion was impossible.

When Dom Leander lay dying it was said that an English bishop sought earnestly to see him.   This may probably have been Godfrey Goodman, who was consecrated to the see of Gloucester in 1624, and who, in 1636, asked, Panzani said, to be allowed to keep an Italian priest to say mass secretly in his house.   In 1640 he was committed to prison for his communications with Rome. Through him, and it is possible to a lesser extent with Mountague, negotiations may have been continued.   But Laud, it is certain, kept out of them.   An Oratorian sent to England in 1635 was forbidden, " on any pretext whatever, to allow himself to be drawn into communication with the Archbishop of Canterbury."   Efforts were made to bribe the archbishop, with money and with the cardinalate, a typical example of the ignorance of England that existed among papal agents.   An account of the archbishop's trial, still in manuscript, tells us that he spoke on this point, " declaring that if he had desired preferment for compliance with the Church of Rome, he might have had more honour in foreign parts than ever he was likely to obtain here, and that it was no outward honour but his conscience that caused him to refuse the Cardinal's hat."

It is clear, on the other hand, that Laud had no desire to persecute.   He was willing to some extent to recognise the jurisdiction of a vicar apostolic over his co-religionists, though he was utterly opposed to the establishment of " any popish hierarchy."   He emphatically declared that the State did not punish Romanists for opinion, but only for disloyalty.   Thus, he said, " When divers Romish priests and Jesuits have deservedly suffered death for treason, is it not the constant and just profession of the State, that they never put any man to death for religion, but for rebellion and treason only ? Doth not the State truly affirm that there was never any law made against the life of a papist, *quatenus* a papist only ? And is not all this State false, if their very religion be rebellion ?   For if their religion be rebellion, it is not only false, but impossible, that the same man, in the same act, should suffer for his rebellion and not for his religion.   And this King James understood very well, when in his Premonition to all Christian monarchs he saith, ' I do constantly maintain that no papist, either in my time or in the time of the late Queen, ever died for his conscience.'"

While this was his attitude towards Romanists ecclesiastically and politically, he was very eager to secure the return of English Roman Catholics to the church of their fathers. At his trial he gave a list of twenty-two persons whom he had himself "recalled from Rome." When he challenged any one to give a better proof of his zeal Hugh Peters "told him there were those ministers that could prove not only twenty-two but two hundred, yea, some above five hundred, that were converted by their diligent and faithful labours in the work of the ministry, and might have recalled more had they not been silenced by him,"—an absurd boast. Laud's converts could be named : and many of them did yeoman service for the English Church. Of these the ablest was William Chillingworth. Laud had known him from his childhood, and he felt a peculiar sorrow at his conversion to Rome by Fisher, the very Jesuit whom the bishop had controverted. In 1632 he returned to England from Douai, much dissatisfied with Roman teaching. Juxon, Laud's successor as President of St. John's College, Oxford, and Sheldon, then a Fellow of All Souls', were urgent with him to reconsider his position, and the former reported to Laud that the "pervert" declared himself ready to take any course for satisfaction that his friends might advise, and to confer with Laud himself or any one deputed by him. Juxon shrewdly suspected Chillingworth to be anxious to be Laud's convert, thinking "all his motives are not spiritual, protest he never so much." At Great Tew, near Oxford, he stayed with the fascinating Lucius Carey, Viscount Falkland, who remained, with every wide literary interest and with considerable freedom of speculation, a sincere Christian of the English Church.

At Great Tew it is probable, as well as through direct intercourse with Laud, the mind of Chillingworth found satisfaction. He returned to the Church of England, and before long he published a vindication of his position in answer to a Jesuit attack. Chillingworth's *Religion of Protestants* (1637) is an interesting illustration alike of the influence of Laud's tolerant spirit and of the broad principles on which it was possible to defend the doctrines of the English Church. It is, above all things, a plea for liberty. It protests against the "presumptuous imposing of the senses of men upon the general words of God, and laying them upon men's consciences together, under the equal penalty of death and damnation." It was an assertion of intellectual honesty and of the welcome which the English Church gave to a free and rational inquiry. *The Religion of Protestants*, as the Church of England knew it, was declared to be "a safe way of salvation." It was a book which was destined greatly to influence the thought of the future; and through it Laud's penetrating insistence on the fact that "the Church of England never declared that every one of her Articles are fundamental in the faith" came to be a prominent thought in the minds of the next generation of theologians. "Nothing is necessary to be believed but what is plainly revealed," was a clear statement; but like all similar statements there were difficulties in the interpretation of it.

Sir Kenelm Digby, a genius and an eccentric, was another in whose conversion Laud took the keenest interest, though not with the same success. The relations between the two men are, however, a happy example of the "goodness and affection" which those who knew him recognised in the archbishop. Throughout, they were spiritual motives alone to which Laud appealed. A touching letter from Sir William Webbe, who had profited by the ministry of John Cosin, then rector of Brancepeth, and who was one of Laud's converts, well illustrates this.

Sir Kenelm Digby.

AUTHORITIES.—Laud's *Works*; State Papers, Domestic; *Strafford Papers;* the correspondence of Panzani, Con, and Rossetti (transcripts in the Record Office); and *The Pope's nuntioes, or the negotiations of Seignior Panzani, Seignior Con, etc.*, London, 1643; Berington, *Memoirs of Panzani;* E. L. Taunton, *The English Black Monks*. On the position of Chillingworth Tulloch's *Rational Theology in England in the Seventeenth Century* (which may be compared with Dr. Gardiner's *History*) sketches the relations of Falkland with the theologians of the time.

CHAPTER V

LAUD'S ADMINISTRATION OF THE CHURCH

AFTER this survey of his attitude towards some of those who stood outside we are in a position to examine and estimate the nature of the work which Laud as archbishop undertook. It has often been asserted that he was a reformer, and that his chiefest interest was the conflict with Calvinism. But it is certain that he would have repudiated any idea of innovation, and that he took no active measures to suppress freedom of speculation on the Calvinistic or any other theology, provided it did not desert the limits of loyalty to the Church. To the world his work seemed to be mainly practical. And there was need of it.

The case of Anthony Bourne and Edward Hewitt, churchwardens of Knottingley, Bedfordshire, is perhaps an extreme one : but that it should be possible showed the need of action. They were charged in the High Commission Court in 1637 with allowing the most disgraceful scandals in Church. It was alleged that in 1634 and the two following years fighting cocks were brought into the chancel of the church of Knottingley, and there fought in front of the altar, in the presence of many spectators who betted and performed "the other offices ordinarily used by cock-fighters." The churchwardens and the minister of the parish were themselves present, with many others "both youths and men, laughing and sporting as spectators at a cock-fight use to do." As we do not know the result of the proceedings taken it is possible that there may be much exaggeration in this tale : but it is certain that in many

Scandals
in the
Church.

cases the grossest irreverence prevailed in the use of parish churches. The churches often "lay nastily"; and the altars were often left in the middle of the chancel, contrary to the Injunctions of Elizabeth, with the result that men lounged upon them or covered them with their hats and cloaks.

Many customs too survived in country places which "a godly and thorough reformation" should have swept away. A curious petition, for instance, reached Laud in 1637 from the parish of Clungunford, Salop, a "spacious wide parish," containing "many very old and ancient people," and having an ancient custom time out of mind that after evening prayer on Easter day the parson should provide a church-feast, in the church, of bread and cheese and ale or beer, for the refreshing of those ancient people that repaired to evening prayer, having received the holy sacrament the same day "in the morning, and also for relief of the poor of the parish that repair thither for relief, and have always had sufficient provision of bread and cheese given them by the inhabitants to serve them and their families a good space afterwards." About fifty years past, the petitioners asserted, it was ordered by the then Archbishop of Canterbury that this feast should be thenceforth kept, not in the church but in the parsonage house. It had been so kept until the last Easter, when Samuel Barkeley, the present rector, discontinued the custom altogether. The inhabitants appealed to the archbishop to have it restored. Laud answered: "I shall not go about to break this custom, so it be done in the parsonage house in a neighbourly and decent way; but I cannot approve of the continuance of it in the church, and if ever I shall hear it be so done again, I will not fail to call the offenders into the High Commission."

The archbishop, indeed, was often unwilling to interfere, whatever his own opinions may have been. For example, a preacher before the University of Cambridge, named Adams, is said to have asserted the necessity of confession to a priest. Rushworth records the investigation of the subject by the Heads, with the result that a majority voted that he had taught nothing contrary to the doctrine of the Church of England. The papers in the case were sent to Laud, but he made no comment on them.

Survival of old customs.

Laud's unwillingness to interfere needlessly.

The case of Welwyn is another instance which shows similar absention where popular opinion regarded the archbishop as a violent innovator. The following extract from the Canway Papers in the Record Office will serve to illustrate this attitude of Laud :

"The same week, sixteen men in the parish of Welling in Hertfordshire, came to their archdeacon, Dr. Holdworth, here in London, to complain of the Parson of their Parish, for having refused the three Sundays before, to administer the Sacrament unto them, only because they would not come upp to receive yt : at the Rayle about the communion table. I heare there hath been greate contention betweene the minister and the Parishioners which the Archdeacon not being able to compose, hee therefore with these sixteen, Parishioners, addresseth his complainte to my Lord Grace of Canterbury, who haveing heard all the differences, referres all back to Dr. Holdsworth, to settle peace between all parties saying, hee wonders the Parson should exact their comeing upp to the rayle to receave the Sacrament, if soe bee the Pewes be conveniently seated in the Church to administer in them."

Laud, it is clear, could not interfere everywhere, and when he did interfere he was by no means always indiscreet. His hands were certainly full.

In the north there was much nonconformity, and especial difficulties arose through the popular practice of endowing lectureships, where the lecturers preached, apart from the Prayer-book services, and not without _{The lecture-ships.} contempt of the parish clergy. Thus in January 1634 Archbishop Neile of York reported to the king that the dioceses of Carlisle and Chester were far from obedient to the directions of the Prayer-book, the clergy often "chopping, changing, altering, omitting and adding." Many, he said, "knew not how to read the service according to the book, and those deemed themselves conformable that did not oppose it." A curious example of the absence of order was to be found in the usage of the two cathedral churches of those dioceses. In each there were parochial as well as cathedral services, and "the service with voices and organs in the choir and the reading service in the body of the church" actually proceeded at the same time, to the confusion of the worshippers. At Bunbury, in Cheshire, was a gross example of the evil of lectureships. The Haberdashers' Company had appointed a preacher, and a curate, and claimed power to dismiss them at pleasure: and they had already been suspended for nonconformity. When Charles received this report he wrote sharp comments on the margin. The cathedral service should be ordered as the archbishop wished; and "see next year that ye give me a good account thereof." On the lecturers he made fuller comment: "I have had the like complaint from the Archbishop of Canterbury, wherefore as I have answered him so I tell you, that I will not endure that any lay person (much less a corporation) have power to place and displace curates or beneficed priests at their pleasure, therefore you may be sure of more than my protection in this."

Neile's letter concluded with an account of the recusants in his provinces: Charles's comment was, "the neglect of punishing Puritans breeds papists." He had in fact already ordered that lecturers should always before preaching read the service, in surplice and hood, and that "if a corporation do maintain a lecturer, he be not suffered to preach until he profess his willingness to take upon himself a living with cure of souls within that corporation." The lectureships had threatened indeed to set up an *imperium in imperio* within the Church of England: the lecturers were the leaders of resistance against Episcopal authority; and the feoffees who had bought up impropriations for the sake of endowing lecturers "kept them in their own hands, and disposed of the profits to such lecturers and ministers, and in such proportions and for so long a time as pleased them." The law was invoked against the corporation of feoffees: and the king's injunctions were reissued when Laud became archbishop. He was determined to suppress "vagrant ministers and trencher-chaplains."

The principles upon which Laud determined to act are expressed with great clearness in his dedication of his Conference with Fisher to the king: "No

Laud's principles. one thing hath made conscientious men more wavering in their own minds, or more apt and easy to be drawn aside from the sincerity of religion pro

fessed in the Church of England, than the want of uniform
and decent order in the many churches of the kingdom;
and the Romanists have been apt to say, the houses of God
could not be suffered to lie so nastily, as in some places they
have done, were the true worship of God observed in them,
or did the people think that such it were. It is true, the
inward worship of the heart is the true service of God, and no
service acceptable without it; but the external worship of God
in His Church is the great witness to the world that our heart
stands right in that service of God. . . . These thoughts are
they, and no other, which have made me labour so much as I
have done for decency and an orderly settlement of the external
worship of God in the Church; for of that which is inward
there can be not witness among men nor no example for men.
Now, no external action in the world can be uniform without
some ceremonies; and these in religion, the ancienter they be
the better, so they may fit time and place. Too many over-
burden the service of God, and too few leave it naked. And
scarce anything hath hurt religion more in these broken times
than an opinion in too many men, that because Rome hath
thrust some unnecessary and many superstitious ceremonies
upon the Church, therefore the Reformation must have none
at all; not considering therewhile, that ceremonies are the
hedges that fence the substance of religion from all the
indignities which profaneness and sacrilege too commonly
put upon it."

Laud did not desire to innovate. He took up the primatial
office with the intention of seeing that the Prayer-book was
observed and that the royal injunctions for the maintenance
of order in the Church were carried out. In this aim he must
depend largely upon the friendly assistance of his colleagues
in the Episcopate.

Of the bishops of Charles I.'s time it is impossible here
to speak particularly. Many names of eminence, such as
Davenant and Hall, both at first more Calvinistic
than "Laudian," but the latter a prominent literary
defender of Episcopacy, must be passed with a mere
mention. But special reference may well be made
to those who supported Laud's policy, because it was through
their action that the Church of England recovered the standard

*His
supporters
among the
bishops.*

of seemliness and dignity in public worship which from the Restoration remained the settled order of her life. Notable examples of these were Neile, Wren, Mountague, Manwaring, and Juxon.

Mountague continued to write after his appointment to the see of Chichester. He prepared in 1638 a book on the doctrine of the Christian altar, in which was "much of the Church's sacrifice faithfully related out of antiquity," and submitted it to Laud's judgment. In the same year he was translated to Norwich, being succeeded by an eminent and saintly priest, Brian Duppa. Manwaring was also a correspondent of Laud's. Wren was more notable. He had been chaplain to Charles on his foolish visit to Madrid, and the king had always a high respect for him. As Bishop of Norwich, and afterwards of Ely, he pleaded and worked for "a uniformity of doctrine and a uniformity of discipline," and he was determined in putting down the lecturers who for their living were obliged to suit their doctrines to those who paid them. Neile, an older man, who rose from see to see till he became Archbishop of York in 1632, represented the adhesion of the clergy of Elizabeth's day to the principles of Laud. He was a man of extraordinary energy and activity, an uncompromising churchman and disciplinarian, who was one of the first to attract the attention of the Puritan Commons as a patron of Cosin and Mountague, and he was named by the House, with Laud, as suspected of Arminianism. When he became Archbishop of York he corresponded constantly with officials of Church and State in the South, and especially with Laud, on matters of Church interest, such as the position of the French and Dutch Protestants employed in the drainage of Hatfield Chase ; with the Council as to the work of the High Commission and the enforcement of the Recusancy laws in his province ; and with the Secretary of State on collections for the royal needs.

The report of his diocese for 1636-37 states that the arch-

Richard Neile, Archbishop of York, 1632-1640.

bishop had not found "any distractions of opinion touching points of divinity lately controverted." He declares himself a "great adversary of the Puritan faction (which he holds himself bound in conscience and duty to God, his Majesty and the most happy established Church to be), yet (having been a bishop eight and twenty years) he never deprived any man but has endeavoured their reformation." Though an old man he continued till his death to be active in political as well as in ecclesiastical business. We find him seizing books upon the River Ouse that belonged to a recusant, hunting for the "pope's traitorous agents," receiving and exercising enlarged powers in the High Commission Court, appearing constantly in the Star Chamber, sitting on the Commission for the government of the English colonies and plantations (April 10, 1636), settling the difficulties in the parish of Newcastle-upon-Tyne, and cordially welcoming Dr. George Wishart (the biographer of Montrose). Till within a fortnight of his death a correspondence was kept up with Laud, Windebanke, and Sir Dudley Carleton. Always an energetic man of business, he was at work up to the last, and his death, October 31, 1640, was felt by the southern archbishop as a severe loss, for he was "a man to be as true to, and as stout for, the Church of England established by law as any man that came to perferment in it."

If these were all friendly to the archbishop, William Juxon, Bishop of London, was one whom he could implicitly trust. As a member of his own college, and his successor as president, he had known him from his youth. He was a man of industry and capacity, who never made an enemy. The bitterest Puritan could not find a word to say against him, nor did he, though he was the staunchest of Laud's supporters and the most orthodox of theologians, ever find his clergy intractable. A contemporary speaks of him as "the delight of the English nation, whose reverence was the only thing all factions agreed in, by allowing that honour to the sweetness of his manner that some denied to the sacredness of his function; being by love what another is in pretence, an universal bishop." Juxon was indefatigable in public work, secular as well as ecclesiastical. On March 6, 1636, he was made Lord Treasurer, an act which, though it was probably in the heated feeling of the time unwise, was certainly intended to benefit the public service as well as to advance the position of churchmen. Laud wrote in his diary: "No churchman had it since

William Juxon, Bishop of London.

Henry VII.'s time. I pray God bless him to carry it so that the Church may have honour, and the king and the State have contentment by it. And now if the Church will not hold up themselves under God, I can do no more."

The visitation articles of these and other bishops, especially perhaps those of Mountague and Juxon, show how scrupulously investigation was made as to the services of the Church, as to the king's requirement that the altar should be placed at the east end of the chancel, and as to the character and activity of the clergy.

At Juxon's first triennial visitation, in 1634, the "articles to be inquired of within the diocese of London" were printed as a pamphlet. They may be quoted as character-istic of the reforming movement rather than as original. Inquiry was made (1) whether before all sermons the minister prayed for the king, queen, and royal family, and all archbishops, bishops, and other ecclesi-astical persons. (2) Whether the prescribed form of Divine service was used in reading public prayers and the litany and in administering the Sacraments, whether the people knelt at the administration of the Holy Communion, whether the minister used the sign of the Cross in baptism, whether he preached once every Sunday or read a homily, whether he wore the surplice and hood of his degree, whether he joined in or allowed any "private conventicles or meetings," and further as to his residence and due discharge of his duties of visiting his people. Moreover, concerning the church whether there was a "font of stone standing in the ancient usual place" and "a convenient and decent com-munion table standing upon a frame with a carpet of silk or some other decent stuff and a fair linen cloth to lay thereon at the communion time," whether it was placed in a convenient place "within the chancel or church as that the minister may be best heard in his prayer and administration and that the greater number may communicate," and if it was in any way "abused to profane uses" out of service, further "have any ancient monuments or glass windows been defaced, or anything else belonging to your church or chapel been at any time purloined?"

Concerning the duties of Church wardens the usual

Visitation articles.

inquiries were made, as to the recusants, and those of other parishes who attended the church, and whether any plays, feasts, banquets, church-ales, drinkings, musters, and showing of arms or any other profane usages had been kept in their church, chapel, or churchyard, and as to any persons of ill life or deniers of the king's supremacy or defamers of the Church and Prayer-book. The "minister, churchwardens and side-men" were required to draw up and present lists of recusants, men and women, of noncommunicants, and of communicants. In the articles for Juxon's visitation in 1640 certain changes occur based upon the new Canons of that year and the questions are more explicit, *e.g.* "Do the chancels remain as they have in times past, that is to say in the convenient situation of the seats and in the ascent of steps unto the place appointed anciently for the standing of the holy table."

The position of the holy table, and its security from profanation, were points which were especially insisted on. A report of Laud's shows how necessary this was. The position "There happened also in the town of Tadlow a of the Lord's table. very ill accident on Christmas day 1630, by reason of not having the communion table railed in that it might be kept from profanations. For in sermon time a dog came to the table, and took the loaf of bread prepared for the holy sacrament in his mouth, and ran away with it. Some of the parishioners took the same from the dog, and set it again upon the table. After sermon the minister could not think fit to consecrate this bread; and other fit for the sacrament was not to be had in that town; and the day so far spent, they could not send for it to another town: so there was no communion."

The practical reform embodied in the requirement of rails, such as dogs could not pass, might seem to need no defence, but in this, as in other matters, one Bishop opponent stood out against the most prominent Williams's *Holy Table.* of Laud's requirements. This was Bishop Williams, whose temper was not improved by disgrace. He lived in great state at the Episcopal manor of Buckden, and Charles disliked "the lustre wherein he lived, the great company that resorted unto him." He clung to the

Deanery of Westminster, and no remonstrance could induce him to put an end to so gross a pluralist scandal. When protest was made his biographer admits that he was " utterly deaf to it." With these failings he had also a theological position which was not popular at court. " He would not unchurch those Christians, but wished them a better mind, that had set up another discipline." And in 1633 he gave order against the action of the vicar of Grantham, who had placed the holy table at the east end, and justified his position by condemning the doctrine of the Eucharistic sacrifice. Heylin, one of Laud's chaplains, wrote against him a book called *A Coal from the Altar*. He replied with a reasoned defence of his position, *The Holy Table : Name and Thing*. Of Laud's feeling towards him his biographer Hacket, afterwards Bishop of Lichfield, writes thus : " Of all men, Bishop Laud was the party whose enmity was most tedious, and most spiteful against his great benefactor Lincoln. He batter'd him with old and new contrivances fifteen years : his very dreams were not without them. I will touch that fault, that great fault, with a gentle hand, because of that good which was in him; because in other things, I believe, for my part, he was better than he was commonly thought ; because his death did extinguish a great deal of envy. I meet with him in his worst action that ever he did, and cannot shun it ; if I should draw him in purposely to defame him, now he is at rest, I were more sacrilegious than if I robbed his tomb."

Laud's friends as stoutly defend him from the attack. He himself asserted his just dealing towards Williams with much emphasis : but Williams as time went on spoke with unconcealed bitterness of the archbishop. " He had best not meddle with me, for all the friends he can make will be too few to save himself." Against Laud's metropolitical visitation he stoutly protested. But the scandals of his own life prevented his having much weight. For a long time a charge of revealing the king's secrets contrary to his oath as privy councillor had been hanging over his head. At a critical point he clearly suborned witnesses : and when the king was enraged against him, and he had failed to win pardon by a bribe, the Star Chamber and

Laud and Bishop Williams.

the High Commission alike sentenced him, the one to a heavy fine, the other to suspension from his ecclesiastical functions. Two years later (1639) he received further sentence in the Star Chamber for some discreditable letters in which he seemed to have used unbefitting language about the archbishop, and in this trial he again perjured himself. For the time he was silenced.

His chief opponent thus removed, the course of Laud's measures may be seen in the annual reports of his province which he sent in to the king. These, with reports also from every diocesan bishop, were required by Charles in the Instructions which he issued in 1634. Each bishop was to give in an account annually to his metropolitan, from which the metropolitan was to "make a brief" of his province, "so that we may see how the whole Church is governed, and our commands obeyed." Among the instructions were those requiring residence of the bishops in their sees, observance of triennial visitations, care of ordinations, and restraint of lecturers and chaplains, with special order as to catechising.

The annual reports of the two provinces sent in to the king.

The first report from Laud noted some nonconformity, which consisted mostly of omitting parts of divine service and refusing to subscribe the Articles; some "seditious" and some "running" lectures. In the next year the archbishop was able to report the beginning of his metropolitical visitation, which had extended over seven dioceses, beginning with his own. It was conducted partly by the vicar general, Sir Nathaniel Brent, and partly by the Dean of Arches, Sir John Lambe. In the diocese of Canterbury there seemed a probability of the creation of a number of new sects through the French, Italian, and Dutch congregations. In the theory of the day, *cujus regio ejus religio*, it would have been strange if those who had been born since the settlement of the congregations in England should have been allowed to continue their separate worship. It was enough that those who fled to England should themselves follow the customs which they had adopted abroad : the next generation might naturally be expected to conform to the church of their adopted country. Nonconformity was evi-

Canterbury.

dently increasing. "I find the greatest part of Wiltshire overgrown with the humours of those men that did not conform." "For Lincoln, my vicar general certifies me, there are many Anabaptists in it, and that their leader is one Johnson, a baker; and that in divers parts of that diocese many both of clergy and laity are excessively given to drunkenness." The Bishop of St. David's noted that some lecturers, "that have with their giddiness offered to distemper the people," had been driven out of the diocese. The Bishop of Gloucester (Goodman) "certifies that he is forced to ordain some very mean ministers in his diocese, to supply cures as mean; yet he professeth, that to his knowledge he never gave holy orders to any unworthy person."

In 1635 there were "yet very many refractory persons to the government of the Church of England about Maidstone and Ashford and some other parts." A few nonconformists were reported from London. The Bishop of Lincoln reported that he had gone over his whole diocese in person, and that there was but one unconformable man, and he "in the High Commission Court and ready for sentence." In 1636 the "Brownists and other separatists" still lingered about Ashford : but the "Walloons and other strangers" had conformed. In this year Laud for the first time noted a recrudescence of the libels of the Martin Marprelate days, a "spreading and dispersing of some factious and malicious pamphlets against the bishops and government of the Church of England." These doubtless were the writings of Prynne, Burton, and Bastwick, of which more is to be said. Charles promised to deal with them. The diocese of Norwich was full of nonconformity: but Bishop Wren had deserved well of the Church for his vigorous action. A report of Bishop Williams, with Laud's comment on it, shows that the archbishop was far from unreasonable in the pursuit of conformity. "There are risen," reported the former, "some differences in the southern part of his diocese, about the ministers urging the people to receive at the rails, which his lordship saith he hath procured to be placed about the holy table, and the people in some places refusing to do so. Now because this is not regulated by any canon of the Church, his lordship is an humble suitor that he may have direction therein. And truly," added Laud, "I think for this particular the people will best be won by the decency of the thing itself; and that I suppose may be compassed in a short time."

The recusants, it may be observed, figure almost as prominently as the Puritans : and notably from the diocese of St. Asaph. "There is a great resort of recusants to Holywell : and this summer the Lady Falkland and her company came as pilgrims thither; who were the more observed because they travelled on foot and dissembled neither their quality nor their errand. And this boldness of theirs is of very ill construction among your Majesty's people." In 1637 the conventicles at Ashford still continued, and the strangers in Canterbury did not resort to their parish churches as formerly. In London nonconformity was growing : twenty-five ministers had been convented before the chancellor. The diocese of Norwich again sent a very full report through the activity of Wren. In 1638 the report as to Ashford was as before, but the foreigners were more obedient. Matthew Wren had found his reward for activity at Norwich in translation to Ely : and he now sent a brief report from his new diocese. The new Bishop of Norwich, Mountague, reported that "the only thing that troubles his diocese is, that the people have been required to come up and receive at the rail which is set before the communion table, and that heretofore many have been excommunicated or suspended for not doing so. For the thing itself," Laud noted, in giving Mountague's report, "it is certainly the most decent and orderly way, and is practised by your Majesty, and by the lords in your own chapel, and now almost everywhere else. And upon my knowledge it hath long been used in St. Giles's church without Cripplegate, London, with marvellous decency and ease ; and yet in that parish there are not so few as two thousand communicants, more than within any parish in Norwich diocese." He added that the account of suspensions was exaggerated, for out of more than three hundred parishes there were "not thirteen either excommunicated or suspended for refusing of this."

In 1639 signs of growing disturbance are very plain. In several dioceses there were many who refused to come up to the rails : there was strange preaching, and many were "utterly fallen from the Church." In the diocese of Oxford some twenty or thirty persons had been refused ordination, but had obtained it elsewhere, a scandal which might well increase nonconformity. Interesting points such as these crop up continually in the reports, illustrating the condition of the Church. Of a like value are the repeated orders for the strict observance of catechising on the Sunday afternoons, intended apparently not only for children but for the parishioners generally. Two points are notable in this year in the report of the Bishop of Peterborough (Towers), as Laud quoted it : "This he saith he finds plainly, that there are few of the laity factious, but where the clergy misleads them. And this I doubt is too true in most parts of the kingdom." And "they have in this diocese come to him very thick to receive confirmation, to the number of some thousands." This was the last report sent in to the king, on January 2, 1640. The troubles were begun.

Archbishop Neile of York sent similar reports from his province. For instance, in January 1636 he reported that in his own diocese he scarcely found a beneficed minister stiffly unconformable. A few poor stipendiary curates have been found unconformable, but most of them, upon being called to account, have submitted themselves. Touching his Majesty's Declaration for settling questions in doctrine, a watchful eye is had, if any fly out, to call them to account. The Declaration touching catechising has brought many of the ministers to perform both catechising and preaching. The command concerning lecturers has so prevailed that many of the clergy that were forward for market-day sermons, finding how negligent the inhabitants were of coming to the sermon, and that their preaching was more desired to draw company to the market than for the comfort of the preaching, resolve rather to employ themselves in visiting neighbour churches that want preaching ministers ; and to all such places where such weekly sermons are permitted (which are very few) the rule is, "Either observe his Majesty's directions in every particular, or have no sermon." For men's having ministers in their houses, some gentlemen that have impropriations but are to find a curate make the poor minister's

York.

living in their houses a part of his stipend, but none such are permitted save conformable men.

The churchwardens, however, were slack in presenting those who would attend sermons but not the Common Prayer : and there was some dislike of the declaration to permit sports on Sunday. For 1636 we have, in Archbishop Neile's report of his own diocese, an instance of his mild measures. He speaks of his treatment of " a poor melancholic, brainsick, unconformable man," who, having petitioned the archbishop to accept a resignation of his benefice, was called to a conference and dismissed with half a year's respite. Curates at poor stipends he desires should be tolerated in gentlemen's houses, provided in their domestic prayers they hold to the Book of Common Prayer.

Of the year 1638 the certificates of all the northern bishops are preserved. The archbishop himself replies to the order to give notice of " any notable alteration, or other accident within his diocese, which may any ways concern either the doctrine or discipline of the Church established," as follows : " I do not find in my diocese any inclination to innovation in anything which concerns either the doctrine or the discipline of the Church of England ; only I find that too many of your Majesty's subjects inhabiting in these parts of Yorkshire are gone into New England, among which there is one Rogers, that had a benefice well worth £240 per annum, gone, whom I have laboured by the space of two years in sundry conferences to reclaim, and refused to suffer him to resign ; but at the last, he going on shipboard for New England, wrote his letter to me, acknowledged that I had given him good counsel but in vain, and prayed me to accept his resignation, for gone he was for New England." Against which is written in the margin, in the king's hand, " An honester man must bee put in place."

The accounts thus given of the condition of the two provinces may be supplemented from what we learn of Laud's metropolitical visitation. This was evidently medi- *The metro-* tated by the archbishop from the first as a great *political* engine of reformation. He knew that he was sup- *visitation.* ported by the power as well as the personal affection of the king, and he determined to make full use of the opportunity.

At the time of his translation Charles had addressed to him a special letter, expressing his "gracious opinion" of the new archbishop's "worth and care both for the good of God's Church and for the king's service," and giving directions for the preservation of all ceremonies, offices, state and dignity as belonged to the archbishop, for "the upholding of the honour and government of the said Church." In instituting a visitation of all the dioceses within his province Laud acted upon pre-Reformation precedent. He does not seem to have had the slightest intention to innovate. But he gave special directions, his biographer and chaplain, Heylin, says, "to his Vicar General to inquire into the observation of his Majesty's injunctions of the year 1629, to command the churchwardens to place the communion table under the eastern wall of the chancel, where, formerly the altar stood; to set a decent rail before it, to avoid profaneness; and at the rails the communicants to receive the Blessed Sacrament."

The archbishop's memoranda for the visitation exist. They are notes written by him for the instruction of Sir Nathaniel Brent, some "general," some "particular," and they are dated February 22, 1634.

Laud's notes for the visitation. Generally, attention was to be given that no school should be kept in any chancel, that strict inquiry should be made into peculiars held by prebendaries or lay persons; that order should be taken for the use of the surplice and other decent ceremonies of the church; that fonts be brought to their ancient places; inquiry as to observation of his Majesty's instructions; seats in cathedrals to be looked to, and chancels severed from the church or other ways profaned to be remedied. The particular memoranda apply to the several dioceses intended to be visited. Under Canterbury and Norwich special inquiry was to be made as to what Liturgy was used by the foreign refugee churches seated in those places, for how many descents they were for the most part born subjects, and whether such as were so born would not conform to the Church of England. In the diocese of Salisbury special attention was directed to the ecclesiastical condition of Reading (the birthplace of the archbishop), and in several places attention was required to be given to circumstances respecting which the archbishop had received private information from persons with whom the Vicar General was to communicate privately, and not to mention their names. In the diocese of Lincoln, the Chancellor of Lincoln was the archbishop's private informant. In some memoranda specially addressed to the Vicar General he is directed privately to charge the archbishop's officers to give good example by being uncovered in prayer and sermon time, by bowing at the name of the Saviour, and by using the chancels with reverence. On the back of the paper, which is now preserved in the Record Office, is a list of the dioceses intended to be visited in each of the years 1634, 1635, and 1636.

Within a few months reports began to come in. An "abstract or brief account" of the proceedings of Sir Nathaniel Brent during his metropolitical visitation of the diocese of Lincoln, exists at the Record Office. He had arrived at Lincoln in August 1634, Bishop Williams having protested in vain against the visitation. He noted in the cathedral church that the communion table was "not very decent," and the rail worse, that the organs were old and naught, and the copes and vestments had been embezzled. In the minster-yard itself were ale-houses, with hounds and swine, kept "very offensively." At Aylesbury and elsewhere, later on, he found complaints against clergymen who solemnised clandestine marriages, and notably against Edward Collingwood, curate of the ancient church of Stow, near Lincoln, who was declared "to marry them with gloves and masks on." *Reports from the Vicar General.*

The report as to the French and Dutch congregations was not unfavourable. Sir Nathaniel Brent reported in March 1634, that their ministers had visited him and entreated him to give the archbishop humble thanks for his honourable and gracious usage of them, and for the grave counsel he gave to them, promising to endeavour to deserve his great favour towards them. "They all say," he continues, "that they will obey his commands as much as possibly they can; that is, they will repair often to the English churches to hear both divine service and sermons, and persuade their congregations so *The congregations of foreign Protestants.*

to do; and say that they hope to induce them to receive the Blessed Eucharist every year in the English churches and will do whatsoever else may be done without the utter dissipation of their own congregations."

The ministers did protest too much, for in truth it was only a compliance of fear. When Laud was dead it was emphatically asserted that the persecuted folk had played the man; and "a relation of the troubles of the three foreign churches in Kent caused by the injunctions of William Laud, Archbishop of Canterbury, A.D. 1634, etc.," was "written by F. B., minister of the Word of God," with the motto, "et quorum pars magna fui." The French services were never again interfered with.

Laud and his Vicar General had a keen eye for dissent, and an impartial. No less care was taken in the visitation about Romanists than about other foreign recusants: inquiry was made whether the parish priests "endeavour and labour diligently with mildness and temperance to confer with, and thereby to reclaim, the popish recusants in their parishes from their errors."

For the decent order of the Church such questions as the following were asked in each parish. Was there a font of stone set up in the ancient usual place, a convenient and decent communion table standing upon a frame with a carpet of silk or some other decent stuff, and a fair linen cloth to lay thereon at the communion time? This had been asked by Laud as Bishop of London, and similar questions with regard to the duties of clergy and churchwardens and the condition of the parishes were now put. But on the whole little was done in the parish churches. The articles of inquiry into the obligations of the cathedral chapters, on the other hand, were minute. The statutes by which the capitular bodies were bound were investigated and searching questions were asked as to their fulfilment. It was found in many cases that the statutes sat very lightly indeed upon the prebendaries, vicars, and choristers. The reply was often of this tenour. "Our book of ancient statutes is neither punctually observed nor indeed acknowledged by most of us to be of any power. Answer will be made, we are sworn to customs as well as statutes, and customs we make and break

The questions asked.

according to our ease." Yet the visitation met with little
resistance, and there can be no doubt that its result everywhere told in favour of decency and order.

If there was some hesitation in certain dioceses as to the
metropolitical visitation, as the letter of Bishop Williams given
in Hacket's *Life* would show, the extension of the power of
visitation to the universities might be expected to arouse considerable opposition, though it was clearly stated that matters
ecclesiastical only were to be the subject of inquiry, and the
college and university statutes were not to be interfered with.
There was some stir even in Oxford, as the letters of Dr.
Potter, Provost of Queen's College, show ; but the university
did not—perhaps hardly could—generally object to the visitation of one who was its own chancellor. But at Cambridge
formal protest was made ; and only a decision of the king in
Council overrode the opposition. The visitation, however,
was never held.

It may be remarked in passing that the relations of
ecclesiastical and civil jurisdiction were at the time very
much complicated. The Council was often engaged   Confusion
on matters that would seem to have been more   of juris-
fitly dealt with by other courts.   Thus, on January   diction.
24, 1638, there was an order of a Committee of the Council,
on which sat both Laud and Juxon, in consequence of the
petition of Arthur Heron, Vicar of Bardwell, Suffolk, complaining against Mr. Barrow, of the neighbouring village of
Barningham, that he made a park of his land to the prejudice
of the vicar, and of St. John's College, Oxford, the patron
of the living, in the matter of tithes. Mr. Barrow's promise
that in no case should the tithe be diminished was ordered
to be registered.

The close connection between Church and State which
was characteristic of the times is very evident in the history
of the Courts of Star Chamber and High Commission. Of
the history of these offshoots of the king's Council it is not
necessary to speak, earlier than the reign of Charles I. It is
sufficient to observe the fact that, though the origin and the
jurisdictions of the two courts were quite distinct, many of
their members were the same, and this tended to the confusion
of their work which has survived in the books even of com-

petent modern historians. The Star Chamber dealt with civil cases which were believed to be either outside the competence of the common law, or, through the condition of the parties concerned, or some special difficulty in the case itself, unlikely to be satisfactorily treated in the ordinary courts. Here then were brought a number of cases of libel, which touched upon ecclesiastical matters. Three of the cases need especial comment here. In 1632, William Prynne, a learned antiquary and lawyer but a man of crabbed and bitter temper, published a book called *Histriomastix*, in which he cast foul reflections, with hardly any disguise, on the queen and the king. He was condemned to stand in the pillory, to lose his ears, and to be imprisoned during the king's pleasure. Laud was a member of the Court of Star Chamber, and he favoured a severe sentence on Prynne. He was laying in store for himself a severe retaliation.

In 1635 Prynne, whose cruel sentence for his former offence had been lightly carried out, published his *News from Ipswich*, in which he definitely reprobated every change which had been introduced during the last few years by the bishops and by the metropolitical visitation. The king and the bishops, he alleged, designed "to change the orthodox religion and introduce popery." Prynne was again summoned before the Star Chamber in 1637, and with him were charged Henry Burton, who had preached two violent sermons against the measures of Laud, and John Bastwick, who had written a mock Litany charging the bishops with being the authors of "ungodliness and unrighteousness, impiety and all manner of licentiousness." The condemnation of the Court was a foregone conclusion. The accused were sentenced, with the exaggerated severity that was in fashion, to punishments which it was never intended literally to carry out. They were to lose their ears, to be imprisoned for life in Guernsey, Scilly, and Jersey respectively, and to pay a fine of £5000 each. The cutting off the ears, revolting though the punishment seems, does not appear to have been done so literally as to be incapable of repetition. That Elizabeth would have dealt with the offenders even more severely is, as Laud said, certain. Laud and Juxon would not vote; but Laud took the occasion to deliver

The Star Chamber.

William Prynne.

an important speech in defence of his measures. A third case was that of Alexander Leighton, who scurrilously attacked the bishops. After a severe sentence he fled, but he was recaptured, and then was scourged and deprived of an ear.

However small may have been the part which ecclesiastics played in these cases, and there can be no doubt that it was very greatly exaggerated in popular imagination; it is certain that the part they took was a grievous error, for which the Church itself had to suffer. Then, as in past ages, clergy could not act prominently in secular affairs without great risk of scandal and danger. And the scandal and danger were not mitigated by the work of the Court of High Commission. This court was designed by Elizabeth to remedy, through its clear and swift procedure, the delays and abuses of the ordinary ecclesiastical courts. Through it she thought to exercise her supremacy in the matter of jurisdiction. Its purview, it would seem, had been extended; and cases of disobedience to the orders which issued from Lambeth were naturally brought before it. Nothing could have been more unfortunate. It is rare that the English people have complacently sanctioned the suspension or deprivation of the parochial clergy for offences unknown to the law but created by archiepiscopal opinion or rescript. The case of the opponents of Laud was no exception to this rule.

Recent investigations tend to the conclusion that the Court of High Commission has, even by eminent writers, been much too severely judged. Its great defects were, in an exaggerated form, those of the other law courts of the time. They were chiefly, the exercise of the "*ex-officio oath*," by which persons holding office in the Church or under the crown could be required to give evidence, in certain cases, against themselves; and the general style of browbeating and unfairness in the treatment of evidence which seems to us to be characteristic of all the tribunals of the time. The greatest modern authority on the history of the period says, "No one who has studied its records will speak of it as a barbarous or even a cruel tribunal." Unhappily the greater part of its records has been destroyed. Sufficient, however, survive to enable

The Court of High Commission.

us to give some account of the part which it played in the Laudian reformation. Its main work, and the main object of its judges, was moral.

During the century which succeeded the Reformation the English Church was engaged in a strenuous, and in the end successful, struggle against wickedness in high places. The moral tone of the courts of Elizabeth and James I. was notoriously low, and it was too faithfully reflected among the nobility and country gentry. There was often difficulty in punishing high offenders, who thought " they were above the reach of other men or their power or will to chastise." This was intolerable to Laud, and from the time when his influence became supreme, " persons of honour and great quality," says Clarendon, " of the court and of the country, were every day cited into the High Commission Court, upon the fame of their incontinence, or other scandal in their lives, and were there prosecuted, to their shame and punishment : and as the shame (which they called an insolent triumph upon their degree and quality, and levelling them with the common people) was never forgotten, but watched for revenge, so the fines imposed there were the more questioned and repined against, because they were assigned to the rebuilding and repairing of St. Paul's church, and thought therefore to be the more severely imposed, and the less compassionately reduced and excused." The cases of which we have record bear out this view. Moral offences of laity as well as clergy were most severely dealt with ; and they were the most numerous cases.

Its action in favour of morality.

Next to them come cases of ribaldry, scurrilous abuse, sacrilege, and the like, the majority of which seem as we read the account of the trials to have been committed by persons of unsound mind. There are many cases too of blasphemy, which were doubtless due either to insanity or to the too literal interpretation, by persons of no education and of unbalanced minds, of the English version of the Holy Scriptures. The cases of suspension for refusal of the new orders are very rare, and degradation almost invariably was the punishment only for moral offences. In one case the Bishop of Rochester was careful to call attention to the charges which were often made against the

Cases of sacrilege and the like.

court, and to note their divergence from the truth. " Let
men know," he said in the case of a clergyman named
Harrison, "that he is not sentenced for not wearing the
surplice, but for drunkenness, profaning of marriages, and
making men live in perpetual adultery, that he is a briber, a
beggar, a drunkard, a Bedlam." Laud added that it was
time to punish such a man as this, "seeing they have sent us
this printed libel from Amsterdam, wherein they accuse us
for conniving with such men," and he read the words,
"although he be the vilest wretch that lives under the sun,
yet if he will wear the surplice, and cross the child with
thumb, he shall be countenanced by you much better than
the best." Other notable cases were those of Leighton, with
whom the High Commission dealt only in degrading him
after his sentence for libel by the Star Chamber ; Ward, who
was sentenced to suspension for contemning the Prayer-book
and committed to prison because he would not acknowledge
his offence ; Barnard, who declared that the English bishops
were Roman Catholics at heart, and no Roman Catholics
could be saved ; Lady Eleanor Davies, who was sentenced
for foolish prophecies, and ought to have been recognised
as insane, and again more severely when, "with a kettle in
one hand and a brush in the other," she entered Lichfield
cathedral church "to sprinkle some of her holy water (as
she called that in the kettle) upon the (altar) hangings and
the bishop's seat, which was only a composition of tar, pitch,
sink-puddle water, etc., and such kind of nasty ingredients."

Whatever may be thought of the wisdom of the acts of
the High Commission, and whatever excuses may be made
for the severity of its judgments, there can be no doubt that
its activity was widely resented. Nor can it be *General
unpopularity
of the
courts and
of Laud.* denied that the vehemence of Laud, his sharp
language and his bitter feeling towards those who
offended against the settled order of the king and
realm, did much, though probably within a limited circle, to
increase the rising animosity towards the rulers in Church
and State, and to direct it, with special violence against the
"urchin," the "little meddling hocus-pocus" (as Bishop
Williams called him) himself. Good was done by the court,
but harm was done also, and good was not done in the right

way. There was chapter and verse for all that was done for the decency and order of Divine worship, but it bore so much the air of being enforced by an unsympathetic power from London that it was bitterly resented, often by country squires and sometimes by country parsons.

In spite of this, the aims of the archbishop were to a very considerable extent realised even during the few years when he was in power. The age needed peace, order, tolerance, settled dwelling-places on a sure foundation. For these he built, and though what he built seemed to be swept away, he had gone deep and built sure. As time went on Reason suggested articles of peace on the lines which he had laid down. It was something also, to have seen clearly where the dividing line came. His measures made it clear to Englishmen that a rigid Calvinism and a Presbyterian hierarchy were alike inconsistent with the principles of the Church of England. Two centuries and a half after his death the order and the worship of our parish churches represent his ideal: and it has been well said by Dr. S. R. Gardiner that "his refusal to submit his mind to the dogmatism of Puritanism, and his appeal to the cultivated intelligence for the solution of religious problems, has received an ever-increasing response, even in regions in which his memory is devoted to contemptuous obloquy."

AUTHORITIES.—The State Papers, Domestic (which are here sometimes quoted verbatim from the abridgment in the Calendars), and the pamphlet literature of the time are the most important. Next to these must be placed Laud, *Works;* Hacket, *Scrinia Reserata;* the correspondence of Laud and Strafford (Strafford Papers); the Visitation Articles of the chief bishops, especially Laud, Neile, Juxon, and Mountague. Much information as to the conduct of the different dioceses, and as to the charges against the bishops, is to be found in the Tanner MSS. (Bodleian Library), notably vols. clxviii., ccxx. Vol. lxx. fol. 124 *sqq.* contain the articles drawn up by the court lawyers against Prynne, Burton, and Bastwick, March 11, 1635. *A New Discovery of the Prelates Tyranny* (1641), by Prynne, contains his account of the trials of himself, Bastwick, and Burton. A full account of the period is to be found in Collier, *Ecclesiastical History of Great Britain*, and there are many documents in Rushworth, *Historical Collection*. See also S. R. Gardiner, *History of England*, vols. vii.-ix.

CHAPTER VI

POLITICAL OPPOSITION TO THE CHURCH

THUS far we have dealt chiefly with the internal history of the Church. We have now to see how the agitation against the measures associated with Laud and his school found expression in Parliament, and how that expression *Interaction of politics* made war inevitable. In one aspect the opposition *and religion.* to Laud's reforms was simply a part of the opposition to the policy of the crown, the policy of James and Buckingham, and of Charles, as seen after Buckingham's death, in his own personal government. "No bishop no king" was a phrase of double meaning. The critical divergence of view between king and Commons led inevitably to an attack upon the Church. No one can think that there would have been a rebellion of Puritans if there had been no rebellion of Parliamentarians. May, the historian of the Long Parliament, even considers that the just constitutional cause of the Commons suffered from the fanatics who would always put religion into the first place in every attack upon the government. But none the less the rulers of the Church were gravely un- *Unpopularity* popular. The country gentry resented the attack *of the* upon what they considered their privileges in *bishops.* Church matters, and resented the new dignity given to the clergy, whom they were too often accustomed to think of as dependents and "hedge-priests." Hacket in his *Life of Williams* says, "The clamour might have warned wisdom to stop. Policy ought to listen abroad to the talk of the streets and the market-places, and not to despise rumours when they are sharpened against the innovating of any discipline."

As early as 1637 it was clear that, in London, for example, the measures of Laud were frequently unacceptable to the people.   There is among the State Papers of that year the petition of the parishioners of All-Hallows, Barking, to the archbishop.   " Of late years," they say, " our Parish Church has been repaired, and the communion table as before placed and railed about according to the laws and customs of the Church of England.   Now there is a new font erected, over which certain carved images and a cross are placed, and also our communion table is removed out of its ancient accustomed place, and certain images placed over the rail which stands about the table, all which, as we conceive, tends much to the dishonour of God, and is very offensive to us parishioners, and also perilous.   We have desired our doctor to give way, that the images might be taken down, yet he refuses so to do. The petitioners pray the archbishop to command that the images may be taken down and the communion table be restored its place."   The doctor in question was Laud's nephew by marriage, Edward Layfield, who (it is probable) introduced the custom of mingling the chalice, which continued at All-Hallows from the archbishop's till a much later time. It is not likely that the petitioners met with any sympathy from Laud.[1]

The feeling in London.

Laud's sharp tongue and his intense activity made him personally unpopular.   Clarendon well says of him that " his greatest want was that of a true friend, who would reasonably have told him of his infirmities, and what people spake of him.   It is the misfortune of persons of that condition that they receive for the most part their advertisements from clergymen, who understand the least and take the worst measure of human affairs, of all mankind that can read and write."   The second sentence of this opinion no doubt expresses the lay feeling of the time as fully as the first ; and behind it there was a great deal of local and family pride, which disliked that influence in

The personal unpopularity of Laud.

---

[1] It must not, however, be supposed that all feeling was on one side.   See the amusing skit, *Some small and simple reasons delivered in a hollow tree in Waltham Forest in a lecture on the 23rd of March last, by Aminadab Blower, a devout bellows-mender of Pimlico, etc.*, 1633.

the country should be counteracted by the importance of ecclesiastical officials who had close links with the court. Political and social feeling were mixed. Thus Mrs. Hutchinson can speak of Laud as leading the van of the king's evil councillors, and as "a fellow of mean extraction and arrogant pride"; and of the clergy in general she says, "The corrupted bishops and other profane clergy of the land, by their insolences grown odious to the people, bent their strong endeavours to disaffect the prince to his honest, godly subjects."

But stronger than this was the feeling of the sincere and powerful body of religious Puritans, men trained in the doctrines of Calvin and Cartwright, sympathetic towards the Scottish Reformation, and determined, The position
of the altars. like their predecessors under Elizabeth and James I., to sweep away all that survived of the doctrine and associations of the pre-Reformation Church of England. Matters such as the order as to the position of the altar seemed to these men at once to attack the vital principles of their faith. And the fact that many of the clergy were of their mind must not be forgotten, nor the position of men like Williams on the same question ignored. When John Carter, minister of St. Peter Mancroft, Norwich, gave his opinion of the lawfulness of reading service at the communion table, now placed at the east end of the church, he evidently felt that he was making a great concession to lawful authority, as he argued that it could not be unlawful to read the service in any part of the church, "being the whole temple is the house of prayer." The authority placed over him, being lawful, ordered him thus to read the prayers, and that on pain of ceasing his ministry. He assured his friends that this was no sufficient cause for leaving the ministry, and so he would consent to obey. This grudging concession shows the temper of the times. As Clarendon says, "On this unhappy subject proceeded a schism among the bishops themselves and a world of uncharitableness in the learned and moderate clergy towards one another. And, without doubt, many who loved the Church, nor did dislike the order and decency which they saw mended, yet they liked not any novelties, and so were liable to entertain jealousies that more was intended than was hitherto proposed."

Bishop Williams, far too vigorous and astute a man to be finally suppressed by his conviction or his imprisonment, was still working behind the scenes. He represented himself as being not so much in disgrace as was popularly supposed. "The king allowed of him in all those things of which he was complained against," he said. Yet he would hold his own. "No king in the world should make him do what Sir John Coke told him was the king's pleasure." He was as ready to ally himself with the political opposition to the crown as with the religious opposition to Laud. In that double opposition there lay a new chance for recovery of power. To see how this was so it is necessary to return to an earlier date. The course of the Parliamentary opposition to the religious measures with which the king sympathised may now be briefly sketched.

Charles's endeavours in 1628 to silence contending parties, followed by his injudicious promotions, completely failed. In January 1629 a Committee of the House of Commons on religion presented its report, and Pym emphatically asserted the supremacy of Parliament. Eliot in a great speech protested against the Declaration, and still more against Laud, and Neile, and Mountague. And in the result the House passed this resolution. "We the Commons now in Parliament assembled do claim, profess, and avow for truth the sense of the Articles of Religion which were established in Parliament in the reign of our late Queen Elizabeth, which, by the general and concurrent exposition of the writers of our Church, have been delivered to us, and we do reject the sense of the Jesuits and Arminians." This meant, as Eliot explained, that though the Lambeth Articles had no Church sanction, they, with their unhesitating Calvinism, were accepted by the Commons as explaining the sense of the Thirty-nine Articles. The laity were to enforce on the clergy, in contradiction to the opinion of the bishops, a new series of dogmas. This was the key to the position. It was felt to be so in 1629; it was proved to be so during the next sixty years. Nor has the idea yet been forgotten. Had the Parliament the right to enforce on the Church, clergy and laity, its own interpretation of documents which the Church and realm had equally received, which were capable of two interpretations, and which

Bishop Williams.

Resolution of the House of Commons, Jan. 1629.

a considerable party accepted in a sense different from that declared by Parliament? Arminianism had become simply a cant name for refusal to accept the whole Calvinistic theology. This famous and revolutionary resolution was followed by attacks on Cosin and on Neile. Cromwell made his first speech, and, as it afterwards appeared, the revolution was begun. The Commons were in a frenzy of excitement: rumours of Jesuit plots were eagerly credited—a Roman agent had spoken after the manner of his kind of 150,000 Romanists in England.

After scenes of the wildest excitement, culminating in the holding of the Speaker (Finch) down in the chair while three resolutions were put, Charles dissolved the Parliament. One of the resolutions was this: "Whosoever shall bring in innovation in religion, or by favour seek to extend or introduce Popery or Arminianism, or other opinions disagreeing from the true and orthodox Church, shall be reputed a capital enemy to this kingdom and commonwealth." *Protestation of the Commons, March 2, 1629.*

Charles, in his proclamation of March 10, 1629, took his stand on the law as opposed to all innovations. He would allow no novelties in the Church; but neither there, nor in matters of State, would he submit to the rule of the House of Commons. It was thus *Charles's reply.* that Charles and Laud stood before the country when the eleven years of personal government began.

It was during these years that Laud was able to work practically unfettered. Church and State went hand in hand. Laud was never above or in advance of his age. He had no desire to invent a new theory of the relations between Church and State. He took such matters in practice as well as in theory very much as *The personal rule of Charles and Laud.* he found them. In his mind the theory of Divine right assumed no prominence. "I was never yet such a fool," he said, "as to embrace arbitrary government." It was enough for him to accept the royal supremacy in the Church as it was established by existing law and custom, and, through his own close association with the king, to use it for the great ends which he hoped to accomplish by its means. Thus Church and king fell together. The events of the years 1629-40, apart from Laud's administration of the Church, may be briefly

summarised.   After the dissolution of Parliament peace was
made with France and with Spain.   In neither case was any
provision made on behalf of the Protestants, for whom the
wars were supposed to have been undertaken.   At the end of
the year came the first critical case in which religious and
political opposition were combined in an offence brought
before the Star Chamber.   Leighton's *Sion's Plea* seemed to
counsel Parliament to kill the bishops by smiting them under
the fifth rib ; it less obscurely called the queen a daughter
of Heth, a Canaanite, and an idolatress.

In 1633 Charles made a progress, for his crowning, to
Scotland, and the ecclesiastical policy of Laud was pressed
on the reluctant country.   It was in the same year
that Prynne suffered for his *Histriomastix* and
Bastwick for his *Elenchus Papismi.*   1634 and
1635 were the years of shipmoney, 1636 that of Juxon's
appointment as Treasurer, 1637 and 1638 showed how strong
was the movement against arbitrary power.   Prynne, Burton,
and Bastwick, when they were sent into exile, were followed to
the sea by sympathising crowds.   Williams's imprisonment
drew a poem of sorrow even from Herrick.   Hampden's trial
aroused intense excitement.   But most important of all, the
Covenant was signed, and the whole fabric so laboriously
reared in Scotland fell to the ground.   The *bellum episcopale*
was ominous on both sides of the Tweed.   The imprisonment
of two noted Puritan lords for refusal to march against the
Scots was significant of the union of Puritanism in the two
kingdoms.   The pacification of Berwick, June 18, 1639,
showed that Charles and Laud had failed in Scotland.   On
the 5th of December, when, on the archbishop's as well as
Wentworth's advice, a Parliament was summoned in England,
it must have been clear to many that failure there too was
not far off.

The news "being spread abroad among the people made
them almost amazed, so strange a thing was the name of Parliament grown," says May.   More amazed were the
king's councillors when they saw the new spirit in the
country which spoke in the Short Parliament.   It was
soon apparent how wide and deep was the national
opposition.   Till Parliament met, with Williams disgraced,

The critical dates, 1633-1639.

Meeting of the Short Parliament, April 13, 1640.

Laud seemed without rival in England. He was indeed secure, as long as the king was safe. Parliament alone could procure his fall, and no Parliament was needed so long as the king could subsist on gifts from the clergy, on the sale of offices, and on legalised but unparliamentary exactions. All was changed by the Scots war that was over and the new Scots war that was planned. Charles hoped that Parliament would take up his cause against the Scots. It was a vain hope. " The Lower House," wrote the Earl of Northumberland, " fell into almost as great a heat as ever you saw them in my Lord Buckingham's time, and I perceive our house apt to take fire at the least sparkle." Petitions of every kind, a means of expressing party feeling skilfully arranged by Pym, poured in on every side. And when the great leader introduced the petitions, he spoke with a force and directness that showed the power behind him. He protested against   *Pym's speeches.* new ceremonies, altars, images, crucifixes, bowings, and other gestures, and against the punishment of those who refused to conform. He spoke severely of the action of the courts : " any other vice almost may be better endured in a minister than inconformity,"—a charge which the records sufficiently refuted. But men's passions were too hot for them to listen to reason ; and it was natural indeed that they should accept for truth the colourable, scarce perceptible, exaggeration of Pym's picture.

The king and the Commons differed on cardinal points. There was no use in denying it ; and the promotion of Manwaring was an evident proof. The House of   *Hall's* Lords took up the same cry, and discussed the   *Episcopacy* appointment in a hostile spirit ; the bishops were   *Asserted.* told that they were no estate of the realm : Bishop Hall had published, with the approbation and assistance of the archbishop, a book entitled *Episcopacy by Divine Right Asserted,* in which, in view of the Scottish rejection of bishops, he argued, on fifteen grounds, for the supreme authority of Episcopacy, as ordered by Christ, and declared the government by bishops " both universal and unalterable," and the non-episcopal system to be of " known newness " and discreditable origin. So plain and straightforward a book, which claimed to represent the clear teachings of the English reformers, could not pass unchallenged. Hall was compelled to beg pardon of the House for saying that Lord Saye and Sele "savoured of a Scottish covenanter," a saying of which it did not take many months to prove the truth : and only the direct message of the king prevented their censuring Manwaring. The king could not come to terms with the Parliament, and on May 5 it was dissolved.

The Dissolution, May 5, 1640.

But the Convocation of Canterbury sat on. On April 22 it had unanimously granted the king six subsidies. It had thus shown itself as clearly on the side of King Charles on the main questions of the day. Its unanimity, too, had proved that the policy of Laud had its support. With an almost pathetic ignorance, if not a bold defiance, of the dangers on every side, Laud was prepared to continue the work of ecclesiastical legislation when the Parliament was dissolved. He had taken the opinion of seven judges on the point, and was informed that "the convocation, being called by the king's writ under the great seal, doth continue until it be dissolved by writ or commission under the great seal, notwithstanding that Parliament be dissolved." On this point, it is to be observed, modern legal opinion has confirmed that on which Laud relied, the constitutional doctrine now being that it is not of necessity that convocation should be prorogued when Parliament is, while the archbishop's prorogation is recognised in determining the meeting irrespective of any other document. Thus fortified the convocations of 1640 proceeded, having the royal license to enact canons[1] and claiming the title of a national synod. The canons passed in London were agreed to at York, and they received the royal assent. They would therefore, having never been repealed, appear to be still in force, though the Act 13 Ch. II. explicitly refrains from confirming them.

The Convocation of 1640.

The king's letters patent declared the occasion of the license in significant words. After referring to the Reformation the declaration proceeds : "and albeit since those times for want of an express rule therein, and by subtle practices, the said rites and ceremonies began to fall into disuse, and in place thereof other foreign and unfitting usages by little and little to creep in ; yet, forasmuch as in our

Licence to enact canons.

---

[1] The canons are printed in Laud's *Works*, v. 607 *sqq.*

own royal chapel, and in many other churches, most of them
have been ever constantly used and observed, we cannot now
but be very sensible of the matter, and have cause to conceive
that the authors and fomenters of these jealousies, though they
colour the same with a pretence of zeal, and would seem to
strike only at some supposed iniquity in the said ceremonies,
yet, as we have cause to fear, aim at our royal person, and
would fain have our good subjects imagine that we ourselves
are perverted, and do worship God in a superstitious way,
and that we intend to bring in some alteration of the religion
here established. Now, how far we are from that, and how
utterly we detest every thought thereof, we have by many
public declarations, and otherwise upon sundry occasions,
given such assurance unto the world, as that from thence we
do assure ourself, that no man of wisdom and discretion could
ever be so beguiled as to give any serious entertainment to
such brain-sick jealousies ; and for the weaker sort, who are
prone to be misled by crafty seducers, we rest no less confident that even of them, as many as are of loyal or indeed
but of charitable hearts, will from henceforth utterly banish
all such causeless fears and surmises, upon these our sacred
professions, so often made by us, a Christian defender of the
faith, their king and sovereign." Then, having observed the
argument that might be drawn from the want of uniformity,
the letters proceeded to state that the king "according to the
Act of Parliament in this behalf, having fully advised herein
with our metropolitan, and with our commissioners authorised
under our great seal for causes ecclesiastical," had granted
leave to the convocations to treat and agree upon canons
"necessary for the advancement of God's glory, the edifying
of His holy Church, and the due reverence of His blessed
mysteries and sacraments." The decay of reverence was
attributed partly to "the inadvertency of some in authority in
the Church under us."

Under this direction the Convocation of Canterbury proceeded to business. Of the details of discussion
we know nothing, for it was agreed that no one Convocations of
should take any private notes in the house; but Canterbury and York.
there appear to have been few dissentients from
the decisions arrived at. But the canons were without demur

subscribed at York, where, says Fuller, "the Convocation is but the hand of the clock, moving or pointing as directed by the clock of the province of Canterbury."

The first canon is an unequivocal declaration that the "most high and sacred order of things is of divine right, being the ordinance of God Himself, founded in the pure laws of human nature, and clearly established by express texts both of the Old and New Testaments." This was explained to mean a rule and command over all persons ecclesiastical and civil, the power to call and dissolve councils, and the care of the Church,—vague phrases which were amplified by a declaration that to bear arms against kings "offensive or defensive, on any pretence whatsoever," is to resist the powers ordained of God. The second canon concerned the observance of the king's accession day. The third was a stringent provision "for suppression of the growth of Popery"; the fourth was "against Socinians." The fifth declared that, as the synod was well aware "that there are other sects which endeavour the subversion both of the doctrine and discipline of the Church of England no less than the Papists do," the "proceedings and penalties" of the canon against Popish recusants shall stand also against Anabaptists, Brownists, Separatists, and the like"; and also against those who resort to sermons but not to prayers.

The sixth canon is the famous one of the "*Et cætera* oath." It was enacted to prevent "all innovations in doctrine and government," and requires all the clergy, school-masters, divinity graduates, and "all that are licensed to practise physic, all register actuaries and proctors," to take the following oath :—" I, A B, do swear that I approve the doctrine and discipline, or government, established in the Church of England, as containing all things necessary to salvation ; and that I will not endeavour by myself or any other, directly or indirectly, to bring in any Popish doctrine contrary to that which is so established ; nor will I ever give my consent to alter the government of this Church by arch-bishops, bishops, deans, and archdeacons, etc., as it stands now established, and as by right it ought to stand, nor yet ever to subject it to the usurpations and superstitions of the See of Rome. And all these things I do plainly and sincerely

The canons of 1640.

The Et cætera oath.

acknowledge and swear, according to the plain and common sense and understanding of the same words, without any equivocation, or mental evasion, or secret reservation whatsoever. And this I do heartily, willingly, and truly upon the faith of a Christian. So help me God in Christ Jesus."

Of the results of this canon something will be said later. It will suffice to note here that among the other canons were some for redressing the abuses of ecclesiastical courts, and urging "the sober, grave, and exemplary conversation of all those that are employed in administration of holy things"; and that the seventh canon, which is "a declaration concerning some rites and ceremonies," confirms Laud's previous action. It is a long and carefully written statement. It begins with a reference to the desirableness of a uniformity of worship as well as of a unity of faith. The position of "the communion table sideway under the east wall of every chancel or chapel is in its own nature indifferent"; so no one should object to it. At the time of "the reforming of this Church from that gross superstition of Popery," all "Popish altars" were demolished, because "of the idolatry committed in the mass"; but Elizabeth ordered that the holy tables should stand where the altars stood, and this had been the custom in the royal chapels, in most cathedral, and some parochial churches. Therefore it was fit that this custom should be made universal, "saving always the general liberty left to the bishop by law during the time of administration of the holy communion." To this practical, there was added the doctrinal statement, "And we declare that this situation of the holy table doth not imply that it is, or ought to be, esteemed a true and proper altar, wherein Christ is again really sacrificed; but it is and may be called an altar by us in that sense in which the primitive Church called it an altar, and in no other."

The direction for a rail to sever the communion tables next followed, and also that the communicants should "draw near" to receive "the divine mysteries," which had heretofore in some places been unfitly carried up and down by the minister. The "doing reverence" at going in and out of church was also advised, but not ordered, "not with any intention to exhibit any religious worship to the communion table, the east, or church, or anything therein contained in so doing, or to perform the said gesture in the celebration of the holy eucharist, upon any opinion of a corporal presence of the body of Jesus Christ on the holy table, or in mystical elements, but only for the advancement of God's majesty, and to give Him alone that honour and glory that is due unto Him, and no otherwise ; and in the practice or omission of this rite, we desire that the rule of charity described by the apostle may be observed, which is that they which use this rite despise not them who use it not, and that they who use it not condemn not those that use it."

This was, undoubtedly, the most important article illustrative of the doctrinal and practical position of the rulers of the English Church at this time. The statement is thoroughly in accord with the documents of the Reformation. Popular Roman teaching that Christ is again really sacrificed was always unhesitatingly rejected by English theologians after the Reformation ; but the appeal of the Reformers to the primitive Church was emphatically repeated.

It is possible that the rest of the canons might have been suffered to come into use if the times had been less disturbed ; but the sixth, by a mere mischance of hurry, set theological passions in a blaze. *Et cœtera !* what might not be meant by that ? Anger and dismay and ridicule alternated. In a few days it seemed as if the whole country had heard of it, and was aroused. The oath, though it had its parallel under Elizabeth, was regarded as a new burden, imposed on unwilling persons by ecclesiastical authority. It was felt that there was no right thus to fetter men's freedom. There was no Parliament to voice the public alarm, but already Charles and Laud had learnt to look for the opinion of the people elsewhere than in Parliament. Ballads and squibs and lampoons were printed and read everywhere. Laud was obliged to give way. By the king's order he directed that the oath "should be forborne" till the next Convocation. It was twenty years before it met ; and the best that could then be hoped of the oath was that it might be forgotten.

The last session of the synod took place on the 29th of May. Its session had to be protected by an armed guard, and

The tumults about Et cœtera.

Charles had hurried on the conclusion.   Goodman, Bishop of
Gloucester, though he signed the canons, shuffled   Bishop
when asked to declare that he had signed *ex animo*.   Godfrey
He could no longer keep up the sham.   He was   Goodman.
suspended and imprisoned; and it appears that he died a
Roman Catholic.   During the last days of the session there
had been serious riots.   On May 9 all 'prentices had been
summoned by an anonymous paper posted on   Strong
'Change, to sack Lambeth Palace.   The train-band   feeling in
from Southwark was ordered to defend it.   At mid-   the City.
night a mob assembled, but failed to force an entrance.   Laud
slept at Whitehall; it was said that he had been obliged to
"take a grey cloak and escape over Thames."   This was but
one expression of the feelings of London.   The city refused to
advance money to the king.   War was ready to break out again;
and on August 20 the Scots crossed the Tweed.   While the
great council of peers met at York to discuss terms with the
rebels, the High Commission Court was attacked, and the mob
tore down all the benches in the consistory court, and cried out
that they would have no bishop and no commission.   The
Libels poured from the press.   Laud as early as 1629   pamphlet
had obtained examples of the virulent attacks that   war.
were being printed and circulated with the object of arousing
popular feeling against him.   Thus he wrote in his diary:
"Two papers were found in the Dean of Paul's his yard
before his house.   The one was to this effect, concerning
myself: Laud, look to thyself; be assured thy life is sought.
As thou art the fountain of all wickedness, repent thee of thy
monstrous sins before thou be taken out of the world, etc.
And assure thyself, neither God nor the world can endure
such a vile counsellor to live, or such a whisperer; or to this
effect.   The other was as bad as this, against the Lord
Treasurer.   Mr. Dean delivered both papers to the king that
night.   Lord, I am a grievous sinner; but I beseech Thee
deliver my soul from them that hate me without a cause."

Day after day letters of accusation and fly-sheets imputing
every kind of crime and folly to him poured from the opposition press.   His diary shows how he noted them and what
he felt.   "The best is," he wrote to Strafford in 1636, "they
have called my Master by the worst name they have given me,

and He has taught me how to bear it." Two years later it is the same. "Within this fortnight I have received four bitter libels. I only tell the king of them, and put them in my pocket." Among those that came out in 1641 are: "All to Westminster: newes from Elizium," "Canterburie's Tooles, or Instruments wherewith he hath effected many rare feats and egregious exploits, as is very well known, and notoriously manifest to all men. Discovering his projects and policies, and the ends and purposes of the prelates in effecting their facinorous actions and enterprises," "Rome for Canterbury, or a true relation of the Birth and Life of William Laud"; "Rome's ABC," "Canterbury's Will," "Canterburie's Amazement; or, the Ghost of the Young Fellow Thomas Bensted, who appeared to him in the Tower," "A Parallel between Thomas Wolsey, Archbishop of York, and William Laud, Archbishop of Canterbury," "Canterburie's Dreame" (a vision of Wolsey), "Mercurie's Message; or, the Coppy of a Letter sent to William Laud, late Archbishop of Canterbury, now prisoner in the Tower," and "Canterbury's Will, with a Serious Conference between his Scrivener and him." This last came when he was in prison, and threatens his death by hanging. "Dost thou not hear," he is made to say, "as thou walkest along the streets, how each school-boy's mouth is filled with a *Give Little Laud to the Devill?*" Many of these libels are still preserved in the Lambeth Library, docketed by Laud himself, with a note of how he got them. "WILLIAM LAUDE—WELL AM A DIVIL" is one anagram; the archbishop wrote—

> He that of this would better English make,
> Shall find a task will make his brain to ake.

But this is somewhat to anticipate. Meantime events in England had moved fast. On October 2, commissioners of the Scots met the king's envoys at Ripon. On November 3 the Long Parliament assembled at Westminster. From that moment it was certain that the measures of Laud had gone as far beyond popular sympathy as had those of Charles himself. What would be the ultimate judgment of Englishmen, or how they would judge when twenty years made the consequences of their actions clear, remained for time to prove.

Meeting of
the Long
Parliament,
Nov. 7, 1640.

Now, a majority seemed to speak in the words of Rudyerd. "We well know," he said in the House on November 7, "what disturbance hath been brought into the Church for petty trifles; how the whole Church, the whole kingdom, hath been troubled where to place a metaphor, an altar. We have seen ministers, their wives, children and families, undone, against law, against conscience, against all bowels of compassion, about not dancing on Sundays. What do those sort of men think will become of themselves when the Master of the house shall come and find them beating their fellow-servants?"

Exaggeration was everywhere, exaggerated anger, exaggerated fear; and there were tales of Popish plots which both Laud and the Commons believed, though they were alleged to be of opposite intent—one to kill the king and archbishop, one through the latter to convert the land to the Pope.

On November 11 Strafford, the devoted friend and ally of Laud, loyal alike to king and Church, was impeached. On November 22 the House of Commons received the holy communion together in St. Margaret's, Westminster; and Williams, who was now released from prison, as Dean of Westminster and ordinary, gave permission for the holy table to be moved into the middle of the church, declaring that "he would do as much for any party in his diocese that should desire it." It was as that of the ordinary that the decision of the Dean and Chapter of St. Paul's had been confirmed in 1633. Their direction was that the altar in St. Gregory's should stand at the east end. Charles himself had declared that the discretion in the matter was "the judgment of the ordinary." Williams, whose decision in a disputed case at Grantham had been much disliked by Laud's party, had now the opportunity of repeating it at a critical time.

The communion at St. Margaret's.

On November 28 Prynne and Burton, released from their exile, were triumphantly welcomed in London. On December 4 Bastwick had a similar reception. On the 10th Windebanke, Secretary of State, whose promotion was due to Laud, fled from England, fearing the construction that might be put upon his relations with papal agents if they were discovered. Next day a petition for the abolition of bishops, signed, it was said, by

15,000 Londoners, was presented to the House of Commons. On the 15th it was stated that the new canons bound neither clergy nor laity, on the ground (which the law did not recognise) that they needed confirmation by Parliament. On the 16th they were declared illegal; and Laud was accused by name in the House of Lords as "an incendiary." On the 18th he was impeached in the Commons and committed to the custody of the usher of the Black Rod. As he left Lambeth for the last time hundreds of poor folk crowded round him and prayed for his safe return.

The next month saw wild disorder in London. Petitions for the abolition of Episcopacy, "root and branch," and for a thorough reformation, were presented to the House. In several churches public worship was irreverently interrupted; in some the new rails were taken away, and the altar moved. On January 23, 1641, the king told the Houses that he would agree that all matters of religion and government should be as they were under Elizabeth, and that the bishops should lose any power injurious to the State; but of their ancient privilege as Lords of Parliament he would never deprive them. It seemed to the Puritan Commons that he was "irremovably fixed to uphold the bishops in their wealth, pride, and tyranny." They retaliated by demanding the execution of a Romanist priest whom Charles, always tolerant and averse from blood, had reprieved. On February 8 a debate of the first importance occurred on the "root and branch" petition. Among the speeches that of Falkland was almost alone in pleading for a liberal interpretation of the supremacy of Parliament over the Church, which was now the rallying cry of the Commons. He was as Erastian as Pym, but he thought that new laws could restrain the clergy from all offence. "I am as confident they will not dare either ordain, suspend, silence, excommunicate, or deprive otherwise than as we would have them." Puritan members spoke much more clearly. It was a revival of the absolute power of the State over the Church which, in the days of Anselm, the Church had successfully resisted. Now, if the Puritans should be content not to abolish Episcopacy or the Book of Common Prayer, it was only by their mere grace and favour that such things should remain.

It was at this time that Bishop Hall put forth his *Humble Apology for Liturgy and Episcopacy*, urging, in a tone much less confident than in his *Episcopacy a Divine Right* (1641), the excellence of the English form of the first and the divine authority of the second. *Hall's Apology for Episcopacy.* Such voices were overborne in the violence of the conflict that was beginning; but already in the House of Commons there were men who saw that the Church was worth defending as well as the king: men like Hyde, to whom the Church appealed as the safeguard of order and decent devotion—like Falkland, whose foresight showed him that the Church, not Puritanism, was the protector of intellectual freedom—as well as like Digby, who thought rather of the Church as a corrupt, but powerful bulwark against democracy. And for the most part the defenders of the Church were as thorough Erastians as Pym. They sought the solution of the difficulties of the day in State interference, not, whence it would eventually come, in the free exercise of religious liberty. A horror of the inquisitorial system of Presbyterianism, the more clearly evident the more Englishmen came to know of the Scots ministers who had drawn up the Covenant and cast down the bishops, was already showing itself.

On February 27, 1641, a numerously signed petition from Cheshire was presented to the House of Lords. "We cannot but express our first fears that their desire is to introduce an absolute innovation of Presbyterian government, whereby we who are now governed by canon and civil laws dispensed by twenty-six *The Cheshire petition. Feb. 27, 1641.* ordinaries, easily responsible to Parliament for any deviation from the rule of law, conceive we should become exposed to the mere arbitrary government of a numerous Presbytery, who, together with their ruling elders, will arise to near forty thousand Church governors, and with their adherents must needs bear so great a sway in the Commonwealth, that if future inconvenience shall be found in that government, we humbly offer to consideration how these shall be reducible by Parliament, how consistent with a monarchy, and how dangerously conducible to an anarchy, which we have just cause to pray against, as fearing the consequences, would prove the utter loss of learning and laws, which must necessarily produce an extermination of nobility, gentry, and order, if not of religion." It was the answer of the conservative feeling of the country to the "root and branch" petition. "If we make a parity in the Church we must come to a parity in the Commonwealth," said a member. Finally, the Londoners' petition was referred to a committee. But the temper of the majority of the Commons was seen more clearly in an order of the House, January 23, 1641, that "commissioners be sent into the several counties to demolish and remove out of churches and chapels all images, altars, or tables turned altar-wise, crucifixes, superstitious pictures, and other monuments of and relics of idolatry." Already the power of the House showed behind it a dangerous approach to mob-law. May tells how "with extreme licence the common people, almost from the very beginning of the Parliament, took upon themselves the reforming, without authority, order, or decency; rudely disturbing Church service while the common prayer was reading; tearing their books, surplices, and things."

On March 15, 1641, a Committee for Religion was appointed by the House of Lords. Its authority was to examine into "innovations," and, it was added, *The Committee for Religion, March 1641.* "if their lordships shall, in their judgment, find it behoveful for the good of the Church and State, to examine after that the degrees and perfection of the Reformation itself." Williams, who in everything was swimming with the tide, was a member of it, and the learned Usher, Archbishop of Armagh, with Hall and Morton, also sat. They were outnumbered by ten earls and ten barons. Some wholesale alterations were suggested, but Hacket, who may be supposed to represent the opinion of Williams, says that those against the Prayer-book were "petty and stale, older than the old exchange." Their temporising measures, however, were soon lost sight of in the rapid march of events.

The bill of attainder gave Strafford into the hands *The Protestation, May 3, 1641.* of his foes, and on May 3 the House of Commons, still alarmed by fanciful popish plots, agreed upon a Protestation, on the precedent of the oath of association taken in Elizabeth's time. After hot debate this was restricted to the maintenance of "the true Reformed

Protestant religion, expressed in the doctrine of the Church of England, against all Popery and popish innovations within this realm contrary to the same doctrine." This seemed to Baillie, the Scots representative in England, to be "in substance our Scottish covenant." On May 10 Charles consented to the bill for the continuance of the present Parliament till it should decree its own dissolution. On the same day he signed the death warrant of Strafford. At that supreme crisis of the king's life two bishops had stood forward predominantly among his advisers. The honest Juxon, "that good man," as Charles always called him, urged him to refuse his assent, "seeing he knew his worship to be innocent"; Williams told him he had two consciences, private and public, and that in this public business the decision of the House of Lords was enough.

The execution of Strafford marked a new step in the division. The House of Lords rejected the bill for the exclusion of the bishops. From that moment the dominant party in the Commons determined to destroy Episcopacy altogether; and Falkland and Selden stood aside from Hampden and Pym. The "root and branch" bill never passed; a resolution was carried on June 16 that "deans and chapter, archdeacons, prebendaries, canons, etc., should be utterly abolished and taken out of the Church." For the position of the bishops there was still a struggle; but on July 5 the king gave the royal assent to the bill abolishing the Star Chamber and the High Commission, and making it illegal for a bishop to exercise coercive jurisdiction or to offer the *ex officio* oath.

Abolition of the High Commission.

Thus the legal but unconstitutional powers conferred by the Tudor and Stewart governments, the exercise of which had been so disastrous for the Church, were stripped from the clergy. It was the last constitutional action in the war of Puritans against the Church. From that moment the will of the great conservative mass of Englishmen was for nineteen years unable to assert itself against the fiery zeal of fanaticism and the powerful advocacy of political change. In the House a few strenuous and determined men ruled; outside opinion in the large towns was swayed more and more by light-hearted mobs. The ribald

Popular squibs in verse and prose.

expression of political and religious sentiment in ballad and broadsheet was irrepressible.   Thus was the destruction of the High Commission welcomed—

> Lament, lament, you bishops all,
> Each wear his blackest gown,
> Hang up your rochets on the wall,
> Your pride is going down.
> The Bishops' Holy Synod, and
> The priests of Baal that there
> Consented and concluded all
> Are now in grievous fear.
> To be deprived of priestly style
> And coat canonicall,
> And quite be banished from this isle
> They fear they must be all.
> Ah ! poor *Et cætera* now is dead,
> Which grieves the bishops most,
> What they would have immortal made
> Has now given up the ghost.
> Alas ! that new begotten oath,
> Like snow against the sun,
> It did begin to melt away
> When the Parliament begun.
> All ceremonies now are cheap,
> And I will tell you how :
> The surplice, hood, and tippet eke
> Are good for nothing now.

Nor were the arts of the "lively emblem" disdained.   A characteristic pamphlet of the year 1641 is *A Rot amongst the Bishops, or a terrible Tempest in the Sea of Canterbury*, in which Thomas Stirry expressed his intention, as the "proud Popish prelates" were become no more than "shroving cocks," to throw a stick at them.   Four quaint woodcuts show as emblems Laud with his legal assistants, and Wren with the devil's hand on his shoulder, navigating a ship named High Commission, and discharging the *oath et cet.* from the mouths of canons ; next comes a storm, which forces them to unload their boat, and then Laud is led to the Tower, from which at last he pitifully looks out upon the gallows—

> For now be sure that all your golden copes
> You must exchange for new-spun hempen ropes,

says the wit who has accompanied the pictures with doggerel comment.

To such gibes there was added a more serious controversy. *Prelacie is miserie* was the tone of many, as it is the title of one, of the pamphlets issued in 1641. *Smectymnuus* (five prominent ministers, Stephen Marshall, Edmund Calamy, Thomas Young, Matthew Newcomen, William Spurstow) attacked Bishop Hall's defence of Episcopacy in March. In May or June John Milton, hitherto known as a poet of no marked Puritan sympathies, published his first pamphlet, *Of Reformation reaching Church Discipline*, a plea for the establishment of Presbyterian government. The Commons were still in committee on the " root and branch " bill ; Bishops Wren and Piers were impeached. And at the same time lay preachers, even women, were springing up everywhere, to the indignation of the older Puritans.

> " When women preach,"—said some, " and cobblers pray
> The fiends in hell make holiday."

More serious objections were met more seriously. Williams endeavoured to discuss points of difference with a view to conciliation. But it was impossible to find a common basis.

The " worthy and learned divines " who met the Bishop of Lincoln in 1641 protested against the Twentieth Article, " Habet ecclesia authoritatem in controversiis fidei," against the view that " works of penance are satisfactory before God," and that " the absolution which the priest pronounceth is more than declaratory," against prayers for the dead, against " monasticall vowes," against " turning of the table altarwise and calling it an altar," against the use of candlesticks, crucifixes, credence tables, and such like, and against the rule that cathedral and collegiate churches should celebrate the holy communion every Sunday, when " might it not rather be added once a month." This meeting at least served to show the importance of the great Puritan orator who had now come into the front rank of those who were determined to carry on the war against the Laudian " reformation."

In March 1637 especial attention was called to the importance of a Puritan clergyman who was before long to become famous. Stephen Marshall, Vicar of Finchingfield, had been reported to Laud in 1632 among the "lecturers" as only preaching on the holy days, and "in every way conformable," in 1636 as guilty of irregularities and want of conformity. Sir Nathaniel Brent reported him within a year as dangerous, but exceeding cunning, and as governing the consciences of all the rich Puritans in his neighbourhood. Three years later he seemed to have become the John Knox of the English Puritan Revolution. In sermons before the House of Commons he laid aside entirely the moderation which had prevented his suspension. From an impressive pulpit orator he became an important party leader. The first of those whose names made Smectymnuus, he was as skilful with his pen as with his voice. On January 23, 1641, a petition that professed to express the opinions of seven hundred Puritan clergy was presented to the House. The signatures had in many cases been affixed to other petitions; but the document none the less had its effect. Stephen Marshall was an adroit, but scarcely scrupulous party manager. He was enthusiastically welcomed by the Puritans in the Commons. In the Committee of the House of Lords which met under the auspices of Williams (see p. 90) he was a prominent member. Archbishop Usher's scheme for a "moderated Episcopacy"—from his own autograph manuscript—was accepted. But such measures were not seriously considered outside the walls of the committee room. Marshall was given £300 a year to preach at St. Margaret's, Westminster. In vain his country parishioners protested. He had not for seven years administered the holy communion there, they said. He had, in truth, other matters on his mind. Political agitation did not well agree with parochial duties.

The summer of 1641 was a time of confusion. In August Charles went to Scotland, hoping to gather a party which should give him back his power. A few days after his departure the "root and branch" bill was first for a time, then finally dropped; and it was clear that a division was arising in the Commons. In the Lords a resolution was passed that "the divine service be performed as it is appointed by the Acts of Parliament of this realm, and that all such as disturb that

Political measures in the autumn of 1641.

wholesome order shall be severely punished according to law." At the end of the month there was an adjournment. On October 21 the House reassembled; and it was evident that there was now a definitely united party of Royalists and Churchmen. A bill for the exclusion of the bishops from the House of Lords was brought in and passed the Commons. The Lords delayed it till the trial of the thirteen bishops who had been impeached should begin.

At that very moment Charles showed the extraordinary want of understanding which at critical times constantly defeated his good intentions. He filled up five vacant bishoprics. Since Laud had been a prisoner in the Tower Juxon had advised the king on ecclesiastical matters. "I thank you," wrote Charles to Sir Edward Nicholas on September 19, 1641, "for putting me in mind of the vacancy of bishoprics; therefore I command you to direct the Bishop of London to send me a list of all the vacant bishoprics, and those notes which he and I made concerning the filling of those places." A month later Juxon sent "several bills for his Majesty's signature for the new bishops." They included bishops for *The appointments to bishoprics, 1641.* Bath and Wells, Chichester, Exeter, Norwich, Bristol, Oxford, Winchester, and an archbishop for York. Some of these were translations; and, probably as an attempt to pacify the Commons, Williams was given the northern primacy. It is a strange comment on the disturbance of the times, if not on the nature of public justice, that the preferment of a bishop who had been convicted of grave offences (see above, p. 58) seems to have excited no comment. Usher, whom the rebellion had driven from Ireland, was given the see of Carlisle; the Puritan Prideaux, Rector of Exeter College, Oxford, became Bishop of Worcester—each an appointment at which Puritan churchmen would not grumble. But Hall and Duppa and Skinner, men who had fallen under the Commons' dire displeasure, were translated to better sees —a token of royal approval which was bitterly resented. And those who desired to abolish or limit Episcopal power still more loudly protetsed.

Events moved rapidly. On November 22 the Grand Remonstrance was carried; on December 1 it was presented, and the king was asked to agree to the exclusion of the bishops. Charles in his reply declared that their presence among the peers was part of the fundamental laws of England. Day by day mobs surrounded the Houses; the Lords debated upon a view that they were no longer free.

Exclusion of the bishops from the House of Lords. The bishops drew up a protest, which Williams was the first to sign, and perhaps to suggest, declaring that as it was with danger of their lives alone that they could attend the House, the Parliament was no longer free, and all its proceedings were illegal. This redoubled the popular tumult. The witty Butler a generation later thus described the scenes that followed:—

> The oyster-women lock'd their fish up
> And trudg'd away to cry "No bishop";
> Botchers left old clothes in the lurch,
> And fell to turn and patch the Church.
> Some cried the Covenant instead
> Of pudding-pies and gingerbread;
> Instead of kitchen-stuff some cry
> A gospel-preaching ministry;
> And some for old suits, coats, or cloak,
> No surplices or service book.

In the Commons Pym impeached all the bishops who had signed the protest for high treason, and they were all arrested. For the most part these accusations were never pressed home. Specific charges were never brought to book. The

The impeachment of Bishop Wren. report of the House of Commons Committee, July 5, 1641, for example, stated that "Matthew Wren, Bishop of Ely, excommunicated, deprived, or punished within the space of two years fifty godly, learned, and faithful ministers," and accused him of "practising superstition in his own person," among other enormities consecrating at the west side of the holy table; but he was never brought to trial. He prepared an elaborate answer to the articles of impeachment, in which he denied a large number of the charges. He argued, from Queen Elizabeth's Latin Prayer Book among other sources, that as to the position of the minister, "north part, north side, and north end were all one"; he declared that he had never called the holy table an altar; he affirmed, that while people made reverence to the empty seat of the king in the Parliament House, it was "no superstition, but a sign of devotion and of an awful apprehension of God's divine presence, to do Him reverence, at the approach into the house of God or unto the Lord's table."

But though the House of Commons soon found that it had arrested far more of its opponents than it could deal with, it did not relax its hand, and the bishops remained in custody. The agitation within and without was not one which a weak king could withstand; Charles made a last desperate effort: on January 4, 1642, he attempted to arrest the five members; on the 5th he went into the city in pursuit of them, and as he drove back a paper was thrown into his carriage— "To your tents, O Israel!"

In fact, if not in name, the war was begun. The king made some concessions, acting no more wisely now than when he had resisted. He consented to the bill excluding the bishops from the House of Lords. And while he consented, petitions were pouring in for the maintenance of Episcopacy, petitions from thirteen English and five Welsh counties, all firm in attachment to the Church government and the Prayer-book, "composed," said the Cheshire petition, "by the holy martyrs and worthy instruments of Reformation, with such general consent received by all the laity, that scarce any family or person that can read but are furnished with the book of Common Prayer, in the conscionable use whereof many Christian hearts have found unspeakable joy and comfort, wherein the famous Church of England, our dear mother, hath just cause to glory." The Kentish grand jury at Maidstone, on March 28, drew up a petition which was presented to Parliament. Its most significant words centred round the "solemn liturgy of the Church," and it spoke of the "interruptions, scorns, profanations, threats, and force of such men who daily do deprave it, and neglect the use of it in divers churches, in spite of the laws established"; and, still more significantly, it went on to pray "that Episcopal government might be preserved, and that all differences concerning religion might be submitted to a synod chosen by the clergy, and means taken to provide against the scandal of schismatical and seditious sermons and pamphlets, and some severe law made against laymen for daring to arrogate to themselves and to exercise the holy function of the ministry—to the advanc-

Petitions in favour of the Church.

H

ing of heresy, schism, profaneness, libertinism, anabaptism, atheism."

The presentation of this petition was treated by the House of Commons as a crime ; and the petitioners were imprisoned.

The House of Commons supreme. It was a crime not to agree with the dominant party. For the High Commission and Star Chamber was substituted the House of Commons. And how this new supreme court was to act was prefigured by the Declaration of April 8, 1642, published in every market town of England and Wales : " The Lords and Commons do declare that they intend a due and necessary reformation of the government and liturgy of the Church, and to take away nothing in the one or the other but what shall be evil and justly offensive, or at the least unnecessary and burdensome ; and on the better effecting thereof speedily to have consultation with godly and learned divines. And because this will never of itself attain the end sought therein, they will therefore use their utmost endeavours to establish learned and preaching ministers, with a good and sufficient maintenance throughout the whole kingdom, wherein many dark corners are miserably destitute of the means of salvation, and many poor ministers want necessary provision." What the bishops had done or failed to do the Parliament was to endeavour. Would it succeed better ?

Moderate though the tone of this was, it was in clear distinctness Erastian, and in probable application Presbyterian. The nineteen propositions sent by the two Houses of Parliament to the king at York on June 1 requested the king's assent to this practically in the same words. The claim was one of parliamentary supremacy. Ecclesiastical interests were on both sides bound to political affairs at their crisis. It was this which made peace impossible.

AUTHORITIES.—Journals of the House of Lords. All the important constitutional documents are given in S. R. Gardiner, *Constitutional Documents of the Puritan Revolution ;* State Papers, Domestic, as before ; Laud, *Works ;* Hacket, *Scrinia Reserata ;* Journals of the House of Commons. The Thomason Collection of Tracts in the British Museum arranges the fugitive literature of the time according to dates. The Canons of 1640 are reprinted in Laud's Wcrks. Throughout the long period of political conflict covered by this chapter S. R. Gardiner's *History of England,* 1603-42, is invaluable.

CHAPTER VII

THE CHURCH AND THE CLERGY BEFORE THE CIVIL WARS

THE years which immediately preceded the Great Rebellion seem, when we read the political history of the time, to have been almost entirely days of strife and confusion. But when we look below the surface we find that quiet religious work was quietly proceeding, and that in all classes there were men of deep piety who cordially approved of the action of those in high place, and that a deep-rooted attachment to the Church of England, "as opposed to Popish and Puritan innovations," existed, which sufficiently explains the warmth of devotion that followed her fortunes during the period of their eclipse, and of enthusiasm to welcome her when she received her own again.

When Charles I. came to the throne old men could still remember the days of Queen Mary, and men still in middle life recalled old customs which had only gradually died out. At the end of his life—he died in 1643 —Dr. Kettell, President of Trinity College, Oxford, would speak of the rood-lofts, and the wafers in the sacrament, which he remembered everywhere. They had become uncommon. The vestments were often preserved, sometimes used, in colleges, as well as in cathedral churches. Old customs of festal use survived even in small parish churches. The parish priest, according to George Herbert, would take order that his church was "at great festivals strawed or stuck with boughs and perfumed with incense." Among church-wardens' accounts are found (as in those of St. Mary's, Reading, where the charge is six shillings, and begins in 1622), "for decking the church at Christmas, Easter, and Whitsuntide, with holly, ivy, rosemary, bays, and green boughs." At Durham the influence of Cosin introduced, so Smart objected, customs "not used in other cathedral churches within this realm, nor in former times used in Durham, as, namely, standing up at the Nicene Creed, *Gloria Patri*, wearing of copes at the second service,[1] . . . setting tapers burning, and not burning, on the communion table." The organs, too, were played there during the administration of the sacraments of holy communion and of baptism. And there were many score of images bravely painted and gilded, says the same distempered critic.

Aubrey tells how, when Lord Saye and Sele came to visit the University of Oxford, there were paintings in the chapel of Trinity of two altars, with much other old work.

Paintings and glass. Of the pictures the eccentric President Kettell said, "Truly, my Lord, we regard them no more than a dirty dish-clout," and thus saved them. Mediæval glass at Salisbury remained in 1629 to provoke the anger of Henry Sherfield, and to lead to his prosecution in the Star Chamber. Laud was at pains to collect and restore the glass in Lambeth Palace chapel; and though the Puritan fear of idolatry had a special distrust of painted windows, the feeling was not at all general in England. At Fairford the famous fifteenth-century glass was preserved entire throughout the Civil War. And though this was unusual, there is enough mediæval glass still remaining in many parts of the country to show how much more there must have been before the war broke out. The Puritan Neal's account of the cathedral church of Canterbury is perhaps exaggerated; but he is too systematic to be incorrect when he speaks of "two candlesticks, tapers, a basin for oblations, a cushion for the service-book, a silver-gilt canister for the wafers, . . . a credentia, or side-table, with a basin and ewer and napkins, and a towel, to wash before consecration," and adds that "on some altars there was a pot called the incense pot, and a knife to cut the communion bread." Heylin, Laud's chaplain, thus describes Manwaring's changes at Worcester :

Decorations and fittings of the altar.

---

[1] In his *Memoranda* Smart contradicts this statement of his *Articles*, for he states that when James I. was at Durham copes were worn at the communion.

"He erected a fair table of marble, standing on four well-fashioned columns; he covered the wall behind the same with azure-coloured stuff, having white silk lace upon every seam, and furnished it with palls and fronts, as he had observed it in his Majesty's and some bishops' chapels; and ordered the king's scholars, being forty in number, who formerly used to throng tumultuously into the choir, to go in rank, by two and two, and make their due obeisances at their coming in."

In Laud's metropolitical visitation, inquiry, as we have seen, was made whether there "was a convenient and decent communion table standing upon a frame, with a carpet of silk or some other decent stuff." A green carpet was purchased for the communion table of St. Mary's, Reading, which cost £2 : 8s. St. Edmund's, Salisbury, had in 1631 "one cloth of red damask and gold for the communion table." Among the articles plundered from St. George's Chapel at Windsor by Parliamentary soldiers when Christopher Wren, brother of the Bishop of Ely, was dean, were "two fair double-gilt chalices with covers, two fair double-gilt flagons, and a bason, gilt, for the bread at great communions." It was alleged against Cosin in the articles of his impeachment, that "at the first Candlemas day, at night, he caused three hundred wax candles to be set up and lighted in the church at once in honour of our Lady, and placed threescore of them upon and about the altar." The offended Prebendary Smart, who has already been mentioned, preached bitterly against all that Cosin had done in that great cathedral. "Our young Apollo repaireth the quire, and set it out gaily with strange Babylonish ornaments; the hallowed priests dance about the altar, making pretty sport and fine pastime with trippings and turnings, and crossing and crouching."

While Puritans made mock there were many in the North, where there survived a traditional affection for ceremonial, who warmly approved. Smart had heard, he said, *Church music.* "A strange speech, little better than blasphemy, uttered lately by a young man in the presence of his lord and many learned men. 'I had rather go forty miles to a good service than two miles to a sermon (*Os durum*).' And what meant he by a good service? His meaning was manifest: where goodly Babylonish garments were worn, embroidered with images, where he might have a delicate noise of singers, with shakebuts and cornets and organs, and, if it were possible, all kinds of music, used at the dedication of Nabuchodonosor's golden image."

The movement was far from generally unpopular. And it was no mere love of show that dictated it. The endeavour to introduce a certain standard of ceremonial, based, as Laud argued, upon the unbroken usage of the royal chapels, the example of most of the cathedral churches, and the custom of Queen Elizabeth's days, was accompanied, it is interesting to note, by a genuine zeal for church building and restoration. In 1636, Archbishop Neile observed that in the past year there had been expended in the archdeaconries of York, the East Riding, and Nottingham, in "repairing and adorning churches," the large sum of £6562 : 15 : 7. Many cases are recorded of the entire rebuilding of churches, such as that of Little Gidding by the Ferrar family. Laud and Juxon were noted as builders and restorers—Abergwili, Lambeth, Croydon, Fulham, all bearing witness to their zeal. All through this period, too, the restoration and refitting of St. Paul's Cathedral proceeded apace. Laud's correspondence is full of references to it, and it was thought that the fines in the High Commission Court were the heavier because they were devoted to that object.

Church restoration.

St. Paul's.

The most famous instance, however, of church restoration is that undertaken by John, Viscount Scudamore, a friend of Laud's, who, after eminent public services, settled down on his country estate and undertook the re-endowment and re-edification of the churches of which he was patron. Having obtained advice from the archbishop and the necessary licence in mortmain to re-endow, he took in hand the rebuilding of the ancient church of Abbey Dore. So "ruinous and mean" was the condition of this "venerable place" that, according to the writer who describes Lord Scudamore's work, one who "well remembered the rebuilding of the church of Door saith Mr. John Gyles, otherwise then called Sir Gyles, curate here before the present church was rebuilt, read prayers under an arch of the old demolished church to preserve his Prayer Book from wet

Abbey Dore.

in rainy weather." The church of Abbey Dore was consecrated, after complete restoration, on Palm Sunday, 1634.
The form used was that of Bishop Andrewes, practically unaltered.   Part of the description of the work done, as
given by Gibson in 1727, illustrates with some fulness the
nature of the attention paid in the time of the Laudian movement to the details of church fitting.   It is to be observed
that Lord Scudamore restored and re-endowed the other
churches of which Gibson writes in the same manner.   In
later years he was a generous protector of the dispossessed
clergy :

"And as the altar there had been profaned, so the communion table here had been pulled down and buried in the
ruines of that church, till, carrying a great deal of stone away
for common uses, it was dug up, among the rest, and
appropriated (if by way of abuse I may be allow'd to call it
so, tho' I tremble at it) to the salting of meat and making of
cheese upon.   Thus it continued for a while, till it was very
strangely (tho' without a miracle) discovered what it were.
Whereupon Lord Scudamore, when he rebuilt this church,
with great awfulness ordered it to be restored, and set upon
three pilasters of stone, where now it stands, the most remarkable communion table of any in these parts, being one
entire stone, 12 foot long, 4 foot broad, and 3 inches thick.
The fine east window over the communion table was made by
Lord Scudamore, and the glass so painted by him, as I have
been told, at the expense of £100."

While such work as this was being done in regard to the
external fabric and internal order of the churches, it is to be
observed that the custom as to public service was
by no means uniform.   In most of the cathedral   Church
churches the holy communion was celebrated   services.
every Sunday and saint's day.   In many of the parish
churches the celebration was at least once a month.   Of
Hacket, when he was Rector of Cheam as well as of St.
Andrews, Holborn ("he resided," said Holdsworth, Master
of Emmanuel, "more upon his two livings than any Puritan
that ever he knew did upon one") it is recorded that he
celebrated the holy communion "monthly, besides other
times, at which, especially upon the Church's festivals, not

only the whole body of the church, but the galleries also would be full of communicants." Lettice, Lady Falkland, in one of her letters from the country, regretfully speaks of only being able to communicate monthly. The Ordination Articles of the bishops are careful to inquire whether there was communion at least at the three great festivals. The Eucharist is constantly spoken of as "the second service," following morning prayer in due liturgical order, generally quite early, and never later than noon.

The rubric ordering notice of intention to receive the holy communion seems to have been widely observed. In the churchwardens' accounts of St. Edmund's, Salisbury, we find it ordered on December 28, 1626, "that every person that shall receive the communion shall on some day of the week before the communion day give notice to the clerk of their purpose to receive, and the clerk shall deliver out a token for every person that will receive, and towards the defraying the charge of bread and wine every person at the time of their receiving shall pay one halfpenny to the churchwardens for the same, and then deliver back their tokens to the church-wardens.

The holy communion.

A catalogue of superstitious innovations brought into Durham Cathedral, 1641, says that "they took for assistants at the communion the whole quiremen and children which communicated not, contrary to the custom and practice of all cathedral churches." On the other hand, the bishops, it would appear from Mountague's visitation articles for the diocese of Chichester, seem to have regarded non-communicating attendance as a Puritan irreverence as well as an attempt on the part of Popish recusants to conceal their dissent from the National Church.

Non-communicating attendance.

The number of communicants, as might have been judged from the communion vessels of the date, was exceedingly large; at St. Giles's, Cripplegate, for example, there were over two thousand communicants. There do not seem to be traces of reservation of the sacrament in church after service, though Thorndike, some thirty years later, seems to regard it as a laudable and even necessary practice, but it appears, from the case of Nicholas Ferrar, that

Number of communicants.

it was occasionally taken from the church after the celebration to communicate the sick.

In the court and in some cathedral churches there were public prayers every day, and lectures also on the week days. Mary Rich writes that, at Warwick House, where Puritan sympathies were strong, "there were daily many eminent and excellent divines, who preached in the chapel most edifyingly and awakeningly to us. In country churches morning and evening prayers were said regularly on Sundays, and often on week days, as George Herbert's example shows; but the bishops did not enforce the obligation, though they inquired into its performance. In some country churches there was only public prayer " on the Lord's day and its eve, and on holy days and their eves, and on Wednesdays and Fridays, our wonted Litany days. The Litany, except in cathedral churches, does not seem on Sundays to have been said or sung as a separate service, but immediately after morning prayer. Bishop Wren, writing to his chancellor, Dr. Corbett, on March, 6, 1635, orders "that ye divine seruice and sermon in every church shall be at the canonicall time in most places observed, namelie, between ye houres of nine and twelve in ye forenoon; and that in ye afternoone the divine service shall begin about three of the clocke."

Daily services.

Catechising, to which there is constant reference in the voluminous papers of Bishop Wren regarding his visitation of the diocese of Norwich, 1635-38, preserved in the Bodleian Library, was made a special feature of Laud's revival of discipline. It was directed to be held everywhere in the afternoon, and it was intended thus to replace the sermons of the lecturers. Its enforcement was a part of that supervision which was designed to control not only the lecturer pledged to the propagation of particular views, but also the chaplains of country squires, men such as Bishop Hall wittily describes:

Catechising.

The chaplains,

> A gentle squire would gladly entertain
> Into his house some trencher-chapellain,
> Some willing man that might instruct his sons,
> And that would stand to good conditions:

> First, that he lie upon the truckle-bed,
> While his young master lieth o'er his head ;
> Second, that he do, on no default,
> Ever presume to sit above the salt ;
> Third, that he never change his trencher twice ;
> Fourth, that he use all common courtesies,
> Sit bare at meals, and one-half rise and wait,
> All these observed, he would contented be
> To give five marks and winter livery.

Sometimes the chaplain was kept in pretence as "a curate to the parson" of the parish ; Laud mentions such a case. All similar cases the bishops were now exhorted to diligently investigate. There was danger of the revival of the pre-Reformation abuse of chantry priests in another form ; and Episcopal supervision was much needed.

The bishops' interference was not received with satisfaction everywhere, and those of the clergy who were interested in the system of lectureships, as propagating their own *and lecturers.* opinions, or in the freedom of private chaplains as a privilege of county families, to which they themselves belonged, expressed strong distaste. We have an example in the diary of John Rous, a Suffolk rector, who carefully noted the king's injunction as to lectureships, but described with disgust the nature of the new preaching of Laudian principles by hot-headed and ill-educated preachers, and joined in the laugh against

> Sir Roger, from a zealous piece of frieze,
> Rais'd to a vicar, but without degrees,
> Whose yearly audit may, by strict account
> To twenty nobles, and his vails, amount.

While lectures were being suppressed, there seemed in the ministry to be undue laxity in another direction. "The country parson is a lover of old customs, if they be good and harmless ; and the rather because country people are much addicted to them, so that to favour them therein is to win their hearts, and to oppose them therein is to deject them." So wrote George Herbert ; and the instance he quoted in illustration was the yearly Rogationtide procession, for the blessing of the fields and the "beating of bounds." The custom was favoured by those in authority as a means of drawing the people together in Christian fellowship and charity. Herrick mentions it; and Montague inquired after the performance in his visitation articles of 1637: "Doth your minister yearly, in Rogation week, for the knowing and distinguishing of the bounds of parishes, and for obtaining God's blessing upon the fruits of the ground, walk the perambulation, and say or sing in English the Gospels, Epistles, Litany, and other devout prayers, "together with the 103rd and 104th Psalms?"

George Herbert's account of the parson's Sunday is like his beautiful picture of the spring; it was a

> Sweet day, so cool, so calm, so bright
> The bridal of the earth and sky,

which the priest spent in devout worship and ministry, in reconciliation and charity. The spirit of his words suggests nothing of the contention which in his time marred the observance of the day of rest. There was, however, nothing more hotly debated—nothing that made a more sharp division between Puritans and "Orthodox"—than the observance of Sunday. James I. had excited strong feelings by his *Book of Sports*. In the earlier years of Charles I.'s reign a literary controversy on the subject had been followed by an attempt on the part of several judges of assize to forbid the custom of Sunday village feasts, and some had actually required the clergy to publish their order in church. The king regarded this as an interference with his prerogative, and the Bishop of Bath and Wells (Dr. Piers) was ordered to report as to the nature of the parish festivals and their observance. His letter, based on the information of seventy-two clergy, throws an interesting light on the customs of Somerset. He described the classes of feasts as "Feasts of dedication, or revel days," "church-ales," "clerk-ales," and "bid-ales."

"The feasts of dedication are in the memory of their several churches. Those churches which are dedicated to the Holy Trinity have their feast on Trinity Sunday; and so all the feasts are kept on the Sunday before or after the saint's day to whom the churches are dedicated, because the people have not leisure to observe them on the week days. . . .

Church-ales are when the people go from their afternoon prayers on Sundays to their lawful sports and pastimes in the churchyard, or in the neighbourhood in some public-house, where they drink and make merry. By the benevolence of the people at these pastimes many poor parishes have cast their bells, and beautified their churches, and raised stocks for the poor, and there has not been observed so much disorder at them as commonly at fairs or markets. Clerk-ales are so called because they were for the maintenance of the parish-clerk ; and there is great reason for them, for in poor country parishes the people, thinking it unfit that the clerk should duly attend at the church and not gain by his office, send him in provision, and then come and feast with him, by which means he sells more ale and tastes more of the liberality of the people than their quarterly payments would amount to in many years ; and since these have been put down many ministers have complained to me that they are afraid they shall have no parish clerk. A bid-ale is when a poor man, decayed in his substance, is set up again by the liberal benevolence and contribution of his friends at a Sunday's feast."

It was natural that Puritans should feel strongly about many of these observances, and it can only have been from The Sabbatarian controversy. a desire to preserve the people's amusements that Charles should have taken the matter so much to heart. Chief-Justice Richardson, who, on the Western Circuit in 1632, had ordered the clergy to put down the games, was summoned before the Council and soundly rated. Laud was sharp with him for his intrusion into clerical matters. "I have been almost choked with a pair of lawn-sleeves," said the judge when he came out. Bishop Piers pressed his victory, protesting against Sabbatarianism, and censuring those who hindered the revels or church-wakes. The king reissued his father's Declaration of Sports, and added strong words forbidding any interference with "the feast of the dedication of churches, commonly called wakes." This declaration was ordered to be read in churches ; but there was the greatest reluctance in many places to obey ; and some of the clergy were actually imprisoned or suspended for disobeying the king's order. This was one of the most unhappy illustrations of the Erastian theory which dominated the State throughout the seventeenth century. It was also a flat contradiction to the policy of the House of Commons, which had already passed bills of a strongly Sabbatarian tendency. There was a divergence of opinion, emphasised by a mass of polemical literature of great erudition and vigour, which nothing could bridge over.

The divergence was even more marked under Charles I. between Parliament and Puritan on the one side, and men of Laud's impatient temper and the king's despotic theory on the other. In the mass of evidence collected against Laud, there is none more characteristic of popular feeling *Its bitterness.* than that of Richard Culmer, a minister suspended by the Dean and some of the prebendaries of Canterbury, sitting as the archbishop's commissioners at his metropolitical visitation, for refusing to publish "the book for Sabbath dancing." Culmer and two other ministers, Player and Heiron, continued so for above three and a half years. Immediately after their suspension, says the evidence, they jointly petitioned the archbishop for absolution at Lambeth, but he, having read the petition, said, "If you know not how to obey I know not how to grant," and departed; and afterward, being divers times severally petitioned by them, he refused to absolve them until the Bishops' War against the Scots began.

"When I petitioned the archbishop one time," said Culmer, "he being in a great rage, said, 'Consideration—I will take nothing into consideration, and if you conform not all the sooner I'll take a more round course with you'; and so saying he threw Mr. Culmer's petition at him violently. So the archbishop suffered me to continue suspended and deprived by the patron, who gave away my living immediately upon my suspension; so I had not one farthing profit of my ministry or living for three and a half years, having myself, my wife, and seven children to provide for."

It is easy to understand the bitter feeling aroused by such action. In some districts for the time it succeeded; the eyes of Laud seemed to be everywhere; Nonconformity was reduced to a minimum. But the opposition was as strong as ever in the background. While the new supervision was having its effect in many parts of the country, many more strictly ecclesiastical rules and customs of Elizabethan, and indeed much earlier, times survived. Private con-

Private confession. fession was far from uncommon. The teaching of typical churchmen was clear on the point. George Herbert spoke of the need of it in some cases : Bishop Bayly in his *Practice of Piety*, a book of extraordinary popularity, emphasised the same view : Donne contemplated the likelihood of such confessions being made before every communion. Among those who are known thus to have confessed are Charles I., Buckingham, Strafford, and Ferrar. The Duchess of Buckingham, says Hacket, had Bishop Williams for " her ghostly father."

Preaching was not regular in every place, and it was for this reason, no doubt, as well as for the propagation of

Preaching. particular opinions, that lectureships were so frequently established. Dr. Kettell, President of Trinity and Vicar of Garsington, rode out every Sunday to preach at his country living. But the lack of rule was the real difficulty of the time, and the demand for a "preaching ministry" was really a protest against individualism. Men could do what they liked. Thus, Tobie Matthew preached incredibly often, Richard Neile, incredibly seldom, when each was Archbishop of York. But the ideal was that of George Herbert : "The country parson preacheth constantly ; the pulpit is his joy and his throne."

In the universities the sermons in the university church were regularly kept up, but were generally, it would appear, more controversial than edifying. Laud had experience of being convented for a sermon which contradicted the prevailing Calvinism, and of being answered in terms which exceeded even the liberal license of the Puritan pulpit. There were sermons also in the college chapels on days of particular obligation to each college. Much that was loose custom was revived and fixed at Oxford under Laud's chancellorship ; and the college chapels, while they retained many curious individual customs, tended to follow the uses of the cathedral churches.

The early seventeenth century was a period strong in con-

troversial divinity. It was a period also of very earnest
effort after a revival of spiritual life. Among the churchmen
of Charles I.'s days there are names of saints that will last
as long as English literature or English religion. So rich,
indeed, is the age in memories of men of learning and devotion that a selection of the greatest names must give an
inadequate picture of the widespread influence of the Church,
if it is not remembered that in many a village the
Herbert was more conspicuous than the Hampden. *The great*
In the court, the city, the country, the cross of Christ   *divines.*
was held up before men by many a great preacher and many a
humble saint. Perhaps no age has afforded more conspicuous
examples of men in high position, or of great literary ability,
turning to the ministry of the Church for the exercise of
their best energies or for the sanctification of their maturest
powers. Names that stand out are those of Donne, Wotton,
Hales, Ferrar, Herbert, Cosin; and all of them, it is notable,
had some special connection with Archbishop Laud.

Donne has been dealt with in the volume which has preceded this; but a brief allusion to his power as a preacher,
at the height of his influence, when Charles I. was
king, must be admitted here. He held large con-   *Donne.*
gregations enthralled. One of those who often heard him
said :

> And never were we wearied till we saw
> The hour, and but an hour, to end did draw.

Walton's description of his preaching is not to be forgotten—
"He preached the word so as to show that his own heart
was possessed with those very thoughts and joys that he
laboured to distil into others; a preacher in earnest, weeping
sometimes for his auditory, sometimes with them; always
preaching to himself, like an angel from a cloud, but in none;
carrying some, as St. Paul was, to heaven in holy raptures,
and enticing others, by a sacred art and courtship, to amend
their lives; here picturing a vice so as to make it ugly to
those who practised it, and a virtue so as to make it beloved
even by those that loved it not; and all this with a most
particular grace and an inexpressible addition of comeliness."

From the time when he took holy orders Donne grew

more and more of a recluse. He lived for his work and in his work; but his influence increased in intensity for the very fact that it was exercised apart from the court or ordinary public life. Charles at times seems to have doubted the nature of his teaching. Once, at least, he sent for his sermon to read it over. But if he doubted, he was soon convinced, and in 1630 we know that the king designed to give him the next vacant bishopric. Laud's feeling is sufficiently evidenced by the fact that when Donne died he preached his funeral sermon.

Donne had been a close friend of the mother of another poet and saint, George Herbert. Herbert, the brother of Lord Herbert of Cherbury, was unlike Donne in looking forward from the first to holy orders; but his brilliant abilities, and their recognition by the University of Cambridge, where he was public orator and Fellow of Trinity, as well as the favour of the king, seemed for a while to turn his thoughts from divinity. But after a time of some hesitation "God inclined him to put on a resolution to serve at His altar." His final resolve was only after "such spiritual conflicts as none can think but only those that have endured them"; and when the living of Bemerton, near Salisbury, was offered to him, it was only the urgent persuasion of Laud, who told him that refusal would be a sin, which induced him to accept it. Now a married man, he was ordained priest, and went to live in his little parish. There he set forth with a holy simplicity the true life of "a priest to the temple." Each day, when he read the morning and evening services "at the canonical hours of ten and four," he had for congregation "most of his parishioners and many gentlemen in the neighbourhood, while some of the meaner sort would let their plough rest whenever Mr. Herbert's saint's-bell rang to prayers." Already a poet of real inspiration as well as of happy conceit, Herbert wrote at Bemerton that picture of the ideal parish priest which is one of the best-treasured and most characteristic possessions of the English Church. The picture is one dictated by a "humble conformity" to the authority of the Church, a simplicity born of a true self-denial and a perfect taste, and a shrewd good sense that mingles very happily with a fervent

piety towards God.   It shows how absorbing the duties of a
parson were found by those who would adequately discharge
them.   So absorbed, Herbert lived but a few years in the
work to which he had given his heart.   He died in 1632,
before the imminence of the troubles which his gentle soul
did not foresee.   Very different was the lot of his friend
Nicholas Ferrar—like him, a man of affairs who
took holy orders and sought a secluded place in   Nicholas
which to worship and work for God.   It was from   Ferrar.
Laud that Nicholas Ferrar, when he determined to serve in
the ministry, sought ordination, and his favour presented the
Ferrar family to the king, and won for them a sanction which,
perhaps, the Bishop of Lincoln would not then readily have
given.   The household at Little Gidding is a beautiful picture
in the disturbed history of the time.   Hacket, chaplain to
Bishop Williams, in whose diocese the village lay, gives perhaps the clearest picture of the life of its inmates.
Williams, he says, at his second visitation found a   Little
congregation of saints at Little Gidding—mother,   Gidding.
son, and daughters all given to God.   All lived a single life,
but Williams would not allow the daughters to take a
vow of celibacy.   Plainly, not fashionably dressed, giving
entertainment only to the poor, living very simply, with
frequent fastings and giving of alms, they kept up offices of
prayer continually.   Twice daily they attended the common
prayer in church, twice in their house they prayed together ;
and all day and all night one or other was engaged in watching
and in "some private holy exercise."   With all this was no
ostentation, but the meekest simplicity.   In their parlour
was hung up this letter of exhortation :

"He that by report of our endeavours will demonstrate
that which is more perfect, and seek to make us better, is
welcome as an Angel of God.   He that by cheerful partici-
pating, and approbation of that which is good, confirms us
in the same is welcome as a Christian friend.   He that any
way goes about to divert or disturb us in that which is as it
ought to be among Christians (though it be not useful in this
World) is a Burthen while he stays, and shall bear his judgement, whosoever he be.   He that faults us in absence for
that which in presence he made shew to approve, shall by a

guilt of Flattery and Slander violate the Bands both of Friendship and Christianity.

> Subscribed :
>
> > Mary Ferrar, Widow, Mother of this Family, aged
> > about Fourscore Years, who bids adieu to all Hopes
> > and Fears of this World, and only desires to serve
> > God."

It was a life of continual self-denial, entirely without ostentation or anything to attract public regard. But in troublous
times it could not pass without suspicion. "Envy
or ignorance," says Hacket, "could guess no better at
it but that it was a *casa professa* or convent pack'd
together of some superstitious order beyond seas, or a nunnery,
and that the sufferance of it looked towards a change in religion."
It was a strange confession that the Church of England could
produce no mortified life, no observance of devotion like that
of primitive days. Bishop Williams was too sagacious and too
charitable to fall into so pitiable an error as to condemn
these holy souls. "God help us if the best Protestants (for
these may be so called) do look like Papists !" He visited
them, gave them his blessing, and bade them proceed in the
name of God. Hacket, remembering the old days, before
the wars scattered the "Protestant nunnery" to the winds,
with the sad contrast before him in the decay of public morals
and private devotion, wrote with true feeling of sympathy and
pathos. He had seen, and he bore record that the family of
the Ferrars had been with Jesus.

The Protestant nunnery.

In his detailed picture there is the spirit of leisure in quiet
days ; and it was this which the Ferrar household made their
own. In this they continued till the death of Nicholas
Ferrar in 1637. Bishop Williams was in prison at
the time, but Nicholas had visited him not long before
his death, and the house retained a loyal affection for him.
On his release in 1640 he again visited Little Gidding, and in
a still kinder spirit than of old. He now permitted the vow
of celibacy which Mary and Anna Collett had taken, and " was
armed to maintain their good resolutions." A bitter attack
had been made upon the house in a pamphlet called *The
Arminian Nunnery ;* Williams defended them, declaring that
he " knew they did practise nothing but what was according

Suppression of the house.

to the law of the Church of England." But the shadows began to close around them. The king visited them in the earlier days of their community life; he visited them again in May 1642, and once more in 1646, just before he gave himself up to the Scots. Before the end of that year soldiers of the Parliamentary army sacked the church and house, and carried away plate, furniture, and provisions. The survivors lingered on at Little Gidding till, before all the original members of the community died, the rules were given up, and the house of peace, as Nicholas Ferrar designed it, ceased to exist.

A considerable literary as well as religious interest belongs to Little Gidding. The beautiful work of binding and the making of concordances were not the only recreations of the household. Dialogues and interludes, discourses, to be recited each day, were made by the members of the family and read aloud in the evenings. These were tales with a moral purpose, but with not a little of romance in them, and they bear the same relation toward the tales in which the age delighted as the poems of Herbert bear to those of the wits of his day. The art is the same, the purpose different. And it is plain that Little Gidding was as good a school of letters as of piety.

The friendship of Nicholas Ferrar with George Herbert was almost entirely one of correspondence. When they left the great world, each lived a secluded life. It was not so with another famous courtier, Sir Henry Wotton. A famous ambassador and wit, poet, scholar, and diplomatist, the friend of Sarpi and of Bedell, he came to end "the errors of his wandering life" at Eton as its provost and a humble minister in the Church of Christ. Pleased to train children in learning and religion, he spent the last fifteen years of his life a retired and cloistered man, paying a few country visits, and yearly a visit to Oxford, and

> Untied unto the world by care
> Of public fame or private breath.

It was his hope that his example might make the children of great men " not ashamed of the surplice " ; and if the distraction of the times did not suffer many of those whom he had taught to enter holy orders, he had at least the satisfaction of leaving an example which spoke eloquently for charity as for learning and religion.

At Eton he made the friendship of the most learned of the Fellows of his society, "the ever-memorable John Hales."
John Hales. Both were sworn foes to religious disputation, men of a large outlook on life and a beautiful tolerance. Both were sincere in their faith. Hales believed " that pride and passion, more than conscience, were the cause of all separation from each other's communion ; and he frequently said that that only kept the world from agreeing upon such a Liturgy as might bring them into one communion, all doctrinal points upon which men differed in their opinions being to have no place in any Liturgy." It was the thought of a scholar, not a practical man of affairs ; and such, too, was his book on Schism, which Laud looked at with suspicion. The archbishop was to Wotton a patron and friend, and he proved himself able to sympathise also with Hales. He sent for him to Lambeth, and they talked long and, it seemed to the chaplains who watched, hotly. Laud spoke earnestly, as he so constantly did, of the care that should be taken to preserve the peace and unity of the Church, disturbed by new doctrines which wits as well as fanatics set abroad. It is plain that he saw that Hales was of his own mind—firm in essentials, tolerant in matters of less import, and when there was a prebend of Windsor vacant he procured it from Charles for the scholarly recluse. But " the archbishop could not without difficulty persuade him to accept, and he did accept it rather to please him than to please himself, because he really believed he had enough before. He was one of the least men in the kingdom, and one of the greatest scholars in Europe."

With such men among her clergy the English Church could meet the times that were to come with courage. She
Robert Herrick and the poets. touched all classes of society and all sympathies. A parish priest like Herrick could enter into all the innocent gaieties of his parishioners, and write verses with the best wits of the town. Eighteen years a country parson in Devonshire, he was deprived in 1647, and went back to London to write and publish poems. The

Restoration gave him his living again, and there he ended his days, dying in 1674 at the age of eighty-three.   Illustrious as a poet among poets, he yet gave his best thoughts to God, and in his " noble numbers " he strove to write simply for simple folk.   In his parish, long after his death, people who could not read or write knew his Litany to the Holy Spirit by heart, and simple verse like his prayers and thanksgivings reached down to simple hearts in times of stress.

> Make, make me thine, my gracious God,
> Or with Thy staff, or with Thy rod ;
> And be the blow, too, what it will,
> Lord, I will kiss it, though it kill.

Words such as these were fit in the days of the Church's distress : so the thoughts of poets turned to prayer.   Religious poetry was characteristic of the age.   Sandys, Crashaw, Vaughan, men of quite different life and circumstances, unite in singing the praises of God in the Church, that home of peace, where are

> No cruel guard of diligent cares, that keep ·
> Crown'd woes awake, as things too wise for sleep :
> But reverent discipline, and religious fear,
> And soft obedience, find sweet biding here ;
> Silence, and sacred rest ; peace, and pure joys.

Cartwright, as poet and preacher, was another of those who sang as they prayed ; and so were George Wither and Giles Fletcher.

The fashion of religious verse hardly survived the Civil Wars, but the characteristic of English religion in the days of the later Caroline divines——the mass of devotional literature——began while Charles I. was king *Cosin's Prayers.* by the publication of Cosin's *Collection of Private Devotions* in 1627.   It was a book written at the first to supply the ladies of the Court with private prayers of their own, so that they should not be attracted by the foreign books that the queen pressed upon them.   Based upon a primer of Elizabeth's time, it provided a systematic course of devotion according to the principles of the Reformed Church.   But its insistence on the sacramental teaching of the Church, and its recognition of prayers for the dead, produced a series of violent attacks from every quarter, lay and clerical, among men of Puritan sympathies. Yet it served its end. A number of editions were rapidly issued, and there can be no doubt that it did much to confirm the attachment of many to the Church of their fathers.

In several books of the time we have a picture of a famous household trained on these lines. At Great Tew, some
Lord Falkland, sixteen miles from Oxford, there gathered a literary and theological society of famous wits. Lucius Carey, Viscount Falkland, the son of the clever spendthrift who had been Lord-Deputy of Ireland and the eccentric Eliza, daughter of Chief Baron Tanfield, had sold the Burford property, which came to him from his grandfather, and settled on his father's property at Tew. Himself a scholar and wit, his friends were wits and scholars too ; but gradually the theological interest came to predominate. He was a great admirer of Donne, whom he eulogised as

> The voice of truth,
> God's conduit-pipe for grace, Who chose him for
> His extraordinary ambassador.

His house, says Aubrey, was like a college full of learned men. Among them were Chillingworth, "his most intimate and beloved favourite," Earle, Eglionby, Hammond, and Sheldon ; " nor," in the phrase of Clarendon, " did the lord of the house know of their coming and going, nor who were in his house, till he came to dinner or supper, where all still met ; otherwise, there was no troublesome ceremony or con-straint to forbid men to come to the house, or to make them weary of staying there ; so that many came thither to study in a better air, finding all the books they could desire in his library, and all the persons together whose company they could wish and not find in any other society. Here Mr. Chillingworth wrote, and formed and modelled his excellent book against the learned Jesuit, Mr. Nott, after frequent debates upon the most important particulars." The letters of
and his wife. Falkland's wife, Lettice Morison, show her to have been one of the most saintly women of the age. Devout, obedient and simple in her religion, following the rules of the Church in prayer and fast and thanksgiving with pious regularity, she found the spiritual experiences of the saints

reproduced in her life, their penitence, their dryness, their
infinite consolations.   The particulars of her life which her
chaplain, Dr. John Duncan, added to the letters when they
were printed in 1648, give a remarkable picture of holiness.
They describe the employments of a great lady who watched
over the poor and sick of her estates, who treated her servants
as friends, and whose plans for education and charity went
far beyond the ideas of her time.   Such lives, it is plain,
could still be lived peacefully in the country, though the land
resounded with the clash of arms.   It was in such a household that Chillingworth framed his tolerant defence of " the
Religion of Protestants " ; there that he solemnly re-affirmed
his belief (which modern writers have again doubted) in " the
doctrine of the Trinity, the deity of our Saviour, and all other
supernatural verities revealed in Holy Scripture " ; and it was
there that, in converse with learned men and with a saintly
wife, Falkland confirmed the faith which led him to take up
the sword for Church and King.

It was the aim of the school to which men such as Falkland and Hammond and Cosin belonged to make clear the
appeal of the Church to every side of life, the claim   Contrast
of religion to rule over all that belonged to the   between these
                                                     ideals and
interest of mankind.   Therein lay one of the   that of the
greatest of the contrasts between the Puritan and   Puritans.
the man of the school of Laud.   To the former life must be
lived ever in the Great Taskmaster's eye, and the task that
He set seemed to involve an elimination of much that was
innocent and healthy.   Puritanism grew in sternness.   Music
as well as dancing, the old-fashioned English amusements of
wrestling and archery, as well as the brutal sports of bull- and
bear-baiting, were excluded from their view of what was lawful to a Christian.   Because they were virtuous there should
be no more cakes and ale.   But theirs, strained and uncharitable though it often became, was a needed protest
against luxury, idleness, and ungodly ways.   The general
relaxation of morals which followed the Reformation had left
its disastrous fruits in carelessness and recklessness among all
classes.   And there was a grandeur about the stern Calvinistic
creed, with all its contrast to the fundamental conceptions of
Christianity, which gave a bracing influence to English re-

ligious life. The thought that all men, apart from any action of their own, were predestinate of God to glory or destruction, "quia voluit," had an immense power over strong and valiant hearts. The voice of God seemed perpetually to call the elect to new acts of service and of vengeance on His enemies. The lot was cast, and the elect, saved without a whisper of their own, must, by every noble inspiration of their souls, give themselves to the work of God without distraction from any human call. To those who sang with Herbert and prayed with Cosin life had a different aspect. The world was full of the beauty and goodness of God. He willed all men to repent and to come to the knowledge of the truth. Art, music, poetry, were His gifts, to be consecrated to His service ; the riches of life, on every side, were His. Nothing that was man's, save only sin, was alien from His love. And as the holy mysteries which He had ordained were instituted to link heaven to earth, so the worshipper must consecrate every beauty of nature as well as every thought of his own heart to the Trinity of Love and Power from Whom all blessings flowed.

How narrow, when we read the intimate details of the daily life of those days, when we compare Herbert and the Ferrars with the Hutchinsons and Mary Rich, seems the division between the two parties, at least in spiritual things. But men who feel most deeply have often fought about trifles. The House of Commons, when it turned to discuss theology, was stirred by the most childish gossip. When Cromwell first raised his voice it was because, in 1629, he remembered that Dr. Beard had told him that Bishop Neile had ordered him, in 1617, not to controvert a preacher who had approved some "tenets of Popery." The preacher was Dr. Alablaster, whom Herrick exalted in his verse. "Men's minds," says Fuller of this time, "were exasperated with such small occasions as otherwise might have been passed over and no notice taken thereof." It is not hard for us now, when the stern simplicity of the Calvinist creed has lost its power, to discern how close, but for it, the pious spirits of both parties were to each other and to God.

AUTHORITIES. —State Papers, Domestic ; the Tanner MSS. ; Cosin's *Correspondence* (Surtees Society) ; Wren, *Parentalia ;* Aubrey, *Brief Lives,* (ed. Andrew Clark) ; George Herbert, *The Temple*, and *A Priest to the Temple;* Works of the writers mentioned in the text ; The Visitation Articles of different bishops ; *Two Lives of Farrar*, edited by Professor Mayor, 1855 ; *Life of Donne*, by Edmund Gosse, with important criticisms by H. C. Beeching, in the *Cornhill Magazine*, 1900, and *The Athenæum ; The Story Books of Little Gidding;* Hacket's *Scrinia Reserata* (Life of Williams) ; *The Returnes of Spiritual Comfort and Grief in a Devout Soul* (Lettice, Lady Falkland), 1648 ; Prynne, *Canterburie's Doome ; A View of the Ancient and Present State of the Churches of Door, Home-Lacy, and Hampstead*, Gibson, 1727 ; *A Laudian Church*, G. M'W. Rushforth, *Guardian*, March 5, 1902 ; C. Fell Smith, *Mary Rich, Countess of Warwick ;* M. E. Palgrave, *Mary, Countess of Warwick ; Churchwardens' Accounts of St. Mary's, Reading* (Garry) Reading, 1893 ; *Churchwardens' Accounts of St. Edmund and St. Thomas, Sarum*, Wilts Records Society, 1896 ; Laud, *Works ; Diary of John Rous, Incumbent of Santon Downham*, 1625-42, Camden Society, 1856.

CHAPTER VIII

THE CHURCH IN THE CIVIL WARS

THE last hope of peace had fled from political as well as religious life. On the 22nd of August 1642 the king's standard was raised at Nottingham. Charles issued
The war begun. a lengthy declaration as a manifesto, in which he said "that nothing but the preservation of the true Protestant religion, invaded by Brownism, Anabaptism, and Libertinism, the safety of our person threatened and conspired against by rebellion and treason, the law of the land and liberty of the subject oppressed and almost destroyed by an usurped, unlimited, arbitrary power, and the freedom, privilege, and dignity of Parliament by force and tumults, could make us put off our long-loved robe of peace, and take up defensive arms." These words, however inadequately they accounted for the origin of the civil war, found an echo in many hearts, and many felt what Walton said in after years : "When I look back upon the ruin of families, the bloodshed, the decay of common honesty, and how the former piety and plain dealing of this now sinful nation is turned into cruelty and cunning ; when I consider that, I praise God that He prevented me from being of that party which helped to bring in the Covenant and those sad confusions that followed it."

In a war of creeds the ecclesiastical machinery naturally demands attention, and the religious life of the New Model
Religion in the armies. must also be considered. Both armies had chaplains. In the king's, each regiment was thus provided, many of those employed being clergy who had been driven from their livings, Fuller and Pearson among

their number. A *Soldier's Prayer Book* was put forth by the king's command in 1648 for the use of his army: it was a book of prayer and praise drawn up on the model of the Common Prayer. In 1643 a special Fast was observed on the second Friday in every month, and a form of prayer for it, incorporating the Prayer against Rebellion of Elizabeth's day, was published at Oxford.

The Parliament had not fixed chaplains, but was very liberally supplied with ministers, who spoke freely against the Church and the bishops. The following passage from the letters of Nehemiah Wharton, quoted in the " Calendar of State Papers Domestic," is characteristic :

" A week later " (September 1642) when Wharton's force reached Hereford, he relates, " Sabbath Day, about the time of morning prayer, we went to the minster, where the pipes played and the puppets sang so sweetly that some of our soldiers could not forbear dancing in the holy choir, whereat the Baalists were sore displeased. The anthem ended, they fell to prayer, and prayed devoutly for the king, the bishops, etc.; and one of our soldiers with a loud voice, said, 'What ! never a bit for the Parliament,' which offended them much more. Not satisfied with this human service, we went to Divine, and, passing by, found shops open and men at work, to whom we gave some plain dehortations, and went to hear Mr. Sedgwick, who gave us two famous sermons, which much affected the poor inhabitants, who, wondering, said they never heard the like before. And I believe them."

After Edgehill most of the ministers in Essex's army went home, and it was in this that Baxter attributed the growth of independency, which Cromwell, from the first, wished to be dominant in the army. Within two years of the formation of the New Model the Independents secured complete control. Dell, Saltmarsh, William Sedgwick, and Hugh Peter were the chief ministers, and they were indefatigable. From 1648 a considerable increase of chaplains occurred, but, though they were well paid, their position remained a precarious one, liable to termination at the will of the commanding officer, on whom depended the precise shade of theology preached.

Independents and Sectaries.

The Independents, however, did not remain without rivals.

A large number of sects sprang up, not unnaturally, from the fact that soldiers claimed to preach indiscriminately, and that attempts to restrict the privilege to ministers ordained by some Reformed Church entirely failed. But toleration was no more complete in the army than outside it. Severe measures were used against Quakers, Fifth Monarchy men, Antinomians, and the like: the limits of permissible opinion were strictly fenced.

The ministers as well as the officers heartily approved of the iconoclasm which marked the progress of the Parliamentary troops. Waller's army did grievous damage at Winchester and Chichester. At the latter place, where painted windows and monuments were destroyed under Waller's eyes, a trooper said, "That if his old colonel in the Low Countries were there and commanded in chief, he would hang up half-a-dozen soldiers for example's sake." It may be added that there is no evidence for, and much to contradict, the often-repeated statement that every soldier in Cromwell's army had a Bible in his knapsack.

When the war began Puritanism presented an unbroken front. Presbyterians and Calvinistic churchmen stood shoulder to shoulder, and Independency had hardly yet begun to lift up its head. Puritanism at its best was indeed a powerful and in many respects a righteous force. Allied, on the one hand, with those who were eager for political freedom, or at least for definite checks on the personal government of the king, and, on the other, with the strong individualist tendencies of the religious men who had been trained in the school of Calvin, it had, in the strength of its protest against luxury and immorality, the "scurf" of the playhouse and the idleness of the cultured classes, a work to do which no other party could have accomplished. Puritanism had the power which always belongs to strong individualist principles when they are keenly felt by masses of men. It was a logical and rational following of the principles of Luther and of Calvin—unlike in outward expression as those principles were, but ultimately the same in essentials—in the reliance of the soul upon God apart from any *media* of communication. The stern simplicity of life which it fostered, the rejection, when pressed to its extreme, of worldly literature and art, was its most distinctive feature, and as such it sank into the hearts of thousands of poor folk, to whom the English Bible was speaking with a tremendous force of literalism and of conversion. In its sternest moments, even in the extremity of its Calvinism, when its divines could joyfully contemplate the damnation of "infants a span long," it was not really far divided from charity and grace. Households trained on its principles were homes of love as well as of discipline, and to them much that was beautiful as well as strong in later English life was not a little due.

Such was Puritanism in its noblest aspect, but in the hands of too many of its upholders it meant no more than bigotry and outrage. As the Parliamentary army set out from London in September 1642 they sacked the churches on their way, burning the communion tables and destroying surplices and prayer-books. Even clergy disposed towards Puritanism did not always escape. Dr.   and at its worst. Featley, of Acton and of Lambeth, of Pædobaptist fame, though he was, as Heyton says, "a Calvinist always in his heart," had his barns and stables at Acton fired by some of Essex's troops after the battle of Brentford. They had heard that he was very exact in his prayer-book services, so at Lambeth they broke open the door of his church, smashed the windows, burnt the rails, and destroyed the font. His subsequent history, it may be noted, was unfortunate. The Committee for Plundered Ministers made short work of him, and though only four of its members out of seventeen were present, turned him out of his living, and he died in prison.

The advance of the Parliamentary forces was too often marked by reckless destruction of church property by the soldiers. At Oxford they stole as much of the college plate as they could get, and fired shots at the statue of the Blessed Virgin with the infant Saviour in her arms over the new porch of St. Mary's church. Later, they hacked to pieces a representation of Christ on tapestry at Canterbury, and made a stone statue of Him a target. The cathedral church of Worcester was foully defiled, and many another after it. Charing Cross was destroyed by order of the Common Council on May 2, 1643. Before that, on April 24, the House of

Commons had appointed a committee "for demolishing of Monuments of Superstition or Idolatry." At its head was Sir Robert Harley. Thus ran the form of its instructions: "By virtue of an order of the House of Commons, and agreeable to a bill passed by both Houses of Parliament, for suppressing of divers innovations in churches and chapels; this Committee doth require you and every of you to take away, and demolish, every altar or table of stone within your church or chapel, and to remove and take away all tapers, candlesticks, and basons from the communion table in the said church or chapel; and to take away and demolish all crucifixes, crosses, and all images and pictures of any one or more persons of the Trinity, or of the Virgin Mary, in your said church or chapel. And this Committee doth further require you to take down and demolish all crucifixes, crosses, images, or pictures of any one or more persons of the Trinity, or of the Virgin Mary, upon the outside of your said church or chapel, or in any open space within your parish; whereof you are to give an account to this Committee before the twentieth day of this present month. To the churchwardens of the parish church or chapel of——, and to every one of them." With such a warrant, the noblest monuments and nearly all the old glass in Westminster Abbey and in St. Margaret's were destroyed.

Iconoclasm by order of the Commons, 1643.

One instance of the manner of doing may suffice. Bishop Hall tells in sad words the "furious sacrilege" which he witnessed in the "reforming the Cathedral Church" at Norwich. "Lord, what work was here; what clattering of glasses, what beating down of walls, what tearing up of monuments, what pulling down of seats, what wresting out of irons and brass from the windows and graves; what defacing of arms, what demolishing of curious stone-work, that had not any representation in the world, but only of the cost of the founder, and skill of the mason; what tooting and piping upon the destroyed organ pipes; vestments, both copes and surplices, together with the leaden cross which had been newly sawn down from over the green-yard pulpit, and the service-books and singing-books that could be had were carried to the fire in the public market-place; a lewd wretch walking before the train in his

Sacking of Norwich Cathedral Church.

cope trailing in the dirt, with a service-book in his hand, imitating in an impious scorn the tune, and usurping the words, of the litany used formerly in the church. Near the public cross, all these monuments of idolatry must be sacrificed to the fire, not without much ostentation of a zealous joy in discharging ordnance to the cost of some who professed how much they had longed to see that day. Neither was it any needs upon this guild day to have the cathedral now open on all sides to be filled with musketeers, waiting for the mayor to return, drinking and tobaconing as freely as if it had turned ale-house."

Such was the nature of the work of Puritanism when it was left to be carried out by mobs. Designed for a purification of the sanctuary, it became merely an occasion of sacrilegious outrage.

All this was done, professedly by authority of Parliament; it was by the same authority that an Assembly of Divines was called together, and that the revenues of bishops and deans and chapters were sequestered for the payment of the Parliament's troops. Political difficulties were added to financial. It was only possible for the Parliament to carry on war by the aid of the Scots, and the Scots insisted on the establishment of Presbyterianism. In January, 1643, the bill for the abolition of Episcopacy was passed by both houses. This was enough to make peace impossible. It was followed up in August 1643, by the sending of English commissioners to Scotland to settle the bases of an agreement; and before this an Assembly of Godly and Learned Divines had met at Westminster. It consisted of 130 clerical and 30 lay members, the latter selected from the two Houses. It was entirely the creature of Parliament, allowed only to consider what Parliament referred to it. It became practically an assembly of clergy of Puritan opinions; very few laymen attended its sessions, and no priest who adhered to the ancient establishment was present. It revised the Articles in a Puritan sense, but it showed no desire to go further than a moderate friendship with Scotland; it required only an engagement to maintain the Scots Church so far as each man should in his conscience "conceive it to be according to the will of God." The assembly

Abolition of Episcopacy, Jan. 1643.

Work of the Westminster Assembly, Aug. 1643.

was not prepared for the full Presbyterian system, for the inquisitorial yoke of the Presbyteries. The establishment of a
Presbyterian ministry, for which the Puritan leaders were
prepared, was very different from the acceptance of the full
Calvinistic hierarchy. The English Rebellion was thoroughly
Erastian in its treatment of church questions—a complete
contrast to the Scots. The House of Commons would never
consent to loose the authority of lay courts over the clergy
or to admit the despotism of the Presbyterian ecclesiastical
courts. But this was still future. Now political necessities
were urgent; and on August 26, the Solemn League and
Covenant abolishing Episcopacy, and vowing an endeavour
towards complete agreement between the two Churches, was
sent from Scotland to Parliament, and to the Westminster
Assembly.

It was subscribed, after several amendments, by both
Houses, and on February 2, 1644, it was ordered to be taken
by all men above the age of eighteen. There was no mis-
taking the significance of this order, for clause ii. of the
covenant ran as follows : "That we shall without respect of
persons endeavour the extirpation of popery, prelacy (that is,
church government by archbishops, bishops, their chan-
cellours and commisseries, deans, deans and chapters, archdeacons, and all other ecclesiastical officers depending on
that Hierarchy), superstition, heresy, schism, profaneness, and
whatsoever shall be found contrary to sound doctrine, and
the power of godliness, lest we partake of other men's sins,
and thereby be in danger to receive of their plagues, and that
the Lord may be one, and His Name one in the three
kingdoms." What view of the covenant was likely to be taken
by even moderate churchmen was clearly expressed
by Fuller. It was incompatible with their loyalty to
church and king. From the year 1643, therefore,
the clergy began to be ejected from their livings, partly as
malignants, or aiders of the king's party, partly for refusing
the Covenant and adhering to the Prayer-book. The number
ejected cannot have fallen far short of two thousand. Baillie,
after describing the means taken to fill the livings, added,
"even then some thousands of churches must vake for want
of men." In October 1644, the Westminster Assembly agreed

Ejection of
the clergy.

to a Directory for Public Worship; on January 3, 1645, it was to come into universal use. The observance of the Christian festivals was abolished. Christmas day, 1644, was ordered to be observed as a fast.

Meanwhile theological disputation flourished on every side, and strange opinions were propagated. A significant example is to be found in the pamphlet which Dr. Daniel Featley, imprisoned as a malignant, wrote against ^{The} Anabaptists. the "new changes never heard of in former ages." His work was entitled "The Dippers dipt, or the Anabaptists duck'd and plung'd over head and ears, at a disputation in Southwark," and was dated *Calend. Jan.* 1645, from a "Prisoner in Peter-house." It was preceded by a vigorous address to the Houses of Parliament. It professed to observe the wildest vagaries among those who now freely preached Anabaptism in England, holding weekly conventicles and rebaptizing hundreds of men and women "in rivulets and some arms of the Thames, and elsewhere, dipping them over head and ears"; and, at a meeting in Southwark, Dr. Featley claimed to have confuted many erroneous and strange opinions, religious, social, and political. A "description of the several sorts of Anabaptists with their manner of rebaptizing" follows. Among them is to be observed in a lively picture the Hemero-baptist, one of a body "who in the summer-time, *quotidie baptizantur* [were christened every day], *senserunt enim aliter non posse hominem vivere, si non singulis diebus in aqua mergeretur, ita ut abluatur et sanctificetur ab omni culpâ.*" These and similar sects, which "have neither root nor order," afforded employment for controversialists, entertainment to the idle, and business for the theological experts of the House of Commons.

Change was everywhere in the air. The churches, the streets, the bookstalls, rang with strange doctrines. Though the Church was practically under suspension, witty and learned writers could still make her claims known by their pens. But the outward aspect everywhere was that of a new world. Amid such changes it might seem that the man whom the Puritan leader regarded as the arch-enemy had been forgotten. Laud had lingered on for three years in prison. In November 1643 the peers had ordered him to send an answer to the articles

against him.   On March 12, 1644 he was at last brought
to the bar.   The doctrine of cumulative treason,
The trial
of Laud. unknown to the law, was brought forward to procure
a conviction.   One of the articles, coming strangely
from the Commons, then in arms against the Crown, charged
him with an attack on the royal prerogative.   The trial was a
wonderful exercise of endurance on the part of the prelate,
who was ready at every point with an answer, with chapter and
verse for all he had done.   But the conclusion was foregone.
When the Lords refused to accept as treason anything not
specified in the Statute of Edward III., the Commons resorted,
as in the case of Strafford, to a bill of attainder.   Never did
Laud stir from his steadfast protestation of loyalty to the
Church of England.   In the last extremity he was firm.   He
thus described his condition.   " My very pockets searched ;
my Diary, my very Prayer-book taken from me, and after used
against me ; and that in some cases not to prove but to make
a charge.   Yet I am thus far glad, even for this sad accident.
For by my Diary your Lordships have seen the passages of
my life ; and by my Prayer-book the greatest secrets between
God and my soul ; so that you may be sure you have me
at the very bottom : yet, blessed be God, no disloyalty is
found in the one, no Popery in the other."

And, so day by day, in answer to each particular charge as
well as to the general, and so strained, indictment, the archbishop spoke in defence of his own religion and honour.   He
repeated his entire obedience to the laws and the religion of
the land.   To the charge of Popery he had a ready answer.
He might have had far more honour and ease abroad than
His defence. ever here in England : " for whatsoever the world
may be pleased to think of me, I have led a very
painful life, and such as I could have been very well content
to change, had I well known how.   And had my conscience
led me that way, I am sure I might have lived at far more
ease ; and either have avoided the barbarous libellings, and
other bitter and grievous stories which I have here endured,
or at the least been out of the hearing.   Nay, my lords, I am
as innocent in this business of religion, as free from all
practice, or so much as thought of practice, for any alteration
to Popery, or any way blemishing the true Protestant religion

established in the Church of England, as I was when my mother first bare me into the world. And let nothing be spoken against me but truth, and I do here challenge whatsoever is between heaven and hell, to say their worst against me in point of my religion; in which, by God's grace, I have ever hated dissimulation; and had I not hated it, perhaps it might have been better with me, for worldly safety, than now it is. But it can no way become a Christian bishop to halt with God."

So again when the House of Commons, casting away all disguise of strict legality, and urged on by the easily manufactured petitions from the City of London, called him to their bar to answer, when the bill of attainder was brought in. "Mr. Speaker," he replied very simply, " I am very aged, considering the turmoils of my life, and I daily find in myself more decays than I make show of; and the period of my life, in the course of nature, cannot be far off. It cannot but be a great grief unto me, to stand at these years thus charged before ye. Yet give me leave to say thus much without offence : whatsoever errors or faults I may have committed by the way, in any my proceedings, through human infirmity—as who is he that hath not offended, and broken some statute-laws too, by ignorance, or misapprehension, or forgetfulness, at some sudden time of action ?—yet if God bless me with so much memory, I will die with these words in my mouth, 'That I never intended, much less endeavoured, the subversion of the laws of the kingdom ; nor the bringing in of popish superstition upon the true Protestant religion established by law in this kingdom.'"

On the 4th January 1645 the Lords passed his attainder : it was the day when they accepted the Directory : "and so the archbishop and the service book died together."   *His attainder.*

It was on Friday the 10th of January that he was brought forth to die. A pamphlet called " A Brief Relation of his Death and Sufferings," printed at Oxford a few days later, expressed the feelings of all those who had come to recognise the steadfastness of his loyalty to the Church when it said : " So well was he studied in the act of dying (especially in the last and strictest   *His execution, Jan. 10, 1645.*

part of his imprisonment) that by continual fastings, watchings, prayer, and such like acts of Christian humiliation, his flesh was rarified into spirit, and the whole man so fitted for eternal glories that he was more than half in heaven before death brought his bloody (but triumphant) chariot to convey him thither. He that had so long been a confessor could not but think it a release of miseries to be made a martyr."

On the scaffold "his great care," says Heylin, "was to clear his majesty and the Church of England from any inclination to Popery." He preached, as it were, a last sermon on the scaffold. "Good people," he began, "this is an uncomfortable time to preach ; yet I shall begin with a text of Scripture, Hebrews xii. 2—Let us run with patience the race that is set before us, looking unto Jesus, the author and finisher of our faith ; who for the joy that was set before him, endured the cross, despising the shame, and is set down at the right hand of the throne of God."

"I have been long in my race," he said, "and how I have looked to Jesus, the Author and Finisher of my faith, He best knows. I am now come to the end of my race, and here I find the Cross—a death of shame." As he spoke of the affliction and its end, he stoutly declared that he would not follow the imaginations that the people were setting up, as the three children would not worship the king's image. "Nor will I forsake the temple and the truth of God to follow the bleating of Jeroboam's calves in Dan and Bethel." The people were "miserably misled" ; the king was "as sound a Protestant (according to the religion by law established) as any man in this kingdom" ; the Londoners had cried round the Parliament house for blood ; his predecessors had suffered before him, St. Alphege and Simon Sudbury—"though I am not only the first Archbishop, but the first man, that hath ever died by an ordinance in Parliament." And then he spoke of his religion and faithfulness to the laws. "What clamours and slanders I have endured for labouring to keep a uniformity in the external service of God, according to the doctrine and discipline of this Church, all men know and I have abundantly felt."

Thus he ended, "I have done. I forgive all the world, all and every of those bitter enemies which have persecuted me ; and humbly desire to be forgiven of God first, and then of every man, whether I have offended him or not, if he do but conceive that I have. Lord, do thou forgive me, and I beg forgiveness of him. And so I heartily desire you to join with me."

Till the very last moment he was pressed by bitter enemies : to them he said that the best saying for a dying man was " Cupio dissolvi et esse cum Christo," and that his full assurance of faith lay in " the Word of God concerning Christ and His dying for us." This was his last prayer : " Lord, I am coming as fast as I can : I know I must pass through the shadow of death before I can come to Thee ; but it is but *umbra mortis*, a mere shadow of death, a little darkness upon nature : but Thou, by Thy merits and passion, hath broken through the jaws of death. The Lord receive my soul, and have mercy upon me, and bless this kingdom with peace and plenty, and with brotherly love and charity, that there may not be this effusion of Christian blood amongst them, for Jesus Christ His sake, if it be Thy will." A moment in silence, and then he said, " Lord, receive my soul," and all was over.

He was buried, with the Church service, in the church of All Hallows Barking, on Tower Hill, where, before the century was over, the graves of many holy men clustered round.

The death of Laud synchronised with an attempt at an arrangement for peace. Commissioners from both sides met at Uxbridge on January 29, 1645; but from the first the religious difficulty was seen to be at the root of the division. Charles was determined to uphold Episcopacy. The Scots were equally determined to overthrow it; and they had the Parliament at their mercy. In vain the clergy at Oxford, the best representatives of the king's side in ecclesiastical matters, drew up a scheme of toleration, by which bishops were to exercise their jurisdiction only by the consent of a council of presbytery. Freedom in ceremony was to be allowed ; and the clergy declared a genuine toleration. "We think it lawful that a toleration be given—by suspending the penalties of all laws—both to the Presbyterians and Independents." That this would have been accepted by the king is practically certain ; but it was not accepted by his opponents. When

The Uxbridge Conference, Jan. 29, 1645.

they came into power it would be seen that there was no toleration for those who did not agree with them. If the king would have yielded further, peace might perhaps have been made; but he stood almost alone in the determination with which he wrote in the summer of 1645. "Let my condition be never so low, I resolve by the grace of God never to yield up this Church to the government of Papists, Presbyterians, or Independents." Already his cause had become hopeless. On June 14 was the crushing defeat of Naseby; on September 13 all chance of help from Scotland was destroyed by the battle of Philiphaugh.

Naseby was a victory for the Independents. Already in the Westminster Assembly they had shown their power. Based

Naseby and the Independents. on the strong individualism of men who had formed their religious convictions anew from the beginning by intent study of the English Bible, and more particularly the Old Testament, wide enough to include men of learning like Milton, whose *Areopagitica*, a plea for the liberty of unlicensed printing (1644), was a protest against the despotism of Presbyterian censorship, and rough country folk whose religious enthusiasm led them into the wildest eccentricities, the Independent party found its great leader in Oliver Cromwell, and its strength in the New Model Army which he organised. It was with this party that Charles now found himself face to face. On May 5, 1646, he entrusted himself to the Scots. Then came months of difficult negotiation. The king

Charles at Newcastle. was willing to allow the establishment of Presbyterianism, for a time, and the suppression of the Independents, in whom men like Baxter as well as the Scots already saw their most dangerous foes; but he insisted on the maintenance of some at least of the sees, as a security for freedom of Church worship and for the continuance of apostolic succession. The matter is worth detailed examination.

At the time of Charles's interviews at Newcastle with the Presbyterian, Alexander Henderson, who tried to persuade him to consent to the extirpation of Episcopacy, it might seem as if the king hesitated for a moment. The following letter to Juxon explains his position; his curious conscience, strained, yet loyal to a fundamental principle, speaks in it characteristically :

"NEWCASTLE, 30*th Semptember* 1646.

"My Lord—My knowledge of your worth and learning, and particularly in resolving cases of conscience, makes me at this time (I confess) put to you a hard and bold task, nor would I do it but that I am confident you Asks advice of Juxon know not what fear is in a good cause.   Yet I hope as to how far he may yield. you believe that I shall be loath to expose you to a needless danger, assuring you that I will yield to none of your friends in my care of your preservation.   I need not tell you the many persuasions and threatenings that hath been used to me for making me change Episcopal into Presbyterial government, which absolutely to do is so directly against my conscience that by the grace of God no misery shall ever make me ; but I hold myself obliged by all honest means to eschew the mischief of this too visible storm, and I think some kind of compliance with the iniquity of the times may be fit, as my case is, which at another time were unlawful. These are the grounds which have made me think of this enclosed proposition, the which as one way it looks handsome to us, so in another I am fearful lest I cannot make it with a safe conscience ; of which I command you to give me your opinion on your allegiance.   Conjuring you that you will deal plainly and freely with me, as you will answer it at the dreadful day of judgment.   I conceive the question to be whether I may with a safe conscience give way to this proposed temporary compliance, with a resolution to recover and maintain that doctrine and discipline wherein I have been bred.   The duty of my oath is herein chiefly to be considered, I flattering myself that this way I better comply with it than being constant in a flat denial, considering how unable I am by force to obtain that which this way there wants not probability to recover, if accepted (otherwise there is no harm done) for my regal authority once settled, I make no question of recovering Episcopal government, and God is my witness my chiefest end in regaining my power is to do the Church service.   So, expecting your reasons to strengthen your opinion whatsoever it be, I rest,

"Your most assured, reall, faithfull, constant friend,

"CHARLES R.

"I desire your opinion in the particulars, as well as in the

general scope of it, and yet mend much in the penning of it.
I give you leave to take the assistance of the Bishop of
Salisbury and Dr. Sheldon, or either of them.   But let me
have your answer with all convenient speed.   None knows
of this but Will Murray, who promises exact secrecy.   If
your opinion and reason shall confirm me in making of
this proposition then you may some way be seen in it, otherwise I promise you that your opinion shall be concealed."

The reply of Juxon and Brian Duppa was a carefully considered document, which expresses very clearly the position of
those who had been long confronted with the Presbyterian arguments and were fitly representative of
the reasoned decision of the theologians of the
English Church.   It characteristically defines the line which
separated the Church from the sects : and it illustrates the
position assumed by the bishops of the restoration.   After
declaring that they spoke "plainly and freely," the bishops
continued :

"The doubt is tending the lawfulness of a temporary compliance in matters of religion, in the state where they now
stand ; that is, as we apprehend it, whether your majesty may
without breach of your oath and with a safe conscience, permit
for some time the exercise of the directory for worship and
practice of discipline as they are now used and stand enjoined
by ordinance.   For resolution, whereof we shall take the
boldness to make use of those grounds which we find laid to
our hand in your Majesty's directions.   For your Majesty's
constancy and fixedness of resolution not to recede from what
you have by oath undertaken in that matter, as it gives us a
great latitude to walk with safety of conscience, in your
endeavours to that end (the rectitude of intention abating
much of the obliquity in all actions), to the full expression you
have been now pleased to make of it, and that what your
purpose is at present in order thereunto, both much facilitate
the work and fit us for a resolution.   Taking therefore your
Majesty's settled determination, touching the Church for a
foundation immovable, and this proposition (in your Majesty's
design), as a means subservient thereunto ; considering also
the condition your Majesty's affairs now stand in, being

destitute of all means compulsory, or of regaining what is lost by force; we cannot conceive in this, your Majesty's condescension, any violation of that oath whereof your Majesty is so justly tender, and that your Majesty doth thereby still continue to preserve and protect the Church by the best ways and means you have left you (which is all the oath can be supposed to require); and that the permission intended (whereby in some men's apprehension your Majesty may seem to throw down what you desire to build up) is not only by your Majesty allowed to that end, but, as your Majesty stands persuaded, probably fitted for the effecting it in some measure.

"And, as your Majesty will stand clear (in our judgment at least) in respect of your oath, which is principally to be regarded, so neither do we think your Majesty will herein trespass in point of conscience; because your Majesty, finding them already settled, and (as it were) in possession, do only (what in other cases is usual) not disturb that possession while the differences are in bearing; or (which is more justifiable) permit that what you cannot hinder if you could; not commanding it (for that may vary the case), but which possibly may be better liked, leaving it upon that footing it now stands, enjoined by authority of both the houses, which is found strong enough to enforce obedience; which intentment of your Majesty would stand more clear, if this point of a temporary toleration were not laid as the principal of the proposition (as it may now seem to be standing in the front), but as an accessory and necessary concession for the more peaceable proceeding in the business.

"The first part, therefore, in the proposition might be for the accommodation of differences by a debate between parties (as it lies in the proposition); and then, that during the debate all things remain *statu quo nunc*, without any interruption or disturbance from your Majesty, provided that the debate determine and a settlement be made within such a time, etc.; and that your Majesty and your household in the interim be not hindered, etc., which, notwithstanding, we humbly submit to your Majesty's better judgment to alter or not.

"We cannot but have a lively sense of the great trouble your Majesty undergoes; and doubt not, but that God, who hath hitherto given you patience in them, will bless you with a deliverance out of them in due time, and make the event of your constant endeavours answerable to the integrity of your Majesty's heart, which is the prayer of

> "Your Majesty's most obedient humble servant,
> "GUIL. LONDON,
> "BR. SARUM.

"FULHAM, *October* 4, 1646."

To this advice Charles was willing to agree. On October 15, he offered to accept the establishment of Presbyterianism for five years, on an engagement that after that "a regulated Episcopacy" should return. This would have preserved the essentials of the Church ; and the reaction, in five years, might well have found expression. Beyond this, in any case, Charles would not go. "How can we expect God's blessing," he said, "if we relinquish His Church?" When his wife urged him to yield he replied in language which she and her advisers could little relish. "I assure you that the change would be no less and worse than if Popery were brought in, for we should have neither lawful priests, nor sacraments duly administered, nor God publicly served, but according to the foolish fancy of every idle person ; but we should have the doctrine against kings fiercelier set up than amongst the Jesuits."

Charles's determination to retain the essentials of the Church.

Stalwart on this point, Charles was on others eager to find a way of escape. He would play Parliament against Army, Army against Parliament. But with neither had he really any common basis of agreement. When he was in the power of the Parliament at Holmby, or in the power of the Army at Carisbrooke, the negotiations always broke down at this point. And this Cromwell saw, and thus he decided—Charles, he said, had hardened his heart : and so he must die.

When the Second Civil War broke out, and an effort was made to rescue the king, the Army had begun to control Parliament. "The soldiers," says Von Ranke, "exercised a sort of police authority, and persecuted malignants and papists ; but what might not be included under these names? The prisons were filled with Royalists, alike Catholic and Protestant ; others were banished and took to flight. Thus, those who desired to introduce universal liberty appeared as the wielders of an absolute, selfish, and oppressive power. Ideas in their nature mutually exclusive were brought, through love of faction and power, to walk hand in hand." Letters of the time amply confirm this description of the judicial historian.

The result of the "Second Civil War" was to prevent all real hope of an accommodation between king and parliament. In the negotiations at Newport, September 1648. Charles was willing to agree to the establishment of Presbyterianism for three years. Beyond that he would not go. He was determined in "the adhering to the Church—from which I cannot depart, no, not in show." He yielded, says our greatest authority, "all that he could reasonably be expected to yield"; and when he was asked to give up his friends to death as well as to permanently disestablish the Church, he had a double reason for firmness. At this point the army intervened. On November 20, they presented a Remonstrance. This declared that the king was but the chief functionary of the State and that if he deliberately abused his trust he must be brought to account, and that it was evident that nothing would bind Charles; and they insisted that he should be brought to trial. From this moment the end was inevitable. Cromwell soon came to see that, to clear the political arena, Charles must go to the block. He appealed to Providence; an infallible indication, says his great apologist, of a change of front. And Cromwell was the one strong man among soldiers and statesmen who saw difficulties but not the way out of them. Even then

Results of the Second Civil War.

Prides Purge.

it needed force to purge the Parliament. On December 6, Colonel Pride expelled all members who could not be trusted to act as the army willed. The house became the mere instrument of the military power. As such, it erected the High Court of Justice, which condemned the king to death as a tyrant, traitor, and murderer, and a public enemy to the Commonwealth of England. At the last religion did not enter into the words of condemnation; but Charles and the people of England knew that it was because he would not surrender the Church that he came to die.

Trial and condemnation of the king.

His last thoughts were given to the one fixed loyalty of his life. He told his little daughter Elizabeth that he was to suffer for the laws and liberties of his country and for main-

taining the true Protestant religion. He bade her read the
sermons of Bishop Andrewes, Hooker's Ecclesiastical Polity,
and Laud's controversy with Fisher. They were indeed the
bases of his own Anglican faith—Andrewes taught the Catholic
verities, Hooker and Laud gave the rational foundation of the
English Reformation as against Geneva and Rome. Then,
says his faithful servant Herbert—

"The king now bidding farewell to the world . . . he laid
aside all other thoughts and spent the remainder of his time
in prayer and other pious exercises of devotion in conference
with that meek and learned Bishop Dr. Juxon who, under
God, was a great support to him in that his afflicted
condition." He was not suffered to rest undisturbed ; but
"when several London ministers wanted to pray with him, in
regard he had made choice of Dr. Juxon (whom for many
years he has known to be a pious and learned divine, and able
to administer ghostly comfort to his soul suitable to his present
condition), he would have none other." It was to
Juxon that he made his last confession, and from
him he received his last communion. In the last
hours of his life, with that steady regularity of devotion which
was the strength of the Anglicanism of the time, he said the
morning prayer of the day. Nothing was varied ; yet the very
lesson of the day, St. Matthew xxvii., spoke directly to his
heart. "Death is not terrible to me," he said, "I bless my
God I am prepared." At the very last he declared that the
hope of religious peace lay in the calling of a national synod :
and he died, he said, "a Christian according to the profession
of the Church of England." So he

bowed his comely head
Down, as upon a bed.

Lord Herbert thus tells how his body was laid to rest. "At
such a time as the king's body was brought out of St. George's
Hall, the sky was serene and clear, but presently it began to
snow and fell so fast as by that time they came to the west
end of the Royal Chapel the black velvet pall was all white
(the colour of innocence) being thickly covered over with
snow. . . . The king's body being by the bearers set down near
the place of burial, the Bishop of London stood ready with the

Service Book in his hands to have performed his last duty to
the king his master, according to the order or form for the
burial of the dead set forth in the book of Common Prayer,
which the Lords likewise desired but could not be suffered by
Colonel Whitchcote, the Governor, by reason of the Directory,
to which (said he) he and others were to be conformable."
And so in silence the last scene closed ; and another pathetic
memory was added to those which men treasured till the young
king's return.

Charles, with all his failings, died for the Church.   Nothing
was more significant of the popular feeling that this was true
than the enormous success of the *Eikon Basilike*,
published February 1649, of which no less than forty-   The *Eikon Basilike*.
seven editions were issued.   It was, almost certainly,
the work of Dr. John Gauden, one of Charles's chaplains.   It
contained some of the king's prayers which had been in the
hands of Juxon ; and with a remarkable skill the writer managed
throughout, in a pathetic fidelity, to convey Charles's true feelings
when he knelt in penitence before God.   If the book contained arguments for kingship it contained ten times as many
for Anglicanism and the system of Laud.   If it showed Charles
at his best, it showed the Church as Laud longed for it to be.

Another apology for the monarchy was put out by the
Royalists at Amsterdam in 1649, entitled *Tragicum theatrum
actorum et casuum tragicorum Londini publice celebratorum*, in
which the great heroes of the Cavaliers were commemorated,
—Strafford, Laud, and the king himself,—and the young king
and his followers were eulogised.   It tried to tell Europe what
the *Eikon* had told England.

Milton's answer, *Eikonoklastes*, October 1649, was little
more than a mere piece of vulgar railing, and proved utterly
ineffectual to stay the horror and pity which the *Eikon* had
evolved.   The *Eikon Basilike* was read everywhere, by every
one : Puritans felt the genuineness of its piety, as churchmen
felt the sincerity of the attachment to the Church which inspired
it.   "There are ways enough to repair the breaches of the
state without the ruins of the Church" wrote the author ; and
when the ruin had come the people of England felt with him.
"Peace itself is not desirable, till repentance have prepared us
for it ;" and to repentance the sufferings which the war entailed

and the repression which followed its conclusion made men most seriously inclined. The execution of Charles made certain the restoration of Church and King.

AUTHORITIES.—Clarendon, *Cromwell's Letters and Speeches ;* Hacket, *Scrinia Reserata ;* the works of the chief divines, notably Laud, Hall ; Warwick, Memoirs ; Herbert, *Memorials ;* Prynne's voluminous pamphlets, especially *Canterburie's Doom ;* Heylin, *Cyprianus Anglicus.* The pamphlet literature of the time must be constantly consulted. Among modern authorities, Gardiner, *History of England* and *History of the Great Civil War* are the guides at every step ; see also Lives of Laud, Juxon, Prynne, Stephen Marshall, Milton, in *Dictionary of National Biography ;* Masson, *Life of Milton ;* Todd, "Letter to the Archbishop of Canterbury on the authorship of *Eikon Basilike."* For religion in the armies, see Firth, *Cromwell's Army.*

CHAPTER IX

THE COMMONWEALTH AND THE PROTECTORATE

1649–1660

THE years that followed the death of Charles I. may here be briefly sketched. The Church of England, the body established from old time under the sanction of the State, on its acceptance of the Catholic creeds and the Apostolic ministry, was no longer recognised by the State. Its worship was illegal, its ministry was *The disestablishment of the Church.* deposed, and it was replaced by a fully established Presbyterian Church. The Universities, the strongholds of the National Church, were purged of all those who would not take the Covenant and accept the new religious order. And throughout England the process was carried out with increasing rigour. The Engagement, offered in 1649, by which a promise was given to be faithful to the Commonwealth as established, without a king and House of Lords, was not much more satisfactory to many of the clergy than was the Covenant. Several changes occurred at Oxford from refusal to take the Engagement, for, writes Calamy the biographer of Baxter, "the moderate Church party and the Presbyterians" rejected it.

After a sketch of the general action of Parliament towards the Church, and of its consequences, the history of the Church from 1649 to 1660 can best be followed by an examination of the religious position of Cromwell, of the ecclesiastical settlement under the Presbyterian system, the treatment of the dispossessed clergy, the nature of the toleration that was allowed by the Government to Christian and non-Christian bodies, and the causes which led to the reaction which restored the Church with the king. At this point it may be well to contrast the systems of Presbytery and Independency.

The former was originally of French origin. The scheme, the heirarchy of elders, the elaborate system of assembly and classes, the strict discipline enforced, were all The Presby- derived from the institution of John Calvin. terians.
Adopted in Scotland through the genius of John Knox, advocated in England by able and influential writers such as Thomas Cartwright, the system was adopted as the ideal of those Puritans of Elizabeth's and James I.'s days, who regarded the Episcopal government of the Church of England as contrary to the word of God. This has been dealt with in the previous volume of this *History of the English Church.* In the reign of Charles I. and up to the triumph of the Parliamentary party through the aid of the Scots, the Presbyterians of England seem to have learnt nothing and to have forgotten nothing. They still desired to establish the system of jurisdiction which was the keystone of the Presbyterian system. It was this which they succeeded in formally setting up by law on June 1646. But it was soon found to be in every sense a foreign system in England.

Objections to it were advanced on two sides. First there were the Erastians, who desired to subject the Church entirely Unpopu- to the State, and were therefore utterly hostile to larity of their the encroaching supervision of the hierarchical system. system of Presbytery. When the system was established by law, ineffectually though it worked, it was found by men of different views from Milton, as well as by the poet himself, that "new presbyter is but old priest writ large." There was a strong feeling against the tyranny of the spiritual courts and the enforcement of civil penalties for spiritual offences. It was a foreign system out of harmony with the instincts of the English people.

Secondly, there was Independency, which divided with the Church the enthusiasm of the really pious English The Inde- folk. It secured the allegiance of Cromwell, Milton, pendents. Vane, the three great names of the later years of Revolution. They would—in theory at least—free the

Church from State control, and yet place religion under the guardianship of the State. Yet their system (which looked back also to Elizabeth's days and the teaching of Robert Brown, the Separatist) was the antithesis of the Presbyterian. Each congregation claimed the right to order all its own business, religious and secular, and to choose its own ministers. All spiritual offences were punished by spiritual penalties alone. It was the logical outcome of individual ideas. Politically it avoided, in theory at least, the danger of a Church-governed State, and it was, as the great German historian Von Ranke observed, essentially republican. It held out hopes of a wider toleration than seemed consistent with the views of other parties. It attracted to itself nearly all those who were not strongly attached to the English Church or the Presbyterian system.

The attitude of these two parties towards the Church was different. The Presbyterians claimed to reform it by substituting a system more purely spiritual but not less ecclesiastical,—one which would enter still more deeply into every aspect of the individual and national life. *Attitude of each towards the Church.* This they claimed to do as in obedience to the direct instruction of Holy Writ, outside the words of which any Church government was unlawful. The Independents, on the other hand, desired to reform the Church in the direction of individual liberty, to loosen the bonds between Church and State, to establish a number of small self-governing societies hardly related to each other by more than brotherly love.

It was natural that the Presbyterian party should come to the front during the earlier stages of the constitutional struggle and of the war. It alone was an organised party, with fixed principles, and a history behind it, and with examples of successful establishment among neighbouring nations. The characteristic expression of their views is to be found in the propositions made at Uxbridge in 1645, in which it was demanded that Charles should take the Covenant, assent to the abolition of the Prayer-book and of Episcopacy, and to the establishment of the Directory of Public Worship and the Presbyterian Church systems. It was a demand based on the conscientious belief that one form of government, with its concomitant expression in worship, had been established by the Long Parliament, a form from which it would be impossible to vary without incurring the Divine wrath.

It is characteristic also that this demand was met by the project of toleration suggested on behalf of the Church, by which the bishops were to continue, but to exercise their power only by the advice of the presbyters, and the Prayerbook was to be revised. Toleration was at the same time offered. " We think it lawful," said the Oxford clergy representing the Church view, " that a toleration be given by suspending the penalties of all laws, both to the Presbyterians and Independents."

It was on the rejection of these terms, or the failure to obtain an agreement or compromise between them, that the Independent party became prominent. It was strong in the army, and every day the failure of the Presbyterian system to root itself in the affections of the country made it stronger ; and it had the supreme advantage of being guided by the greatest man in England, in force and will, Oliver Cromwell, the Lord General who had led the armies of the Parliament to victory, and whose firm insistence had brought the king to the block. When the king suffered, the final position of these two parties was not certain ; but during the next few months, step by step, the Independents, through the army, which since the New Model was strongly of their party, came into power. The history of the events which brought this about belongs to politics, not to religion. It is our part here rather to sketch the general attitude of Parliament towards the Church.

Three clergy lists have recently been printed. They contain the names of those clergy dealt with by Parliament as " superstitious, innovating, scandalous, or malignant." The first on the list, it may be noted, is Dr. Layfield, of All Hallows Barking, the Church in which Archbishop Laud was buried. To this is appended a list of Puritan lecturers nominated or sanctioned by the Long Parliament up to the outbreak of the Civil War, and after that there is a list of the Parliamentary sequestrations of Royalist clergy from the beginning of the war, with the names of those who were appointed in their places, in each case the action being that of Parliament. How minute and inquisitorial the action of the House was is

General action of the House of Commons with regard to the Church.

shown by these lists. It assumed the patronage of the Crown, of all the ecclesiastical corporations, both sole and aggregate, and of Royalist private patrons whenever it could with any appearance of justification. Complete chaos seems in some counties to have been introduced into the ecclesiastical arrangements by these means. The Church had been entirely disestablished and disendowed; and, though in August 1645, and March 1646, Presbyterianism was definitely established by law in its place, it was found impossible to carry the system into operation in many parts of England—by no means only those which during the war were favourable to the king. The Calvinistic system was felt by the people to be both foreign and inquisitorial. Theoretically it had the adhesion of the Universities, when they had been "purged" by Parliamentary Commissions with armed men at their backs; and in London and Essex it was practically founded; but in the north it hardly existed, even in name.

Beside these detailed lists has been placed a very interesting and significant collection of financial *data*, showing what became of the Church lands. After the money used by the Parliament for military purposes, and after the extremely large deductions for salaries and expenses, and the small sums paid to the dispossessed clergy, very little, in proportion, went to the support of a "God-fearing clergy." It seems clear that if the revolution had been completely carried out, it would have resulted, as it had done in Scotland a century before, in the utter impoverishment of the religious establishment.

There was great difficulty in procuring a proper sustenance for the Ministry. The Parliament, by ordinance of April 1, 1643, confiscated all the real and personal property of all persons, ecclesiastical and civil, who had taken up arms against the Parliament or voluntarily contributed towards the king's army, and with it two-thirds of all the property of Roman Catholics. The sums thus secured, and the property, were placed in the hands of committees and sequestrators, named for all the English shires, who were to remit the money for the use of the Parliament. None of this money seems to have been directly employed in the maintenance of the ministers now placed in

(1) The payment of ministers.

the parishes; and at the same time some allowance was occasionally made, as will be mentioned later on, for the dispossessed clergy and their families.

At the same time there were many expressions of an aversion to the tithe system. The controversy of the early years of the century had now sunk down from Tithes. learned men to the people. The Independents were inclined to regard it as carnal, contrary to the spiritual life in its freedom. In May 1646, a body of about two thousand persons from Buckinghamshire and Hertfordshire petitioned the House for the abolition of tithes; they were sternly rebuked by the Speaker, who told them that they knew not the laws of God or the realm, and must go home and obey both.

On August 6, 1649, a proposal to declare the payment of tithes compulsory was rejected by the House of Commons. During the Commonwealth considerable interest was shown in the question. Some desired to get rid of such payments as unspiritual, some because they did not wish to pay. A proposal for their abolition was made in Parliament, July 15, 1653, but it was rejected. A voluntary system, however, continued to be strongly advocated, and a committee considered the subject. In November 1653 the question was further complicated by a proposal to abolish private patronage, as leading to simony and to scandalous appointments. When the Instrument of Government ordered the maintenance of an Established Church it seemed to propose at least the commutation of tithes. But as to their abolition Cromwell stated that "he was but one, and his Council allege it not fit to take them away." So the matter rested.

The second subject on which it is well to observe the general attitude of Parliament, before dealing in detail with special aspects of it, is that of toleration. The (2) practical results of the financial question affect this Toleration. very closely. It has been shown by minute investigation that there is no justification for the view that real toleration was granted. Schoolmasters who were not certified to belong to the dominant religious order were dismissed, under command from Parliament. Up to 1653 or 1657, there was no legislative grant of toleration, and Presbyterianism remained the legally established form of religion.   Practical toleration came to be enjoyed by the Independents when Cromwell was in power, but legally and practically they stood in much the same position with regard to the established State Presbyterian system as their successors stand to-day in regard to the Church of England.

The history of toleration during these years is an interesting one.   The facts do not seem to justify the attacks made on Charles I., whose views of toleration, inadequate though they were, were sincere, and were formally sanctioned by the religious advisers to whom he referred the matter at the crisis of his fate.   A very one-sided view of the subject also is given when the literary advocates of toleration are ignored.   Among them were not only prominent Independents, but Churchmen, as sound and as prominent as Hammond, whose sermons would be a revelation to some of those who throw stones at the Caroline divines. It should not be forgotten that pamphlets and sermons, as well as Parliamentary speeches, had a real influence on the acquisition of such toleration as was secured.   The chief force which worked for toleration was perhaps, in the long run, not the interaction of Presbyterian and Independent thinkers, nor the views of Churchmen, such as were shown in the Oxford opinions presented at the time of the treaty of Uxbridge, nor the supremacy of Cromwell, but the determined Erastianism of the Long Parliament.   In other words, the claim made by Parliament to decide every religious matter for every class and every individual, to upset churches and replace them, to turn out ministers, to say what men should teach and what they should be paid for teaching, worked in the long run for toleration.   This is the view of important historical writers. Perhaps it did, but, if so, it was very largely by the reaction that it caused.

Influence of theories of toleration.

Three strong influences, however, were at work.   Besides the deep-seated Erastianism of the age, conspicuous in the Long Parliament, and the rooted affection of the majority of Englishmen to the Church with her settled liturgy, was the indomitable individualism of Oliver Cromwell.

So far we have been dealing with general characteristics. We must now turn to consider the period in more detail.

Some judgment of the character of the great Protector is necessary before we begin to consider his ecclesiastical policy.

Oliver
Cromwell. The mists of partisanship have now lifted, and we need not take sides violently like our fathers. Dr. Gardiner, with his impartial record, has enabled us at least to dethrone the demigod of Carlyle's fervid imagination. On the other hand, we are not able to accept the diatribe of Clarendon :

" Cromwell, though the greatest dissembler living, always made his hypocrisy of singular use and benefit to him ; and never did anything, how ungracious or imprudent soever it seemed to be, but what was necessary to the design," wrote the immortal historian of the Great Rebellion. We cannot accept such a judgment ; but the facts that are now before us enable us to understand more clearly than was possible fifty years ago, how it was easy for a contemporary critic honestly to form such an opinion, or that in which the same great writer expresses his final judgment. " He had some virtues which have caused the memory of some men in all ages to be celebrated, and he will be looked upon by posterity as a brave bad man."

The first point which confronts us when we begin to examine Cromwell's religious position is his attitude towards toleration.

His attitude
towards
toleration. And here it is difficult to avoid the dilemma of either convicting him of gross inconsistency or regarding him as a pure opportunist. Passage after passage from his letters and his speeches may be quoted to show his assertion of the right to complete freedom in belief. " Sir, the State in choosing men to serve it, takes no note of their opinions," he wrote to Major-General Crawford in 1643, when there was some question of the employment of an Anabaptist. In the same spirit he concluded his famous letter to Speaker Lenthall on the capture of Bristol. " And for brethren, in things of the mind we look for no compulsion, but that of light and reason." What did the Parliament men fight for, he said in dissolving the first protectorate Parliament (January 22, 1655), but " for a just liberty, that men should not be trampled upon for their consciences ? Had not they laboured but lately under the weight of persecutions, and was it fit for them to sit heavy upon others ? Is it ingenuous to ask liberty and not to give it? What greater hypocrisy than for those who were oppressed by the bishops, to become the greatest oppressors themselves so soon as their yoke was removed? I could wish that they who call for liberty now also, had not too much of that spirit, if the power were in their hands." With this may be compared many passages in the extremely lengthy oration with which he opened the second Parliament of the Protectorate on September 17, 1656.

"That which hath been our practice since the last Parliament hath been to let all this nation see that whatever pretensions be to religion, if quiet, peaceable, [they may enjoy] conscience and liberty to themselves, [so long as they do] not make religion a pretence for arms and blood. Truly we have suffered them, and that cheerfully, so to enjoy their own liberties." On these words there follow, it is true, some involved sentences from which it might not be difficult to produce the meaning of a very restricted toleration, but on the whole the speech may be, as it was doubtless intended to be, interpreted in favour of liberty.

But, on the other side, there are words as strong and acts much stronger. In his speech which he addressed to the two Houses on January 20, 1658, he still harped upon the winning and maintaining of "our spiritual liberties as Christians," and claimed that the Petition and Advice had given "liberty for all those that are of the Protestant profession among us; who enjoy a freedom to worship God according to their consciences"; but five days later, in the banqueting house at Whitehall, in that sad speech in which he seemed half ready to confess that all his work had been in vain, he alluded with unconcealed severity to the "malignant Episcopal party." It was this party, in other words the party of those who adhered steadfastly to the Church of England, which he was at all times determined to shut out from toleration. "That the Royalists had religious ideals of their own was a provocation," it has been said by an impartial authority of Cromwell's later attitude as Protector, "which made it easy to deny them the toleration which they had hitherto virtually enjoyed." What that toleration was we shall afterwards inquire : here we only quote the statement as a true expression of the real divergence between Cromwell and Churchmen.

Its limitations.

The possession of religious ideals different from his own was an intolerable crime in his eyes. He could never really allow freedom of belief to Irish Romanists, or Scottish Presbyterians, or English Churchmen.

Of his attitude towards those with whom he disagreed, conspicuous examples are, of course, the cases of the Roman Catholics and the Quakers. "I meddle not with any man's conscience. But if by liberty of conscience you mean a liberty to exercise the mass, I judge it best to use plain dealing and to let you know, where the Parliament of England have power, *that* will not be allowed of." So after Drogheda he cynically wrote, "I believe all their friars were knocked on the head promiscuously, save two"—and they were killed later in cold blood. "Your clergymen," he wrote to the Governor of Kilkenny, "if they fall into my hands know what to expect"—that is, if a surrender was not agreed upon. At Carrick "we took a Popish Priest, who was caused to be hanged." It was a consistent action based on a consistent belief. The last time a Romanist was executed in England for the offence of being a priest, it was by Cromwell's orders. The exception to this rigid attitude is to be found in the sale of the Scottish Presbyterian prisoners to the Roman Catholic Republic of Venice. With regard to the Quakers there is much that is interesting to be said. The sum of it is that though Cromwell did not desire to persecute them, and indeed sympathised with the true religious feeling which he saw in George Fox, he did not stop their persecution, though it was often illegal. The Puritan position, as he himself saw it, was the only real Christianity for him.

That Cromwell ever realised the possibility of a toleration of any but Puritans it is difficult to believe. And there was every excuse for his blindness. Few, save the Anglican theologian Dr. Hammond, and the Puritans Milton and Vane, at all grasped the idea which we all now hold. The liberty of conscience, which Cromwell considered a "fundamental," was a liberty at the discretion of the "person" whom he regarded as, with Parliament, an essential feature of the constitution. It was a great thing to desire so much, when Presbyterians wrote that "to let men serve God according to

His practice.

their own consciences was to cast out one devil that seven worse might enter." Toleration, wrote another, was "the devil's masterpiece," and he said that, "if the devil had his choice whether the hierarchy, ceremonies, and liturgy should be established in the kingdom, or a toleration granted, he would choose a toleration." Bad as the order of the Church of England was, toleration, thought many of the Puritans, was infinitely worse. And Cromwell was unable to overcome this feeling among his supporters.

He could never rise to the sublime conception of toleration which was preached by Hammond, the great theologian of the persecuted Church. What he would give, as, in plain words enough, he told the first Parliament elected under the provisions of the Instrument of Government, was liberty of conscience, under the control of the Lord Protector. And the terms of the Instrument of Government were these : "That the Christian religion contained in the Scriptures be held forth and recommended as the public profession of these nations ; and that as soon as may be a provision less subject to scruple and contention, and more certain than the present, be made for the encouragment and maintenance of able and painful teachers for instructing the people, and for discovery and confutation of error, hereby, and whatever is contrary to sound doctrine ; and that until such provision is made the present maintenance shall not be taken away or impeached.

Under the Instrument of Government, Dec. 16, 1653.

"That to the public profession held forth none shall be compelled by penalties or otherwise, but that endeavours be used to win them by sound doctrine and the example of a good conversation.

"That such as profess faith in God by Jesus Christ (though differing in judgment from the doctrine, worship, or discipline publicly held forth) shall not be restrained from, but shall be protected in, the profession of the faith and the exercise of their religion, so that they abuse not this liberty to the civil injury of others and the actual disturbance of the public peace on their parts : provided that this liberty be not extended to Popery or Prelacy, nor to such as under the profession of Christ hold forth and practice licentiousness."

What then was the form in which Cromwell thought that

liberty of conscience could be realised? He looked for the formation of a federated religious body, which should be Puritan in its essential principles, excluding English Churchmen and Romanists, and which should labour under State control to advance the righteousness of the people. Uniformity he did not expect : agreement even, in more than general principles, he perhaps hardly desired. "All that believe," he said, "have the real unity, which is more glorious because inward and spiritual." Practically this State control held the seeds of future disaster. It was this control of the religion of the country by the State which made Cromwell's policy so offensive to the Scots. It was the severity of that control which gradually inspired all England with longing for a Restoration of Church and King.

His ultimate opinions.

A striking proof of this is to be found in the address drawn up by the Sectaries in 1656, and presented to Charles II. in exile by "an Anabaptist of special trust among them." While they pleaded against the erection of "any such tryannical, popish, and anti-Christian hierarchy (Episcopal, Presbyterian, or by what name soever it be called) as shall assume a power over, or impose a yoke upon, the consciences of others, and for perfect liberty of worship, they were fully prepared for the maintenance of that which is called the national ministry," though they were anxious to avoid any share in the payment of it. But no rule could be so bad, they were agreed to declare, as that under which they were groaning, and to which they had been led by taking up arms "only to restrain the excesses of government."

Results of Cromwell's policy, uniting divergent sects, and ultimately in favour of the Church.

"We must confess," they cried, "that we have been wandering, deviating, and roving up and down, this way and that way, through all the dangerous and untrodden paths of fanatic and enthusiastic notions, till now at last, but too late, we find ourselves intricated and involved in so many windings, labyrinths, and meanders of knavery, that nothing but a divine clue of thread handed to us from heaven, can be sufficient to extricate us, and restore us. We know not, we know not, whether we have juster matter of shame or sorrow administered to us, when we take a reflex view of our past actions, and consider into the commission of what crimes, impieties, wickednesses, and unheard of villainies we have been led, cheated, cozened, and betrayed by that grand impostor, that loathsome hypocrite, that detestable traitor, that prodigy of nature, that sink of sin, and that compendium of baseness, who now calls himself our protector."

Doubtless these good Protestant sectaries did protest too much; but there was truth in their complaint that the oppressive rule of Cromwell gave them no religious liberty. The Parliaments, they say, were broken reeds; the army a rod of iron to bruise. And then: "If we go to him who had treacherously usurped, and does tyrannically exercise an unjust power over us, and say to him, Free us from this yoke, for it oppresseth us, and from these burdens, for they are heavier than either we are, or our fathers ever were, able to bear; behold, in the pride and haughtiness of his spirit, he answers us, You are factious, you are factious; if your burdens are heavy, I will make them yet heavier; if I have hitherto chastised you with whips, I will henceforward chastise you with scorpions. Thus do we fly, like partridges hunted, from hill to hill, and from mountain to mountain, but can find no rest; we look this way, and that way, but there is none to save, none to deliver. . . . When we looked for liberty, behold slavery; when we expected righteousness, behold oppression; when we sought for justice, behold a cry—a great and lamentable cry—throughout the whole nation." So they spoke, and they voiced the opinion of churchmen as well as of those who had long neglected her teaching.

Such being the feelings of the sectaries, who had hoped that the war would give them religious freedom, and who in the event found themselves, as they thought, betrayed, we may naturally inquire, what was the religious system which the Commonwealth and the Protectorate set up, and what religious disabilities existed under it? We may then fitly collect special facts which emphasised public dissatisfaction and prepared the way for the restoration of the Church.

The essential fact underlying the religious changes of this period, which witnessed the triumph of Puritanism, is that English Puritanism was never genuinely Presbyterian. The inquisitorial system associated with Scottish Presbyterianism was odious to the English

The religious system, 1646-60.

people. The Presbyterian party came to the front as a strong, aggressive, imperious body in the Long Parliament, and in the war itself, "but none the less it was an abrupt and startling and illogical expansion from the basis of English Puritanism." No one has more truly expressed this than the saintly Baxter: "Though Presbytery generally took root in Scotland, yet it was but a stranger here, and it found some ministers that lived in conformity to the bishops' liturgies and ceremonies (however they might wish for reformation), and the most that quickly after were ordained were but young students in the universities at the time of the change of Church government, and had never well studied the points on either side; and, though most of the ministers then in England saw nothing in the Presbyterian way of practice which they could not cheerfully concur in, yet it was but few that had resolved on their principles; and when I came to try it, I found that most that ever I could meet with were against the *jus divinum* of lay elders, and for the moderate primitive Episcopacy, and for a narrow congregational or parochial extent of ordinary churches, and for an accommodation of all parties in order to concord."

While this was the general feeling even among Puritan students of divinity, a definite Presbyterian system was established in England by law. After long discussion among the Assembly of Divines at Westminster, which first met on July 1, 1643; and after debates on the same subject, oft renewed, in the House of Commons; on July 7, 1645, the Assembly submitted to Parliament its "Humble Voice concerning Church Government." The House then debated the details of the erection of the Presbyterian system, and passed an order for the election of elders, which was eventually accepted by both Houses on August 19. This was the first step in the establishment of the Presbyterian system. It provided "that all parishes and places whatsoever, except peers' chapels, shall be brought under the government of congregational, classical, provincial, and national assemblies." On September 26, 1645, a list of persons was drawn up who should act as "triers" of these elected elders in the twelve classes of London, and on February 20, 1646, it was resolved that the

[margin note:] Presbyterianism in England.

choice of elders throughout England should be made forthwith. The classes for London were thereupon devised, and county committees were left to do the same work in the shires. But the power of jurisdiction, so essential to the perfected system, was stoutly resisted. The House of Commons hesitated to allow an unlimited jurisdiction to the eldership. Already it seemed that new presbyter would be but old priest writ large. Bayly characteristically wrote on October 14, 1645: "Great wrestling have we for the election of our presbyteries. It must be a Divine thing to which so much resistance is made by men of all sorts, yet by God's help we will very speedilie see it set up in spight of the devill." Finally, on March 14, 1646, an ordinance passed both Houses, of which the following were the most important clauses :

1. Be it ordained that there be forthwith a choice made of elders throughout the kingdom of England and dominion of Wales in their respective parish churches and chapels.

2. Notice of the election to be given by the minister in the public assembly the next Lord's day but one before.

3. Electors to be members of the congregation who have taken the National Covenant, being over age and not servants.

Thus Presbyterianism was legally established. But it was found impossible to carry the system into operation. In the universities, when they had been purged by Parliamentary Commissions, not without the assistance of armed force, something more than a mere theoretical adhesion was given. In London and in Essex the system seems to have come into practical working. But in many parts of England—and those by no means only where the Cavalier interest was strong—it was found impossible to establish it at all. The North of England would have none of it.

The clergy everywhere regarded it with little cordiality. The London clergy said, "We have seriously pondered the present state of things, and find ourselves, whether we act as is required or act not, to be in a very great strait." At best they yielded ungraciously. The example of the parish of St. Botolph without Aldgate is a good illustration of the difficulties introduced into the parochial system by new methods of appointment and of government. Matters were little mended when the Protector and the Council, after dispossessing Anglicans, had to intervene between Presbyterians and Anabaptists. It was but scantily that the classical presbyteries were accepted by the country at large, and with great reluctance. Yet, doubtless, the system would eventually have been enforced but for the triumph of the army. It was Independency which prevented the real establishment of Presbyterianism; and still more it was the Erastianism of the Long Parliament, and the strength of secular feeling as against both Independent and Presbyterian. Still more, we should say, it was the stolid aversion of the English people to a type of Church government so inquisitorial, and the steadfast loyalty that lay behind all to the Church of England.

Presbyterianism, then, was the legal Church government of England from 1646 to 1660, if it may be admitted that a legal establishment can be made apart from the concurrence of the Crown. But at least from 1649 a practical freedom was enjoyed by Independent congregations.

The establishment of Presbyterianism involved the disestablishment of the Church and the deprivation of her loyal ministers. These were dealt with, in the first case, by the Committee for Scandalous Ministers (or for Preaching Ministers), first nominated on December 12, 1640, which was concerned with the dismissal and replacement of any clergy who in any way adhered to the king's party in Church or State—of the "delinquents," in the language of the day. "Delinquency" was an offence vague enough and capable of wide extension. It was, however undefined, a complete cause for the sequestration of a benefice. To this were added charges such as Popery, or scandalous life. These offences, originally dealt with by a short-lived Committee for Scandalous Ministers, were, from the beginning of the war, allotted to the Plundered Ministers' Committee, who, acting under general authority of the House, punished by sequestration.

The committee for scandalous ministers.

Gradually the powers of all the other committees established for dealing with religious matters were accumulated on the Committee for Plundered Ministers. It became a board of ecclesiastical commissioners to provide for an ecclesiastical system which the House of Commons had set up, without any security for the enjoyment of the endowments of the disestablished Church.

This committee having, of course, ceased to exist as a Parliamentary Committee when Cromwell ejected the Rump, was replaced in September 1654 by the Trustees for Maintenance, established by Act of Parliament. This new body acted in entire subordination to Cromwell and his Council. When they proposed any new endowment or augmentation of livings—which came to be their chief duty, for the ecclesiastical revenues were spent very largely on military purposes and on the "office expenses" of the trustees and those whom they employed, leaving a comparatively small sum for meagre pensions to the dispossessed clergy and for salaries for the intruded ministers—they acted always "by way of report to the Protector and Council ; and quite as often they had simply the duty of registering the grants made *mero motu* by Cromwell with the Council, or even by the Council itself."

Little indeed was done by this committee, and, when Cromwell's second Parliament met the new ecclesiastical establishment was still inadequately provided for. That Parliament planned, but did not act. After Cromwell's death—to complete the story—when the Long Parliament met again in May 1659, it re-established the old Committee for Plundered Ministers. This made report to the House, "guided, apparently, by a wish to discredit the whole administration of the Trustees and Cromwell from the time of the Protectorate." Confusion might have been worse confounded if it had not been for the return of the Church with the king.

What, then, was the position of the Church during this period? It was made practically impossible for any Episcopalian clergyman to hold a living. From 1641 it was regarded as "an open violation of their covenant," says Bishop Hall, for a bishop to ordain. In March 1654 a Commission of thirty-five persons was appointed to examine all who wished to be presented to any benefice. The object of this Commission was to prevent any man who had been ordained by a bishop from obtaining a living : and the kind of questions asked of candidates shows that it

Proscription of the Church clergy,

must have been very difficult for any intelligent man to satisfy his examiners. One man was examined for seven weeks, and then dismissed. Another was asked, "What is the breath of the soul? What is the heat of the soul? What is the sense of the soul?" Another was required to say the year, the day, and the *hour* when he was called by the Holy Ghost: and he was rejected because he did not give answer *definite* enough. Such tales were told. No doubt they were exaggerated, but they had a substantial foundation of truth.

And during this period the use of the Book of Common Prayer was illegal. The choir service, "so unedifying and offensive," as Cromwell had called it at Ely, where he had so long collected the tithes for the Dean and Chapter, was silenced. The cathedrals were in many cases utilised as military storehouses, if not for stables. Parliament had melted down the bells for cannon, and sold the organs where a purchaser could be found. By Act of Parliament passed on August 24, 1653, only marriages solemnised before a Justice of the Peace were declared lawful. It was reported by Major-General Worsley on February 9, 1656, that he had "inflicted deserved punishment upon several persons unduly and pretendedly married contrary to the law, and the persons that married them"—a reference doubtless to those who were married by priests of the Church. Our parish registers, in consequence of this Act, show almost a complete blank for seven years in regard to matrimony. None the less, as Clarendon spitefully notes, even the Protector himself yielded to the sentiment in favour of a religious ceremony. The weddings of his two unmarried daughters in 1657, says Clarendon, "were celebrated at Whitehall with all imaginable pomp and lustre; and it was observed that though the marriages were performed in public view according to the rites and ceremonies then in use, they were presently afterwards in private married by ministers ordained by bishops, and according to the form in the Book of Common Prayer; and this with the privity of Cromwell, who pretended to yield to it in compliance with the importunity and folly of his daughters," which did not save Dr. Hewet, who performed the marriage of Lord Fauconberg to Cromwell's daughter Mary, from execution for a plot with which he had very little concern.

and of the Prayer-book.

The observance of Christmas day was discouraged in every possible way, with the result of riots at Canterbury, Ipswich, and elsewhere in 1648. In 1650 the Council of State reported "a wilful and strict observation of the day commonly called Christmas day." On Christmas day, 1656, Evelyn received the Holy Sacrament "at Dr. Wilde's lodgings" in London. On the same day in 1657 a congregation worshipping privately was arrested as they were receiving the Holy Communion, for observing "the superstitious time of the Nativity."

John Evelyn thus describes the scene in his Diary: "December 25. I went to London with my wife, to celebrate Christmas day; Mr. Gunning preaching in Exeter Chapel, on Micah vii. 2. Sermon ended, as he was giving us the Holy Sacrament, the chapel was surrounded with soldiers, and all the communicants and assembly surprised and kept prisoners by them, some in the house, others carried away. It fell to my share to be confined to a room in the house, where yet I was permitted to dine with the master of it, and the Countess of Dorset, Lady Hatton, and some others of quality who invited me. In the afternoon came Colonel Whaly, Goffe, and others, from Whitehall, to examine us one by one; some they committed to the marshal, some to prison. When I came before them they took my name and abode, examined me why, contrary to an ordinance made that none should any longer observe the superstitious time of the Nativity (so esteemed by them), I durst offend; and particularly be at common prayers, which they told me was but the mass in English, and particularly pray for Charles Stuart, for which we had no Scripture. I told them we did not pray for Charles Stuart, but for all Christian kings, princes, and governors. They replied, in so doing we prayed for the King of Spain too, who was their enemy, and a papist; with other frivolous and ensnaring questions, and much threatening; and finding no colour to detain me, they dismissed me with much pity of my ignorance. These were men of high flight, and above ordinances, and spoke spiteful things of our Lord's Nativity. As we went up to receive the Sacrament the miscreants held their muskets against us, as if they would have shot us at the altar, but yet

Of Christmas day.

M

suffered us to finish the office of Communion, as perhaps not
having instruction what to do in case they found us in that
action."

Nothing in all the Puritan *régime* was felt more severely by
the people, we may be sure, than these two acts—the practical
abolition of Christian marriage and the prohibition
of the observance of the feast of our Lord's Nativity.

The marriage law.

With regard to the latter, Whitelocke especially notes
that he strongly advised Cromwell against enforcing the prohibition, pertinently observing that it was "contrary to the liberty
of conscience, so much owned and pleaded for by him and his
friends." But the destruction of any observance of Christmas
was a cardinal point. As early as 1644 a pamphlet defending
the observance (*The Feast of Feasts, or the celebration of Christ's
Nativity founded on the Scriptures*) had been issued, but
without effect on the Puritan conclusion. Calamy, preaching
before the House of Lords in 1647, denounced it as equally
superstitious and profane ; and Cromwell "gave way to it, and
those meetings [for the celebration of Christmas] were suppressed by the soldiers." There was too, it need hardly be
added, a special cruelty in the refusal of Christian marriage
rites to the poor. In England the sanctity of the marriage
service of the Church had always been regarded with a special
reverence. In 1076 the Council of Winchester under Lan-
franc had declared that marriages made without the blessing
of the Church were invalid, and of the nature of the sin of
fornication : and the rule had never been repealed. It was
the marriage tie which dominant Puritanism was determined
to sever from any religious sanction.

Already on Christmas day 1655 Evelyn had recorded
that "the funeral sermon of preaching" was delivered by Dr.
Wilde. From thenceforth, with very few exceptions, "the
Church was reduced to a chamber and a conventicle, so
sharp was the persecution." But the fervour of devotion was
increased rather than diminished : so notes the same pious
observer. Entries in many a private diary of those days show
with what eagerness the services of the Church were sought
when they were proscribed under heavy penalties.

The condition of the deprived clergy during these days
was always precarious, often full of danger. In 1714 the

Rev. John Walker published his notable collection, *An Attempt towards recovering an Account of the Numbers and Sufferings of the Clergy of the Church of England,* Condition of the deprived clergy. *Heads of Colleges, Fellows, Scholars, etc., who were sequestered, harassed, etc., in the late Time of the Grand Rebellion.* It was based on the most careful investigation, and though of course it is not strictly contemporary, there is no reason to accuse its author of more than a few almost inevitable mistakes. From this we obtain our fullest information. Nearly all the bishops underwent imprisonment : almost all the clergy were reduced to extreme poverty. It is true that the committees had power to give one-fifth of the income of the sequestrated benefices to the extruded incumbents ; but the restrictions on this were so severe that, as the accounts show, it was not often awarded. The incumbent was required peaceably to surrender his house and property, without words of dispute or anger even from his wife or children ; he was obliged to remove from the parish, taking an oath, if required, to obey orders of the committee as to his future residence ; and, lastly, it seems to have been required that the claim should be made by a wife in person, which would exclude bachelors and widowers from all pension.

Till 1655 it was possible in some cases for the dispossessed clergy to obtain employment as schoolmasters, tutors, and chaplains. Many went abroad. Some lived in obscurity in England. Some, like the future Arch- Sufferings of the clergy. bishop Tenison, "studied physic for the disturbance of the times." Many suffered very severely. There are pitiful tales in Walker's book of the cruelty of ejection—a cruelty hardly paralleled when under Charles II. the intruded ministers were dispossessed. Examples may be found in the cases of Dr. Piers, Bishop of Bath and Wells, and Dr. Raleigh, his dean. The former, from his opposition to Chief Justice Richardson, was notorious as an enemy to Puritans (see above, p. 108). He was one of the bishops who withdrew under protest from the House of Lords from the debate on the bill for depriving the bishops of their seats ; and in consequence he was impeached and imprisoned. When the bill was passed he was released, and he retired to

Cuddesdon, in Oxfordshire, where he was reduced to such extremity as to be forced to beg for any post as curate to keep his children from starvation, a request which was not complied with. He lived, however, to be restored to his see, and died, still bishop, at the age of ninety-four. His son William, Archdeacon of Taunton, had his living sequestered, and was imprisoned for giving the name of Charles to a boy to whom he stood sponsor. Dr. Walter Raleigh, Dean of Wells, was also sequestered, and imprisoned as a malignant. He had been among the defenders of Bridgwater, and on the capture of that place by the Parliament was sent to his living of Chedzoy "upon a poor contemptible horse, with his legs tied under the belly of it," to be shown as a criminal to his parishioners. Imprisoned at Wells in the deanery, under the charge of a shoemaker, he was murdered by his jailer, who had been threatened with dismissal if he should allow any liberty to his prisoners, and regarded Dr. Raleigh as the cause of the rebuke. The jailor was acquitted, and the clergyman who read the Church service at the dean's funeral was imprisoned for the rest of his life.

Most of the clergy were ejected from their livings. But there were not a few instances of the kindly feeling that still prevailed among right-thinking men. At Kidder-minster the old vicar lived on in the vicarage house without any molestation, while Richard Baxter, who was called to preach in the town in 1640, and remained there sixteen years, continued to labour among the people with what his biographer terms "an unprecedented success." Baxter throughout the troubles preserved the affection of all good men. He had himself had few scruples as to conformity to the Church, of which he was an ordained priest, and whether as preacher, army chaplain, or minister to individual souls, his efforts were directed always to the encouragement of charity among all men. Of sectaries he was a zealous opponent; he believed, indeed, that "friars and jesuits were their deceivers, and under several vizors were dispers'd among them." He endeavoured at Kidderminster "to keep his people as free from any concern in the public changes as was possible." He kept them from taking the Covenant, and he spoke and preached against the engagement. He regarded

Richard Baxter at Kidderminster.

Cromwell and his adherents as traitors, "but yet he did not think it his duty to rave against them in the pulpit." Living in charity with all men, he was able to bring the ministers of Worcestershire during the troubled days to an "agreement for Church order and concord." Thus some, like Hacket, at Cheam, lived in retirement. To the last moment he had read the Common Prayer in London, even when a soldier held a pistol to his head and commanded him to cease, to whom he replied that "he would do what became a divine, and he might do what became a soldier"; and in later days he once said the burial service by heart at the funeral of a noted Puritan, whose friends expressed themselves much affected, and were greatly surprised to learn that what they had admired was "the very office of the poor contemptible Book of Common Prayer." When he was forcibly prevented reading the Prayer-book he "even still kept up the use of it in most parts, never omitting the Creed, Lord's Prayer, confession and absolution, and many other particular collects, and always as soon as the Church service was gone absolved the rest at home." L'Estrange, too, though he had been a colonel in the royal army, and was an eminent writer on behalf of the Church, lived at peace in "the vales of rural recess."

For the ten years following the execution of Charles I., Juxon, who had attended him on the scaffold, lived at Little Compton in Warwickshire, where he had bought the manor some years before. Whitelocke, who had *Juxon.* known him for many years, tells how he lived like a country gentleman, diverting himself with a pack of hounds, which Cromwell refused to interfere with, and which "exceeded all other hounds in England for the pleasure and orderly hunting of them." Hard by Little Compton is the still standing Chastleton House, a beautiful Jacobean mansion built in the first decade of the seventeenth century. Here, it is traditionally recorded, Juxon used every Sunday to read the Common Prayer; and several relics of the distressed time, and of the Martyred King, still recall the bishop's days of retirement. He was able to assist many of the poorer clergy. The Verney letters, and his own, tell of the sad straits to which Cosin was put in the Low Countries, and Morley with him. The correspondence between the former and Sancroft throws an interesting light on their difficulties and on the spirit in which they were met. "I am right glad to hear still," wrote Cosin in February, 1656, "how firm and unmoved you continue your own standing in the midst of these great and violent storms that are now raised against the Church of England, which, for my part, notwithstanding the outward glory and dress that she had, be in these evil times taken from her, yet I honour and reverence above all the other churches of the world: for she bears upon her, more signally than any other that I know does, the marks of Christ, which, when all is done, will be our greatest glory."

Sancroft, who had been deprived of his fellowship at Cambridge between June 27 and August 13, 1651, for refusal to take the engagement, was living quietly on his property at Fressingfield, and writing vigorous attacks on the dominant Puritanism of the day. The first, which he published in 1651, was called *Fur Prædestinatus*, a supposed dialogue between a Calvinist preacher and a thief condemned to the gallows who declared that he was predestinated to do what he had done. An English translation appeared in 1658. It is a vigorous attack on Calvinism as subversive of morality, with reference to the works of all the leading Calvinist doctors. This was followed by *Modern Policies taken from Machiavel, Borgia, and other choise Authors by an Eye-Witness,* which reached a seventh edition in 1657. It is an equally vigorous attack upon Puritan politics and religion. He declared that "all news in religion, whether in doctrine or discipline, is the common screen of private design." Ralph Brownrigg, Bishop of Exeter, was a notable support to such men, and to him, under initials, Sancroft dedicated his second book. Great care was taken to continue the Episcopal succession, and the king's ministers abroad as well as the bishops in concealment were keenly interested and in constant correspondence on the subject. A fragment of a letter from Dr. Duncombe to Hyde, among the Clarendon Papers, and dated July, 1655, is concerned with the consecration of bishops to the vacated sees in England. Among the names of fit men suggested is that of Sheldon.

While thus the clergy were for the most part interested chiefly in ecclesiastical matters, some of those who were afterwards in high office in the Church were (as was said of medieval bishops such as Roger of Salisbury) *magni in sæcularibus*. There are few more amusing histories than that of Captain Peter Mews, afterwards Bishop of Winchester, who ran many risks as a Royalist agent in Scotland, yet still always endeavoured to keep up his studies even while he "with inseparable duty" followed the fortunes of the king, and was much disliked by the "Presbyterian gang" as a stalwart son of the English Church. He applied through the Princess of Orange for the post of Philosophy Reader at Breda, but Hyde warned him that a man was needed "that hath not been a truant from his books." To such, and stranger, shifts were the banished clergy put. But amid all their strange surroundings the clergy, indeed, were never more active during the whole century than at this period when they were persecuted. Wits like Abraham Wright satirised the preaching of the day in sermons which it was difficult to distinguish from their prototypes. An anonymous writer even dared to satirise the proceedings of the Committee of Triers, which was now set up to examine the qualifications of all who desired to serve in the ministry of the anomalous church system established. *The Examination of Tilenus before the Triers in order to his intended Settlement in the Office of a Public Preacher in the Commonwealth of Utopia* is a powerful and humorous indictment of the fashionable theology. The grace of conversion, the Triers are made to assert, is not resistible, else were man stronger than God ; and in the text that "God would have all men to be saved," "*All* is to be understood *non de singulis generum* but *de generibus singulorum*, not for *all of every kind*, but for *some few* only of every sort and nation." There is hardly exaggeration in this play of wit.

The places of the dispossessed clergy were filled by men who, for the most part, had but inadequate theological training. A weaver appeared in the pulpit with a sword by his side. Tinkers, cobblers, saddlers, coachmen Their successors. took on them the ministry of the Word. At Sampford Peverell the intruded minister, who had been a ship's carpenter, left behind him a table that he had made, at least a useful occupation. It is said that Arthur Okeley, rector of West Mersea, could not write his name. In fact, from 1649 to 1660 it can scarcely be said that a definite church system existed.

Cromwell's determination was, as he said to Ludlow, to reform the Church and the law. He was prepared to show both ministers and lawyers their mistakes, but they were not ready to accept his dictation. So the years went on to the inevitable reaction.

In November 1654 the House of Commons appointed a committee to confer with the Protector on the subject of the ecclesiastical settlement. In 1652 Dr. John Owen and his supporters had produced fifteen fundamentals of Christianity which excluded Quakers and Unitarians ; Churchmen and Romanists were already excluded. Baxter would have been satisfied with the Creed, the Lord's Prayer, and the Ten Commandments ; Cromwell appeared to desire a still wider toleration. In December a wrangle occurred as to whether the " Protector should have a negative voice to any Bill compelling attendance on the services of the Established Church." " Every one desires to have liberty," said Cromwell, " but none will give it." On January 12, 1655, it was resolved by the House that the " damnable heresies " to be exempted from toleration should be enumerated by the Protector and Parliament. While there was no serious proposal to extend liberty of worship to the Church, it remained an open question whether toleration could be extended to the Society of Friends. On February 15, 1655, the Protector put out a verbose proclamation which congratulated the nation on the free course of the Gospel in its midst, but declared that all disturbers of public or private worship, such as " Quakers, Ranters, and others," should be punished by the civil magistrates. Later on, in August 1656, Cromwell intervened to free a number of Quakers who had been arrested. The clergy of the Church were more effectually silenced. The Plundered Ministers' Committee met with cases of refusal to take the Solemn League and Covenant or of the employment of the Prayer-book. In September 1655 it was ordered that

The ecclesiastical settlement.

Persecution of Churchmen.

after November 1 no Royalist " was to be suffered to keep in his house any of the ejected clergy as a chaplain or a tutor for his children, under pain of having his fine doubled ; and no such clergyman was to keep a school, preach, or administer the Sacraments, celebrate marriage, or use the Book of Common Prayer under pain of three months' imprisonment for the first offence, of six months' for the second, and of banishment for the third."

This severe rule was probably not stringently enforced. None the less it was repeated on November 24, in the following terms :

" His Highness, by the advice of his Council, doth publish, declare, and order, that no person or persons do, from and after the first day of January 1655(6), keep in their houses or families as chaplains or school-masters for the education of their children, any sequestered or ejected minister, fellow of a college or schoolmaster, nor permit any of their children to be taught by such, in pain of being proceeded against in such sort as the said orders do direct in such cases ; and that no person who hath been sequestered or ejected out of any benefice, college, or school, for delinquency or scandal, shall, from and after the said first day of January, keep any school, either public or private ; nor any person who after that time shall be ejected for the causes aforesaid, shall preach in any public place, or at any private meeting of other persons besides his own family, nor shall administer baptism or the Lord's Supper, or marry any persons, or use the Book of Common Prayer, or the terms therein contained, upon pain that every person so offending shall be proceeded against as by the said orders is provided."

Order of Nov. 24, 1655.

It was the last act of Archbishop Usher to petition for some concession to the clergy of the Church. Cromwell seemed for the time inclined to tolerance ; but the rule of the major-generals was not a light one.

Of the religious condition of England during the suppression of the Church an important illustration may be given here. An interesting episode in the history of the Commonwealth and Protectorate is formed by the negotiations which led to the readmission of the

The question of Jewish toleration.

Jews, banished since the time of Edward I., to England. It is one which throws a valuable side-light upon the religious history of the time, and it affords an illustration, from an unexpected quarter, of the nature of Cromwell's views of toleration.

The return was prepared by a series of literary discussions. Busher's *Religious Peace*, published in 1614, pleaded for the admission of Jews to toleration. It was republished in 1646. Roger Williams, in his *Bloudy Tenant of Persecution*, 1644, was no less emphatic ; and Hugh Peters was of the same mind. Several petitions were offered to Parliament which included the same demand. In 1650 Menasseh ben Israel published his *Hope of Israel*, with a somewhat fulsome dedication to the English Parliament. The pamphlet, though widely read, was vigorously attacked. It was claimed by Puritan writers that the Jews should only be admitted under conditions which should tell directly in favour of their conversion. And Menasseh appears to have taken no further steps for some time. It was after this that Cromwell himself took up the matter, and it is clear that he was actuated by reasons of political expediency. In 1654 a Jewish envoy, brother-in-law of Menasseh, visited England, probably at the direct invitation of Cromwell, and petitioned for the restoration of the Jews to England on religious and commercial grounds. The Protector especially recommended the petition to the Council, but they would take no action. Cromwell, however, did not let the matter end there. He conveyed to Menasseh that his personal presence in England "would be not altogether unwelcome." In October 1655, Menasseh arrived in London, and published his *Humble Addresses*, in which he defended his people against the charges of usury, of slaying children, and of converting Christians, and pleaded for absolute freedom for Jews to settle in England, and to follow their religion "whiles we expect with you the hope of Israel to be revealed." The result was a tempest of expostulation and calumny. "Not a single influential voice in England was raised in favour of" the proposals ; and Prynne, who was followed by many less learned, if not less bitter, controversialists, published in his wonderful *Demurrer* a laborious and virulent opposition to the scheme, on historical as well as religious grounds.   Undeterred, Menasseh presented his petition in person to the Council of State, and Cromwell gave him his unhesitating support.   The Council, not daring openly to refuse, advised the calling of a special conference of learned men to consider the petition : "Whereupon," in Menasseh's words, "it pleased his Highness to convene an assembly at Whitehall of divines, lawyers, and merchants of different persuasions and opinions.   Whereby men's judgments and sentences were different."

It was decided, in fact, that there was no law of England forbidding the Jews' return.   But, on the other hand, the religious opposition of Puritans, now embittered by the many pamphlets published, was strongly against concession ; and the English merchants as vigorously protested against the admission of new rivals in trade.   Cromwell himself strongly supported their petition, but only by ending the conference did he prevent its voting formally against his wishes.   Shortly afterwards—the date is uncertain—the Protector gave his personal assurance that the Jews should be free to settle and to worship privately "by way of connivancy," as a Royalist news-letter tells on December 31, 1655.   So the matter ended, while Cromwell lived.   It may be added that at the Restoration the London merchants made the strongest efforts to induce the king to withdraw the connivance, but Charles was too much indebted to Jewish money-lenders (one of whom he knighted) to take any such steps, and eventually toleration was promised to the Jews by the king in Council so long as they lived peaceably and without scandal to the Government. The old bitternesses and hostilities were dying away in men's hearts ; but the treatment of the clergy by the State was still far indeed from religious liberty.   The fact seemed emphasised as the older clergy died.

> The connivance at their return.

As the years went on not a few of the dispossessed clergy passed away.   In 1656 died one whom even Presbyterians were ready to declare "the most reverend and learned father of our Church," James Usher, once Archbishop of Armagh.   He had lived a long life of controversy.   His first book, *De Ecclesiarum Christianarum successione et statu*, was presented in 1613 to James I. as the

> Archbishop Usher.

first-fruits of the learned University of Dublin, of which the author was the first scholar. His Calvinism was toned down by his scholarship. Through an English merchant at Aleppo he secured a copy of the Samaritan Pentateuch and an important MS. of the Old Testament, and up to the end of his life he was engaged in studies in the Semitic tongues and in early Church history. At the time of Strafford's trial he was in England, and it was through him that the king sent his last messages to the earl on the eve of his execution. The Irish rebellion drove him from his country, and Charles gave him the bishopric of Carlisle. During the wars he spent much of the time at Oxford; he declined to sit in the Westminster Assembly, and his library was seized by the Parliament. He then spent some time in retirement in Wales, and later returned to London, where he was preacher at Lincoln's Inn, whence he was summoned to assist the king in the negotiations for the Treaty of Newport. His scheme for a "moderated Episcopacy" attracted much attention, and it seemed that even Cromwell would at least dally with his suggestions for an ecclesiastical reunion. Usher turned from the bitter contests of the day to talk of his manuscripts, of the Septuagint and the Syric version, of the history of Episcopacy, and of the letters of St. Ignatius. He was universally beloved; and when he died he was given a public funeral in Westminster Abbey. It was characteristic of the financial difficulties of the Protectorate that his daughter was obliged to pay for the funeral to the extent of £600, and that a grant that had been promised for her provision was withdrawn from her as a "malignant." Tolerant though Usher was, he was firm in his adherence to the Prayer-book, and it was his last sorrow that men declared that he believed the Church service to have been justly abolished, a charge which he repudiated as "a shameless and most abominable untruth."

Within six months of Usher died another noted prelate who had fallen on evil days, Joseph Hall, "late Lord Bishop of Norwich," as the preacher of his funeral sermon in St. Peter Mancroft, described him, "who upon the 8th day of September 1656, *anno ætatis suæ* 82, was gathered to the Spirits of the Just that are made perfect." His life, it was said, was "a demonstration that prelacy and piety are

Bishop
Joseph Hall.

not such inconsistent things as some would make them," and "he was noted for a singular wit from his youth ; a most singular rhetorician and an elegant poet ; he understood many tongues, and in the rhetoric of his own he was second to none that lived in his time." He had lived at the end in great poverty, but without complaint, devoted in study and ready to preach in any church "till he was first forbidden by men, and at last dis-inabled by God." When first he was a bishop men had taken him for a favourer of the Puritans, and he tells in his autobiography that "the billows went so high that he was three times upon his knees before the king," and that he told Laud that rather than be subject to "the slanderous tongues of his informers he would cast up his rochet." It was his lot before he died to be an example of constancy to the principles of the Church.

Signs of reaction were visible on every side. Baxter's system of voluntary associations was beginning to spread, a reaction against the severe and exclusive Presby- terian order. "These churches begin to see," wrote an acute observer, "that they have been fooled under the specious pretence of liberty of conscience to betray the civil liberties of their own native country." It was the natural result of the triumph of the sects and of the illegal and unconstitutional acts of Cromwell. He grew careless of strict legality, being convinced that he owed account only to God. Men began to see that his rule was as much personal, perhaps as arbitrary, as that of Charles I.

Signs of reaction.

Popular opinion indeed was beginning by the year 1658 to set rapidly against the government of the Protector. There can be no doubt that it was not merely arbitrary government and acts more illegal (if the expression be allowed) than those of Charles I., not even the suppression of the worship and the religious customs of the great majority of Englishmen, but the contrasts between the pride and glory of the upstarts in power and the depressed condition of the people at large, which affected the popular mind. Even in the household of Cromwell godliness, it would seem, was at a discount. His chaplain, the saintly John Howe, found it difficult to instil religion into his court. "My call hither," he wrote to Baxter, "was a work

Cromwell's household.

I thought very considerable—the setting up of the worship and discipline of Christ in this family. . . . But now at once I see the designed work here hopelessly laid aside. We affect here to live in so loose a way that a man cannot fix upon any certain charge to carry towards them as a minister of Christ should; so that it were as hopeful a course to preach in a market, or in any assembly met by chance, as here." He speaks sadly of "the affected disorderliness of this family as to the matter of God's worship" in the same letter. Those who did not live at Court were struck by manners other than those which distressed the conscience of the sensitive young Puritan. The Verney letters show that while honest Sir Ralph was in prison, his brother Henry was enjoying the luxury in which the "lords" of Cromwell's family revelled. "My Lord Fleetwood" and "my Lord Claypole" were great men in their pleasures; but the recreation of the loyal gentry and the poor were forbidden. Racing and card-playing, "a lude life" and "ill hours" were the joys of Master Henry Verney with my Lord Claypole and many another of his company. And meanwhile England was under a cloud of severe repression.

How severe it was the State Papers of the last four years before the Restoration abundantly show, and it was severe without being uniform. Disorder, indeed, was the chief characteristic of those years, when government was most oppressive. The Council did everything, and did it very ill. One day we find them ordering on the petition of the Mayor and Corporation of Gloucester, "that the late cathedral, with its utensils, cloisters, churchyards, library, etc., be henceforth enjoyed by them, for the preaching of the Word, education of children, and other public uses." On another there is referred to them the petition of the inhabitants of Wells for the use of the Cathedral Church, which is "much in decay in the covering, windows, and other parts," and needs immediate repair. Similar complaints were common; there was no money to repair the churches, and it was no man's business to do it. "Everywhere," it was said by a Puritan, "the Prelatical party is the most numerous, dissatisfied, closely working, though complying."

All the more urgent it seemed to those in power to keep

The severe repression.

up the severe laws against Popery and Prelacy. The Parliament of 1657 petitioned that toleration should extend to neither of these false faiths, and passed a very severe Act against recusants. On the other hand, liberty almost reached license. The inhabitants of Abbotsley parish, Hunts, were allowed liberty for any godly person whom they may procure to preach in the public meeting-place of the town, whereunto they may be summoned by a bell, and the incumbent and others concerned were not to interfere. Yet the persecution of the Quakers did not cease. They complained that they were "beaten, stoned, stocked, hauled out of our synagogues, cast into dungeons and noisome vaults, denied food for days together, not allowed pen, ink, and paper, and a legal trial refused or postponed for months or years." "Search the records," they said, "for you will hardly find so many in prison for conscience sake since the days of Queen Mary as now is in your day."

The end was clearly not far off. In March 1658 Cromwell put forth a proclamation that all cavaliers and papists must retire from London under pain of being proceeded against as delinquents; and 800 horse were quartered in St. Paul's, to be ready in case of a rising. The Protector died on September 3.

At every opportunity the people began to assert their attachment to the Church. Thus, when a minister at Luton refused to allow a burial with the Prayer-book service, the church was forcibly broken open and the old service was read. When Cromwell died it became more and more difficult to restrain public feeling. At Bagendon, in Gloucestershire, the minister who had been put in under "his late Highness's broad seal," was forcibly ejected by the parishioners, the former minister being restored. Almost to the last the restored Rump went on legislating as though Presbyterianism were to endure for ever. On March 14, 1660, they passed an Act "for approbation of ministers of the Gospel to benefices," and two days later one "for ministers and payment of tithes." But if their ears were shut the ears of England were open. At every street corner broadsheets proclaimed that the tyranny of the sects was dead, and that the Church should have her own again. A petition, claiming fifteen thousand signatures, was presented to Parliament on April 27, 1659, protesting, *inter alia*, against tithes, but protesting very pertinently: "Is this our rest and the end of our work, and is this the Reformation that must be the price of so much blood? To set the magistrate in Christ's throne to try and judge who are fit to be his Ministers, and to send out and restrain whom he thinks fit, and to force a maintenance further, even from those that for conscience sake cannot hear them nor own them ; but for Christ's sake, to whom the kingdom belongs, are made to testify against both magistrate and minister as intruders into Christ's place?"

Prynne, who had learnt some wisdom since his old enemy had gone to the scaffold, voiced the public feeling in his crabbed style, in "A short, legal, medicinal, usefull, safe, easie prescription, to recover our Kingdom, Church, Nation, from their present dangerous, distractive, destructive confusion, and worse than Bedlam madnesse," and "the Republicans and others' spurious good old cause briefly and truly anatomised." Monk for a while hesitated as to Church as well as king. "As to a government in the Church, the want whereof hath been no small cause of these nations' distractions," he said to the reassembled Parliament on February 21, 1660, "it is most manifest that if it be monarchical in the State, the Church must follow and Prelacy must be brought in." But he professed to believe that moderate Presbyterian government, with a sufficient liberty for conscience, was the best solution. "Resolved," wrote a wit in "Several Resolves prepared by the Commanding Junto to pass the House," "that there be a restraint upon Presbytery as well as Popery and Prelacy, because it somewhat resembles Christianity."

Richard Cromwell's brief rule ended in a torrent of squibs and lampoons ; the "good old cause," as the soldiers called it, was laughed at on every side : the end of the drama, that had had so many tragic scenes, was pure comedy. No movement in English history was more popular than that which brought back the Church with the king. Of what followed we do not now speak ; but it must be remembered that if the majority of the nation was afterwards proved to desire new safeguards against another revolution, and to think

Richard Cromwell.

that they could be found only in intolerance, the Restoration itself came with a declaration of freedom beyond that which Cromwell had ever granted. The declaration from Breda contained these words :

"And because the passion and uncharitableness of the times have produced several opinions in religion, by which men are engaged in parties and animosities against each other which, when they shall hereafter unite in a freedom of conversation, will be composed or better understood ; we do declare a liberty to tender consciences, and that no man shall be disquieted or called in question for differences of opinion in matters of religion, which do not disturb the peace of the kingdom ; and that we shall be ready to consent to such an Act of Parliament, as upon mature deliberation shall be offered to us, for the full granting of such indulgence."

Toleration promised at the Restoration.

We have passed away, in these concluding observations, from the great Protector himself ; but in the months that followed his death his spirit appeared still to brood over the disturbed scene. It was his indomitable insistence which caused the execution of the king. It was his strength of will and absence of sympathy or foresight which made the difficulties of the Puritan rule insoluble. Puritanism, some modern writers tell us, was incarnate in him. It was he, certainly, who more than any one man, was responsible for its fall.

AUTHORITIES. — Tanner MSS., Bodleian Library ; Evelyn, *Diary ;* Calendar of State Papers, Domestic ; Pamphlet literature of the time ; Shaw, *History of the English Church,* 1640-66 ; Clarendon, *Great Civil War;* Cromwell's *Letters and Speeches ;* editions of Carlyle and Stainer ; Walker, *Sufferings of the Clergy ;* Bailli　 *Letters ;* Clark Papers, ed. Firth (Camden Society) ; Clarendon Papers, ed. M　 Wolf, *Menasseh ben Israel.* Among modern biographies of *Cromwell,* th　 S. R. Gardiner, C. H. Firth, and John Morley. Among pamphlets on t　ion of the sects not favoured by the Protector should be especially not　 *Dissertation of the present sufferings of above* 140 *of the people of God　are now in prison,* 1660. Among refutations of the Covenant, etc., William Prynne, *Concordia Discors,* 1660. See also "Troubles in a City Parish under the Protectorate," *English Historical Review,* x. 41 *sqq.,* and Calamy's *Abridgment* of Mr. Baxter's *History of his Life and Times,* 1702. Details of the later years of Usher and of Hall are found in the *Life and Death of* . . . *Dr. James Usher* (a sermon), by Nicholas Bernard, 1656, and *Death's Alarum* (a sermon), by John Whitefoote, 1656, and in the autobiographical memorials in Wordsworth's *Ecclesiastical Biography,* vol. v. ed.

1810. The *Life of Hacket*, by Plume (ed. Walcott, 1865), and the Lives of Juxon, Hammond, Hall, Usher, in the *Dictionary of National Biography*, give information. As to the establishment of Presbyterianism, the formal terms may be observed in the *Ordinance of the two Houses*, published 1645 (1646) by John Wright. The best account of the condition of a diocese during the interregnum is that in the *Diocesan History of Bath and Wells* (W. Hunt), chap. viii. *Tilenus the Trier* was printed by R. Royston at the Angel in Fire Lane ; the copy in the possession of the present writer has, in a contemporary hand, on the title page, " John Aston," which may possibly be the name of the writer. *The copie of a paper presented*, etc., London printed by A. W. for Giles Calvert, at the Black Spread-eagle, at the West end of Paules, 1659. Speech printed by S. Griffin, 1659 (1660), on the order of " his excellency the Lord General."

CHAPTER X

THE CHURCH OF THE RESTORATION

THE Restoration meant much more than that, after a few months' unrest under an impossible government, Oliver Cromwell's successor was Charles Stewart. The Church was restored with even fewer conditions than the king. Statesmen were fearful, but their fears were groundless. When, in 1659, Thorndike published his *Epilogue to the Tragedy of the Church of England,* in which he reiterated, clearly and unhesitatingly, the doctrines which the school of Laud had inherited from the divines of the Reformation and their historical ancestry, Catholic custom was to his mind still the unbroken rule of the Church: the historic Episcopate, the use of confession and of prayers for the dead, the restoration of the *Epiklesis* on the elements, for these he pleaded. His principle was the appeal to the Holy Scriptures as interpreted in the primitive church; outside this there was no compromise possible for churchmen. Such statements alarmed the cautious Hyde, the faithful counsellor of the exiled Charles as of his father, and afterwards famous as Earl of Clarendon. "What do our friends think of the book?" he asked, "and is it possible that he would publish it, without ever imparting it or communicating with them?" The king, he said, was apprehensive of danger; reports reached England from his court that "any Episcopacy, how low soever, would serve the turn and be accepted."

Some of the London clergy and laity "that adhered to the late king," drew up a declaration, in which they declared that they regarded their sufferings as inflicted by God, "and

therefore do not cherish any violent thoughts or inclinations
to those who have been in any way instrumental
in them." Baxter said publicly that moderate
men could be easily satisfied. He, and many with
him, made no exceptions to the doctrines of the Prayer-
book. It seemed that the Presbyterians—so the French
ambassador wrote to Cardinal Mazarin on April 1, 1660,
—were still in power. But the Presbyterian system, as we
have seen, had never taken root in the country. The differences among other religious bodies, whom Presbyterians and
churchmen alike contemptuously described as "sectaries,"
prevented any possible union on the basis of Independency,
even if the essentially republican nature of the Independent
system had made it possible as the religious establishment of
a restored monarchy. The grievous exceptions which the late
government had continued to make to a religious toleration
left no precedent for a scheme which would allow freedom to
all. If the lines upon which religion should be settled had
been submitted to argument, it is probable that no conclusion
would ever have been arrived at. But the matter was settled,
as a revolution generally settles such matters, without compromise.

Possibilities of a settlement.

The first factor in the settlement was the king himself.
Charles had been brought up in the strict Church of England
system, which was the centre of his father's ideas.
He had undergone among the Presbyterians of
Scotland uncomfortable experiences, involving, to
a man of his supple dishonesty, considerable personal humiliation. He had mixed continually during his exile with Roman
Catholics, and the Commonwealth had done its best to make
England believe that he was already a papist.[1] But he had
kept up the English services in what was termed his private
chapels, and his advisers were for the most part sincere
members of the English Church. The matter did not touch
him very nearly. From his boyhood he was utterly dissolute
and corrupt. "His religion was Deism, or rather that which
is called so; and if in his exile, or at his death, he went into
that of Rome; the first was to be imputed to a complaisance

The views of Charles II.

---

[1] The publication in 1650 of *The King of Scotland's Negotiations at Rome*
rendered it necessary to publish a full refutation of the charges in 1660.

for the company he was then obliged to keep, and the last to a lazy diffidence in all other religions, upon a review of his past life, and the near approach of an uncertain state." Such is the judgment of Dr. James Welwood, writing in 1700. And it is indubitably correct. If it is true that the Presbyterian ministers who went over to see him at the Hague were befooled by listening to him at his prayers for a heart "constant in the exercise and protection of thy true Protestant religion," and tender to nonconformists, the sorry jest was one which he must thoroughly have enjoyed. He offered liberty, no doubt gladly and honestly, but he would certainly oppose no personal convictions to the wishes of the majority of Englishmen, for fear he should "go on his travels again."

And the opinion of England, or of the strongest party in England, was soon manifest. Charles II. was proclaimed in London on May 8, 1660, by order of the newly-elected Convention. On the 12th he was proclaimed at Durham. A typical parish register adds, "on which day I, Stephen Hogg, began to use again the Book of Common Prayer." The king's first Sunday in England was spent at Canterbury, where the Common Prayer was again read in the cathedral church. On the 29th of May he entered London in triumph.

On the king's return an Act was passed restoring to their benefices all clergy who had been deprived since the rebellion began, if they were not concerned in the king's death, or Anabaptists; and this was carried out, with some popular tumult, within a few weeks in many parts of the country. Where the Episcopalian incumbent, however, had died, or where he had remained during the interregnum, accepting the religious changes, no alteration was at first made.

The Restoration, May 29, 1660.

From the day of the king's formal restoration, petitions poured in from the Episcopalian clergy, seeking the royal favour. Two days after he returned to London the Lords and Commons petitioned for the proclamation of a day of thanksgiving. The London ministers requested the restoration of "the former ecclesiastical, civil and military government." Newcastle-on-Tyne hoped that Charles might "be the instrument to unite a divided church." The ministers of Exeter and Devon expressed their

Petition as to the Church.

joy that to his zeal for the Protestant religion "is joined a
pitiful heart towards tender consciences," and hoped that he
would protect "the young and weak of the flock who cannot
pace it with their older brethren." Totnes left to the king
"the settlement of the Church." North Wales hoped for a
"resettlement of the Church." The mass of petitions that
poured in with regard to Church preferment, recommendations
of clergy by eminent men, and the like, showed, within the
first month of the king's restoration, how certain men regarded
the restoration of the Church, and that practically without
conditions. Within a month, too, the king had authorised
the use of the Book of Common Prayer. On the 28th of June
a solemn thanksgiving was held "for the happy return of his
Majesty," and Gilbert Sheldon, once warden of All Souls'
College, and a warm supporter of Laud in Oxford, now dean
of the Chapel Royal, preached before the king at Whitehall.
In marked contrast to the fulsome words in which the
Presbyterian Speaker of the Commons had assured Charles
that he was ranked for his sufferings among the martyrs of
Christ ; Sheldon earnestly and soberly spoke of David's deliverance and thanksgiving as a pattern for king and people. "A
sad bargain it is," he said, "to save wealth, honour, crowns,
and sceptres, life itself, anything we have, at the loss of our
God, at the expense of our soul ;" and as before the Rebellion,
there was "open, public, and national sin," so now true
gratitude involved doing good ; "an horrid sin it is, instead
of thanking God to sacrifice to Bacchus, to express *publicum
gaudium per publicum dedecus*" [a public joy by a public dis-
honour]. A right note was struck for the new reign, but it
was not followed.

The first great public ceremonial of the restored Church,
restored almost before men had taken in hand its restoration,
was the consecration of five bishops in Westminster Abbey.
Of those who had held sees before the war there survived
many notable men. The appointment of Juxon to the primacy,
vacant since that day when the friend and patron of his youth
had died on the scaffold, was inevitable. He was the
closest link with memories which the loyalists of the
Restoration felt to be sacred. His election was
confirmed in Henry VII.'s chapel, on September 20, 1660,

Appoint-
ments to
bishoprics.

amid a great concourse of clergy and laity, and every sign of rejoicing and thankfulness. All men loved him. Long before, the great Falkland had said that "he never knew any one that a pair of lawn sleeves had not altered from himself, but only Bishop Juxon." He was, all through his life, what Charles I. had called him above all others, a "good man." But he was now infirm as well as aged, and he took no part in the consecrations to any of the vacant sees. Besides him there remained several who had suffered : Wren, who had been in prison nearly twenty years ; Piers, who had been impeached with Wren, but like him never brought to trial, and several others. One also there was who had been consecrated in the chapel of Magdalen College, Oxford, when the war was at its height, on April 28, 1644,—Accepted Frewen, Bishop of Lichfield, now raised to the Archbishopric of York.

On October 28, 1660, in Henry VII.'s chapel, Gilbert Sheldon was consecrated to London ; Humfrey Henchman to Salisbury, George Morley to Worcester, Robert Sanderson to Lincoln, George Griffith to St. Asaph. The new bishops. On December 2, seven more bishops were consecrated ; on the Feast of Epiphany four more. One of these was Edward Reynolds, consecrated to Norwich, a notable Puritan, who after putting before the king his opinion as to the position of the Episcopate, cordially accepted the new settlement. Another was John Gauden, the author of the *Eikon Basilike*, who had, though then secretly, done more, perhaps, to bring about the Restoration than any other man save Monk. He had preached at St. Paul's on February 28, 1660, before the lord mayor and Monk, a very subtle sermon in which he hinted, without saying it, what was in every man's thoughts, that the return of the monarchy was "the right method of healing Church and State." Concerning Church he said, "the perfect healing of the Church and religion, as Christian and reformed (whose divisions, hurts, and deformities are many), will hardly be done without calling those spiritual physicians together, after the primitive pattern, in ecclesiastical synods or national councils, who are best skilled in the true state of health in the nature of the diseases, and in the aptest remedies, which in religion ought to be only humane and

charitable, convincing with meekness of wisdom, and healing
as much by prayers and tears as by reasonings and persuasions.
I confess I cannot see how a committee of Parliament for
religion is proper for this work." He had then, as in his
famous book ten years before, the art of catching what was in
men's minds. All were weary of the State ruling the details
of Church government. It had not succeeded when Charles
I. was king, or when the Long Parliament established Presbyterianism, or when the discredited Committee for Plundered
Ministers had returned again with the Rump. Let the details
be left to the clergy. Puritans were content, churchmen
jubilant. Charles had before his return made several Puritan
clergy his chaplains, Baxter among them. It was between
these men and the bishops, after many preliminary discussions, that a conference was arranged.

But first Charles, seemingly anxious to fulfil his Breda
pledge, issued a Declaration of Indulgence, promising several
concessions to the Puritans. Dated on October 25,
1660, this declaration by the king concerning
ecclesiastical affairs stated that his residence abroad
enabled him to testify the approval by foreign divines of the
Church of England. He intended to call a synod, but
meanwhile seditious pamphlets are published, and his own
declaration, made when under constraint in Scotland, is un-
reasonably printed and dispersed; and the jealousies of
faction delayed a synod for the present. He declared his
resolution to support the government of the Church of
England, but promised to appoint divines of both parties
to review the Prayer-book, to waive minor points of ceremonies, and to excuse subscription to canonical obedience as
a condition of ordination. The Declaration was brought
before Parliament in the form of a Bill, and was
rejected by the Commons. This showed at once
the temper of the people, and their determination to
allow no alteration in the standards of the Church. The promised conference then must decide what could be done.

Meanwhile the election to the new Parliament showed
plainly the force of the Royalist reaction. For the city of
London, it is true, only Presbyterians and Independents were
returned; but in most cities as well as in the counties, strong

Royalists and churchmen were elected. Before the Parliament met, the promised conference began at the Savoy. It had been prepared for by an address from the nonconformists, asking for the abolition of kneeling at the Communion and other customs of the Church, as well as for the revision of the Prayer-book. A reply of the bishops had declared the book to be practically faultless, but consented to its revision " by such fit persons as his Majesty shall think fit to employ therein," and whereas the Puritan had desired an approximation in the services to the model of the foreign Protestants they replied that "the nearer both their forms and ours came to the liturgy of the ancient Greek and Latin churches, the less they are liable to the objections of the common enemy."

A royal commission was issued on March 25, 1661, The Savoy Conference. to twelve bishops and twelve Puritan divines; and to nine other divines on each side as assistants. The commissioners were given authority to advise upon and review the Book of Common Prayer ; comparing the same with the most ancient liturgies which have been used in the Church in the primitive and purest times, to consider the several directories, and rules and forms of prayer, and the objections raised to them, and avoiding all unnecessary alterations to make such reasonable corrections and amendments as should be agreed upon to be needful or expedient for the giving satisfaction to tender consciences. Meanwhile the king was crowned, and not only Parliament but Convocation, legally summoned after the ancient manner, met.

Charles was crowned at Westminster on April 30. Juxon was too infirm, as well as "lame of his hands," to undertake the whole office of consecration and coronation, and The coronation, April 30, 1661. the greater part of the office was said by the Bishop of London. But the primate presented the king to the people, asking their assent, in the old form. And again he performed the unction, on the palms of the hands, the breast, and between the shoulders, "at the bending of both arms," and on the crown of the head. He blessed the sword, which was put on by the Lord Chancellor; he laid the crown on the altar, blessed it, and placed it on the king's head—"at which all the peers present put on their coronets" —he put the ring on the king's finger, and delivered to him the two sceptres; and he pronounced the final benediction. The service used was practically identical with those used since that date, except that the oath was strengthened when offered to James II., and that certain insertions were made at the coronation of William and Mary. The oil of anointing was consecrated by a special form. The archbishop was "vested in a rich ancient cope."

The "Savoy Conference" met on April 15, under the presidency of Sheldon, Bishop of London, but it was then adjourned at his desire for the preparation of the Presbyterian objections to the Prayer-book. On May 4 these were presented in writing, and the serious business of the Conference began. Baxter had already drawn up a revised liturgy of his own composition. The objections show that the Puritan position had not materially altered from what it had been at the Hampton Court Conference, or from the terms submitted to Bishop Williams (see above, p. 93). Polite words were used of the Prayer-book: but it was suggested that as it was originally drawn up in a form designed to propitiate the papists, "by varying as little as they well could from the Romish forms before in use," so now it might be composed anew, so "as to gain upon the judgments and affection of all those who in the substantials of the Protestant religion are of the same persuasion with ourselves." Objection was taken to Lent, Saints' days and their vigils, the Apocrypha, and the use of the words "priest" or "curate" and "Sunday," and it was requested that "no part of the Liturgy need be read at the communion-table except when the Holy Supper is administered," and that all reference to baptismal regeneration be removed from the Prayer-book. The surplice, the sign of the cross in baptism, and kneeling at communion, were excepted against as in 1604, and special objections were made in detail to several passages in the Prayer-book, and notably to the rite of confirmation as administered by the bishops. Detailed answers were given by the bishops in writing, and eventually a discussion took place. The line of resistance which the bishops took was generally purely defensive. "They had nothing to do," was their declaration, "till the others had proved that there was a

Puritan objections at the Savoy Conference.

The attitude of the bishops.

necessity for alteration, which they had not yet done." They
assumed the position of rulers of the Church, prepared to
entertain all serious objections, and fully competent to decide
upon them.   It was a claim which absolutely conflicted with
the presumed equality between the parties with which the
conference was supposed to have begun.   The popular feeling
was so evident that the bishops found themselves able to
assert their old authority, and skilful assistants supported
them.   The most notable of Baxter's antagonists were the
learned Pearson, afterwards Bishop of Chester (1673-84); and
Dr. Peter Gunning, afterwards Bishop of Chichester (1670-74)
and Ely (1675-84), "well read in fathers and councils."   The
latter was "vehement from his high imposing principles and
ever zealous for Arminianism and formality and church pomp,"
says Baxter, who argued with him at the Savoy.   He certainly
desired more ceremonial.   He was spoken of as "the incom-
parable hammer of the schismatics"; and the victory was his.
The final report to the king was "that the Church's welfare,
that unity and peace, and his Majesty's satisfaction, were ends
at which they were all agreed; but as to the means they could
not come to any harmony."

The Presbyterians presented a petition to the king at
the end of the conference, praying that none might be
punished for not using the Prayer-book till it had been revised.
But the matter had now passed into the hands of Parliament and of Convocation.   The spirit of Parliament was
intensely Royalist and bitterly opposed to the *The Royalist*
dissenters.   They declared that no petition for any *Parliament*
alterations in Church and State could be allowed to *feeling of*
be presented unless approved by three justices of *the country.*
the peace; and they passed a resolution which formed an
ominous precedent for a century of legislation and strife.   No
one was to be admitted a member of the House who had not
received the Holy Communion.   The aim of this was quite
clear.   The House believed that the disasters and struggles
of the century were due to the intrusion into the government
of the country of interests out of sympathy with the National
Church.   The reigns of the later Tudors had established the
principle that Romanists should be excluded from the conduct
of national affairs.   The great rebellion had shown, it was

thought, that those who dissented on other grounds might be equally dangerous to the peace of the country. Parliament considered it certain that the nation wished to be ruled only by members of the Church of England. But who was a member of the Church? The test of baptism was insufficient, that of confirmation unsatisfactory. No one who dissented on conscientious grounds from the Church would communicate at her altars. This seemed certain. The test was simple, and it appeared to be sure. It was not designed to narrow the limits of the Church, but to make plain who were desirous to abide within those limits.

The House of Commons proceeded to make its intentions still more clear, by passing a Bill for Uniformity, enjoining the use of the Book of Common Prayer, in the form annexed to the Bill. This, it should be observed, was the book issued in 1604, in which the alterations from the last fully authorised book had received no sanction from either Parliament or Convocation. The House, clear as to its own and the people's wishes, followed in the way of the Long Parliament, acting on purely Erastian principles. Happily the House of Lords preferred to wait for the result of the Savoy Conference and the revision of the Prayer-book, which Convocation was known to be about to undertake. By the summer of 1662 it was certain that the Church would be re-established in substantially the same position as it held in the days of Laud. It was almost equally certain that the principles of its rulers would be those on which he and the bishops of his school had interpreted the system and the formularies of the Reformation.

The Bill of Uniformity passes the Commons.

The restoration of the bishops to their full constitutional power had been prepared by the publication in 1660 of *An Apology for the Ancient Right and Power of Bishops to sit and vote in Parliament as the first and principal of the three estates of the Kingdom*, quoting Dr. Davenant's "determination at Cambridge" on the thesis, "Civil jurisdiction is by right granted to ecclesiastical persons," Archbishop Williams's speech in the House of Lords in defence of the bishops' right to sit and vote, with two speeches of Lord Newark's, also in 1641, on the same subject. There was indeed at the Restoration little opposition to their re-

Restoration of the bishops' powers.

covery of their full powers.   Though Pepys thought that after
the end of the Savoy conference, "the king would now be
forced to favour Presbytery or the City would leave him," he
was a few months later compelled to observe that "the
bishops carry themselves so high that they [the City] are never
likely to gain anything upon them."

On October 10, 1661, royal letters were issued to the
Archbishop of Canterbury directing the Convocation to revise
the Prayer-book and submit any suitable alterations. Meeting
Similar letters were issued to York (November 22), of the
in consequence of which delegates were appointed Convocations,
to act on behalf of the Northern Convocation. 1661.
Thus the two Convocations acted together as a National
Synod.   The Canterbury Convocation appointed eight bishops
to act as a committee of revision.   Of these the most
prominent member was John Cosin, Bishop of Durham,
whose chief study for over forty years had been in liturgies;
and his chaplain, William Sancroft, a minute and careful
scholar, was appointed to correct the printing of the book.
Bishop Wren and Bishop Gunning were other important
members of the revision committee.   The work practically
took from November 21 to December 20, on which day
the Book of Common Prayer, as revised, was accepted and
signed by the clergy of both Houses and both provinces.

In the revision something like six hundred alterations were
made.   Many of them were purely verbal : but others had a
distinct bearing on the controversies of the last The revision
thirty years.   In the first place, great emphasis was of the
now laid, by means of changes of phraseology, on Prayer-book.
the distinction between the episcopate and the priesthood,
and on the priestly character of the ministry.   The use
of the term "church" instead of "congregation" was also
emphasised.   A commemoration of the departed was added
to the prayer for the Church in the communion service;
additions were made to the baptismal and confirmation
services, and an office for the baptism of "such as are of
riper years," necessary in consequence of the laxity of the last
two decades, was inserted.   The rubric as to the ornaments
of the church was revised so as to agree exactly with the Act
of Parliament to which it referred, ordering "such ornaments

of the church and of the ministers thereof to be retained and be in use as were in this Church of England by the authority of Parliament in the second year of King Edward the Sixth." The "black rubric," at the end of the communion service, was inserted, in a form altered from that in the Second Prayer-book of Edward VI. (at the instance, says Burnet, of Peter Gunning), and denying a "corporal presence." A rubric was added, directing that "if any remain of that which was consecrated it shall not be carried out of the church," but shall be there consumed. A new preface to the book, written by Robert Sanderson, Bishop of Lincoln, was inserted. This declared the wisdom of the Church of England "to keep the mean between the two extremes," and justified the alterations. The revision is spoken of as rejecting all those proposals which secretly struck "at some established doctrine, or laudable practice of the Church of England, or indeed of the whole Catholic Church of Christ," but as endeavouring to do what "might most tend to the preservation of peace and unity in the Church, and exciting of piety and devotion in the publick worship of God, and the cutting off occasion from them that seek occasion of cavil or quarrel against the Liturgy of the Church."

It was admitted that the revisers could not expect, "in such variety of apprehensions, humours, and interests as are in the world, to please all; nor can [they] expect that men of factious, peevish, and perverse spirits should be satisfied with anything that can be done in this kind by any other than themselves." Indeed all the chief objections of the Puritans had been entirely overruled. Baxter and those who acted with him felt that the rubric declaring the salvation of baptized infants was in itself sufficient to prevent their conforming. It needed only the action of Parliament formally to create the inevitable schism.

After two months' consideration by the king and council the Prayer-book was submitted to Parliament. It was by the unquestioned exercise of synodical power that the Prayer-book was drawn up and approved. The book so approved was then by authority of Parliament imposed on the whole nation. On April 16, 1662, the Commons accepted the alterations without debate,

Nature of the work.

Its acceptance and enforcement by Parliament.

while asserting their right to consider them. In the House
of Lords the alterations were read over but in no way discussed, and a vote of thanks was passed to the Convocation
for the pains taken in the matter. On May 19 an Act of
Uniformity was passed ordering the revised book
to be read in all churches and chapels from St. *The Act of Uniformity.*
Bartholomew's Day. It was ordered that all persons
who were not in holy orders by Episcopal ordination should
be deprived of any benefice they held : and that all should
be deprived who would not use the book : and all clergy
and schoolmasters were required to make a promise to conform to the book, and a declaration of the illegality of taking
up arms against the king. The House of Lords endeavoured
to allow a dispensing power to the king, but the House of
Commons decisively rejected it. The national voice had
spoken, and it would allow no appeal. The ministers of
the Church must be those, and only those, who accepted
Episcopal ordination and the general sense of the Prayer-
book as the Reformers designed it.

"The Presbyterian ministers expressed their disapproba-
tion," says Clarendon, "with all the passion imaginable."
Their natural feeling of dismay and disappointment
that the declaration from Breda should not be *Presbyterian protests.*
interpreted as offering a consideration for tender
consciences within the Church, but rather outside it, would
be intensified by the words in which the Speaker had presented the Bill to the king. "We cannot forget the late
disputing age, in which most persons took a liberty and some
men made it their delight to trample upon the discipline and
government of the Church. The hedge being broken down,
the foxes and the wolves did enter, the swine and other
unclean beasts defiled the temple. At length it was discovered the Smectymnuan plot did not only lend itself to
reform ceremonies but sought to erect a popular authority of
elders, and to root out Episcopal jurisdiction. In order to
this work, church ornaments were first taken away, then the
means whereby distinction or inequality might be upheld
among ecclesiastical governors ; then the forms of common
prayer, which as members of the public body of Christ's
Church were enjoined us, were decried as superstitious : and

in lieu thereof nothing, or worse than nothing, was introduced.   Your Majesty having already restored the governors and government of the Church, the patrimony and privileges of our churchmen, we hold it now our duty, for the reformation of all abuses in the public worship of God, to present unto your Majesty a Bill for 'the Uniformity of public prayer and administration of the Sacraments.'   We hope the God of order and unity will conform the hearts of all people in this nation to serve Him in this order and uniformity."   It was clear that Parliament was absolutely determined in its action; and the efforts of the king and of the Presbyterian ministers were equally unavailing to stay its course.

The nonconformists almost with one accord adhered to their conscientious objections to the church services and St. Bartholo-   doctrines.   On St. Bartholomew's Day, 1662, some mew's Day,   eighteen hundred, as Baxter computed, or two 1662.   thousand, as Calamy, left their places.   The loss of so many good men was grievous, but now that the mists of controversy have cleared away it is impossible to regard it as other than inevitable.   When the majority of the Church and nation were agreed as to the limits of the Church, and, notably, insisted on the necessity of Episcopal ordination, it was impossible that men not so ordained and differing on important points from the doctrines of the Prayer-book should continue to hold office in the Church and to neglect her commands.   Comprehension could only have been achieved by the sacrifice of convictions on both sides, and this was a sacrifice which men's consciences happily would not allow them to make.   When the Act of Uniformity was enforced the Church was left in a position to carry out her system consistently, and those who left her for conscience' sake were free to teach and worship as they willed.   But, unhappily, Parliament would not allow the settlement to be permanent.   From definition it advanced to persecution.

At first, however, it seemed that settlement would satisfy the Anglicanism of the nation and its legislature.   The The   Puritan ministers for the most part withdrew in beginnings of   dignified silence.   The Church resumed her ordi-persecution.   nary methods of action.   The crown proceeded to act upon its ecclesiastical powers as if no rebellion had ever disturbed them. On October 14, 1662, the king issued a letter to the archbishops, to the effect that, the extravagance of preachers having much heightened public disorder, and still continuing so to do, through the diligence of factious spirits who often dispose men to jealousy of the government, and young divines in ostentation of learning handling the deep points of God's eternal counsels, or wrangling about gestures and fruitless controversies, his Majesty, to put a timely stop to these abuses, has followed the example of former kings and drawn up directions for preachers, to be communicated to every minister.

On August 22, 1663, a proclamation directed the observance of the statutes requiring attendance at church under penalty of a shilling fine for each absence without reasonable excuse, condemning Sunday trading and dissipation, and ordering the proclamation which the king had issued the day after his return to London against vicious and debauched persons to be read monthly in every church or chapel for the next half year. Charles was advised to exercise to the full the ecclesiastical prerogatives of his predecessors. The exercise was made the more acceptable by the memory which now gave to the crown a peculiar sanctity in the eyes of churchmen. *Proclamation requiring attendance at church, Aug. 22, 1663.*

The Church came back bound by a new link to the crown, a link forged by the execution of Charles I. and the publication of the *Eikon Basilike*. On the evening of March 25, 1660, some soldiers came to the Exchange and effaced the inscription that had been placed where once the statue of the king had stood, "*exit tyrannus, regum ultimus, anno libertatis Angliæ restitutæ primo, annoque Domini* 1648." The air rang with shouts of "Long live the king": men knew that Charles I. was not to be the last of their monarchs, and instead of a tyrant they deemed him a martyr.

On January 25, 1661, a proclamation was issued by request of Parliament, which ordered January 30 to be kept as a day of fasting and humiliation, to show "the abhorrence of the nation at the act of those wretched miscreants, who, usurping the power of Parliament and reducing the army, erected a prodigious and unheard of tribunal, by which the late king was condemned to death and publicly *The canonisation of Charles I.*

o

murdered." A form of prayer for use on the day was drawn up by Brian Duppa, Bishop of Winchester. It offered praise and thanks to God " for the glory of His grace that showed forth in His anointed our Sovereign King Charles," and besought that " by a careful, studious imitation of this Thy blessed saint and martyr, and all other Thy saints and martyrs that have gone before us, we may be made worthy to receive benefit by their prayers, which they, in communion with the Church Catholic, offer up unto Thee for that part of it here militant." This form was revised in January 1662, and a third revision was completed when the Convocation formally issued the service, with that for the 29th of May, in thanksgiving for the restoration of the king. These were annexed to the book of Common Prayer by the authority of the crown, Parliament being content merely to order the observance of the days. It may be noted here that the service underwent further changes on the accession of James II., when the tone of loyalty was, under the influence of Sancroft, heightened. The popular feeling, it is clear, went with the services; and it was encouraged by preaching on the " sufferings " and " martyrdom " of the king, which had more than a touch of extravagance. Churches before long came to be dedicated to the memory of the king. Seth Ward, Bishop of Exeter, writing to Archbishop Sancroft on September 1, 1665, spoke of his consecration of a church at Falmouth " by the name of Charles Church, *in memoriam Caroli regis et martyris*," varying from a form already used, " out of the honour which every true son of the Church owes to his memory (the only person canonised for a martyr by it)." He was to consecrate a few days later a church at Plymouth, " which by an Act of the Long Parliament (made in the beginning of it) is to be called by the name of Charles' Church. I was ashamed," he added, " that those hypocrites should, besides the making him a martyr, canonise him by a prolepsis, and that having so fair an opportunity I should not give testimony to his glory." This " canonisation," certainly a popular act, had important religious and political consequences.

It was designed not only to commemorate a martyr but to emphasise such views as are to be seen in the advice he had given in the days of his imprisonment, to his son now on the throne. "If you never see my face again, and God will have me buried in such a barbarous imprisonment and obscurity wherein few hearts that love me are permitted to exchange a word or a look with me, I do require and entreat you, as your Father and your king, that you never suffer your heart to receive the least check against, or disaffection from, the true religion established in the Church of England. I tell you I have tried it, and after much search and many disputes, have concluded it to be the best in the world, not only in the community as Christian, but also in the special notion as reformed : keeping the middle way between the pomp of superstitious tyranny and the meanness of fantastic anarchy. Not but that, the draught being excellent as to the main, both for doctrine and government in the Church of England, some lines, as in very good figures, may haply need some correcting and polishing, which might here easily have been done by a safe and gentle hand, if some men's precipitancy had not violently demanded such rude alterations as would have destroyed all the beauty and proportions of the whole. The scandal of the late troubles which some may object and urge to you against the Protestant religion established in England, is easily answered to them or your own thoughts in this, that scarce any one who hath been a beginner, or an active persecutor of this late war against the Church, the laws, and me, either was, or is a true lover, embracer, or practiser of the Protestant religion established in England, which neither gives such rules, nor ever set such examples before."

It was this advice which the Church desired by her formal action to give to the new king. Every point in it was emphatic in the desire of the Church now as of the king whose blood had been shed, as churchmen believed, for the Church's sake. "Some correcting and polishing" perhaps was needed : but that must come from those who had the interests of the true Protestant religion at heart, that is, from the bishops and clergy who adhered to the principles which they had maintained before the wars against Papist and Puritan alike. Those who fought against the Crown could not, the Church taught, be loyal to the Constitution. It was a view which the pulpits were tuned to make emphatic and

Lessons intended by the canonisation.

impressive.   It represented not only the views of the Church
but those of the parliamentary representatives of the people.

The sermon preached before the House of Commons in
St. Margaret's, Westminster, on January 30, 1662, by Dr.
Lessons from
his life. Hardy, and printed by the House's desire, shows
how warmly the Parliament had already taken up the
cause of the Church—the preacher congratulated the
country that they had now "an House of Commons made up
of gentlemen, and those both faithful subjects to their king
and zealous friends to the Church,"—and how studiously the
character of the royal martyr was commended as an example
to his son.   "Unspotted either with incontinence or intemper-
ance, so that even his most malicious enemies could not lay
either to his charge ; indeed, he was an exemplary pattern of
the contrary virtues."

Charles II. showed no signs of a desire to follow such an
example.   While he was on the whole scrupulous in attending
divine service and long-suffering in the matter of sermons, he
resented any personal address or personal application.   He
would talk theology with preachers, but there was never any
doubt as to his real character.   The devotion to his father's
memory cast but a dim reflection indeed on the "Merry
Monarch."   And while the veneration of Charles I. intensified
the popular feeling against the dissenters, it did not, as was soon
Charles's
failure to
obtain
toleration. seen, involve the recognition of any extra-legal power
in the crown.   Charles II. was genuinely anxious
to satisfy the nonconformists.   It was impossible
that the law should be carried out entirely without
friction.   Some of the dissenting ministers thought it still to be
their duty to preach : and Edmund Calamy was imprisoned
for thus disobeying the law.   The ministers presented a
petition for toleration ; and the king promised to urge Parliament to make an Act enabling him to exercise his "dispensing
power" in the matter.   But the House of Commons in the
next session, February 1663, vigorously protested against any
project of "establishing schism by a law," and the king was
unable to proceed.

AUTHORITIES.—For list of authorities, see end of Chap. XI.

CHAPTER XI

SHELDON AND SANCROFT

WITHIN a few months of the settlement of the Church Juxon and Sanderson passed to their rest. Gilbert Sheldon, Bishop of London, was elected archbishop on June 6, 1663. He had already been in practical possession of the powers of archbishop, owing to Juxon's age and infirmities. No bishop of his time has been so variously judged. Burnet spoke of him as having "little virtue and less religion," a judgment little less than grotesque on one who was the intimate friend of Falkland, Hammond, Clarendon, Sanderson, and Juxon, and to whom Charles I. had intrusted his solemn vow to restore all Church lands and lay impropriations held by the Crown if he should be restored to his "just rights." At the restoration Brian Duppa had written to him, "You are the only person about his Majesty that I have confidence in, and I persuade myself that as none hath his ear more, so none is likely to prevail on his heart more, and there was never more need of it." He fully deserved the confidence reposed in him. He strongly reproved Charles II. for his evil life, and refused to admit him to the Holy Communion; and eventually, in 1667, he entirely lost the king's favour on account of his consistent attitude. The memoirs which he left behind him, and which appear to have perished, would doubtless afford a vindication from his own standing-point of his policy in many matters where it has been severely criticised. Without them, we must look for the most intimate portrait of him in the *History of his own Time*, written by Samuel Parker, Bishop of Oxford, who was at one

Sheldon, Abp. of Canterbury, 1663-78.

His character.

time his chaplain. " As he came in due time to the manage-
ment of public affairs," he writes of Sheldon, " being a man of
great abilities, and was present at the most remarkable occur-
rences ; so transacting everything with a peculiar strength and
penetration of judgment, without doubt the commentaries he
wrote upon all affairs were excellent. . . . He was a man of
eminent piety : for though he was frequent and assiduous in
prayers, yet he was not such an admirer of them as some are,
nor did he so much regard the bare worship as the use that
was made of it ; and therefore he judiciously placed the sum
of religion in a good life."

A sober, just, and chaste life constituted, he was constant in
repeating, the essentials of piety—a lesson much needed by
the age of Charles II. It was no matter of what church
wicked men were, so the archbishop would say ; and, on the
other hand, " he greatly delighted himself with this saying,
and always spoke it with exultation, *Do well, and be merry*."
A kindly, gracious, hospitable man, simple in his life, and
very clear and determined in his judgments, is the impression
which he makes on those who read his letters and those of his
friends. He lived entirely for the Church, continuing the
example of celibacy set by his most recent predecessors in
the archiepiscopal office. The direction which Church affairs
took up to his death in 1677 was largely due to his initiation,
and, indeed, the characteristics of Church life up in the age of
Anne may to a great extent be traced to the influence
exercised by the opinions and policy of Sheldon, a disciple of
Andrewes and Laud, and a close friend of Lord Chancellor
Clarendon.

In the same year as Juxon there died also another prelate
greatly beloved, Robert Sanderson. He was one of those who
were ejected from Oxford, where he was Regius
Professor of Divinity, by the Parliamentary Commissioners. During the Commonwealth he had lived
in retirement, corresponding frequently with Piers, and with
the saintly Hammond, visiting London sometimes (as when,
" in sad coloured clothes, and God knows, far from being
costly," he met Walton, who describes their long talk in his
inimitable way), studying continually and recreating himself
with " the study of old records, genealogies, and heraldry."

Bishop
Sanderson of
Lincoln.

Sheldon knew his virtues, as those of one who would fulfil the primitive conception of a bishop's office, "not made up of ease and state, but of labour and care"; and it was at Sheldon's request that Charles II. at the Restoration nominated him to the see of Lincoln. He played, as we have seen, an important part in the Savoy Conference. As bishop he had time only to show himself careful in restoring the Episcopal palace and augmenting poor benefices, and in being so noted for his "condescension and obligingness to the meanest of his clergy," says Walton, "as to be known to most of them."

One of the first acts of Sheldon as archbishop was the recognition of an important constitutional change. The Convocation of 1663 was the last to exercise the ancient right of taxing the clergy. The "four subsidies" they granted were both a heavy burden on them, says Burnet, and yet an inconsiderable addition to the king's revenue. By a verbal agreement between Sheldon and Clarendon, which was recognised though not explicitly mentioned in an Act of Parliament 1665, the clergy henceforth ceased to tax themselves, and as a consequence claimed, and have since exercised without dispute, the right to vote for members of the House of Commons. It was (as, in later days, the constitutional historian Gibson, Bishop of London, justly said to Speaker Onslow), "the greatest alteration ever made in the constitution without an express law." It prevented the practical divergence between clergy and Commons being emphasised, as it was at the close of the Short Parliament, by a grant to the crown from the clergy when the laity refused all supplies. But the primacy of Sheldon was marked by events and changes which were of consequence more immediate and obvious—by the unhappy legislation of a bigoted Parliament against dissenters, by the terrible disasters of the plague and the fire, and by the completion of the work of restoration and order in the cathedral and other churches of the land.

End of separate clerical taxation.

To consider first the period of disaster and recovery, we must observe how heavily the weight of distress had fallen on the Church and the nation. In 1665 London, and the country in a less degree, was devastated by the great plague, a visitation more terrible than any

The plague, 1665.

since the Middle Ages. During the whole of the horrors of that terrible time, Sheldon remained at Lambeth, and by charitable distribution preserved many lives, while, says Le Neve, " by his affecting letters to all the bishops [he] procured great sums to be returned out of all parts of his province." The Bishop of London worked hard to keep up the spiritual provision so urgently needed. Letters of the time speak of him as threatening with expulsion pastors who left their flocks; and it is clear that in the absence of some of the clergy the nonconforming ministers often did a noble work. Baxter's pamphlet of spiritual instruction was widely circulated. All over the country there were the same tales of horror and distress ; and, no less, of the simple heroism of the ministers of God. The great fire which followed destroyed a large number of churches, and St. Paul's was burnt almost to the ground. Sancroft, then dean, preached a striking sermon, which he called *Lex ignea, or the School of Righteousness*, before the king, full of solemn appeal ; and Dr. Hardy, of St. Martin's-in-the-Fields, made the fire the occasion for a vigorous denunciation of the national sins.

The fire of London, 1666.

It was long before the churches were rebuilt. Hardly, indeed, had the work of re-edification imposed by the Civil War been half carried out before this new demand came upon the liberality of church folks. It was nobly responded to. The reign of Charles II. was a great age of church restoration. Almost every cathedral church had been dismantled, many had been practically destroyed, during the war. Salisbury was a bright exception. There the loyal gentry had, during the whole time when there was no bishop or dean, kept their fabric in good order at their own cost. But in most places all that savoured of bishops had perished. The fact that the chapel which Laud had built at Abergwili was an essential part of the house preserved it from destruction, but the ancient Episcopal chapel at Auckland Castle was utterly destroyed. St. Paul's, as a sermon of the period says, was debased, defiled, and almost ruined during the Commonwealth, being made " at once a den of thieves and a stable for beasts." The necessary work was at once put in hand. Sheldon himself gave

Church restoration.

The restoration of St. Paul's.

over £4000 before and after the fire.   On April 18, 1663, a commission was issued to Sir John Robinson, Lord Mayor of London, the Archbishops of Canterbury and York, Lord Chancellor Clarendon, Lord Treasurer Southampton, and numerous other persons to employ, for the repair of St. Paul's, the arrears of church moneys granted to certain trustees for that purpose, and empowering them to keep a register to receive voluntary contributions from the nobility, clergy, etc. All the money was to be paid to Sir John Cutler, appointed receiver ; it included a proportion of the fines in the pre-rogative courts, etc., and that obtained by briefs for a general collection.   The committee were to view the decays of the church, estimate the repairs required, inquire into all moneys subscribed for the church under former commissions, into the embezzlement of bells, ornaments, etc., belonging to it, and to compel composition or payment; to take charge of materials brought for the work, attend to the accounts, agree on a form of patent for collections in that behalf, appoint ordinances for its future preservation, and to treat of all matters for furtherance of the great work.

This summary shows that extensive work was intended even before the fire.   Some progress seems to have been made.   Considerable sums were collected ; and only a week before the fire the dean had summoned a number of repre-sentative churchmen to discuss the needed restoration of " that ancient and venerable church."   Evelyn, who wrote this in his diary, says that the design of a great cupola was already in Wren's mind and his own.   The fire gave the great opportunity ; and the first stone of the new work, en-trusted to the greatest of English architects, whose design was chosen by the dean because it was " the most awful and artificial," was laid in 1675.   Twenty-five years later the masterpiece was completed.   To Sancroft, Sheldon, and Henchman belongs the credit of choosing " a design hand-some and noble and suitable to all the ends of it and to the reputation of the city and nation."   In generous contribution the dean rivalled the archbishop, and Parliament made the great work possible by putting a tax on every chaldron of coal brought to the port of London, and giving the proceeds to the cathedral church.

Throughout England meanwhile the work of church restoration had proceeded. One typical instance may suffice. It
was on Christmas eve, 1669, that Bishop Hacket dedicated
the restored cathedral church of Lichfield, "with
all fitting solemnity," says his biographer, "that he
could pick out of ancient rituals." He had found
it desolate and ruined; the roof off, the lead and timber, the
stalls and glass, all gone; and the very day after his arrival
he set his coach-horses to work to clear away the rubbish.
On the restoration over £20,000 was spent, a great part of
which came from Hacket's own munificence.

Lichfield cathedral church.

The officers of the restored Church indeed showed no
lack of gratitude; it was the very characteristic of Sheldon's
primacy that the clergy were generous in giving to the church.
The archbishop himself set the example. It was calculated,
by one who was not naturally his eulogist, that he gave in his
lifetime £72,000 "to public pious uses." Unhappily his
memory, with little justice, has been linked with the most
bitter of the retaliatory measures of those who restored the
Church. Popular feeling, so strongly represented in Parliament, had its way; and the blame was cast unfairly on the
clergy.

The nature of the opposition by which the Church was still
met, and which may account for, though it does not excuse,
the severity of the legislation, may be judged from
the scandalous and indecent pamphlets published
under the name of Ralph Wallis the Cobbler of
Gloucester, which contain a collection of libels against the
clergy of the neighbourhood unsurpassed for foulness. It was
some satisfaction, doubtless, to the Church party that they
were able to answer the "Room for the Cobbler of Gloucester
and his wife with several cartloads of abominable irregular
pitiful stinking priests" (1668), by "the Life and Death of
Ralph Wallis" in 1670; but there are many pamphlets of the
same sort, if not so outrageous, which show the bitterness of
sectarian feeling and the indecency of its expression. Popular
writing of this kind was just what would affect a House of
Commons composed of men still smarting under the losses
inflicted by the war, and resentful of the days of subjection to
a ministry of local artisans. The feeling is represented in

Coarse attacks on the Church.

Butler's *Hudibras*, the wittiest expression of popular dislike of the insincerity and the ludicrousness of Puritan excess. But the dislike, and its manifestations, naturally went deeper.

The hot fit of cavalier loyalty was largely made up of bitter resentment against those who had oppressed and impoverished the country gentry and replaced the ancient services of the Church, to the great discontent of the edu- cated laity, by extemporary services of varying character. Unhappily the clergy were not averse from the spirit which moved the Commons, though most of the bishops showed much personal kindness to the conscientious dissenters. A petition was addressed to Parliament, which is preserved among the Tanner MSS., for repression of the Anabaptists, for an increase of the shilling fine on those who did not attend church, for the improvement of small livings, and the like. The Parliament dealt with Church questions in a very drastic temper. Like the loyalist Parliaments of Henry IV., it regarded dissenters as a political danger; like the leaders of the Long Parliament it attached great importance to tales of plots which were probably no real danger to the Government; and it showed itself much more solicitous for the Church's power than was the Church herself. In 1664 an Act was passed against conventicles, which became known as the First Conventicle Act. By this, every person who should be present at a religious service other "than is allowed by the liturgy or practice of the Church of England," was made liable to fine and imprisonment, and on a third conviction to trans- portation. The power under this Act was placed in the hands of the justices of the peace, who were often in- competent to exercise it with any pretence of consideration; but it seems that the Anabaptists and Quakers, whom Pres- byterians and Independents, no less than churchmen, regarded as noxious enemies of the Christian faith, were the chief sufferers by the Act.

This was, however, only a beginning. In 1666 was passed the "Five Mile Act," levelled directly against the dissenting ministers who had not subscribed the Act of Uniformity. It directed that all such should take the oath against the lawfulness of bearing arms against

Legislation against dissenters.

The persecut- ing Acts.

Conventicle Act, 1664.

The Five Mile Act, 1666.

the king, and against endeavouring alteration in Church or State, or they were not to "come or be" within five miles of any town in which they had acted as "parson, vicar, or lecturer," etc. The Act was obviously a purely political one, as no religious test was demanded, and the Parliament might claim that if it pressed hardly on the deprived ministers it could only be because they were enemies to the political settlement which the majority of the nation supported. But though the argument would be strictly true, the Act, like all other inquisitorial measures, was a grave infringement of true liberty of conscience, religious as well as political; because religion and politics could not truly be separated in the mind of a religious man of Charles II.'s day.

It is certain that some of the bishops, notably Earle, Bishop of Salisbury, opposed the Act; Burnet says that Sheldon and Ward "acted and argued most for it." The king still spoke, as at the opening of Parliament in 1667, in favour of toleration of the dissenters; but the House of Commons was obdurate, and petitioned for a more strict enforcement of the law against them. The Lord Keeper Bridgeman had an interview with Baxter, probably by Charles's orders, with a view to a scheme of comprehension for the Presbyterians and of toleration for the Independents. Baxter proposed that all who had been ordained by forms other than those of the Church should be admitted to be ministers by the following form: "Take thou legal authority to preach the Word of God and administer the holy Sacraments in any congregation of England where thou shalt be lawfully appointed thereunto." Ceremonies were to be "left indifferent and the liturgy altered." Dr. Wilkins, who represented a new body in the Church, which came to be called the "Latitude men," agreed with these proposals; but, again, the House of Commons would not hear of them, though they had the support of the noble lawyer, Sir Matthew Hale.

None the less the nonconformists remained strong in the country. Calamy's list of the deprived ministers shows how wide was their influence, and a letter of the time says that in some places the dissenters had "arrived at such insolence as to break open church doors and get into the churches, to vent their sedition and rebellion."

Amount of nonconformity.

A violent literary controversy also sprang up in which eminent writers on both sides took part, notably Simon Patrick, whose *Friendly Debate* represented a churchman arguing with a dissenter with much success. Its large sale showed that the Church had the popular ear. Samuel Parker's *Ecclesiastical Polity* was an able and witty defence of a completely Erastian theory which confuted dissent on the ground that the king had an absolute power over religion. But neither local disputes nor literary controversy disturbed the judgment of the Royalist Parliament. A proposal that the king should be empowered to arrange a new conference was re- The Cabal jected by 176 to 70 in the Commons; and the Ministry, Ministry of the Cabal, though for a time it procured 1667. the non-enforcement of the laws against dissenters, was quite unsuccessful in its endeavour to secure political aid by this means. Charles indeed was tending more distinctly than before to acceptance of Roman Catholicism. Secret negotiations had long been conducted with Rome, though with tepid interest on either side. The formal alliance with Louis XIV. was more serious: though the public knew nothing definite of its religious objects, they were at least suspected.

In 1670 the Second Conventicle Act greatly increased the distress of the dissenters, for though its penalties were not quite so severe, it was much more stringent in its inquisition. It was the last formal Act against Protestant noncon-formists, and the support of it by Sheldon and Ward shows that the bishops were willing to go far indeed towards persecution.

The Cabal Ministry was unpopular in Parliament, and their attempt to gain support by a policy of toleration was quite unsuccessful. Towards such a policy they were led by external no less than internal considerations. In 1669 Charles found himself obliged to return to his alliance with France, and this implied that some toleration should be granted to Roman Catholics in England. The Charles's king himself became more and more strongly in- leanings clined towards that faith, and he prepared to make Rome. a definite agreement with Louis XIV. on the understanding that he should declare his conversion to Romanism. A long negotiation led to the Treaty of Dover, 1670, by which it was

agreed that a war with Holland should be followed by a
Declaration of Indulgence and by the king's acknowledgment
of his change of faith. Of all this Parliament and the country
were in entire ignorance, and they were certain to break out
in fury so soon as the secret should become known. Nor
was there any real bond of union in the Ministry. They
were agreed only, as Von Ranke says, in the desire to strengthen
the royal prerogative by moderating the Uniformity laws, with
the help of France, and during the excitement caused by a
foreign war. In religion their views were widely divergent.
Lauderdale was a Presbyterian ; Ashley, what was then called a
philosopher ; Buckingham, if he had any opinions at all,
an Independent ; Arlington, a moderate Romanist ; Clifford,
a zealous one. Ashley, the friend of Locke, and Buckingham, a debauchee, who professed a sympathy with the
Puritans, were anxious to lessen the power of the Church
and to give toleration to the dissenters : in this Lauderdale,
from the point of view of a Scots Presbyterian, agreed.
Clifford and Arlington, on the other hand, had for chief idea
the reunion with Rome. Arlington suggested three points
as necessary in an agreement—the security of the ecclesiastical estates that had passed into lay hands, communion in
both kinds, and the introduction of English hymns at mass.
Little did any of them understand the temper of the Parliament and the people.

On March 15, 1672, the king issued a new Declaration of
Indulgence, which showed his persistence in a policy of
toleration. It was suspected that its aim was
solely to benefit the Romanists, but on the face of
it, it was a just and wise offer. The clergy of the
Church were required exactly to obey the Prayer-
book, but it suspended all penal laws against dissenters,
allowing Protestants to meet in public, and Romanists in
private. Determined to retain to the full the powers exercised
by the Long Parliament, the House of Commons
at once requested the king to recall his declaration
as illegal, and to his reply, claiming his act as a
natural consequence of his ecclesiastical power,
answered as follows : "Your Majesty having claimed a power
to suspend penal statutes in matters ecclesiastical, and which

*Declara-
tion of
Indulgence,
1672.*

*Condemned
as illegal
by Parlia-
ment.*

your Majesty does still seem to assert in the said answer to
be entrusted in the crown, and never questioned in the reigns of
any of your ancestors: in this we humbly conceive your Majesty
hath been very much misinformed, since no such power was
ever claimed or exercised by any of your Majesty's predecessors; and, if it should be admitted, might tend to the
interrupting the free course of the laws, and altering the legislative powers, which have always been acknowledged to reside
in your Majesty and in your two Houses of Parliament."
The king was forced to withdraw his declaration, and the
hope of toleration was at an end.

The attempt indeed made the country full of suspicion,
and Parliament passed the Test Act 1673, to guard against
the repetition of the danger. The aim of the Act,
it is clear, was entirely political, and directed against   The Test
the Romanists. It ordered that in "future no one   Act 1673.
should be admitted to any office or public position unless he
abjured the doctrine of transubstantiation and declared that
in the sacrament after consecration there is the substance of
bread and wine." The Act was one of those many in English
history (like the anti-Lollard statutes) which were intended far
more for the convenience of the State than for the benefit of
the Church. There were political reasons for it, but there
was no religious demand for it. And in its effects on Church
order it was disastrous. By it nonconformists had   Its effects.
to qualify for office, and the receiving of certificates
from the clergy was in every way a most offensive and impo-
litic abuse. By the Test Act the selfishly Anglican Parliament
raised up hundreds of enemies to the Church, and definitely
committed the dissenters to political opposition. The
Commons were ready to pass a toleration Bill for Protestant
dissenters, but the Lords refused it. Charles openly scoffed.
When the Test Act was passed he said that he would purge his
court of all Catholics except his barber, whom he would keep
in spite of all their Bills. A prorogation of Parliament soon
after the Duke of York's papist marriage, and the dismissal of
Shaftesbury, caused the new nonconformist and anti-Catholic
party to become of great importance. Shaftesbury had already
made friends with the Protestant and patriotic party, and
throughout the year 1673 was preparing for his dismissal by

announcing himself as the avowed enemy of the papists, and in danger of attack from them.   On November 9, 1673, he was dismissed : before three weeks were over the king and the French ambassador, Ruvigny, had endeavoured to win him back, but failed ; and when Parliament met on January 7, 1674, he was at the head of a party which was determined to stop the growth of papist influence.   Shaftesbury moved an address to the king, desiring that a proclamation might be issued ordering all papists and reputed papists, except householders and peers' servants, to withdraw ten miles from London.

The French ambassador thus reported his speech : " Lord Shaftesbury made a speech to excite the assembly, saying that he knew well there were in the suburbs of London more than 16,000 Catholics who were resolved to strike a desperate blow, and that no one could be sure of his life while such people were in liberty at the gates of the city, and that it was necessary to think seriously of the means of preventing a massacre which might take place any day."

This was the beginning of the great anti-papist agitation which — in the hands of its originators almost entirely a political trick—sacrificed so many innocent lives and nearly overturned the monarchy.   The address was agreed to, and the king was requested to order a day of fasting.   So vehement was the language of the party that the king prorogued Parliament on February 24.   When the Houses reassembled in 1675 Shaftesbury led the opposition to the new Test Bill, by which a further declaration of passive obedience was to be required from every officer of Church and State.   Nothing of any very great importance happened for some time, owing to the prorogations of Parliament, and in February 1677 Shaftesbury, by a mistaken argument that the Parliament was in reality dissolved, got himself into trouble, and was imprisoned in the Tower for a year for contempt of the House.   He returned to public life in February 1678, at the very height of Danby's power and the king's success.   After four years' strenuous advocacy of the claims of the Duke of Monmouth, Charles's reputed son, as a Protestant candidate, and after encouraging the worst excesses of the popish plot, Shaftesbury found the tide turned, and he fled the country.

Influence of Shaftesbury.

While these events were happening, Sheldon died at Lambeth, on November 9, 1677. To the surprise of many, William Sancroft, Dean of St. Paul's, was his successor. It was said that James, Duke of York, recommended him to his brother, as less vehement in his Protestantism than most of the prominent ecclesiastics of the day, but there was never any doubt of the sincerity of his attachment to the Church of England. He had refused the bishopric of Chester in 1668, being determined to devote himself entirely to the restoration of his cathedral church. In that great undertaking nothing, great or small, was done without his sanction. It was now so far advanced that it was possible for him to withdraw without harm to the work. As archbishop, he showed the qualities of gentleness and consideration which his predecessor had lacked. Dryden describes him as

Sancroft, Abp. of Canterbury, 1678-91.

> Zadock the priest, whom, shunning power and place,
> His lowly mind advanced to David's grace.

He was consecrated in Westminster Abbey on January 27, 1678. One of his first acts was a strenuous but ineffectual effort to bring back the Duke of York to the English Church. A few weeks later the terrors of the Popish Plot distracted the country; and nothing was thought of but "the Church and king in danger."

Nothing shows more clearly the disturbed condition of English feeling, the wild unrest which the Rebellion had fostered and the persecution of dissenters had increased, than the miserable history of the Popish Plot. "For months the whole town," as Burnet says, "was inflamed." The king, it seems, was one of the few people who saw from the first that Titus Oates, who came forward with an elaborate story, was a liar; but he declared that this did not prove the whole plot imaginary. Parliament, and indeed the whole country, was led away, and innocent blood was shed like water to appease the popular terror. Sir Edmund Berry Godfrey, justice of the peace for Westminster, a zealous Protestant and "esteemed the best justice in England," was found murdered; and there were rumours of the lives of noted preachers being sought. One account

The Popish Plot, 1678.

of the plot says that " Doctor Stillingfleet haveing beene attempted by a fellowe in a gentile habitt, who brought a counterfeit letter, as from the Bp. of London, to desire him to come to him in the evening, and brought a coach to carry him, intending to have served him as Sir Edm. Godfrey was, but was prevented ; partly an extraordinary businesse would not permit him to go out, and partly jealousie, which made the Doctor answer him—if hee could goe hee would make use of his owne coach, which made the fellow vanish, and the Doctor waiteing on the Bishop the next day, found the letter and pretence wholly counterfeit. Thereupon, on Sunday, about 40 persons as guard waited on the Doctor to church and home." It is an illuminative picture of the terrors of the time. Bishop Herbert Croft published his sermons on Popery in 1679 as a "legacy to his diocese," evidently in great fear of death from the Jesuits. The pulpits rang with the denunciation of Popery : but the clergy took no active part in pressing the plot. It is certain that there was a real Roman Catholic conspiracy in 1678. Charles at the moment was the great impediment in the way of the realisation of the Romanist hopes, which centred round the Duke of York. Sir Edmund Berry Godfrey knew of a secret meeting of the Jesuits at the duke's house, and it is possible that they were concerned in his murder. But the more moderate Romanists took no part. The wiser and more charitable observers, like Gilbert Burnet, saw that, so far as the mass of the papists were concerned, it was an invention ; but it was used even by Sancroft in his sermon before the Peers, November 13, 1678, as an occasion for strong language against the Jesuits as "devils of sedition and faction, of fraud and rebellion."

One of the most deplorable results of the national frenzy was seen in the action of Parliament, which was as eagerly anti-Popish as it was anti-Puritan ; and the Bill

Results of the Plot.

which was passed by the Commons required (in Burnet's words) "all members of either House, and all such as might come into the King's court or presence to take a test against Popery ; in which not only transubstantiation was renounced, but the worship of the Virgin Mary and the Saints, as it was practised in the Church of Rome, was declared to be idolatrous." Evelyn

records that even in the Commons "several good Protestants scrupled" at the charge of idolatry against the
Roman Catholics, and Bishop Gunning argued against it
in the House of Lords. But eventually the test was
accepted, and even Gunning took it, "though he wished it had
been otherwise worded." The Duke of York only was
exempted. A proposal to exclude him from the succession
was long debated : and in the midst of the confusion Danby,
the king's chief minister, who had given a tacit support to the
Church, was impeached.

To this the public interest gradually turned ; and the trial
was found to involve a point of constitutional usage of some
interest to the Church. Had the bishops the right
to vote in a trial for treason, if not in the judgment   The bishops
at least in the preliminaries? Burnet says that, in   *and the
impeachment
of Danby.*
face of the strong feeling of the House of Commons,
they were willing to abandon their right ; but it is more
probable that their feeling was due to a doubt of their position
by canon law. Anyhow, the king would not suffer them to
withdraw ; and Burnet says "he was so set on maintaining the
pardon [which he had given Danby] that he could not venture
such a point to the votes of the temporal lords ; and he told
the bishops that they must stick to him, and to his prerogative,
as they would expect that he should stick to them if they came
to be pushed at." Dr. Stillingfleet, one of the most learned
writers as well as famous preachers of the day, distinguished
himself by his advocacy of the bishops' constitutional rights.
The decision at which the House of Lords arrived was that
the lords spiritual have the right to stay in questions of blood
till the vote of guilty or not guilty is taken, a conclusion which
repeats that of the Constitutions of Clarendon and represents
the rule of canon law.

The unpopularity of the minister who was believed to be
concerned in a base subservience to France was reflected on
the bishops, whom the king had commanded to support him.
And the nonconformists (again to follow Burnet) took occasion
to sharpen their attacks upon the Church. A literary warfare
burst out in which some of the clergy, by "the heat of their
tempers and the hope of preferment, were driven to many extravagances," from whom, however, Burnet admits that several

good men stood aside. The Exclusion Bill, which designed
the exclusion of James Duke of York from the crown, was a
project which affected the Church, men declared, at least as
much as the State. Thus a witty speaker expressed the
situation : "You shall have the Protestant religion,
you shall have what you will to protect you, but you
must have a popish king who shall command your
armies and navies, make your bishops and judges. Suppose
there were a lion in the lobby, one cries, 'Shut the door and
keep him out.' 'No,' says another, 'open the door and let us
chain him when he comes in.'" When the Bill came to the
Lords, all the bishops in the House voted against it. But the
feeling remained no less hot against the papists : and naturally
it was followed by something of a reaction in favour of the
Protestant dissenters. The House of Commons passed a
resolution that the recusancy laws ought only to be carried out
against Romanists, and another that the laws against dissenters
ought not to be executed.

The Exclusion Bill, 1681.

The Parliament at Oxford in March 1681 was dissolved
without any discussion of Church questions. After the dissolution the king put forth a declaration to explain his
action, and in it he reiterated his "affection to the Protestant religion, as established by law." This declaration
was to be read in all churches, Burnet says, at Sancroft's
proposal. It might be taken at least to reassure the
people on the part of the king that the Church establishment would be undisturbed. Nor can it be said that some
such security was unnecessary. Negotiations with Rome were
suspected by many, and it now became certain that Charles
would have a Romanist successor. And, on the other side,
the dissenters were active. Typical of the unrest, shown also
in a thick crop of pamphlet literature, is a letter
(among the Tanner MSS.) to Bishop Lamplugh of
Exeter, complaining of a training school of "factious
and seditious preachers" at Lyme Regis, and asking
for a commission from the king (for the place was a peculiar)
to the Archbishop of Canterbury to visit, "as he did effectually
visit Poole, which hath wrought good reformation there": the
chief preacher was Ames Short, and the letter adds a copy of
the articles of communion, or new covenant, signed by his

Unrest and disturbance in the country.

followers. With plots on every side, with "petitioners" to the king to summon Parliament and "abhorrers" of any such interference with his prerogative dividing the country, and rumours of conspiracies and even of civil war, the interests of the Church seemed for the time to be subordinated entirely to politics; and the impression is confirmed when we read the declaration published after the Rye House Plot. In this the principle of non-resistance, or passive obedience, was formally inculcated; and it appeared to be fully accepted. It was indeed the doctrine which both the experience of the war and the philosophy of Hobbes seemed to enforce. A new experience, and a new philosophy, were soon to discredit it.

The execution of William Lord Russell for his share in a plot which was assumed to have the king's death for object, was an emphatic assertion of the view which the clergy upheld. "He died," as Von Ranke says, "for the right of resistance, which had become to him a sort of religion," "behaving himself," said the Duke of York, "like a stout man but not like a good Christian." On the same day (July 21, 1683) the University of Oxford formally condemned "certain pernicious books and damnable doctrines." Among them was Hobbes's *Leviathan*, which was condemned because it based the conclusion of non-resistance on premises which were most unorthodox to the mind of the university. It seemed as if confusion were over everything. Only those saw clearly who, like Burnet, wished for salvation in a monarchy of strictly limited powers, or who, like Sancroft, thought all active resistance a sin.

Condemnation of Hobbes's *Leviathan*, 1683.

That Sancroft could act boldly in Church matters was shown in April 1684 by his suspension of Wood, Bishop of Lichfield, for gross neglect of his duties. Eighteen years before, when he had been dean of Lichfield five years, his bishop, Hacket, spoke of him as "the phrenetique who sides altogether with Puritans, and told me to my face I did more harm than good in re-edifying this church," and was anxious that the Bishop of Durham might oblige him to keep his residence as prebend of Durham, and thus "call off our most untractable and filthy natured dean." He had made court to the Duchess of Cleveland and through her obtained in 1671, on Hacket's

Suspension of the Bp. of Lichfield, 1684.

death, the bishopric of the diocese in which he had been found so troublesome. As favoured by the court he doubt less thought his position secure, but Sancroft, though he held extreme views of the duty of obedience in politics, never hesi tated in a matter of ecclesiastical duty. The instrument of suspension, which is preserved in Sancroft's register, was read in Lambeth Palace Chapel on July 19, 1684 : and the Bishop of Lichfield remained under suspension for two years.

Similarly, the archbishop altogether declined to sanction a pardon, about which the king wrote to him, to the Archdeacon of Lincoln, who had been convicted of simony. Thus exact in his ecclesiastical duty, Sancroft refrained altogether from intervention in politics : a letter of his on the subject of the formation of a European Protestant League is an admirable example of wise counsel.

As the king's reign drew to an end there were signs of change everywhere. Burnet records the death of many bishops and the increase of persecution of dissenters, who were proceeded against "not only for going to conventicles, but for not going to church, and for not receiving the sacrament ; the laws made against papists with relation to these particulars being now applied to them."

On a sudden came the end which all England had dreaded Charles's life seemed to many the only thing that stood between the kingdom and Popery or civil war. In the midst of a life of "inexpressible luxury and profaneness, gaming and all dissoluteness, and, as it were, total forgetfulness of God"—so Evelyn describes the last Sunday of the king's life—Charles was struck down by apoplexy. Bishops hurried into the crowded sick-room. Eye witnesses have preserved vivid details of the last days of Charles II. Sancroft "made a weighty exhortation, in which he used a good deal of freedom." Ken, then Bishop of Bath and Wells, spoke "as one inspired," and he took some broken words of acknowledgment of sin to justify the absolution. But a few hours later all the bishops were turned from the room, and Charles ended his miserable life with a death-bed declaration of his conversion to the Church of Rome.

If, so long as he lived, Charles never turned from his evil ways, it was certainly not for want of clear language of ex-

Death of
Charles II.,
Feb. 6, 1685.

hortation.   Nothing, for example, could be stronger or more
pointed than Stillingfleet's sermon preached before
the king on February 24, 1675, and "printed by his   His
Majesty's special command" on "Lest any of you be   character.
hardened through the deceitfulness of sin."   Very clear and
plain indeed was the language, and it was not heeded at all.
Sermons on Christian evidences and faith were equally common,
and equally disregarded.   Sheldon and Sancroft had both
spoken clearly to him.   Frampton had directly addressed him
in a sermon, and Charles had told him, "that I cannot allow of."
Ken had refused to give up his house to his mistress, Nell
Gwyn, when she came with him to Winchester.   There was
no lack of warning and plain speaking : but Charles made a
mock of all.   At one moment he would gravely reprove
Frampton for saying that atheism was tolerated at Court.   At
another he replied to Lord Halifax, who had told him that he
was "the head of his church," "that he did not desire to be
the head of anything, for indeed he was of no church."   His
was a pitiable end ; but men hoped there was a death-bed
repentance.

With the death of Charles II. the end of an epoch in the
history of the English Church is distinctly marked.   Protestant
dissent had come to be clearly recognised as a fact
in English religious life.   The Church had passed   Character of
through a fiery trial and had had time to reconsider   the Church
the bases on which her reformation had been   his reign.
founded.   Thus, with full deliberation she had reiterated her
conviction that it was essential to the fulness of church life
that the threefold ministry should be continued and reverently
used and esteemed ; and that only those could be her lawful
ministers who had received Episcopal ordination.   The Presbyterian theory of Church government had been thoroughly
weighed and was rejected, and the Independent system had
found even less favour.   The established doctrines and laudable practices of the whole Catholic Church of Christ were
adhered to.   The English Church stood firm against the
influence of Geneva or of Scotland.   Was this an approximation towards the Roman position ?   Was there a prospect of
reunion, or of submission ?   This was the question which the
next reign was to solve.

AUTHORITIES.—State Papers, Domestic, in the Record Office ; Guizot, *Life of Monk*, with the documents appended ; Tanner MSS., in the Bodleian Library ; Calamy, *Abridgment of Baxter's Life ;* Burnet, *History of his Life and Times*, ed. Osmund Airy ; Cardwell, *Conferences ;* Sheldon MSS., in Bodleian Library ; Dolben Papers ; Clarendon Papers ; Lathbury, *History of Convocation ;* Lords' *Journals*, vol. xi. ; *Canmore's Journals*, vol. viii. With regard to the revision of the Prayer-book there is a whole literature of investigation, history, and reprint, the results of which are usefully summarised in the *History of the Prayer-book*, by Procter and Frere (1901), additional note, pp. 204, 205 ; see also Cosin, *Works*, vol. v., and *Correspondence*. The original MS. of the Prayer-book as subscribed by Convocation was published in facsimile, 1891 ; Bishop Samuel Parker's *Commentarii* (translated as *History of his own Time*, by T. Newlin, 1727) ; Clarendon's *Life ;* Salmon, *Examination of Burnet* (1724) ; D'Oyly, *Life of Sancroft ;* Historical MSS. Commission, XIV Report, Appendix 10, part 2 ; *Life of Robert Frampton*, edited by Evans, 1876. On the Popish Plot, see *The whole series of all that hath been transacted in the House of Peers concerning the Popish Plot*, London, 1681, and a thorough examination in *The Popish Plot*, by John Pollock, 1903. The sermons quoted (which have not hitherto received the attention they deserve as showing the trend of popular opinion) are *David's Deliverance and Thanksgiving*, Sheldon, 1660 ; *Healing the Hurts of the Nation*, Gauden, 1660 ; *Lex Ignea*, Sancroft, 1666 ; *Lamentation, Mourning, and Woe*, Hardy, 1666 ; *A Sermon before the King, February* 24, 1675, Stillingfleet, 1675 ; *The Legacy of the Right Reverend Father in God, Herbert, Lord Bishop of Hereford, to his Diocese, or a short determination of all controversies we have with the Papists*, 1679 ; *A Sermon preached to the House of Peers*, Nov. 13, 1678, Sancroft, 1678. Among modern books, Perry, *History of the Church of England ;* Plumptre, *Life of Ken ;* Stoughton, *Church of the Restoration ;* L. von Ranke, *History of England chiefly in the Seventeenth Century ;* Foxcroft, *Life of George Savile, Earl of Halifax*.

CHAPTER XII

THE ROMAN PROJECT AND THE REVOLUTION

THE suspicion with which James had long been regarded
seemed to disappear as soon as he became king.   In the few
words he spoke to his council when he took the
oaths, he declared that " he would endeavour to
maintain the government both in Church and State,
as by law established, its principles being so firm for monarchy,
and the members of it showing themselves so good and loyal
subjects, that he would always take care to defend and support the Church of England."   The words were written down,
the king approved them, and they were circulated throughout
the country, and received with an unbounded enthusiasm.
Typical of the Church's relief was the address from the
diocese of Bath and Wells.   They had sown in tears, they said,
and reaped in joy.   James had replaced his brother as "a
most tender nursing father to the Church and people of
England," which, they added, "to our unspeakable consolation,
does illustriously appear in that auspicious promise your
Majesty has made, of protecting our established religion, the
greatest concern we have in this world."

The Church, indeed, felt that it deserved the king's support
and favour.   That the clergy had remained firm in adherence
to the right of hereditary succession was unquestionably one
of the chief causes of the failure of the Exclusion Bill.   It
might well have seemed that James must know the strength
of the Church and the wisdom of making no attacks upon
her.   But he was injudicious as well as conscientious, and it
was not long before he showed that he was a Romanist heart

*The welcome
to James II.,
1685.*

and soul, and eager to proselytise. The second Sunday after
his accession he went in state to the Roman mass. When the
Duke of Norfolk, who bore the sword of state before him,
stopped at the door, James said : " My lord, your father would
have gone farther." " Your Majesty's father would not have
gone so far," was the duke's answer. Within a few days the
publication of some papers warmly advocating the claims of
the Roman Church, which were said to have been found in a
strong box of the late king's, showed the new king's desire for
the conversion of England. James, a few days later, repeated
his promise, but with a significant warning to Archbishop
Sancroft, and Compton, Bishop of London. " My lords, I
will keep my word, and will undertake nothing against the
religion established by law, assuming that you do your duty
towards me ; but if you fail therein you must not expect that
I shall protect you. I shall readily find the means of attain-
ing my ends without your help."

Two months later, when the coronation was solemnised
with maimed rites, there being no communion, the king's
isolation from the national sympathies was again emphatically
asserted. Yet when James met his first Parliament
he repeated his assurance of favour and defence of
the Church. This was on May 19. In less than
a month the king had to meet a rebellion against his throne.

*His
coronation.*

On June 11, 1685, the Duke of Monmouth landed at
Lyme Regis. His supporters put him forward as a true
adherent of the Church of England, and his rebellion
as a crusade against Popery. But the king's speeches
and declarations had for the time stilled all sus-
picions ; and foremost among those who opposed the insur-
rectionary force was the old cavalier, Peter Mews, Bishop of
Winchester, as stout a loyalist as he was firm in the church
principles of Laud. The clergy to a man refused to accept
Monmouth as a deliverer. His troops, when they were driven
back on Wells, spoilt the cathedral church of its lead roof,
and did other damage. The chapter book, under date of
July 1, 1685, thus records the sad work : " The civil war still
grows. This cathedral church has suffered very grievously from
the rebel fanatics, who have this very morning laid hands upon
the furniture thereof, have almost utterly destroyed the organ,

*Monmouth's
rebellion.*

and turned the sacred building into a stable for horses." It seemed to the clergy as if a Puritan rebellion had come again. But it did not last long. Within a month its leader was a prisoner, and on July 15 he was beheaded on Tower Hill.

From the ecclesiastical point of view there are many curious illustrations in the insurrection of contemporary Church life. Monmouth, as was natural in the case of a man of life so notoriously profligate, conspicuously failed to win the support, at any stage of his ambitious career, of prominent churchmen. He posed as a Protestant champion, received a Bible from the little maids of Taunton, and was always very scrupulous in going to church. But his religion went no further. He was declared to have preached during his last campaign, but he assured Tenison of the contrary: " 'No,' said the Duke, 'I never preached; nobody preached but Ferguson, and he very foolishly many times. That man,' says he, 'is a bloody villain.' "

The Ferguson in question was a hack writer, who had been turned out of his living for nonconformity, and was a plotter of base type. In fact, though Monmouth at the last claimed to be a defender of the Church of England, his career did not support the claim. When he visited Chester in 1682, the mob who favoured him signalised their affection by breaking into the cathedral church, destroying the windows, mutilating the monuments and the font, and tearing up the vestments, completing their entertainment by drinking damnation to the king and the Duke of York. When at Chichester the preacher took for his text, "For rebellion is as the sin of witchcraft," etc. (1 Sam. xv. 23), Monmouth in haste departed from the unwelcome and appropriate discourse. Church and king were alike the enemies of the bastard duke. In prison and on the scaffold Ken and others endeavoured to make him acknowledge his sin in taking up arms against the sovereign, but he would not answer them according to their wish. That they at least were consistent was to be proved before long.

Congratulatory addresses poured in from every side; and Jeffreys brutally executed the king's vengeance on the deluded rebels. Alice Lisle, the widow of a regicide and member of Cromwell's house of lords, was one of those who suffered in the bitter persecution. She

The results of the rebellion.

had sheltered a dissenting minister named Hickes, who had fled to her Hampshire house from Sedgmoor, and though there was no proof of any complicity or sympathy on her part with the rebellion, she was condemned and executed as a traitor. At the Revolution the attainder was set aside on the ground that "the verdict was injuriously extorted and procured by the menaces and violences and other illegal practices" of the Lord Chief Justice. The rebellion was made the occasion of searching for nonconformist ministers and suppressing conventicles. Lord Clarendon, the king's brother-in-law, wrote that he was assured at Coventry, "that there has not been a conventicle in this town for above a year, and that executing the law upon nonconformists in making them pay has brought them all to Church."

James now thought that he was secure on the throne and could proceed at once to action. Charles II. had long designed a reunion with Rome, and took money from France to prepare it ; but he had so far as possible kept his project secret. James was of another mould. He was obstinate and headstrong. It began to be said openly that all tests must be repealed ; and the clergy, says Burnet, began to open their eyes. On November 9 Parliament reassembled, Alarm at the king's action. and the king informed them that in the necessary increase of the forces he had employed officers who had not complied with the provisions of the Test Act. The House of Commons addressed the king in protest against his action, and Henry Compton, Bishop of London, moved in the House of Lords to appoint a day to take the king's speech into consideration. James in haste prorogued the Parliament.

The temper of the nation was shown by the eagerness and generosity with which subscriptions were provided for the sufferers by the Revocation of the Edict of Nantes ; National Protestantism. and no less by a marked revival of controversial teaching. One of the first steps of James had been to prohibit preaching upon points of controversy. But no one heeded the order. The Romanists were working eagerly and openly, and the English clergy were not slow to reply. One of the most important disputes that occured was that between Dr. Thomas Tenison, rector of St. Martin's-in-the-Fields, and the head of the Jesuits then settled in the Savoy, who wrote under the name of Andrew Pulton. This produced a mass of pamphlets, of which the summary is to be found in " A true account of a conference held about religion, September 29, 1687, between A. Pulton, a Jesuit, and Tho. Tenison, D.D., as also of that which led to it and followed after it "; and " Mr. Pulton considered in his sincerity, reasonings, and authority." Tenison complained of attempts to convert his parishioners, and declared that he had been obliged to act on their behalf. He mentioned in passing a fact curious indeed if true, that during the Commonwealth " a Roman Catholic got in " to his father's benefice. James was pressing members of Parliament to agree to the repeal of the Test Act and the penal statutes; and the more those private interviews became known the more boldly, says Evelyn in his Diary, did the clergy preach " against their superstition and errors." And thus not one proselyte of importance was made. Ken preaching at Whitehall boldly attacked the Roman doctrines, and exhorted his hearers to remain steadfast in the English Church, " whose doctrine for Catholicism and soundness he preferred to all the communities and churches of Christians in the world."

While public feeling in England was thus heated by events within the land, it was further disturbed by sympathy with the Huguenots who had escaped from France. The Huguenot immigration. Many of these conformed to the Church so soon as they settled in England; as years went on they became an important Protestant influence, tending to the revival of Calvinist teaching, and from the first they served to stimulate the Protestant enthusiasm of the country. Some interest in this connection belongs to the somewhat later case of Nicholas Mallarhé, ordained by Richard Kidder, Bishop of Bath and Wells. Objection was made to him as having been a nonconformist, and as having exercised dissenting (Huguenot) ministry. He was a man sixty years of age, and a schoolmaster, and his object appears to have been to combine his teaching work with the holding of a benefice. The objections, which Kidder considered pedantic, were finally overruled, and he was ordained priest by the authority of two bishops.

While controversies of this kind were rife James took a further step by establishing a Court of High Commission, which it was clear was intended to deal with clergymen who

New Ecclesiastical Commission, 1686. withstood the action on which he was determined. Jeffreys, Lord Chancellor, was appointed to preside, and the king nominated as members the Archbishop of Canterbury and the Bishops of Durham (Lord Crewe) and Rochester (Sprat). Sancroft declined to serve, and though he gave as reason his great age and infirmities, he made public declaration that he could have no part in a spiritual commission of which a layman was the head. He had taken care minutely to examine the question of the legality of the Court, and decided against it. James, though he could not formally punish the refusal, contemplated summoning the archbishop before the commission for censure, and forbade him to come to court. When Sancroft recommended the famous preacher South for the bishopric of Oxford, James nominated Samuel Parker, once chaplain to Archbishop Sheldon, upon whom he thought he could rely. Lord Crewe had succeeded Compton as Dean of the Chapel Royal when the latter was dismissed for his speech in the House of Lords; and two other bishops were believed to be at least tolerant of the court policy. A first step, and one which was soon abandoned, was a renewal of persecution of the dissenters. Under this revived inquisition Baxter was tried by Jeffreys, who treated him with savage brutality, and sent him to prison.

James now took a further step, as it seemed, to legalise his action. The question of his power to dispense from the The dispensing power. obligations of the Test Act was brought before the judges in the case of Godden *v.* Hales, a collusive action brought against an officer in the army who had not taken the test, and the decision was in favour of the officer and really of the king. From that moment Romanists were everywhere appointed to office; and from the State James proceeded to attack the Church. Already several communities of Romanist religions were settled in London, and chapels were being built in many country districts. But no step was taken without protest. Frampton, preaching at the Whitehall, "showed the difference between Popery as modify'd here and as he had seen it abroad," and in a later sermon denounced the persecution which was already beginning when Bishop

Compton had been suspended; whereupon James complained to Sancroft, who stoutly defended his brother prelate. Even Burnet, so ready to decry the merits of his cloth, admits that "many of the clergy acted now a part that made good amends for past errors. They set themselves to study the points of controversy, and upon that there followed a great variety of small books that were easily purchased and soon read." The contest was close. Fortified by the decision in Hales's case, the king now pressed on if possible to establish Romanists in the Church. Edward Sclater, rector of Putney and Esher, received the king's dispensation to hold his benefices, though he declared himself a Roman Catholic. At Oxford a determined attempt was made to capture the university. In May 1686 Obadiah Walker, Master of University College, a man of some learning and the author at least of a pious tractate, *Of the benefits of our Saviour Jesus Christ to mankind* (1680), as well as of other works, with several fellows of his college, received the royal license to "absent themselves from Church and common prayer, and from administering the Sacrament of the Lord's Supper as used in the Church of England, and from taking the oaths of supremacy and allegiance," with a license also to print and sell Romanist books. In December the king appointed a lay-fellow of Merton, John Massey, to be Dean of Christ Church, dispensing him from the laws. It had not been unknown in England since the Reformation for a deanery to be held by a layman; but the dispensation from all religious obligations, in the case of the most important headship in the University of Oxford, was felt as an outrage upon the national Church. The Roman mass was now said in two of the Oxford colleges. Less objection was felt to the appointment, already mentioned, of Samuel Parker to the see of Oxford; but the fact that he published a cogent argument against the Test Act (the common sense of which would now be fully admitted, but which seemed then obviously to be a bid for the king's favour) made churchmen regard him with suspicion. But still more strongly resented was the appointment of Dr. Thomas Cartwright, then Dean of Ripon, to the see of Chester. He was a man of poor reputation, and believed to be willing to help James in his design. So he proved.

Attempt to Romanise Oxford.

His diary shows him to have constantly met the king's Roman clergy; and at a time when the king was much enraged against the other bishops he was especially praised by him as "a prelate of proved loyalty." He was a strange contrast to his predecessor, Bishop Pearson.

James now proceeded openly against those who opposed him. Samuel Johnson, formerly chaplain to Lord Russell, was degraded from his orders and was put in the pillory, whipped, and fined for an address in which he had exhorted the army not to obey popish officers. The order to the Bishop of London to suspend Dr. Sharp, a prominent London clergyman, for a sermon against Popery was a still more remarkable attempt to exercise despotic power over the Church. The bishop saw Sharp, and informed the king of his loyalty and obedience. No heed was taken of this, but the bishop himself was summoned before the High Commission. On this court were Sprat, Bishop of Rochester, and Crewe. Cartwright was added later. The king compelled the court to pronounce Compton guilty of disobedience to the royal order, and suspended him from the exercise of his office.

James's headlong attacks on the Church.

Fortified by this success, the king now began to prepare a further advance by granting a toleration to dissenters. A time was chosen when the bishops, it seemed, were especially anxious to maintain their impartiality, for they joined to their condemnation of Rome a direction to churchwardens to present all those who did not communicate at Easter. James made an attempt to unite both oppositions to the English Church. On April 4, 1687, he issued a Declaration of Liberty of Conscience, by which the execution of all penal laws in ecclesiastical matters was suspended, and also all tests and oaths. The king added a promise to maintain the bishops and clergy in the free exercise of their religion, and owners of property which had once belonged to churches or abbeys in their enjoyment of it.

Declaration of Liberty of Conscience, 1687.

The Declaration had two fatal defects on the face of it. In the first place, it was far in advance of public feeling; and in the second, it was illegal. And, besides this, it was very clearly, as the last clause showed, designed as a step towards the establishment of the Roman Church. Addresses

thanked the king for his charitable declaration, but they were
drawn up and signed, with few exceptions, by men in whom
neither dissenters nor churchmen had confidence.   In return
the king lavished honours on sectaries of every kind.   Some,
such as William Penn, who held generous toleration as a
principle, were honest ; but more were bitter and treacherous.

In spite of apparent satisfaction in different parts of the
country, the Declaration was received by the majority of
Englishmen with silence and distrust.   The dismissal of
several court officials increased the feeling of dismay ; and
James gave still further occasion by "touching for the king's
evil" in Bath abbey, with a form of Roman authority.   No
warning had been given, and Bishop Ken did not think it
wise to oppose the king's act ; but he preached on the following Sunday, treating it as simply a matter of charity,
" which ought to be the religion of the whole world."

A crisis was at hand.   In September, 1687, the king
arrived, on progress, at Oxford, and occupied the Royal
apartment at Christ Church, under the roof of his Magdalen
subservient Romanist dean.   He had come to College,
Oxford.
crush the resistance of a private corporation, which
was teaching a lesson in constitutional procedure to the whole
of England.   At Oxford the highest doctrine as to passive
obedience had long been inculcated.   James was determined
to enforce it to the bitter end.   On March 24 the President
of Magdalen College had died ; a few days later the Bishop
of Oxford announced to one of the Fellows that "the king
expected that the person he recommended should be
favourable to his religion."   On April 5 a Royal mandamus
required the Fellows to elect and admit one Anthony Farmer,
a man of ill repute, who was not eligible by the statutes.
The college, acting under the advice of Peter Mews, Bishop
of Winchester, the visitor, represented that they could not
disobey their statutes.   The king retorted that he must be
obeyed.   No further order having been received before the
last day allowed by the statutes, the Fellows, on April 15,
elected John Hough, B.D., one of their society.   On the
following day he was admitted by the Visitor.   The king
demanded an account of what had been done ; the College
replied with an expression of their confidence that "a loyal

society can never suffer in the hands of so generous and gracious a prince for what they have done out of a conscientious discharge of the trust reposed in them by their founder." They were cited to appear at Whitehall; and, after argument, the Ecclesiastical Commission declared the election void. An inhibition was issued against any further elections to the foundation, and on August 14 the king ordered Samuel Parker, Bishop of Oxford, to be admitted President.

It was at this point that James appeared in Oxford. He summoned the Fellows before him and told them to "get you gone, and immediately repair to your chapel, and elect me the Bishop of Oxford forthwith, or else you shall know what it is to feel the weight of a king's hand." The Fellows did not fear the weight of a king's hand; "the papists," said Hough, "have already got Christ Church and University College; the present struggle is for Magdalen, and they threaten that in a short time they will have all the rest"; and they determined that whatever was done should be done by force. The king sent down the Ecclesiastical Commission, with the subservient Cartwright at its head; they overruled all objections, expelled the President and Fellows, and put others in their places. Within a few days Bishop Parker, the intruded president, died, professing himself still sincere in "adherence to the principles of the Church of England, in opposition to those of the Roman Catholic Church." Ten days later the intruded Fellows admitted as his successor the Romanist Bonaventura Gifford, titular Bishop of Madaura. The college was "filled apace with popish priests and others of the Roman communion," and the chapel was used for their services. The king seemed to be victorious. But the resistance of the College won the attention and the admiration of all England; and when the fears of the Revolution that was at hand penetrated the obstinacy of the king, on the 25th of October, 1688, the lawful President and Fellows were restored to their places amid signs of universal joy. Magdalen College has the undying honour of beginning the lawful resistance to the illegal acts of the king. The example was followed by a more famous body of illustrious men.

James's failure to overawe the college.

Sancroft had been watching events with the acutest distress. The trials of the Church did not, as he wrote to the king's eldest daughter, Mary, Princess of Orange, make him in the least degree depart from his loyalty to the throne, but he was determined in no way to compromise the rights of Englishmen in their religion. The king ordered him to stop the afternoon catechising by the clergy, in which he declared that attacks were made upon Roman teaching. The archbishop refused ; and he joined, as a governor of the Charterhouse, in a refusal to admit a Romanist, by the king's orders but contrary to law. James *James's order to read his Declaration in churches.* was now determined to put his power to a supreme test. On May 4, 1688, the king in council ordered that the royal Declaration of Toleration should be read in all churches during divine service. Sancroft took prompt measures. He summoned a meeting of the more notable London clergy and requested all the bishops to come at once to town. The king's brother-in-law the Earl of Clarendon, John Evelyn, and other loyal laymen, were also consulted. It was decided not to obey ; and the decision was based, as Sancroft records, among the memoranda he has left of the discussion, not on "any want of tenderness towards dissenters, but because the Declaration, being formed on such a dispensing power as at pleasure set aside all laws ecclesiastical and civil, appear to me illegal." Illegal such a Declaration had been formally declared to be in 1672 ; and the clergy were determined to refuse any consent to it now.

On May 18, two days before the Declaration was to have been published, seven bishops met the archbishop at Lambeth, and with them six divines, Tillotson, Stillingfleet, Patrick, Tenison, Sherlock, and Grove. A series of resolutions was drawn up explaining the reasons *The seven bishops.* on which the bishops refused to obey. When they might have left the decision to each individual parish priest, they acted as befitted their position as shepherds of the flock, "an heroic act," says White Kennett, "becoming the character of bishops of the Church of England, who dared to be confessors, as their predecessors had been martyrs, for the Protestant religion." A petition was drawn up to be presented to the king, stating the reasons for the refusal, concluding that the

Declaration was one " of so great moment and consequence to the whole nation, both in Church and State,

that your petitioners cannot in prudence, honour, or conscience, so far make themselves parties to it as the distribution of it all over the nation, and the solemn publication of it once and again, even in God's house, must amount to in common and reasonable construction." It was signed by Sancroft, Lloyd, Bishop of St. Asaph, Turner of Ely, Lake of Chichester, Ken of Bath and Wells, White of Peterborough, and Trelawny of Bristol. These were the only bishops present at the decision. Peter Mews had been stayed by sickness, and Frampton arrived half an hour after they had gone to Whitehall. " I am sure," said the archbishop, " our brother Robert of Gloucester, with his black mare, are on the gallop "; but the hour was late and they could not tarry. The bishops on the same evening after ten o'clock presented the petition to the king. Sancroft being forbidden the court, was not with them. " This is a standard of rebellion," said James, " I did not expect such usage from the Church of England." " We will honour you, but we must fear God," said Trelawney and Ken. " I will be obeyed," said the king. " God's will be done," they answered.

In the morning Frampton wished to go himself to the king to associate himself with his brethren, but Sancroft dissuaded him. " There will come a time, brother,"

he said, " when your constancy and courage may do the Church more service." In a few hours, in spite of the archbishop's precautions to secure secrecy, what had happened had become known everywhere. On the Sunday the churches were thronged. Only in four London churches was an attempt made to read the Declaration. At Whitehall it was read by a choirman ; at Westminster, when Sprat, Bishop of Rochester, who was dean, began to read it, the people began at once to leave their seats, and by the time he had done he was left alone with the choir and the Westminster boys. It was the same all over England. Very few would read, and, says the biographer of Frampton, " one that did was left by his whole congregation, who all follow'd an ancient lady out of church." Not one read in the city or University of Oxford : probably not thirty read in all

England. A week passed, and on the second Sunday still fewer read it. Then James determined to punish the bishops. On May 27 Sancroft was ordered to appear before the council on June 8. The other bishops received similar summons. After repeated examination, and when they declined to enter into their recognisances to appear in Westminster Hall to answer the charge that should be preferred against them, they were committed to the Tower. As they went by water the banks were thronged with people, who knelt and begged their blessing. When they came to the Tower the bell was tolling for evensong, and they went in, the people thronging after them. So when the words of St. Paul sounded in their ears, exhorting them to be worthy of their office, "in much patience, in affliction, in distresses," they gave thanks to God, Who had called them to suffer. Day after day eminent men flocked to see them. Frampton was with them daily, and as he left, the people would press round his coach and ask his benediction. One Sunday he preached at St. Stephen's Wallbrook, "and going thence the people on both sides of the way to his lodgings in Barge Yard kneel'd down to have his blessing."

On June 15 the bishops appeared before the King's Bench, and were let out on bail till the 29th. Every day the public demonstrations of sympathy increased. When they passed to Westminster Hall the people crowded about them and knelt to be blessed, and when any of them walked through the streets they were at once surrounded, "the people," says Lord Clarendon, "thinking it a blessing to kiss any of these bishops' hands or garments." They were charged with conspiracy to diminish the royal power by writing and publishing their petitions. The king's honour, said the attorney-general in opening the case, must be vindicated by the trial. The defence pleaded the illegality of the Declaration, and showed that the private presentation of the petition was neither false nor malicious. The jury spent the whole night in discussion; and at ten o'clock on the morning of the 30th of June, when the court and every approach to it were crowded with an excited throng, gave the verdict of not guilty. The enthusiasm which spread the news over London reached the soldiers in the king's camp at Hounslow, spread all over the land, and was echoed in

The trial, June 29, 1688.

addresses of congratulation and celebrated with bonfires. A medal, which seems to have been designed by Sancroft himself, was struck to celebrate the victory. The bishops were the heroes of the whole nation, and Sancroft was looked on everywhere as the champion of the freedom of Englishmen and their Church.

In nothing were the calmness and confidence in which they had acted seen more clearly than in their quiet return after the exciting days of imprisonment and trial to the ordinary work of their spiritual office. During the next few weeks Sancroft was doubly active. He issued instructions to his suffragans " of things to be more fully insisted upon in their addresses to the clergy and people of their respective dioceses," urging caution against " all seducers, and especially popish emissaries," and " a very tender regard towards our brethren the Protestant dissenters." He made some attempts also to suggest comprehension, but without success ; and he issued a warning against deceivers, among them naming " four persons, exceeding all the rest in confidence, who assume to themselves the titles of bishops of remote places, where they have no flocks, and under pretence of being the pope's vicars in this realm, address themselves to a party of men styled by them lay-Catholics, who separate themselves indeed from our communion, but yet in right and according to the law of this land and the discipline of the primitive Church belong to our care." The first of these documents is thought to have been drawn up under the influence of Ken : and the others also may very likely have been revised by him. It is certain that their trial drew the bishops very closely together, and that they acted during the next few months with one accord.

The bishops' action after their acquittal.

In September James received warning of the intended invasion of the Prince of Orange. On September 21st he issued a declaration of his determination to maintain the Church of England in her powers and privileges. On September 28 he gave an audience to several bishops whom he had summoned. He said nothing but some vague words of favour and confidence. Ken replied that " his Majesty's inclinations towards the

Their last advice to James.

Church and their duty to him were sufficiently understood before, and would have been equally so if they had not stirred one foot out of their dioceses." This was satisfactory to no one, and on October 3, Sancroft, at the head of the bishops, visited the king. They recommended him to withdraw all his dispensations; to restore the President and Fellows of Magdalen; to fill the vacant bishoprics; to prohibit the "four foreign bishops, who style themselves vicars apostolical," from invading the lawful ecclesiastical jurisdiction; to abolish the ecclesiastical commission; to call a Parliament "for the purpose of securing the uniformity of the Church of England, the liberty of conscience, and the liberties and properties of the subject, and for establishing between himself and all his people a mutual confidence and good understanding"; and lastly, to permit the bishops to offer him "such motives and arguments as might, by God's grace, be effectual to persuade him to return to the communion of the Church of England, into whose most Holy Catholic faith he had been baptized and educated, and to which it was their earnest prayer to God that he might be reunited."

James took part at least of the advice. But when he asked the bishops to declare their abhorrence of the invasion, "they told him," says Bishop Sprat, "they could not do it, for the prince might have a just cause of war, for what they knew." Nor would they "declare a dislike" of the invasion. Sancroft, however, willingly prepared a prayer for the restoration of public tranquillity, and so well, says Burnet, that even those who wished for the prince might well have joined in it. Compton, Bishop of London, had already joined in the invitation which had been sent to William, and yet when James questioned him as to the share of the bishops in the matter, he said, "I am sure my brethren will say that they have taken as little part in it as I have." The other bishops, who did know of his share, of course replied when they were questioned that they had not joined at all. James did his utmost to secure the support of the archbishop; and Evelyn seriously warned him not to be entrapped into furthering the designs of the papists. On November 5 William of Orange landed at Torbay. Two days earlier, after several interviews with the king, Sancroft had

The invasion of William of Orange.

drawn up a declaration that he had never incited or encouraged the invasion, but he had refused to repudiate the declaration that had been put out in William's name. At every step in the great national crisis the archbishop stood forward as a true leader of the Church, loyal to the king, but firm in his attachment to law. On November 17 he went with the facile Lamplugh, whom James had now made Arch-

bishop of York, and with Turner of Ely and Sprat of Rochester, to strongly urge the summoning of a "free Parliament," advice which the king took.

On December 10 the queen fled with the baby prince, and on the next day the king followed. Sancroft then joined in signing the order to the fleet to abstain from any hostility towards the Dutch, and on December 11 joined in the meeting at the Guildhall which invited the help of William to secure peace and a parliamentary settlement. At this point he stayed. He would give no further support to the Revolution, feeling the obligation of his oath of allegiance too strongly to assist in any act that might deprive James of the crown. He alone of all the bishops would not wait on William or attend in the House of Lords. No new king, he declared, could be appointed by law, but only "by force of conquest."

Matters had indeed gone beyond his intervention. Strong men held the helm of State, and would carry the bark through the troubled waters. Sancroft knew that he must give up all for conscience' sake. "Well," he said to a friend, "I can live on £50 a year," and he boldly announced to the prince that he did not approve of some things that had been done by

him. A large meeting was held at Lambeth to discuss the situation; but when the convention on January 22, 1689, voted the throne vacant, Sancroft was not present. On the day of the proclamation of William and Mary, as king and queen, Henry Wharton, the archbishop's chaplain, prayed for them at evensong in Lambeth Palace chapel; his diary tells that Sancroft, "with great heat, told him that he must thenceforward desist from offering prayers for the new king and queen, or else from performing the duties of his chapel, for as long as King James was alive no other persons could be sovereigns of the country." He was expressing the settled judgment of many of his Episcopal colleagues and many of the clergy, that a crowned and anointed king could not lawfully be deposed by his subjects. It was clear that whatever might be the political result of revolution, England was in danger of a new religious schism.

AUTHORITIES.—State Papers, Domestic; Tanner MSS., including Sancroft's Papers; D'Oyly, *Life of Sancroft;* Howell, *State Trials.* The case of Alice Lisle, the only one in the "Bloody Assize" of which we have full details, and the other cases, are fully examined in the *Life of Jeffreys*, by H. B. Irving (1898). See "Matters of Fact at the Time of the Revolution," by Bishop Sprat, in Gutch, *Collectanea Curiosa*, vol. ii. Autobiography of Bishop Kidde (in Cassan, *Bishops of Bath and Wells*). The proceedings and trial of the seven bishops were published verbatim in 1689. The actual petition, as well as a draft for it, presented by the bishops to the king, and another copy, with additional signatures, and also a full account of the proceedings, all in Sancroft's own hand, are among the Tanner MSS. A number of important documents, chiefly from the Tanner MSS., are printed by Gutch in *Collectanea Curiosa*, vol. i. (1781). Bishop Cartwright's Diary was published by the Camden Society, 1843. The documents relating to Magdalen College were collected and edited by Dr. J. R. Bloxam (Oxford Historical Society, 1886). Dean Plumptre's *Life of Ken* is full and valuable (2nd edition, 1890). Historical MSS. Commission, on Earl of Dartmouth's Papers, contains some facts of importance. See also *A Compleat Collection of Papers relating to the Great Revolution in England*, 1689. Perry and Stoughton, as before. Lathbury, *History of the Non-Jurors*. An interesting sketch of the chief interests and chief men is to be found in *Life in the English Church*, 1660-1714, by Canon Overton, 1885.

CHAPTER XIII

THE REVOLUTION SETTLEMENT AND THE NON-JURORS

It was his attack on the Church which had cost James his crown. It might have seemed as if the Church would be the chief gainer by the Revolution which overthrew him. It was far otherwise. Again Erastianism came to the top of the tide. Parliament formally accepted the unhistorical theory of an original contract between king and people, in opposition to the theory of Divine right originally developed as a counter-blast to the papal doctrine in politics. James was declared to have broken the contract; and the throne was conferred, without any pretence of religious sanction, upon the Prince and Princess of Orange.

Sancroft gave a commission to his suffragans, which virtually empowered them to crown the new sovereigns, and *Coronation of William and Mary, April 11, 1689.* Compton, Bishop of London, crowned them on April 11, 1689. In the coronation oath, by Act of Parliament, an additional safeguard was inserted, by the use of the words "the Protestant Reformed Religion established by law." James had not regarded his attack on the Church as contrary to his oath : it was clear that the oath must be made stricter ; and before long the Act of Settlement made the security of the Church still more certain by the provision that the sovereign must be a member of it. The king and queen took the oath separately, and vowed to preserve to the bishops and clergy all their legal rights.

William's views of the Church of England were well known to some of the English clergy. He had told Burnet that all he desired was a toleration for those who would not accept Episcopacy, and the abolition of the surplice, the sign of the cross in baptism, and the customary bowing to the altar. He was himself a Dutch Calvinistic Presbyterian, and he had expressed before he came to England a strong dislike to the High Church party (as it may now be called). Ken, who had been his wife's chaplain, had remonstrated with him on his evil life. His adviser in church matters was the bustling, thick-skinned, but industrious and well-intentioned Gilbert Burnet. A Scottish Presbyterian by birth and training, like several other notable English prelates since the Reformation, he never lost his sympathy with the Scottish Puritan theology, though he came to hold what was known as the Low Church, or Latitudinarian, position. He was the first to be nominated by William to a bishopric, and he was consecrated to the see of Salisbury on March 31, 1689, by the bishops of London, Winchester, Llandaff, and St. Asaph. A second adviser was soon found in a man of gentler character but practically the same theological views, John Tillotson, who was appointed Dean of St. Paul's on the election of Stillingfleet to the see of Worcester. These were William's best advisers. Mary was reduced to entire submission. She wished well to the Church, as she had wished well to her father; but she could give to neither more than prayers and tears.

The character and opinions of William III.

Burnet.

Tillotson.

The first acts of the reign showed the policy that would be followed. They were the deprivation of several of the old bishops, the appointment of new bishops, and the preparation of a revised Prayer-book to conciliate the Protestant dissenters. Parliament decided that the clergy must take the oaths to the new sovereigns, under penalty of deprivation. The position of the primate was quite certain from the first. He would do no act which might imply his assent to the Revolution. The House of Lords had summoned him to attend on March 23; he had taken no notice. On August 1 he was suspended, and on February 1, 1690, he was deprived. With him were deprived five bishops, Lloyd of Norwich, Turner of Ely, Frampton of Gloucester, White of Peterborough, Ken of Bath and Wells. Thomas of

The non-jurors.

Worcester and Lake of Chichester, who also refused the oaths, died before the government had issued the order, and White before it was carried out. Five of the famous seven bishops who had withstood James to the face gave up their sees rather than break their oaths to him. About four hundred of the clergy followed their examples. The bishops put out a *Vindication* of their conduct, in which they appealed as evidence of their loyalty to the country to their former resistance to "Popery and arbitrary power." By midsummer 1691 the deprivations had been carried out, and the schism of the non-jurors was a recognised fact.

The course taken by the non-jurors in declining the oaths of allegiance to William and Mary, in resenting the added oath of abjuration, in continuing to stand apart from formal recognition of the government of Queen Anne or the Georges, was a necessary and logical consequence of the doctrine of passive obedience or non-resistance. That this forgotten doctrine was held almost if not quite universally by the clergy in the seventeenth century is not to be disputed. Archbishop Laud, in whose mind the doctrine of Divine right, reaching him not alone through English political thoughts but from Bodin and from his "Master Aristotle," was clearly opposed to any notion of mere arbitrary power or of any contradiction of the law, had gone but a short way on the path followed by Sibthorpe and Manwaring and Cowell, and pursued with greater enthusiasm by the zealots of the Restoration, notably by the Oxford authorities who condemned the political philosophy of Hobbes. But to his successors passive obedience seemed a plain following of the precepts of the Gospel. It did not involve consent to an illegal act, as was evidenced by the unhesitating protest of the seven bishops, but it decisively forbade resistance to evil or unlawful commands. Suffer, do not consent, was the teaching of the Church : it seemed to men like Ken to be a plain adherence "to the doctrine of the Cross." But the theory, logical and consistent though it might be, would hardly have had so many martyrs if it had not been touched by something of a romantic and personal enthusiasm. That was given, there can be no doubt, by the veneration for the memory of the "Martyr King"; and it was continued by the

Political consistency of the non-jurors.

extraordinary fascination which all the later Stewarts, in spite of their weaknesses and crimes, were able to exert. Between the principles of passive obedience and hereditary loyalty and the claims of a foreign prince of aggressive ambition, and of (in the phrase of his warmest admirer) "a disgusting dryness," there seemed no question for men of honour who could not reason to the ultimate issue of political theory. No wonder that more than four hundred clergy could not abandon the convictions of their lives. The non-jurors at least had not changed their principles or stifled their convictions. It was a favourite taunt that others had. Thus a MS. "Epitaph on Passive Obedience," among the Rawlinson Papers, says :

> In hope of sudden resurrection
> Certain and sure beneath this stone
> Passive obedience lies interr'd
> By Church of England men averr'd.
> She was not long since in great favour
> As any doctrine of our Saviour
> With Burnet, Stillingfleet, and Patrick,
> Tho' some will tell you 'twas but a trick
> To curry favour with the Crown,
> And make Preferments all their own :
> For when she brought them into danger
> They all, with one consent, bid hang her,
> Therefore she was arraign'd and try'd
> Condemn'd and sentenc'd, thus she died.
>
> *Ætatis* 1689.
>
> Beware ye Christian doctrines all
> And set before your eyes her fall,
> Beware and see how you contest
> With that supreme grace, Interest ;
> For her great crime upon her trial
> Was anti-Christian self-denial.

Such squibs were circulated everywhere, and the inconvenient consistency of the non-jurors, set forth in such guise, provoked indignant retort.

But this was not the only or the most powerful sentiment of the non-jurors. Loyalists they were, but far more they were men who "realised far more vividly than most of their contemporaries the existence of the Church as a distinct spiritual society, with laws of its own, whose connection with the State, however beneficial, was

Their religious principles.

purely accidental; and, as a consequence, they insisted on the independence of the Church of any power on earth in the exercise of her purely spiritual power and authority." Whoever might be the monarch, the ejection of lawful bishops from their sees simply by the authority of the State, and the filling of the sees not canonically vacant was a violation of the constitutional rights of the ecclesiastical estate. Passive resistance in such a case may well have seemed imperative. It was not until the ejected bishops had died that any consistent men could accept the ecclesiastical settlement of the Revolution. And it was not until the old line of sovereign had died out, and until political theory had advanced, through the irresistible influence of world-wide change, to a new standing-point, that the non-juring body which believed itself to be the unalterably loyal Church of these islands became merged again in the general religious and political life of the nation. For many years survivors of the famous seven bishops marked by their firmness the consistency of the party which they led.

The non-jurors, so long as he lived, admitted with the deepest respect the leadership of Sancroft, the deprived archbishop.

Sancroft. He lived in strict retirement at Fressingfield, engaged in study and in ministry to the non-juring laity. The papers of Archbishop Laud had long been in his hands, and with the help of his chaplain, Henry Wharton, he prepared them for the press, evidently with an anxious desire to vindicate the memory of his great predecessor and at the same time to show his kinship, religious and political, with him. A man of indefatigable laboriousness, he remained a student to the end. One of his most intimate friends described him as "the most pious, humble, good Christian I ever knew in my life. His hours for chapel were at six in the morning, twelve before dinner, three in the afternoon, and nine at night, at which times he was constantly present, and always dressed. His usual diet, when it was not fast day, was two small dishes of coffee and a pipe of tobacco for breakfast; at noon chicken or mutton, at night a glass of mum and a bit of bread, if anything." His friends said of him, as Nelson tells, "that the most greedy worldling never enjoyed half that solid complacency in the most lucky and fortunate acquisitions, as his grace did, in being reduced to the mean circumstances of a private life." He died on November 24, 1693. His dying words truly expressed the lesson of his life, "What I have done, I have done in the integrity of my heart."

Next to Sancroft, Ken certainly stood nearest to the hearts of the faithful non-jurors. He had publicly, from his Episcopal chair in the cathedral church of Wells, asserted his right to be the sole pastor of his diocese and his readiness to continue all his functions. Like Sancroft, he remained in possession of his palace till the last possible moment. After that he lived till March 19, 1711, in seclusion, chiefly at Longleat, the pensioner of his friend, Lord Bath. While Sancroft was prepared to authorise the continuance of the non-juring succession, Ken was anxious to end it, and would on no account enter upon any course which might accentuate the differences between the non-jurors and the "swearers." So firm and so notorious was his attachment to the political principles of the non-jurors that when three of the deprived bishops, with Dr. Wagstaffe and other clergy, were arrested in 1696, he also was brought up with them before the Privy Council, though the charge against them was only the absurd one of issuing a "charitable recommendation" on behalf of the "extreme want" of the families of the deprived clergy. But Ken was never extreme. He did not, like Sancroft, regard the Church from which the non-jurors had cut themselves off as in schism, though he was never willing to take the oaths, and when Queen Anne was anxious to restore him to his see, his scruples no less than his infirmities prevented him from yielding to her wish. In his later years he returned to communion with the National Church, and he communicated in Wells cathedral church to show his acceptance of Hooper, who then occupied the see. He died on March 19, 1711, at Longleat. His tomb is outside Frome Church, the inscription, which he wrote for it, is, " May the here interred Thomas, late Bp. of Bath & Wells, and uncanonically deprived for not transferring his allegiance, have a perfect consummation of bliss, both of body and soul, at the great day, of which God keep me always mindful."

Bishop Lloyd of Norwich was made of sterner stuff. It was he who determined that the succession must be continued,

Ken.

and to him Sancroft, in February 1692, delegated his metropolitan powers.   Hickes, the deprived dean of Worcester, was sent over to St. Germain to ask James to
nominate two bishops.   He left the nomination to
Sancroft and Lloyd; and, at the choice of the archbishop
and his delegate, Hickes, with Wagstaffe, deprived chancellor of Lichfield, were consecrated by Lloyd, Turner, and
White, on February 24, 1694.   They took for titles, though
they never seem to have claimed any territorial jurisdiction,
two of those allowed by the Act of Henry VIII. for suffragan
bishops, Thetford and Ipswich.   The new consecrations
aggravated the bitterness of separation.   Hickes, a man of
great learning and of true piety, was yet a born fighter.   Ken
said that he showed zeal to make the schism incurable.   It
was shortly after the consecration that Dr. Sherlock turned
round on his *Case of Allegiance*, which had advocated passive
obedience, took the oath, and was made Dean of St. Paul's.
The controversy which ensued employed the best wits on both
sides, but it widened the breach.   Hickes wrote continually
and with vigorous bitterness, and he denounced those who
returned to communion with much freedom; and he took the
step of obtaining the assistance of two Scottish bishops in the
year of his own death to continue the succession, which would
otherwise have expired with him.   Very different was the
conduct of the mild and saintly Kettlewell, whose wisdom and
holiness all the non-jurors revered.   He never regarded himself
as separated from the Church of England, though he would
accept only the ministrations of the deprived clergy; but he
died in 1695, before the differences among his party became
irreconcilable.   White and Turner died in 1698.   Charles
Leslie, ablest and most skilful of controversialists, lived to a
much later time.   Another famous non-juror, Frampton, after
some petty persecutions, was allowed to live quietly at Standish
in Gloucestershire, attending the parish church, reading the
service, but omitting the names of the royal family, giving alms
and keeping his house as "a Bethel, an house of God."   He
died on May 25, 1708.

A man of a different mould was Denis Grenville, the
youngest son of the famous Sir Bevil.   He had married the fourth
daughter of Bishop Cosin, and he always had royal influence

The
non-juring
succession.

at his back, and had been made Dean of Durham in 1684, in spite, it is said, of the opposition of Sancroft.
His career was not altogether uneventful. He had *Denis Grenville.* been actually arrested for debt, when he was arch-deacon of Durham, within the precincts, and was imprisoned. He did his utmost to keep up the customs which Bishop Cosin had upheld in the cathedral church, and as dean he introduced weekly communions, and the like. He found it, so he told Dugdale in 1683, "a very hard game these twenty years." His most valuable work was a design to "make the cathedral the great seminary of young divines for the diocese, and to this end to invite ingenuous young men to be minor canons."

These, and many men of obscure but saintly life, were losses which the Church of England could ill bear. The Latitudinarian and Erastian tone which spread over the Church from the Revolution till the Wesleyan movement was due largely to the withdrawal of so many men of vital piety and self-devotion. The transparent honesty of their conduct more than condoned the weakness of their intellectual position. Men honoured, if they did not imitate, those who had gone out, like the clergy during the Commonwealth and the non-conformists in 1662. The lives of Sancroft, Ken, and Frampton had a keen attractive power.

Personal attachment to the "deprived Fathers," the permanence of political and religious principles, and the strongly-marked anti-national characteristics of William III. count for much when we come to explain the strength of the non-juring party. But probably more than has hitherto been estimated is due to the logical training of the universities and its result in the position taken by leading men at Oxford and Cambridge. Recent researches enable us to sketch briefly the position of the non-jurors at the two ancient seats of learning.

High churchmen and cavaliers were the natural product of seventeenth-century Oxford: but none the less it was the resistance of Oxford quite as much as the stand of the seven bishops that emphasised the feeling of *Non-jurors at Oxford* the whole nation against the illegal Romanising of James II. Yet, in the home of old loyalties men who had resisted the king to the face so far as a passive obedience would go, suffering deprivation for their loyalty to law and statutes, now suffered a second time for conscience sake. Dr. Thomas Smith, who had submitted to the election of Bishop Parker at Magdalen, went out later when the papists came in, returned on the "Restoration Day" of the college, October 28, 1688, and went out again when the oaths to the new government were enforced. He was the great friend and literary adviser of Hearne, who calls him "one of the best scholars that were ever bred in Magdalen College and indeed in this university." He remained to the last "an undaunted confessor of the poor, distressed, and afflicted Church of England, and always stood stiff and resolute to the doctrines of it as laid down in our articles and homilies." Thomas Crosthwaite, who was one of the nest of non-jurors connected with St. Edmund Hall, lived on in Queen's College after he had lost his Fellowship. Dr. John Mill, who became Principal of the Hall, had, it is true, taken the oath, but with many hesitations. These lines were sung about him :

> Wilt thou take the oaths, little Johnny Mill?
> No, no, that I won't ; yes, but I will.

St. Mary Hall, too, was also for some time a seat of the High Church and the Pretender's interest ; and when men were silenced elsewhere a bold preacher could still give out his text at St. John's—"James the Third and Eighth : *But the tongue can no man tame.*" It was hardly till George III. brought his wife to see the college that there was any perceptible slackening in the Jacobitism of the House which cherished the tradition of Laud. From Baliol five fellows were expelled at the Revolution as non-jurors. All over Oxford men of like opinion lived on, in college rooms, or in their own houses, and kept up the tradition of scholarship associated with the first leaders of secession. Dr. Richard Rawlinson, a notable benefactor to St. John's and the Bodleian library, eventually received Episcopal consecration on March 25, 1728, having been ordained soon after George I.'s accession by a non-juring bishop. Hearne, losing his preferments, remained still in Oxford, doing more than any man since Matthew Parker for the study of English historians.

At Cambridge in many cases the ejections were later.

Thomas Baker, the famous historian of St. John's College, retained his Fellowship till the accession of George I.   Eminent Cambridge writers, such as Hilkiah Bedford, who had accepted livings, came forward earlier as sufferers.   St. John's at Cambridge, the college of the wonderful boy-scholar Ambrose Bonwicke, was as consistently Jacobite and non-juring as St. Edmund Hall at Oxford ; and not a few other colleges contributed many names to the list of those who would not take the oaths to the new sovereigns. The influence of the universities, where it is hardly too much to say that the intellectual interests of the time were almost entirely centred in the non-jurors, must have been considerable.   For a time they confirmed the schism, and their indirect influence tended to perpetuate the principles, political and theological, which the sensitive consciences and sensitive logic of the seceders of 1689 had urged them to carry to the legitimate conclusions.   To the non-jurors and the universities were due notably the interest in questions of liturgiology and the endeavours towards reunion through which the age of Anne showed most clearly its attachment to the idea of a learned and Catholic Church.

In spite of what has just been said it must be admitted that the popular feeling for the non-jurors was doubtless often somewhat contemptuous.   Men of no scrupulous sensitiveness mocked at them.   "Our old fool the bishop is one of the opposers," said a Gloucestershire parson ; but Frampton showed him that with his action at least lay the merit of consistency.   Of those who at first refused and later accepted the oaths, the most prominent was Dr. William Sherlock, who became Dean of St. Paul's ; of him a non-juring writer says, that "for some reasons now in print, but one more prevalent perhaps and now in the grave, he thought fit to comply."   The buried reason was his wife. It was indeed a great sacrifice that the honest men who "went out" for conscience sake laid upon themselves.   They were practically without exception condemned to extreme poverty : and it is a striking testimony to the reality of their religion that while they differed in no respect from the doctrines or discipline of the Church, they were content to give up all that they loved, to remain exiles from her fold, and yet to enter upon no intrigue against the political settlement which was the sole cause of their separation. Their renunciation seemed to them, as Kettlewell expressed it in a treatise and then in his will, an adherence to the communion of the Church of England "as it adheres to the doctrine of the Cross."

At least as interesting as the clergy who gave up their benefices were the laity who retired from the communion of the Church. Robert Nelson, who remained a non-juror for twenty years, was a devoted son of the Church. As a foremost supporter of the societies which endeavoured the reformation of morals, and as one of the chief founders of the two oldest church societies (see below, p. 314), he did more valuable work for religion than any other man of his time. Busied continually in works of public and private beneficence, he was also an author of extraordinary popularity. He was biographer of Bishop Bull, the author of an admirable book of private devotion, and the expositor of the Church's Biblical and Catholic heritage in his *Festivals and Fasts*. Samuel Wesley tells of him that he would begin the day with Ken's hymns, thus:

> He oft, when night with holy hymns was worn,
> Prevented prime and wak'd the rising morn.

With him the separation from the public services of the National Church never caused a breach of unity in charitable work. Tolerant, loving, sympathetic, it was natural that he should at last return, with the sanction of Ken, to the outward communion of the Church. Henry Dodwell, who gave up the Camden Readership at Oxford within a year of his election to it, because he would not take the oath, lived till 1711, but conformed during his later years. The friend of Hearne and Cherry, two laymen typical of different sides of the party, the antiquary and the conscientious country gentleman, Dodwell was regarded by some at least as "the great lay dictator" of the non-jurors. A letter of White Kennett, who was at one time priest of his parish, illustrates the position that he took with regard to conformity. Kennett complains of his continual opposition. "I could have more charity for his learning and other talents," he wrote, "if his example of dissenter did not disturb the peace of my church and parish." In spite of all that had been done to carry out the work of the parish in the best way, "he will neither join himself nor suffer any upon whom his judgment can have any influence." On the one side, it was clearly regarded as inexcusable to hinder the service of the Church for a mere political scruple. Dodwell thought differently, and could not separate his politics from his religion. He was a man of undoubted and vast learning, but eccentric and unwise, a "sacerdotalist" who ran into extremes where mere reason could hardly attempt to follow him. Francis Cherry, "the idol of Berkshire," drew up clear reasons for the position which the non-jurors assumed, and no one was more glad than he when the death of the bishops who had been deprived of their sees made it possible for him and his friends without inconsistency to return to the worship of their parish churches. They continued to express their dissent in various ways from the reading of the State prayers, but they had returned to the communion of the National Church.

With this return the practical influence of the remaining non-jurors on English religion sank into the background. The historical importance of the schism ends with the death of Bishop Hickes in 1715.

From this digression we must return to the history of the Revolution settlement as it affected the Church. The places of the deprived bishops were filled from 1689 by the advice of Bishop Burnet. During the first two years of the new reign fifteen bishops were consecrated; Burnet says complacently that they were generally looked on as the learnedest, the wisest, and the best men that were in the Church. The Revolution bishops. And, indeed, several of them were notable men. Patrick, learned and devoted; Stillingfleet, erudite and conciliatory; Tillotson, moderate, gracious, charitable; Sharp, whom King James had attacked, and who was a sincere churchman and an industrious prelate; Cumberland, learned in science; Hough, bold in resisting oppression,—all these men were worthy shepherds of the flock. Their characteristic attitude was toleration, and many of them were eager, like William himself, to advance to a comprehension of the dissenters. The real difficulty lay, as it always lies, not in any harsh spirit of division or uncharitableness, but in a real opposition of principles. The question of ordination lay at

the root of the separation. The more moderate clergy did
not disparage the ministry of the Presbyterians and
Independents : strict churchmen like Sheldon and
Sancroft, indeed, had lived in kindly charity with
the dispossessed ministers ; but the general feeling of English
churchmen, as it had grown up through and after the wars,
was expressed by the saintly Ken, and asserted in the preface to
the Ordinal. The English Church's ordination was authentic,
"being by men ordained in an uninterrupted succession on the
primitive bishops, as they were by the Apostles, and the
Apostles by Christ." And Ken made the Church of England
say, "Would you have me disown the right succession of the
power ministerial, conferred by Episcopal hands unto this
day ? "

Question of comprehension.

On the other hand, King William was pledged to assist the
dissenters. In his Declaration he had said that he would
"endeavour a good agreement between the Church of England
and all Protestant dissenters, and cover and secure all those
who would live peaceably under the government from all persecution upon the account of their religion." To toleration
all were agreed. But many desired to widen the limits of the
Church, to take measures that her banished ones should be
restored to her. The diversity of opinions was an obvious
difficulty. Conscientious men held their opinions conscien-
tiously, and on account of them they had separated : different
concessions would be needed to recall Presbyterians, Independents, Baptists, Socinians. Yet the time seemed ripe for a
comprehensive measure. Sancroft had prepared for it, Compton was sympathetic, Tillotson and Burnet were inspired with
a wide charity and a peaceable spirit.

The first step was taken in the House of Lords, where a
Bill for Union, or Comprehension, was introduced and passed.
In the Commons it had a different fate. "The
Church party," says Dalrymple, "were by far the
most numerous " there, and the House, in the words
of Burnet, "was much offended with the Bill of
Comprehension as containing matters relating to the Church in
which the representative body of the clergy had not been so
much as advised with." They petitioned the king to call a Convocation : the House of Lords joined them, and then they

Bill for union rejected by the Commons.

proceeded to pass the Toleration Bill.   By this all Protestant dissenters who should not deny verbally or in writing the doctrine of the Holy Trinity as declared in the Thirty-nine Articles were freed from all restrictions as to worship.   Their teachers were required to subscribe the articles and to register their places of worship. Thus happily was a great advance made towards the removal from the State of the stigma of intolerance of Protestant dissent.   In the case of Romanists it still remained.

Toleration Bill.

The Convocations were now summoned, and a commission was granted to ten bishops and twenty clergy to prepare the business for them.   Tillotson, it seemed, would be the guiding spirit, and he was known to be in favour of recognising foreign Protestant orders, of revising the Prayer-book and canons, and reforming ecclesiastical courts and ceremonies.   Power to prepare a scheme was granted to the commission in a warrant dated September 4, 1689, reciting " that whereas the particular forms of Divine worship, and the rites and ceremonies appointed to be used therein, being things in their own nature indifferent and alterable, and so acknowledged, it is but reasonable that upon weighty and important considerations, according to the various exigences of times and occasions, such changes and alterations should be made therein, as to those that are in place and authority should from time to time seem either necessary or expedient.

Commission for the new Convocation.

" And wheras the book of canons is fit to be reviewed, and made more suitable to the state of the Church ; and wheras there are divers defects and abuses in the ecclesiastical courts of jurisdiction, and particularly there is not sufficient provision made for the removing of scandalous ministers and for the reformation of manners either in ministers or people ; and wheras it is most fit that there should be a strict method prescribed for the examination of such persons as desire to be admitted into Holy Orders, both as to their learning and manners, their Majesties out of their pious and princely care for the said order, edification, and unity of the Church of England, committed to their charge, for the reconciling, as much as is possible, of all differences among their good subjects, and to take away all occasions of the like for the future, have thought fit to authorise, impower, and require the said commissioners or any other nine or more of them (whereof three are to be bishops) to meet from time to time, as often as shall be needful, and to prepare such alterations and amendments of the liturgy and canons, and such proposals for the reformation of ecclesiastical courts, and to consider of such other matters as in their judgment may most conduce to the ends above mentioned, so that the things by them so considered and prepared may be in readiness to be offered to Convocation at their next meeting, and when approved by them may be presented to their Majesties and to the two Houses of Parliament, so that, if it shall be judged fit, they may be established in due form of law."

The Earl of Nottingham, who was supposed to be in sympathy with "High Church" principles, but who had introduced the Comprehension Bill into the House of Lords, wrote to the Archbishop of York and other members of the commission (which, it may be noted, included the "old cavalier," Mews of Winchester), as follows : "The king commands me to acquaint you that he has thought fit to issue a commission under the great seal of England to you and several bishops, deans, and others of the clergy, to prepare such alterations and amendments of the liturgy and canons, and such proposals for the reformation of ecclesiastical courts, and to consider of other such matters as may most conduce to the good order, edification, and unity of the Church of England, so that their resolutions may be in readiness to be offered to the Convocation at their next meeting, and, when approved by them, may be presented to his Majesty, and the two Houses of Parliament ; so that, if it shall be judged fit, they may be established in due form of law. I am further commanded to acquaint you that the bishops and clergy, in and about the city, think the 3rd of October next the most convenient day for the first meeting, in or near London, at which you are desired to be present."

The instructions of the government.

On the 3rd of October some twenty of the commissioners met in the Jerusalem Chamber. Eighteen meetings were held, and the results were presented to the Convocations which met on November 21. A practical agreement was arrived at, which, it is hardly too much to say, would have revolutionised the Prayer-book. It was proposed to modify the order as to the saying of morning and evening prayer; to substitute minister for priest, Lord's Day for Sunday; it was rendered lawful to dispense with the surplice and with kneeling at the communion and with the sign of the cross in baptism; a useful explanatory note was added to the Athanasian Creed; and a suggestion was made with regard to the Nicene Creed, with a view "to our maintaining Catholic communion." A considerable process of alteration was applied to the prayers, and the collects were amplified in an extraordinary manner, especially when Tillotson " gave them the last touches of his natural and flowing eloquence "; rubrical changes appeared to sanction the consecration of the holy communion by persons not in priest's orders; and a "conditional" reordination of Protestant ministers was suggested : modifications were also made in the communion and confirmation services which suggested doctrinal change. Finally, an order, more in keeping with the general feeling of pious churchmen, was given that in every great town or parish there should be a monthly communion, and in every parish at Christmas, Easter, Whitsunday and " some Lord's day soon after harvest ": and ministers were required to exhort to frequent communion.

Proposals of the commission.

Before Convocation met the nature of these proposals seems to have been known; and Burnet, who was in favour of them, describes the general feeling thus : " It was said that the Church was to be pulled down and Presbytery to be set up; that all this now in debate was only intended to divide and distract the Church, and to render it by that means both weaker and more ridiculous, while it went off from its former ground in offering such concesssion." It was clear that there would be hot debate. The king's message to Convocation, which was delivered by the Earl of Nottingham, was as follows :

The meeting of Convocation.

" His Majesty has summoned this Convocation not only because it is usual upon holding of a Parliament, but out of a pious zeal to do everything that may tend to the best establishment of the Church of England, which is so eminent a part of the reformation, and is certainly the best suited to the constitution of this government, and therefore does most signally deserve and shall always have both his favour and protection ; and he doubts not but that you will assist him in promoting the welfare of it, so that no prejudices, with which some men may have laboured to possess you, shall disappoint his good intentions or deprive the Church of any benefit from your consultations. His Majesty therefore expects that the things that shall be proposed shall be calmly and impartially considered by you, and assures you that he will offer nothing to you but what shall be for the honour, peace and advantage both of the Protestant religion in general, but particularly of the Church of England."

This message was prepared on November 4 ; but before Convocation met on November 21 it was clear that the proposed changes had no chance of success. A Presbyterian's letter of that date thus describes the collapse which ensued on the election of a prolocutor : "Our convention for settling religion is likewise broken in pieces, for our Presbyterian party hoped Dr. Tillotson would have been chosen prolocutor, or their man, as they call him, but the vote being between him and Dr. Jean [Jane, canon of Christ Church, Oxford], the latter had it. Dr. Tillotson was one that would have granted us all we could have wished for both in the alteration of the liturgies, prayers, ceremonies, and all ; but this Jean is so stiff for the Church of England, that he will grant nothing. Dr. Fairfax made a proposal that some changes might be made in the Lord's Prayer, as that the first part, viz., 'Our Father which art in heaven,' was not grammar, and, therefore, ought to be 'Our Father which is in heaven' ; and that the petition 'Lead us not into temptation,' ought to be put out, as the making God the author of sin. This was not regarded, and Baxter, and all the other Presbyterian good men, will, we are afraid, decline meeting any more."

The prolocutor, when presented to the Bishop of London, who presided over the Convocation, ended his speech with the sentence, famous in English constitutional history, *Nolumus leges Angliæ mutari.* The result was that the business of the Prayer-book was never brought forward. Important pamphlets on both sides had already been published ; one of

them, *Vox Cleri*, recalled the fact that the last revision had
conciliated no one, and that what would now conciliate dissenters would alienate loyal Church folk. "What though
there be some few that are really but causelessly offended at
our ceremonies, must we for their sakes give offence to the
Church of God? Is it necessary that a parent should yield
to a disobedient child on his own unreasonable terms?" The
Houses met for actual business on December 4,
and they did little but wrangle, chiefly on the   Without
question whether in an address to the king the   result.
Church of England should be described as a Protestant
Church. In the end the more correct phrase, "the Protestant
religion," was used. Finally the session came to an end
without tangible results.

It would have been natural to appoint Compton to the
primacy when Sancroft was deprived, but William had seen in
Tillotson the simplicity and submissiveness which
he desired. Reluctant to accept the high office, "a   Tillotson as
                                                       archbishop.
man of extraordinary piety and a great lover of
peace," he warmly supported the efforts made for the reform
of morals and the inauguration of missionary effort, and he
was a constant and admired preacher. In other respects it
may be said that his primacy had no history. He never
summoned Convocation; and, for himself, he studied to be
quiet. He died on November 22, 1694; and his successor
was a man of temper not unlike his own, Dr. Thomas
Tenison, who in 1691 had been made Bishop of Lincoln.

Tenison, though not so much beloved, was a man of much
stronger mould, of the same comprehensive sympathies and
of piety as sincere as Tillotson. Evelyn in 1683
regarded him as "one of the most profitable   Tenison,
                                               Abp. of
preachers in the Church of England, being also of a Canterbury,
most holy conversation, very learned and ingenious"; 1695-1705.
and added, in his Diary, "the pains he takes and care of his
parish (St. Martin-in-the-Fields) will, I fear, wear him out,
which would be an inexpressible loss." He had taken considerable part in public affairs, having been present when the
seven bishops drew up their declaration, and having come
forward prominently in controversy during the reign of James
II. He was a warm advocate of comprehension. In 1683

he had published *An Argument for Union,* in which he urged the dissenters to "do as the ancient nonconformists did, who would not separate, though they feared to subscribe"; but he limited the possibility of union to the Presbyterians and possibly some of the Independents; as for "Arians, Socinians, Anabaptists, Fifth-Monarchy men, sensual Millenaries, Behmenists, Familists, Seekers, Antinomians, Ranters, Sabbatarians, Quakers, Muggletonians—they may associate in a caravan, but cannot join in the communion of a church." His opinion, in fact, agreed with that of Camber, who, writing to Patrick, declared that the Independents as a body were "incapable of anything but toleration, and cannot be taken in but by such concessions as will shake the foundations of our Church." In the see of Lincoln Tenison had done well. Kennett says that he "restored a neglected large diocese to some discipline and good order."

Elected to the archbishopric at the beginning of 1695, he remained primate of all England for twenty years. He did nothing to modify the Erastian character of William III.'s dealings with the Church. He was content to issue royal injunctions and to acquiesce in the abeyance of the constitutional power of the clerical estate. The Trinitarian controversy and the Convocation controversy were no very serious disturbances to the even tenor of his way. He was content to sit at Lambeth and be quiet. His close personal association, however, with the royal family exposed him to considerable comment. Queen Mary, who had excused him when he preached a funeral sermon for Nell Gwyn, had him for her minister on her deathbed, and the glowing eulogy which he delivered after her death was met by very severe criticism from Ken, on the ground of her undutiful conduct towards her father. On the other hand, helped by the letter which Mary wrote to her husband in her last illness, he severely reproved William for his adulterous life, and having received his promise of amendment, preached a sermon "concerning holy resolution," which was printed by the royal command.

Reserving for later treatment the controversies and the religious and philanthropic work, which were the chief features of the ecclesiastical history of William's reign, we may note that at its close the non-juring schism was widened by an ill-judged Act, which showed how little regard was paid by the government and the clergy whom it favoured to the conscientious scruples of the seceders. On the death of James II. in 1701 the original cause of disunion ceased; no one had taken oaths to his son. It was probable that the non-jurors would now be willing to take the oaths to William as *de facto* king; but an Act of Parliament was passed which required all the clergy to abjure King James's son and his descendants, and to declare William to be rightful and lawful king. This the high Tory principles of the non-juring clergy would not suffer them to accept: the schism remained unhealed, and the numbers of the non-jurors were increased.

The condition of the Church on other grounds was far from satisfactory. There were some serious scandals. In 1699 Thomas Watson, Bishop of St. David's, one of those appointed by James II., "one of the worst men that I ever knew in holy orders," says Burnet, was deposed for simony. Jones, who had been translated by William III. from Cloyne to St. Asaph in 1692, escaped, with difficulty, a similar fate.

William, during the later years of his life, made some endeavours to conciliate the Church. He appointed a commission of six prelates (Tenison, Sharp, Burnet, Lloyd of St. Asaph, Patrick, and Stillingfleet) to advise him in Church appointments, and he became reconciled to the Princess Anne. But in the former case the practical result was that the Church became controlled by the Whig bishops, and the division between the Episcopate and the clergy was widened. And it was not until the king's death, on March 8, 1702, that Anne's influence was perceptible.

William's commission of bishops.

With the death of the Dutch king the dangers which the Revolution settlement had brought home to the Church were at an end. The religious sympathies of James II. and William III. had equally threatened the national character of the established English religion. James would have brought the Church again, and unconditionally, under the sway of the Roman pontiff; William would also have swept away the distinguishing features of Anglicanism by assimilating the principles of the ecclesiastical constitution to those of the foreign Protestant bodies. But the feeling of the Church was at once strongly

Strong national feeling of the Church.

national and strongly conservative. Doctrine and organisation of a definite type were essential parts of her system, as Englishmen understood it, and these they had shown a fixed determination to preserve. Thus the Revolution, though it caused a schism which was in many respects both dangerous and unnecessary, left the Church, after a few years of unsettlement, undisturbed in its position and in the character which it had borne since the Reformation of Elizabeth's day.

AUTHORITIES. — D'Oyly, *Life of Sancroft;* Birch, *Life of Tillotson;* Burnet, *History of his own Time; Autobiography of Bishop Patrick;* Ken's *Works;* Nicholas, *Defence of the Doctrine and Discipline of the Church of England;* Lansdowne Collection, Kennett MSS. (British Museum); Stillingfleet MSS. (in possession of the Stillingfleet family); Tanner MSS. and Rawlinson MSS. in Bodleian Library; State Papers, Domestic, in Record Office; *The Letters of Dean Grenville* (Surtees Society); *The Life of John Kettlewell,* prefixed to his works, 1719, by Francis Lee, Bishop Hickes, and others. The alterations suggested in 1689 by the committee for the revision of the Prayer-book were printed by order of the House of Commons in 1854, and are also to be found in the revised Liturgy, edited by John Taylor, 1855. Among modern books may be mentioned, as above, Perry and Stoughton, Lathbury, *History of the Non-Jurors;* and Overton, *Life in the English Church;* also *Dictionary of National Biography,* especially articles on Tillotson, Tenison, Stillingfleet; and Overton, *The Non-Jurors.*

CHAPTER XIV

THE REIGN OF QUEEN ANNE

In Queen Anne the Church welcomed a sovereign who was in thorough sympathy with her principles. The grand-daughter of Charles I. and of Lord Chancellor Clarendon, she seemed to inherit their sober and sincere churchmanship and their warm affection for the national Church. Taught by Bishop Compton, guided in her spiritual life by Archbishop Sharp, she endeavoured to live as a consistent member of the Anglican communion, and to use her great opportunities for the glory of God and the good of the Church. Conscientious, affectionate, easily influenced, she was in political matters sometimes moved from acting on the principles which she held in her heart, or, more probably, she had schooled herself by the experiences through which she had passed to observe with strict self-repression the position of the constitutional sovereign of a limited monarchy. In religion, on the other hand, she did not move an inch from the principles of Charles I. and Laud and Sancroft. Her husband, Prince George of Denmark, was a Danish Lutheran, and she was deeply attached to him, but she showed no desire to bring the English Church nearer to the Protestant bodies. There can be no doubt that to the end of her life she felt deeply the deprivation of her father and her brother, but she was content to accept the judgment of her spiritual advisers that her own position was fully justified, and she was fully determined to preserve to the Church the position which the coronation oath, so lightly regarded by James II., guaranteed. If James, her brother,

255

"the old Chevalier," would have accepted the teaching of the English Church she would have welcomed him to England, and, if she could not abandon the throne, would have done her utmost to secure his succession. But so long as he remained a Romanist she felt her position to be justified, and she strove to rule according to her conscience for the good of her people and the Church.

It was not only in small matters that the queen at once showed her feelings. She treated the ministers of the Church with scrupulous respect, refused to receive the Holy Communion till after the "bishops, priests, and deacons," according to the rubrical direction, and strictly obeyed the rules of the Prayer-book. And she carried her principles out in a very practical manner. At her coronation by Tenison the sermon was preached by Archbishop Sharp. Immediately on her accession she dissolved the Whig commission of bishops to advise on preferments. At the end of the first session of her first Parliament she spoke with remarkable clearness : "I hope that such of my subjects as have the misfortune to dissent from the Church of England will rest secure and satisfied in the Act of Toleration, which I am firmly resolved to maintain, and that all those who have the happiness and advantage to be of our Church will consider that I have had my education in it, and that I have been willing to run great hazards for its preservation ; and therefore they may be very sure I shall always make it my particular care to encourage and maintain the Church as by law established, and every the least member of it in all their just rights and privileges ; and upon all occasions of promotion to any ecclesiastical dignity I shall have a very just regard for such as are eminent and remarkable for their piety, learning, and constant zeal for the Church."

It was not long before Anne showed how fully she meant her words. On the celebration of her birthday, February 7, 1704, she sent a message to the Commons, "that having taken into her serious consideration the mean and insufficient maintenance belonging to the clergy in divers parts of the kingdom, to give them some ease she had been pleased to remit the arrears of the tenths to the poor clergy, and for an augmenta-

Queen Anne's Bounty.

tion of their maintenance she would make a grant of her whole revenue arising out of the first-fruits and tenths, as far as it should become free from incumbrances, to be applied to this purpose. And if the House of Commons could find any proper method by which her intentions to the clergy might be made more effectual, it would be of great advantage to the public and acceptable to her Majesty." The first-fruits and tenths of all benefices which had formerly been paid to the popes had been secured to the crown by an Act of Henry VIII. The actual sums paid were still based upon the valuation of Pope Nicholas IV., and did not represent the value of the livings in the sixteenth century; but none the less the relief to the poorer clergy was considerable, and the benefit to the Church of the erection of a corporation to administer the fund now created was very great. The increase in the endowments of benefices rendered possible by Queen Anne's Bounty has been a material help to the Church in meeting the increased demands upon her during the two centuries that have succeeded the generous gift. The queen's known interest in all that concerned the Church was also an encouragement to those who in Parliament laboured to promote her welfare. The Act passed in 1710 for building fifty-two new churches in London had her warm approval. It was not, however, fully carried out, only twelve new churches being built in accordance with its provisions.

The interest of Church history in the reign of Queen Anne is mainly political. With the exception of the controversy which raged for several years in Convocation, and the discussions as to the social position of the clergy, *Political influence on Church history.* there is nothing to attract special attention in the life of the Church besides the close connection which she now acquired with questions of public policy. The important part played by the Church in the national resistance to the measures of James II. had been followed by an attempt to define the position of dissenters with regard to the Church and the State on a liberal basis of toleration. But the State was far from ceasing to interfere in matters of religion. Extremely severe laws against the Roman Catholics had been passed under William III., and the legislation of Charles II.'s reign still stood in the way of a full recognition of the political rights of dissenters. The Parliaments of Charles II.'s reign were quite determined that the government of the country, central and local, should be entrusted only to members of the national Church. It was plain that popular feeling on the subject had scarcely diminished in the forty years which had elapsed since the Restoration. But it was equally certain that the legislation had not proved entirely effective. The Test and

Scandal of the Test Acts. Corporation Acts, for example, could, as regards their original intention, be evaded. The holy sacrament had, by the horrible profanation of which unconscientious dissenters did not hesitate to be guilty, become a mere "pick-lock to a place." By a single or an annual communion a man who in every respect dissented from the Church could qualify himself for office. The scandal was shocking to all serious minds. There were two ways of avoiding it. One was that suggested by Bishop Samuel Parker in the reign of James II., the repeal of the Test Act, on the ground that to require assent to a metaphysical dogma of disputed interpretation from a layman ignorant of the rudiments of theology was a mischievous absurdity. The other was to find some way by which the intention of Parliament should be effectively carried out, without the possibility of evasion by men less sincere in their religion than in their ambition or desire to serve the State. For the abolition of all tests none save a few wise and generous thinkers, like John Locke, were as yet prepared.

The question of "occasional conformity" had been raised several times, without exciting much public interest. The pamphlet by the brilliant dissenter Daniel Defoe on the subject, published in 1701, passed unheeded. It was called "A Short Way with the Dissenters," and was a bitter satire on the laws against them. It had little if any effect. But in 1702, on the accession of Anne, the question was revived and became a matter of the keenest debate. A Bill was intro-

The Occasional Conformity Bill. duced into the Commons' House which, after profession of strong feeling against persecution for conscience' sake, declared the intention of the law of England that the country should be ruled only by churchmen, and the evasion of it which had been found possible; and enacted that any person bearing office who should resort to a conventicle should forfeit £100, and £5 for every day that he should continue in office afterwards. Though passed in the Commons, the bill met with strong opposition in the Lords. Some regarded it as designed solely to further the Tory interest in towns; others feared the creation of an army of spies, the aggravation of local animosities, and eventually the withdrawal of the toleration that had already been granted. The bill was passed, however, but in a much modified form. It seemed impossible to arrive at a conclusion which should satisfy both Houses. A conference was held, in which the Commons repeated their arguments as to the intention of the legislature, the evasion of the law, and the scandal to religion, and the Lords reiterated their belief that the scandal could be stopped by a small penalty, with an incapacity for office. This certainly would have been ineffective, and a crop of spies would as readily have found work. Eventually the Lords adhered to their amendments, and the Bill was lost. Before the end of the year it was revived, and again it was sent by a large majority up to the Lords. Bishop Burnet spoke strongly against it, avowing that he had himself been an occasional conformist abroad, and approving of the action of dissenters who communicated from time to time in church. Tenison supported him, and nine other bishops. Archbishop Sharp, on the other hand, with five bishops, were *The rejection.* in favour of the Bill. It was again rejected by the Lords; and the return of a Whig majority to the Commons in 1705 prevented its revival.

When the new Parliament met, the queen reiterated the statement of her affection to the Church and her determination to support it; but an agitation in the country, fostered by Tory politicians for party purposes, was claiming support, and a debate was actually held in the *"The Church in danger."* House of Lords on the question whether the Church was in danger. It was voted that the Church was not in danger, and the Houses passed a joint resolution which was afterwards embodied in a royal proclamation. It ran as follows : "That the Church of England, as by law established, which was rescued from the extremest danger by King William III. of glorious memory, is now, by God's blessing, under the happy reign of her Majesty, in a most safe and flourishing condition ; and that whoever goes about to suggest or insinuate that the Church is in danger under her Majesty's administration is an enemy to the queen, the Church, and the kingdom." The agitation thus raised in the country and discussed in Parliament was continued in the press, the pulpit, and Convocation. Benjamin Hoadly, afterwards a scandal to the Episcopate for his non-residence, then a city rector, attacked the chief Tory and High Church doctrines in trenchant fashion, and was reproved by Bishop Compton in consequence; and controversy surged round him and the subjects which divided the parties of the day. Convocation was the scene of passionate disputations, and after a severe rebuke from the queen its sessions were suspended.

At the beginning of 1708 a change was apparent. Passing under new influences Anne was induced to take a step more favourable to the High Church party. Without previously consulting the council she nominated Dr. Blackall to the see of Exeter, and Sir William Dawes to that of Chester. Both were good men, but their views on politics and Church discipline differed entirely from those of the Whig bishops. Their appointment was followed by a recrudescence of the controversy on Divine right, which showed how entirely Church feeling was for the time entangled in political considerations. Months of dreary controversy passed : they culminated in the famous case of Dr. Henry Sacheverell.

This energetic and aggressive ecclesiastic, a fellow of Magdalen College, Oxford, had already attracted attention by his vigorous attacks on dissenters and Latitudinarians, and those who differed from him in politics and religion, when, in the autumn of 1709, he sprang into national notoriety. On August 15 he preached the assize sermon at Derby, and on November 5 he preached at St. Paul's before the Lord Mayor. The latter sermon had been preached before at Oxford, when Hearne, the Jacobite antiquary, described it in his Diary as upon "'in perils among false brethren,' in the prosecution of which words he did with a great deal of courage and boldness shew the great danger the Church is in at present (notwithstanding the Parliament has voted it to be in none) from the fanatics and other false brethren, whom he set forth in their proper

The Sacheverell sermons.

colours." One of his hearers thus described the scene at St. Paul's :

"Dr. Sacheverell, your mighty Boanerges, thundered most furiously against the fanatics for condemning the king of high treason against his supreme subjects, as he expressed it. He spoke very freely of the Toleration Act, and charged the mayors and magistrates with want of zeal for the Church, and played particularly and expressly upon the Bishop of Sarum. . . . All the congregation were shaken again at the terror of his inveterate expressions. The Whigs, says he, are conformists in faction, half conformists in practice, and nonconformists in judgment. Formerly they laboured to bring the Church into the conventicle, now they labour to bring the conventicle into the Church, which will prove its inevitable ruin." The sermon contained also a pointed reference to the Whig ministry, and especially to Godolphin. It was proposed to print the sermon, but the Court of Aldermen rejected the proposal. None the less it was issued a few days later, with a dedication to the Lord Mayor. On December 13 the House of Commons declared both sermons to be "malicious, scandalous, and seditious libels, highly reflecting upon her Majesty and her government, the late happy resolutions, and the Protestant succession." The next day the author was summoned to the bar, and an order was passed to impeach him. Personal feeling as well as party politics was now concerned, and the projected trial became a public question of national interest. Sacheverell was, as Hearne says, "a man of much noise but little sincerity," and he made the utmost of the occasion. His lodgings were surrounded by admiring crowds, he was prayed for in churches, belauded in sermons. When he drove to his trial in Westminster Hall a multitude followed him with cheers and good *His trial* wishes. When the queen drove back from the hall, where she went privately to hear the trial, the crowd surrounded her coach and called out "God bless your Majesty and the Church. We hope your majesty is for Dr. Sacheverell." A riot was raised in London, and the guards were called out. After a long trial the Lords voted Sacheverell guilty, and the *and sentence.* farce was concluded by a ridiculous sentence. He was suspended from preaching for three years, and his two sermons, with the declaration of the Oxford Convocation of 1683, in favour of passive obedience, were burnt by the hangman.

Several of the bishops, notably Archbishop Sharp, had voted in his favour. The queen, though she maintained a

The popular agitation ending in a Tory triumph. judicious silence, was suspected to approve of what he had said. High Tories everywhere were delighted with the fiasco of trial and sentence. He became a public hero, and when he went down to Shropshire

he had a triumphant progress. At Oxford he was received by the city sheriff and five hundred people ; at Shrewsbury, it is said, by fifty thousand. The hasty action of the Whigs— inspired no doubt by the rage of Godolphin, whose nickname "Volpone" had been used in the sermon at St. Paul's— had, in fact, made him a martyr. It seemed incredible that it should be thought worth while to impeach a hot-headed preacher unless there was a real design to depress the Church. The popular delusion was even more widespread, as it was certainly more rational, than at the time of the popish plot. It had a remarkable effect upon the elections. In November 1710, a large Tory majority was returned, and until the end of Anne's reign the government was entirely in the hands of that party.

Of direct effects on the position of the Church there were few, at first, from this extraordinary frenzy. Sacheverell's first sermon after his suspension had a great sale, and he received the crown living of St. Andrew's, Holborn. He preached before the House of Commons on May 29, 1713, and the sermon was printed by order of the House. With this commemoration of the Restoration, on the principles of passive obedience and non-resistance, which had before been condemned, he reached the culmination of his triumph. It might have been fancied that he expressed the opinions of the Church, and that the nation had been converted to accept them. Thus the incident was closed so far as the Church was concerned.

With the triumph of the Tories the queen believed herself to be emancipated ; she spoke to several persons, Burnet tells us, of the captivity she had endured. Fashion followed the court. It was the mode to be High Church ; and, happily also, the queen's example encouraged virtue as well as churchmanship. But still the political effects were the most prominent. The Tory party used the enthusiastic Church feeling of the country to enable it to carry bills against the dissenters which were designed to make permanent the Tory triumph at the polls.

In 1713 was passed the Occasional Conformity Act, and the Schism Act soon after. The first was passed without demur, in spite of the hot opposition it had pre- The viously met with. Thus the government of the Occasional Conformity country seemed to be placed securely in the hands and Schism of churchmen. But, like all such party legislation, Acts, 1713-14. the Act was quite ineffectual. It did not even succeed in placing the government in the hands of the Tories for any length of time. In 1714 the Schism Act followed. It represented the climax of the political elevation of the Church. It was ordered that no person in Great Britain should keep any public or private school, or act as tutor, without first subscribing the declaration to conform to the Church of England, and obtaining a license from the bishop, which was to be dependent on a certificate of communion and of having taken the oaths. The grounds on which so drastic a measure was advocated were characteristic. It was declared that the dissenters were the irreconcilable enemies of the Church, having shared with the papists in the toleration granted by James II., and that their schools were a danger to the universities and to the Church. It was carried, and the bitter feeling against the Church was thereby greatly strengthened. It was a time of dispute and confusion. There is no wonder that it turned the heads of some. Swift in his journal to Stella tells how the "old Bishop of Worcester," Hough, who had so stoutly defended his rights at Magdalen against James II., now "pretends to be a prophet." He went to the queen to prove to her "out of Daniel and the Revelation, that four years hence [this was in 1712] there would be a war of religion, that the King of France would be a Protestant," and the like. Harley was said to have "confounded him sadly in his own learning; which made the old fool very quarrelsome," adds Swift.

Tattle of this sort did not strengthen the Church.

Legislation in the interests of a party sensibly weakened her. For the moment Church and State seemed to stand together in united strength. But the whole edifice so laboriously reared, the edifice of Tory power based upon the insincere support which statesmen like Harley and St. John gave to the most exclusive claims of churchmen, depended entirely on the life of the Queen. Anne to the last was simple and sincere, patient of advice, deeply in earnest to do good. She would have welcomed a settlement of the succession which might make the Church secure. But she was careful to remain within the strict limits of her constitutional position. Her death was comparatively sudden. On August 1, 1714, she passed away, and George Louis elector of Hanover, came in, like Charles II., without any conditions.

Death of Queen Anne, August 1, 1714.

With the death of Anne the period inaugurated by the accession of her grandfather closes. During the whole of the years 1625 to 1714 it may be said that the Church and her interests were the most important factors in the national history. Pure politics, finance, economics, military and naval affairs, had, in different degrees, prominence in the settlement of great political crises. But behind them stood the question which for ninety years was an acute one, what part should the Church play in the national government. For many years an Erastian theory was dominant. Its expression passed through many different phases, but the results of it were everywhere apparent. The State claimed to foster, to protect, to provide, or to control, the exercise of the spiritual apprehensions of the people. The age of the Stewarts was *par excellence* the age of "the Establishment." At first the State sought the supremacy, more or less disguised, over the Church; and then, when experience had shown difficulties, endeavoured to use the Church for the ends of political party.

Political character of her reign.

The close and inevitable alliance, which was the legacy of Queen Elizabeth, between loyalty to the State and devotion to the Church, was the motive force of church history, judged from its political aspect, during the years from the accession of Charles I. to the death of Queen Anne. The Church, on which this

The position of the Church, 1625-1714.

influence was acting, passed through strange vicissitudes. It was involved in the fall of a dynasty, and in the triumph of a party. It suffered on both sides from religious opponents of its doctrine and order. But throughout it preserved the treasure committed to it in an unbroken adherence to the principles, which, in reliance on primitive tradition and the history of the Church Catholic, the reformers had reiterated for the guidance and the limitation of the Anglican Church. Through years of struggle against foes and of more dangerous protection by undiscerning friends, the Church endeavoured to reach the freedom which had been promised her in the old laws. *Ecclesia Anglicana libera sit :* neither in the restricted nor in any wider sense was the promise of Magna Carta yet fulfilled. But great churchmen and pious thinkers had still pointed towards the light. Even in the worst times of popular patronage, the old note of self-denial and of apostolic mission could be plainly heard. Yet, unhappily, disputes, internal and external, did much to drown it. The history of Convocation is a critical example.

AUTHORITIES.—State Papers, Domestic ; Burnet, *History of his own Time ;* Dean Swift, *Works,* notably his *Sentiments of a Church of England Man* and *Last Four Years of Queen Anne ;* Kennett's *Works* and *Life ; Life of Archbishop Sharpe ;* Sacheverell's Trial in Howell, *State Trials,* vol. xv. ; *The wisdom of looking backwards, to judge the better of one side and t'other by the speeches, writings, actions, and other matters of fact on both sides for the four years last past* [Kennett] 1715 ; The Harley MSS., in *Portland Papers* (Historical MSS. Commission) ; Stillingfleet, *Works* and *Life,* by Bentley. Very interesting sketches of the lives of all the chief clergy are given, from a very complete study of all the materials, by J. H. Overton, in *Life in the English Church,* 1660-1714.

CHAPTER XV

ERASTIANISM AND THE CONVOCATION DISPUTES
(1689–1715)

THE relations of the Church with the State during the reigns of William and Mary and of Anne may very obviously be

The royal power and the Convocations, 1689-1714.

contrasted. The Erastianism of William was foreign to the temper and training of his successor. Nevertheless, though with every difference in detail, each reign was marked by an association of State and Church which was dangerous if not disastrous to the latter. Under William III. there was no question that the State ruled the Church; under Anne the same servitude continued, though the fetters were disguised with flowers. This was partly due to the action of the State; partly it was due to the errors of the Church. The note of Erastianism is distinctly audible in the warrant addressed to Compton, Bishop of London (November 26, 1689), on the opening of the Convocation of Canterbury. The license to confer upon matters seems to be limited to those which the Sovereign " shall propose or cause to be proposed." After the reform of the liturgy and other questions, the further power of discussion is limited to all such " other matters as their Majesties shall think necessary and expedient for advancing of the honour and service of Almighty God, the good and quiet of the Church, and the better government thereof, with liberty and authority to draw out forms, rules, orders, ordinances, constitutions, and canons on such matters as to them shall seem necessary and expedient for the purposes above mentioned, and to set them down in writing

and, from time to time, to deliver them unto the king to the
end that he, as occasion shall require, may thereupon have the
advice of Parliament." But if much of this may be explained
as warranted by constitutional forms, the same can hardly be
said with much truth—though there were precedents for them
—for the royal injunctions, which were the characteristic
instruments of William's government of the Church.

On July 27, 1688, Sancroft had issued letters of advice to
the bishops, which showed, as the letter, probably, of one of
his chaplains expresses it, " that the storm in which
he is does not affright him from doing his duty, but Sancroft as archbishop.
rather awakens him to do it with so much the more
vigour ; and, indeed, the zeal that he expresses in these
articles, both against the corruptions of the Church of Rome
on the one hand, and the unhappy differences that are among
Protestants on the other, are such apostolical things that all
good men rejoice to see so great a prelate at the head of our
Church, who in this critical time has had the courage to do
his duty in so signal a manner." The document which
Sancroft addressed to his suffragans showed, indeed, the
apostolic fervour with which he guided the province of
Canterbury. It urged the clergy often to read over their
ordination vows, to be resident, to be diligent in catechising
and in performing the daily office, in visiting the sick, and in
observing the holy days and their eves, the Ember and
Rogation days, and the seasons of Advent and Lent. It
required them to exhort the people to frequent communion,
and it gave sound advice as to their attitude towards Romanist
and Protestant dissenters.

A letter such as this, coming from the primate of all
England, was a seemly incitement to the performance of
clerical duty. But less appropriate are similar
words of advice when addressed by the State to The king intervenes.
the Church. As example may be given a letter
from the king to the Bishop of London, to be circulated
throughout the provinces of Canterbury and York. "We
require you to examine into the lives and learning of those
desiring to be admitted in holy orders, to see that the clergy
are resident in their livings, and to admonish them to
religiously observe the canon as to sober conversation. You

shall order the clergy to preach frequently against those
particular sins and vices which are most prevalent in this
realm, and on every Lord's day on which such sermon shall
be preached they shall also read such statutes as are provided
against such sins; these statutes we have ordered to be
printed, together with this letter, that they may be transmitted
by you to every parish in the realm. You shall also require
all churchwardens to impartially present all those guilty of
adultery and fornication."

There were special circumstances, notably the king's adulterous life, which gave an air of insincerity to such a letter as
this: yet it doubtless was not without good result, in aiding
the religious societies and those for the reformation of manners
which were then springing into importance. It was the
method of advising rather than the nature of the advice which
was unfortunate. The Church was to be ruled by royal
injunctions. So again in 1695 another series was issued by
the king and despatched through Archbishop Tenison to the
bishops. It ordered that the canons with regard to ordination be strictly observed, and it added further directions as
to pluralities and non-residence, the performance of divine
service, catechising, visiting the sick, commutations
of penance, and the like. The king ordered the
injunctions to be conveyed to the bishops, and
added, "as we esteem it a chief part of our princely care to
promote the true religion as it is established in this Church, and
in order thereunto, we have determined not to dispose of any
Church preferments in our gift but to such of our clergy as we
shall have reason to believe do live most exemplary and preach
and watch most faithfully over the people committed to their
charge, so we assure ourselves that these our pious intentions
will be effectually seconded by you and the rest of our bishops."

This assumption of direction in the matter of the practical duties of the clergy was followed in the same month
by a paper of Directions on the Trinitarian controversy. A
number of Socinian pamphlets had been met by Sherlock's
Vindication of the doctrine (1693), and then by Dr. South.
Oxford rang, as so often, with the vigorous language of the
opponents: and then the royal Directions stepped in to order
that there must be no dispute at all. No preacher whatsoever

was to presume to deliver any other doctrine concerning the
blessed Trinity than what is contained in the Holy Scriptures
and is agreeable to the three Creeds and the Thirty-nine Articles
of religion.   Whoever may have written the Directions, their
language was singularly inept, and the intervention of the
royal power was on every ground to be regretted.   The
advisers of William III. were not content to leave
him to deal with his wars and his policies and to   William's
advisers.
allow the Church to be governed by her own
ministers.   Not only did they thus bring him forward in
the direction of purely ecclesiastical questions, but they were
busy, as may be seen by several papers among the public
records, with suggestions as to fit persons for preferment.
Some of these suggestions have considerable interest, for
example, one that never more than one foreigner at the same
time shall have preferment in the same church, "lest the
English be discouraged," recalls the abuses of the Middle
Ages, and pointedly reprehends the custom of rewarding
Dutchmen who had not received Episcopal ordination with preferments which were not *beneficia curata* (with cure of souls).
No case, it may be observed, is known of one who had not
been ordained by a bishop being admitted to minister in the
English Church.   Another of the proposed rules for better
and more equal distribution of church preferments, which,
it is observed, will free the king from a great deal of importunity, is that the prebends of Westminster should be limited
to the ministers of London and Westminster; and that the
minister of St. Margaret's Westminster, shall be always, as
at present, one of the prebendaries, "because the House of
Commons go to that church, and therefore it is fit there
should be encouragement for a good preacher."   Similarly
one prebend, at least, in every cathedral church, should be
bestowed on some minister in the city of that cathedral church.

Proposals of this kind were often unobjectionable : not so
was the method of ruling the church by means of royal
injunctions, for this practically involved the abeyance of the
Church's provincial and representative bodies.   Nor were
these the only instances of unconstitutional or extra-con-
stitutional action.   Thus, for example, the king summoned
the bishops, while Parliament was not sitting, to meet together

to give advice about the best course to be taken for preserving the religion established by law and for suppressing the growth of Popery. Stillingfleet's undated memorandum on the subject is among the papers of his family. He pointed out that the real difficulty lay in the fact that the laws were quite strong enough, and he advised the bishops to return thanks, express their readiness, and prepare such proposals as may be judged convenient "after the ancient legal way."

The history of the Convocations during the reigns of William and Anne is important and significant. Constitutional forms

The history of the Convocations. survive, and are made the subject of hot contest: the example of party organisation and vituperation is borrowed from the political assemblies of the nation, but practically little is accomplished save the elucidation of some problems of historical interest. In spite of the submission of the clergy, the power of the Convocations had been exercised with considerable freedom under the Stewarts, the notable instance being the enacting the canons of 1640, which received the royal assent, and have never been repealed, though they were condemned by a resolution of the Long Parliament, and the grant of supplies to the king by the clergy when the House of Commons had withheld them. The arrangement between Sheldon and Clarendon (see p. 199) had abolished part of these powers : but the legislative power, under royal authority, remained untouched. Its exercise in popular opinion was, it must be admitted, not calculated to inspire respect. It had been thus described by an opponent, R. Bernard ("A short view of the Prelaticall Church of England," 1641):

"There is a provincial assembly for the province of Canterbury, which consists of the archbishop, the president, of all the other bishops under him, deans, archdeacons with others, and of the two ministers chosen out of every diocese called the clerks of the Convocation. These clerks should be chosen freely, by the publique consent and voice of all the ministers in every diocese, but the prelates propound whom they list or like best for their purpose, and do ask voices, which are given to them of many through fear, so as the choice is not free as it ought to be. That which is intended to be done there is contrived and hammered in the head of the archbishop, and some few with him, to which the rest of the bishops do consent. In the Lower House the priests, parsons, and vicars (those clerks) sit there to gaze one on another and to tell the clock, waiting for their lessons from their lords the prelates. There is no freedom of voices ; they dare not consult among themselves to promote the cause of Christ and to reform abuses. The better sort are the fewest and are either overawed by the greatest or borne down by the worst." When the bishops had the confidence of their clergy, and the king had the confidence of the bishops, this was not an unfair picture of the proceedings ; but matters were reversed under William III. The king, by the accident of having to nominate fifteen bishops, had the Upper House at his command : the Lower House was inspired by feelings utterly opposed to those of the Calvinist king and the Latitudinarian prelates.

For several years after the abortive attempt to revise the liturgy the Convocations were not allowed to exercise their powers. Pamphlets of various complexions had shown the popular interest in the questions. *A Letter from a Minister in the Country*, for example, had argued temperately, but with considerable historical inaccuracy, on behalf of the alterations proposed, with a view to comprehension. With equal good feeling, a letter to a friend relating to the present Convocation, probably written to Dr. Kidder (Ken's intruded successor at Bath and Wells), and dated November 27, 1689, asks, " Are a few excepted passages in our liturgy and two or three ceremonies in our worship things of so great value that we must for the sake of them still maintain those discords and divisions in Church and State which have so long harassed both almost to utter ruin ? " On the other side, *Remarks from the Country* retorted upon this letter, and *Vox Cleri* pointed out that all the proposed concessions when suggested by Stillingfleet in 1681 had been " thrown, as it were, with spite in his teeth," and that Baxter had declared " forty sinful particulars in our communion," and wittily criticised the country minister as a country wit. It was answered, with reasons for comprehension, some petty raillery of the " superstitious devices " of " prostrations at the Eucharist and the like inventions," with

Beginning of the Convocation controversy.

an alarmist suggestion that "the king and Parliament will be
greatly displeased with the clergy unless they consent to some
alterations and abatements in order to a legal comprehension,"
and with an indignant remonstrance at the comparison by
Vox Cleri of the two previous opponents to Don Quixote
tilting at windmills and to *Fur prædestinatus*, Sancroft's slave
of Calvinistic necessity. Pamphlets such as these showed the
vivacity of public interest in 1690.

In 1697 the whole question of the right, powers, and privileges of Convocation was opened by *a Letter to a Convocation
Man*, written probably by Sir Bartholomew Shower,
The Letter to a Convocation Man, 1697. a Jacobite lawyer of eminence. This important
pamphlet argued, first, for the need of a session of
Convocation, from the growth of infidelity and the
claim of foreign Socinians and anti-Trinitarians ("see how
the wind blows from Holland") that the English Church
was of their party. Upon this it proceeded to discuss the
power of the Assemblies of the Church. It admitted that
"Convocation cannot assemble without the assent of the
king : his writ is necessary in order to it," but it asserted
that the Convocation and Parliament stood in this regard
exactly on the same footing. "The one of these courts is
of the same power and use with regard to the Church as
the other is in respect to the State," and in the one as in the
other, "the prerogative power of assembling them by writ
doth not import a power of licensing or confining them in
their debates, any more than it doth in the case of a Parliament." And as to the validity of canons passed with royal
assent, the writer claimed "that they need no confirmation
of, or by the Parliament, provided they do not impugn
common law, statutes, customs, or prerogative." "To confer, debate, and resolve, without the king's license, is at
common law the undoubted right of Convocation." Such
powers were claimed as the undoubted and the necessary
rights of the English Church. The pamphlet was a manifesto of the High Church, and notably of the Jacobite party.

It was answered by Dr. Wake in *The Authority of Christian Princes over their Ecclesiastical Synods asserted.*
Wake's reply. Wake argued that the Convocations could not even
treat of canons without a royal license : they could neither

meet nor debate but by the king's leave. From among the smaller debaters who continued the strife rose the brilliant figure of Francis Atterbury, a student of Christ Church, for whom his party soon came to feel an admiration and loyalty which was little short of personal affection. It appears that the materials for his smart attack were prepared by Dr. Matthew Hutton of Aynho, the correspondent of Henry Wharton : and historically the work was an advance upon its predecessors. It showed the clear distinction between the ecclesiastical summons to the Convocations and the summons in virtue of the *præmunientes* clause. But it went on to the unwarrantable conclusion that the clergy's right to meet was indefeasible, and that their power to enact was not touched by the submission under Henry VIII.

The later stages of the dispute were marked by the publication of much antiquarian and controversial matter. Burnet, Hody, Kennett were concerned, and all were notable Whigs. Burnet confessed that he was "not The controinclined to expect much from the assemblies of versy spreads. clergymen," and Swift dealt in later years very merrily with him on the point. The most important pamphlets published in the years 1701 and 1702 were concerned with later developments of the controversy, especially with the archbishop's right to prorogue the Convocation. The *Forma Convocationis Celebrandæ* itself argued against Atterbury. *The Power of the Lower House of Convocation to adjourn itself Vindicated* was a somewhat clumsy historical argument that the Lower House was not tied by the archbishop's writ to a particular place of session, and therefore could not be bound by a writ of prorogation : a good deal of special pleading led to the conclusion, which had no particular relation to the premises, that "the springs of these unhappy differences lie no lower than in an observation of the steps taken, of late years, towards suppressing the right and very being of Convocation." This was met by a lengthy refutation, *The Right of the Archbishop to continue or prorogue the whole Convocation*, which fully established the power of the archbishop.

It is now time to speak of the action of the Houses to which the earlier of these pamphlets led up and upon which

T

the later ones were based. At the beginning of 1701 the

Practical
action of the
two Houses.

Convocations were again allowed to meet. Dr. Hooper, Dean of Canterbury, who eventually became Bishop of Bath and Wells when Dr. Kidder was killed in bed by the fall of a chimney, was chosen prolocutor of the Lower House, and the claim was at once asserted that the archbishop " could no more legally prorogue the Lower House of Convocation than the Speaker of the House of Lords could order an adjournment of the House of Commons." On these lines the Lower House drew up a report in which it claimed to be prorogued only by its prolocutor and declared that it need not adjourn when the Upper House did : also that its custom was not to attend the bishops till it had first met in session. Before, however, this was discussed a schedule of prorogation had been presented from the archbishop, " a method of adjourning," says the authorised report of the proceedings of the Lower House, " never thought of before the Convocation of 1689." The reply of the archbishop—for the prorogation was not pressed—claimed, as president of the Convocation, the sole power of adjourning the whole body. The Lower House voted " that this was not a satisfactory answer, and desired " a free conference," " a word that never appeared in the acts of any former Convocation," says Kennett. The bishops refused it, and declared that the controversy must be continued in writing.

At this point the Lower House took a further step to assert rights, which had certainly in this case been exercised before,

Attacks on
Toland and
Burnet.

by censuring (in the phrase of their narrative) " a detestable book call'd *Christianity not Mysterious*, writ by Toland," and asking the bishops' concurrence and advice as to the suppression of that and similar books. The Upper House, by the mouth of the archbishop, declared that no judicial steps could be taken without royal license, and severely censured the Lower House. The reply was that they had not asked for judicial censure, and that if it was needed license could be obtained for it. The Convocation was adjourned to May 8 by the archbishop, but the Lower House adjourned to a different day. On May 8, after another censure, the prolocutor presented another reply, carrying the war into the enemy's country. Though the archbishop had declared the proceedings of the Lower House null, he yet received this paper, and a committee of five bishops was suggested to meet ten of the Lower House and inspect the acts of the present Convocation. This the Lower House declined : but it proceeded to offer a representation as to the sense of Burnet's exposition of the Thirty-nine Articles, as tending to "introduce such a latitude and diversity of opinions as the Articles were framed to avoid." From this point an unseemly wrangle began, the two Houses being at issue as to what points were to be discussed and how they were to be discussed : whether the Bishop of Salisbury's book, or the supposed irregularity of the action of the Lower House. The hot-headed Burnet said that the conduct of the prolocutor was "according to his usual insolence," and Dr. Hooper replied that "what my lord of Salisbury was pleased to think, he was not much concerned at." On June 24 the Convocation was prorogued when Parliament ended. Wrangle between the Houses.

In the next Convocation, at the beginning of 1702, it was determined to register the claim of the Lower House as to prorogations, by putting on the minutes the phrase, "*prolocutor continuavit et prorogavit quoad hanc domum.*" This led to a new crop of pamphlets,[1] and the disputes would doubtless have become as hot as during the previous year had not the prolocutor died. The archbishop declined to authorise the election of a new one, for the king's death had been held by the lawyers to end the Convocation. The conclusion of the whole matter seemed to be reached in Wake's revision of his former work, in which he admitted the distinction between the writ to the archbishop and the *præmunientes* clause, and emphasised the effect of the Act of Submission (1532).

But the reign of Anne showed that the Lower House was not silenced or convinced. The attitude of Queen Anne's first Parliament has been already described : the Lower House of the Convocation of Canterbury affords a fit parallel. The question of the prorogation was at once reopened : Archbishop Tenison, on November 13, 1702, repeated to the Lower House the assertion of his right, but agreed to the appointment of a committee of bishops. This committee offered the Lower House "the privilege of Renewal of the dispute under Anne.

---

[1] See list among the *Authorities* for this chapter.

meeting in committees between the sessions, and that when there was business before the House the archbishop should so order the prorogations as to allow time for the ordering and finishing it." The Lower House replied by reiterating the claim of right : the Upper retorted by rejecting it. The Lower then asked that the question might be submitted to the queen, who should be asked to appoint a tribunal to decide it. This the bishops refused, and they desired the Lower House to remember that the Church was Episcopal, and that deference was due to the bishops.

It was at this critical point in the heated discussion that the House of Commons passed a resolution (November 21, 1702) that they would "on all occasions assert the just rights and privileges of the Lower House of Convocation." The House, strongly Tory, felt in deed so strongly against the Episcopate, which William III had packed with Whigs, that one of the members wittily said : "One would be provoked by the late behaviour of the bishops, to bring in a Bill for the toleration of Episcopacy, for, since they are of the same principles with the dissenters, it is but just, I think, that they should stand upon the same foot."

Action of the House of Commons.

Thus the Lower House seemed to have the victory in their hands. They sent up a resolution that they had been as-persed and that they judged the order of bishops to be of divine apostolical institution. In a further resolution of December 15 they asked the bishops to concur in the resolution and to make a declaration against Arian and Erastian opinions. The bishops were placed in a considerable difficulty. The greater number of them certainly did not believe in the divine apostolical institution of their order. In Burnet's words, "The Lower House looked upon what they did in this matter as a master-piece, for if the bishops complied with them they gained their point, and if they refused it, they resolved to make them who would not come up to such a positive definition pass for secret favourers of Presbytery." The Lower House also petitioned the queen to decide the question of right : and she returned answer that she would consider it. At length on January 20, 1703, the archbishop replied that while

The question of the divine institution of Episcopacy.

the preface to the Ordinal certainly spoke of three orders of the ministry, no canon or rule respecting discipline or doctrine could be passed without the royal license.

At the beginning of the next session the Lower House turned to practical matters, complaining of the licentiousness of the press, and the defects of the law as to Church rates : and in the spring they submitted another document, which called attention to the decay of Church discipline, the lack of due performance of divine service and the holy communion, and other spiritual neglects and moral defects. This was regarded as an attack on the bishops, and Burnet sharply observed that nothing was said of the greater abuses of which the lower clergy were guilty.

In the autumn of 1704 the Lower House returned again to the charge, and specially to the question of intermediate sessions, held by the Lower House when the Upper House was not sitting. The disputes continued in 1706 ; and the queen was advised to write to the archbishop stating her concern at the differences. She added that she endeavoured to preserve the constitution of the Church, "but that she was resolved to maintain her supremacy and the due subordination of presbytery and bishops as fundamental parts thereof." Whereupon the Convocation was prorogued. The Lower House had continued their policy of censuring books, calling the attention of the Upper House especially to a sermon of Mr. Hoadly's as contrary to the Homilies. In 1707 both Houses concurred in an address to the sovereign declaring the Church to be safe under her rule ; but a prorogation soon followed, declared apparently under the impression that the Lower House would protest against the terms of the union with Scotland.

The queen's intervention, 1706.

Against this prorogation the Lower House at its next meeting vigorously protested, saying that there was "no instance, 1531-1705, of a writ of prorogation issuing during the session of Parliament to dismiss the clergy met in Convocation." Their representation brought upon them a severe condemnation. In a letter to the archbishop the queen was induced to say of the representation that it was "untrue in point of fact, and amounts to a plain invasion of our royal supremacy which is

Protest against prorogation.

reposed in us by the law and constitution of the Church of England," and to threaten "to use such means for punishing offences of this nature as are warranted by law." When the Lower House was summoned by the archbishop to hear this letter read the prolocutor did not appear. He was declared contumacious, and was compelled to submit. Nothing further happened in this session ; and at the next meeting of Parliament Convocation was not allowed to meet at all.

So stood the unprofitable but not uninteresting or unimportant constitutional question when the Sacheverell case and the Tory reaction changed the face of public affairs. The Convocation of 1710 met under very different circumstances from those in which the last had ended. On January 25 the letters of business were received, the matters to be submitted having previously been arranged by the queen's order under the direction of Archbishop Sharp. On January 29 the subjects were conveyed to the Houses by the queen's letter. They were as follow :

"The drawing-up a representation of the present state of religion among us, with regard to the late excessive growth of *The queen's* infidelity, heresy, and profaneness. The regulating *letter of* the proceedings in excommunications, and reforming *business, 1710.* the abuses of commutation money.

"The preparing a form for the visitation of prisoners, and particularly condemned persons. For admitting converts from the Church of Rome and such as shall renounce their errors. For restoring those who have relapsed.

"The establishing rural deans, where they are not, and rendering them more useful than they are.

"The making provision for preserving and transmitting more exact terriers, and accounts of glebes, tithes, and other possessions and profits belonging to benefices.

"The regulating licences for matrimony, according to the canon, in order to the more effectual preventing of clandestine marriages."

Atterbury was now prolocutor, and the paper which he *The case* drew up on the first head was rejected by the Upper *of Whiston.* House. But the attention of the House was again turned aside to the censure of books, and the work of William Whiston, Professor of Mathematics at Cambridge, who had been removed from his post, and who now dedicated his *Historical Preface to Primitive Christianity Reviewed* to the Convocation, was censured by the Lower House as "directly opposite to the fundamental articles of the Christian religion." The bishops agreed in the condemnation; but the question whether condemnation was possible by Convocation was submitted to the queen for the opinion of the judges.

The judges were consulted, and with them the law officers of the crown, and they, by ten to twelve, gave opinion that Convocations had jurisdiction in cases of heresy, but that there was a right of appeal, not removed by any statute, to the sovereign, from all ecclesiastical as well as civil courts, in virtue of the supremacy by which the queen was "over all persons, in all causes, throughout her dominions supreme." Convocations, they concluded, might try the case, but they added the following judicious safeguard: "This being a matter, which upon application for a prohibition on behalf of the persons who shall be prosecuted, may come in judgement before such of us as have the honour to serve your Majesty in places of judicature, we desire to be understood to give our present thoughts with a reserve of an entire freedom of altering our opinions, in case any records or proceedings, which we are now strangers to, shall be laid before us, or any new considerations, which have not occurred to us, be suggested by the parties, or their counsel, to convince us of our mistakes."

The judges' opinion of the rights of Convocation.

When the opinion was received the bishops proceeded first to censure the book, and to submit the censure to the queen. But no action whatever was taken; months after, the queen professed to have lost the document, and the whole matter then came to a lame and impotent conclusion.

Other matters, however, were considered. The Lower House entered upon the project of building new churches, thanking the Commons for their action; and the Commons resolved "that they would receive all such information as should be offered in this case by the Lower House of Convocation; and would have a particular regard to such applications as should at any time be made to them by the clergy in Convocation assembled, according to the ancient usage, together with the Parliament."

The autumn of 1711 brought the whole matter of the subjects suggested by the queen to a deadlock; for the Lower House, acting under the advice of Atterbury,

Deadlock in 1711. claimed, and persisted in the claim in spite of precedents to the contrary, that everything must be begun anew after a prorogation, according to the custom of Parliament. Nor was anything else done, even a declaration on the validity of lay-baptism falling to the ground between the two Houses.

Before the Convocation of 1714 met Atterbury had been made Bishop of Rochester; but the disputes were not yet at rest. There was a difference as to the address to be presented to the queen, and she received the address of the Lower House separately. Some progress was, however, made with regard to the matters named by the queen in 1711, when, in 1714, the Houses were again diverted to the consideration of the heresies of Mr. Samuel Clarke on the doctrine of the Holy Trinity; but, owing to a disagreement between the Houses, no conclusion was arrived at when the queen died.

Thus abruptly and unsatisfactorily does the history of Convocation break off at the death of Anne. If any con-

A futile contest. clusions can be drawn from it they must be that the clergy displayed considerable learning, interest, vivacity, and independence; that the unhappy policy of appointing bishops for political reasons, and out of one particular party, led inevitably to a deep rift between the higher and lower clergy; and that the public interest in the questions of constitutional right, though not unintelligent, was largely determined by political considerations. In the powers of Convocation what was needed was definition; but this in the heated political atmosphere it was impossible to obtain.

AUTHORITIES.—On the question affecting Convocation, see *A Letter from a Minister in the Country to a Member of the Convocation*, 1689 ; *A Letter to a Friend relating to the present Convocation*, 1690 ; *Remarks from the Country upon the Two Letters*, 1689-1690 ; *Vox Cleri, or the Sense of the Clergy concerning the making of Alterations in the Established Liturgy*, etc. 1690 (this contains an account of the proceedings of the Convocation, with the documents, resolutions, etc.) ; *An Answer to Vox Cleri*, 1690 ; *A Letter to a Convocation Man concerning the Rights, Powers, and Privileges of that Body*, 1697 ; *The Authority of Christian Princes* . . . *with particular respect to the Convocation of the Clergy of the Realm and State of England*, by William Wake, D.D., 1697 ; *Rights, Powers, and Privileges of an English*

Convocation, by Francis Atterbury, D.D., 1700 ; *Reflections on a Book entitled
the Rights, etc.* by Gilbert, Bishop of Sarum, 1700 ; Kennett, *Ecclesiastical
Synods and Parliamentary Convocations*, 1701 ; *Forma sive descriptio Convocationis celebrandæ, etc.* n.d. ; *The Power of the Lower House of Convocation to adjourn itself, etc.* 1701 ; *The right of the Archbishop to continue or
prorogue the whole Convocation*, 1701 ; *A narrative of the proceedings of the
Lower House, drawn up by order of the House* [written by Dr. Hooper], 1701 ;
The present state of Convocation, etc. 1702 ; *The Case of the Schedule stated*,
1702 ; *The Parliamentary original and Rights of the Lower House, etc.* 1702 ;
A Faithful Account, etc. (two numbers), 1702 ; *A Summary Defence of the
Lower House, etc.* 1703 ; *The Pretended Independence of the Lower House,
etc.* 1703 ; *The state of the Church and Clergy of England in their Convocation*, by William Wake, D.D., 1703 ; Gibson, *Synodus Anglicana ;* Nicholson, *Correspondence ;* Lathbury, *History of Convocation ;* Wilkins, *Concilia*,
vol. iv.

CHAPTER XVI

THE CHURCH IN RELATION TO POLITICAL THEORY
AND TO LITERATURE

THE close association between politics and religion which had marked alike the personal government of Charles I. and the rule of Commonwealth and Protector, though it received a severe blow at the Restoration by the legal acceptance of dissent from the religion established by law, and a blow still more severe by the Toleration Act of the Revolution, remained till the death of Queen Anne an important feature in the national history. While men were searching for a satisfactory theory which might define the relations of Church and State in practice their spheres were constantly confused. It is well before we speak of the theory to note how closely the practice was related to it during the years of the later Stewarts.

Instances have already been given of the interference of William III. and Anne, directly or indirectly, in what may be regarded as the specially spiritual work of the clergy. It must not be imagined, that even after the Restoration, there were no precedents for such action. On October 14, 1662, for example, a letter was addressed by the king to the archbishops which is thus summarised in the Calendar of State Papers : "The extravagance of preachers has much heightened the disorders, and still continues so to do, by the diligence of factious spirits, who dispose them to jealousy of the government. Young divines, in ostentation of learning, handle the deep points of God's eternal counsels, or wrangle about gestures and fruitless controversies. To put a timely stop to these abuses he has, as

The State and the Church, 1662.

done by former kings, drawn up directions for preachers, which are to be communicated to every minister." To this letter were annexed directions concerning preachers : " None are in their sermons to bound the authority of sovereigns, or determine the differences between them and the people ; nor to argue the deep points of election, reprobation, free will, etc.; they are to abstain as much as possible from controversies ; catechise the children according to the Prayer-book ; stir up the people to the practice of religious and moral duties ; at afternoon service to expound the Church Catechism and prayers ; read publicly the Canons and Thirty-nine Articles twice a year ; no minister is to preach without special licence from the archbishop or bishop. Attendance at Divine service on the Lord's Day is to be enforced, and frequenters of taverns and unlawful sports punished according to law."

Such a letter was indeed a close imitation of some of the instructions issued by Charles I. to Laud. A later one, of 1665, follows on much the same lines. In July, during the height of the plague, Arlington wrote to the Bishop of London that the king was informed that many incumbents and lecturers had deserted their posts and that nonconformists had thrust themselves into their pulpits, and preached sedition and doctrines contrary to the Church ; wherefore the bishop is ordered to prevent such mischiefs to Church and State. On the other hand, instances were not wanting of a scrupulous observance by the civil authorities of the rights of the Church. During the period of discussion about the revision of the Prayer-book in 1662, for example, at a conference between the Houses of Parliament a suggestion was brought forward to make a provision for "reverend and uniform gestures and demeanours to be used at the time of divine service" ; but it was agreed that this was a matter for the Convocations, and they were requested "to prepare some rule or canon for that purpose, to be humbly presented unto his Majesty for his assent." Other and less trivial examples might be quoted ; the general attitude of Parliament towards the Church is indeed well illustrated by the position assumed during the early years of Queen Anne. (See above, p. 276.)

When we pass from practice to theory we find the field occupied by one great writer, whose work has an influence as

widespread as profound ; and with whose opinions all political
and ecclesiastical writers of the age found themselves compelled to deal, whether in support or
in opposition. We have seen (above, p. 213) the
view which was taken by the University of Oxford of the
works of Hobbes. Though his great work deals hardly more
than indirectly with the Church, it must receive
at least brief mention here. Of the rights of sovereigns it was his cue to argue for the most part, as he said,
from "the principles of nature only," in other words, from
experience : he would make a distinction of Christian politics,
as depending "much upon supernatural revelations of the
will of God," and thus, in his elaborate manner—
often, very plainly, with his tongue in his cheek—
he considers whether Christian sovereigns are
absolute in their own territories, immediately under God, and
then rejects the assumptions of "a vicar of Christ constituted
of the Universal Church" : he dismisses metaphorical,
spiritual, or ecclesiastical interpretations of "the kingdom of
God," and decides that it is a civil kingdom in which the
Christian sovereign is the representative of God, and His
prophet. From this he was able, by quaint and devious paths,
to pass to the definition of a Church as "a company of men
professing the Christian religion, united in the person of one
sovereign ; at whose command they ought to assemble, and
without whose authority they ought not to assemble." This
leads to an identification of the Church in each country with
the civil commonwealth : and it involves an explicit denial of
the existence of "such universal Church as all Christians are
forced to obey," and an emphatic declaration that "there is no
other government in this life, neither of State nor religion,
but temporal ; nor teaching of any doctrine, lawful to any
subject, which the government both of the State and of the
religion forbiddeth to be taught." Thus "temporal and
spiritual government are but two words brought into the world
to make men see double and mistake their lawful sovereign,"
and so the civil sovereign is chief pastor of the Church as
well as chief ruler of the State. As such he has power to
ordain what pastors he please, and they are simply his ministers,
in the same manner as are the civil magistrates, and derive

Political theory.

Hobbes.

In the Leviathan.

from him their "right of teaching, preaching, and other functions pertaining to that office." It is sovereigns alone who have their authority *jure divino :* and bishops ought to describe themselves as "by the favour of the king's majesty bishop of such a diocese." And from this Hobbes, that there might be no doubt of his position in regard to the existing Church of England, claimed for every Christian sovereign authority "not only to preach (which perhaps no man will deny), but also to baptize and to administer the sacrament of the Lord's Supper, and to consecrate both temples and pastors to God's service." No sooner has he decided that the sovereign is head of the Church than he falls into the temptation, which no seventeenth-century controversialist seems able to avoid, of arguing with Bellarmine, from which he emerges only to conclude that this subjection to the sovereign, whether he be Christian or infidel, in no way touches anything "necessary to salvation."

The *Leviathan* was published in 1651, and was well known, to all who had time amid the distractions of practical politics to study religious and political theories, before the Restoration brought its author into something of The Church intimacy, as well as favour, with the king. There feeling could be no doubt how the Church would receive evoked by the book. such doctrines ; though Hobbes quaintly identified his opinions with those of some of the strongest among the Royalist clergy, telling Aubrey "that Bishop Manwaring preached his doctrine, for which, among others, he was sent prisoner to the Tower." Aubrey adds, "there was a report (and surely true) that in Parliament not long after the king was settled some of the bishops made a motion to have the good old gentleman burnt for a heretique." The worthy biographer exaggerates, for the clergy were content to attack Hobbes with their pens, which they did, indeed, without intermission for more than half a century. But it seems certain that, in spite of what were regarded as the effects of his teaching, in the growth of immorality which Burnet speaks of with so much vehemence, he was not regarded as outside the Church, for he received the sacrament from Pearson and made his confession to Cosin when he thought he was dying, and in the autobiographical note which he wrote two years before his death he spoke of himself as a sincere Christian.   Such was not the opinion of those who dealt only with his books.   Bramhall, Seth Ward, and many other notable ecclesiastics plunged into the fray, and later men repudiated his Erastian theories as at once unconstitutional and un-Christian.

In 1673 Clarendon, then in exile at Moulins, wrote, and in 1676 the press at Sheldon's Theatre, Oxford, printed, his *Survey* of Hobbes's *Leviathan*, to confute the "odious opinions" therein contained.   Notably he excepted against the view that the sovereign is the judge of what is to be believed, even to "the sole power of determining the point of transubstantiation," while the subject may believe or not in his heart, as he chooses : for this indeed was a grave encouragement to hypocrisy.   On the chapter "Of Power Ecclesiastical" he had much to say, and that chiefly in vindication of the power committed by Christ to His ministers "of instructing and preaching and using the keys."   No king, he argued, could be rightly jealous of this power, "for there is neither bishop nor priest who pretends to any power of jurisdiction inconsistent with the king's supremacy in ecclesiastical as well as temporal matters."   Most of all he resented the contention of Hobbes that a man might at his sovereign's command deny Christ while still believing Him.   It was in short the essential immorality of Hobbes's doctrine that most conspicuously affected Clarendon : but there was a special animosity in his mind because it seemed to him that Hobbism approximated very closely to the casuistry of Rome.   This view is to some extent illustrated from history in the treatise which he left, entitled *Religion and Policy and the Countenance and Assistance each should give to the other, with a Survey of the Power and Jurisdiction of the Pope in the Dominions of other Princes*.   This was completed in 1673, just before the examination of Hobbes, but it was not published till 1811.   After a survey of earlier papal history and a more full account of the council of Trent, Clarendon dwelt with especial severity on the political action of the Jesuits, urging the necessity of their expulsion from any country "where any moderation is intended to be exercised."   He recalled the fact that Alexander VII. had refused all help to the exiled Charles II. unless he should become a Roman Catholic, and he urged that if an oath of

Clarendon's criticism of it.

abjuration of the political power of the popes were required
from all Roman Catholics in England the penal laws might be
suspended. "For if that subjection to the pope were once
disclaimed and rooted out, their other errors are not dangerous
to the State." He advocated the licensing of "ecclesiastical
teachers," for the Romanists, "of the mildest and most peaceable dispositions, without leaving them to be supplied by a
foreign mission, which will always supply men who shall be
more solicitous to advance that interest than the peace of their
country, because they have a greater dependence upon it."

But while Clarendon thus stoutly defended the English
Church and State alike against foreign aggression, and while he
asserted in explicit language the constitutional doctrine of the
royal supremacy, he would have as stoutly resisted
Bishop Burnet's Erastian view of the dependence   Wide
of the Church on the State. Little though Burnet   influence of
would have symbolised with Hobbes, it is difficult   Hobbes's
                                                     Erastianism.
to distinguish the practical result of their doctrines. When
Burnet asserted that "the independence of the Church upon
the State" was Popery, a pamphleteer replied, "if this
be Popery, all the great men almost this Church and nation
ever produced were papists," and asked, "if the Church be not
a distinct and independent society from the State upon what
power and rights stands it in the times of persecution? What
had it before it was encouraged by the State, and does its
establishment by the State take away any authority that it
enjoyed before?"

There was indeed no lack of independence in the Church,
when ecclesiastics could withstand James II. as did the seven
bishops, or answer Charles II. as did Wren, "Sir, I
know the way to the Tower." But in the condition   Views of
of religion, "so twisted," as Halifax wrote in *The* Halifax
Character of a Trimmer, "with that of government that it is
never to be separated," it was not surprising that not only
should theory be hesitating but practical action be confused by
the conduct of self-seeking men, who, as the same wit says,
"did practice to bow at the altar only to learn to make the
better bow at court." The position of dissenters, papist and
Protestant, was a standing difficulty in the elaboration of a
coherent political philosophy. Hobbes would cut the gordian

knot by his unmitigated Erastianism.   But the practical condition of affairs led the majority of theorists to hold with
Halifax, that it was wise "to use the means of reclaiming such
of the dissenters as are not incurable, and even of bearing to a
degree those that are, as far as may consist with the public
interest and security"; as well as, with the same writer in his
Letter to a Dissenter, to consider the claims of the Church of
Rome as impossible to reconcile either with a free toleration
or with the rights of the national Church or king.   The end

Swift.   of the century not unnaturally saw an impatience
of theory which was consummated in the reign of
Anne and in the contemptuous indifference of Swift : "Nor do
I think it wholly groundless," he wrote in 1708, in the irony of
a robust common sense which refused to discuss any but
practical issues, "or my fears altogether imaginary, that the
abolishing of Christianity may perhaps bring the Church into
danger, or at least put the senate to the trouble of securing
another vote."

It is to be observed that the strong Church feeling, linked
to high Toryism, of Anne's reign is evidenced largely by the
Influence of   publication of historical works which had in all
historical   matters a conservative tendency.   Clarendon's
writing :   *History of the Rebellion and Civil Wars*, published
Clarendon
and Collier.   in 1702-3, was read with avidity as a defence of
"Church and King."   Jeremy Collier's *Ecclesiastical History
of Great Britain*, of which the first volume appeared in 1708
and the second in 1714, was a learned, critical, and powerful
work on the continuous history of the Church, which, written
by a nonjuror, was to a considerable extent regarded as a
vindication of High Church views, and was severely criticised
by bishops of the opposite party, Nicholson, Kennett, and
Burnet.   These works did not stand alone.   There was a
general interest in historical studies, as may be seen from the
work of Wharton, Wake, Kennett, and Brokesby ; and it was
frequently made useful for party purposes.

Whatever, then, may have been the views of party leaders
or of intended ecclesiastics as to the relations between Church
and State, a hard line of aggressive assertion was taken up—
in spite of the personal sympathies of Charles I. and Anne,
at the beginning and end of the period respectively—with

more and more effect by the statesmen of the seventeenth and eighteenth centuries. Not a few of the ancient constitutional rights of the Church fell into abeyance; Erastianism came to rule public policy almost undisputed.

But all the while ecclesiastical writers upheld the traditional views of the Church's position, not only in relation to the English crown, but in regard to the larger, universal body of which the Church formed a part. Thus the preface of the Prayer-book, written in 1662, speaks explicitly of the whole Catholic Church of Christ as having claims to the obedience of Englishmen. It was but following the teaching of Laud and of Hammond, who at the very crisis of the Civil War, in his *Practical Catechism*, written in 1644, urged not only obedience in every particular or national Church, but faithfulness within the fold of the Church universal. Nor was this belief in the essential unity of the Church weakened by the least hesitation as to her fundamental teaching. No one could exalt the importance of a " right faith " more than did the teachers of this school; but with it, as Hammond's writings so clearly show, they pleaded for a wide charity and tolerance. So the Church had held on during the darkest days of her suppression. Bramhall, in his pious and scholarly writings, and notably in his *Vindication of the Church of England*, 1654, asserted the essential unity of the Catholic Church, and submitted himself to its judgments; and Thorndike, just before the Restoration, declared his obligation to the whole Church as well as to the Church of England. In the same spirit Pearson, in his famous *Exposition of the Creed*, insisted upon, and elaborated, the doctrine of the unity of the Holy Catholic Church, emphasising the unity of discipline and government as depending upon the Episcopal order.

It was on this principle that the divines of the Restoration accepted, and defended, their position; and their writings on the subject, sometimes purely ephemeral, often controversial, not rarely bitter, find their appropriate summary and completion in Barrow's famous treatise on the Unity of the Church, in which he explicitly asserts the essential order of the one Episcopate and the one priesthood, and in his *De regimine Episcopali*, in which he declares the rejection of

Churchmen's theory of the English Church.

Hammond.

Bramhall.

Barrow.

U

Episcopal rule, where orthodox and lawful bishops are established, to be, "in the proper sense of the word, a deadly schism."

Opposing views: Sanderson.

It is true that the teaching was not perfectly homogeneous, even in the years to which we have restricted our inquiry; and a discourse, published in 1688, and attributed (probably correctly) to Bishop Sanderson, while it appears to regard bishops as essential to the Church, yet seems, tentatively, to recognise "the Protestant Churches" as occupying a lawful position. In the same sense might be quoted a private letter of Cosin's, written from Paris during his exile in 1650, in which, while declaring in regard to the foreign Protestants "their boldness, presumption, and novelty in setting up themselves, without any invincible necessity, against the apostolical practice and perpetual order of God's Church till their days," he declines to decide that their ministrations and order are altogether null and invalid.

Cosin.

A passage even more emphatic may be added from Baxter, who writes of those whom he considered extreme churchmen: "It is the judgment of these men that I now speak of, that a prelate is essential to a Church, and there is no Church without them; and that their ordination is of necessity to the essence of a presbyter; and that those that are ordained without them (though some will except a case of necessity) are not ministers of Christ. Hereupon they conclude that our congregations here in England are no true churches, except where the presbyter dependeth on some prelate, and the ministers ordained by presbyters only are no true ministers; and they will not allow men to hear them, or communicate with them, but withdraw from our congregations like Separatists or Recusants. And the same note many of them brand upon all Reformed Churches abroad that have no prelates, as they do on us; so that the Church of Rome is admirably gratified by it." But these opinions, though after the Revolution they became more popular, cannot be said, on a careful survey of the theological literature of the period, to have represented the teaching of the leaders, and still less of the formal decisions, of the English Church. The principle of the preface to the Ordinal was adhered to, and the majority of theologians held Episcopacy to be *jure divino* an institution of the Church.

Some such examination of the theory, external and internal,

of the Church has seemed necessary not only for its intrinsic importance, but because of the great influence exercised by the Church of England at this time in the literary world. That the literature of religion outnumbered the literature of other subjects is beyond possible question. Religious subjects could always, it would seem, find readers and hearers; and it was ecclesiastics who were, with a few greater exceptions, the most eminent men of letters of the age. Of these something must now be said.

This will be fitly introduced by a short reference to the distinguished names of Whichcote, Cudworth, Smith, and More, men who lived and wrote through the time of civil and religious stress which preceded the Restoration. The Cambridge school took an interest rather than an active part in the political disturbances of the time. If one of them spoke of Milton as *infamis et non uno laqueo dignus,* others were content to stand aside, and to enunciate sound principles—to take up, in fact, very much the position which Halifax assigned to his "Trimmer." Whichcote's failure to influence public opinion was due to a great extent to the fact that he had an imperfect conception of the corporate character of the Church, and of its divinely regulated and spiritual life. To this may be due the fact that he retained his position as provost of King's College, at Cambridge, throughout the Commonwealth and Protectorate. At the Restoration he was removed from the provostship by the king's order, but, says a contemporary, "though removed he was not disgraced or frowned upon." He continued in active clerical work, with short intervals, till his death in 1683.

The Cambridge Platonists.

The work of these men in attempting a philosophy of religion was a real step in advance. What was implicit in earlier English thinkers—the idea of the Divine illumination of human reason—was set forth in plain terms by Whichcote (1609-83), Smith (1608-52), and Culverwel (died 1651). And, most of all, they set themselves to show the force of Divine truth, "as it unfolds itself in the purity of men's hearts and lives." Theirs was the true answer to Hobbes, though they did not openly controvert him. But Cudworth (1617-88) and More (1614-

The work of the Cambridge School.

1687) dealt with him more directly. And the work of the whole school was, says Burnet, their warm admirer, to "examine further into the nature of things than had been done formerly." Men "of narrower thoughts and fiercer tempers" called them Latitudinarians, and the term indeed pointed to something in their position which made them differ from traditional Anglican theology. As Burnet says, "they loved the constitution of the Church and the liturgy, and could well live under them; but they did not think it unlawful to live under another form. They wished that things might have been carried with more moderation. And they continued to keep a good correspondence with those who had differed from them in opinion, and allowed a great freedom both in philosophy and in divinity; from whence they were called men of latitude."

The Cambridge school had two distinctive marks. In the first place, it designed to set up a rational Christian philosophy in opposition to that of Hobbes; in the second, while maintaining a firm and even bitter opposition to Popery, it desired to destroy, as far as possible, all divisions between Protestants rather by ignoring than by discussing them. "All the differences in Christendom," wrote Whichcote, "are about institutions, not about morals." Smith, Cudworth, Henry More, each in different ways looked for a union that was "above all sects." But their attachment to the English Church was sincere. More loved its "decent grandeur and splendour," and thought "that it would be a sorry exchange to accept of presbytery instead, which would prove but a democratical papacy." The direct influence of the school on practical religion was not great. It is rather as modern Platonists, as an important landmark in the history of modern philosophy, that they are remembered. A greater fame belongs to pure men of letters.

Poetry does not claim during this age any but the briefest reference in what is not a literary history of the Church; but

Poetry.

a few names there are which should not be passed by without comment. The poems, fervid and exquisite, of Crashaw (1613-49) belong to the period before the wars. George Wither (1588-1667) does not deserve the hard words of Aubrey, that "he was an easy rhymer and no poet." On the contrary, there was true fire and rapture in his pious verse ; he saw the Church in her spiritual aspect and hymned her as he saw. A volu-minous writer, he succumbed to the perils that surround fluency ; he was as little consistent in his political as in his poetical standard. For long a staunch churchman, he came, when the Parliament triumphed, to attribute the Church's fall to her avarice and pride. His verse belongs to the earlier part of his life, but he survived till after the Restoration, an example of the way men wavered in the troubled times. Ken (1637-1711) is in everything a contrast to Wither. His fame belongs not to his poetry but to his life ; he was a prolific but most uninteresting writer of verse ; and yet he has left two compositions, the Morn-ing and Evening Hymns, that are perfect in their own style, and as popular, probably, now as when they were written more than two hundred years ago. They have, like the verse of Herbert, the true restrained note that belongs to the devout piety of the English Church. But her literary strength lay in other fields.

The age of the Restoration gave to English religion two great writers who did not conform to the Church. Baxter (1615-91) refused a bishopric and withdrew into a dignified seclusion. Of the parties of his day he wrote that both were to blame. "I will not be he that will justify either of them," he said. "I doubt not but the headiness and rashness of the younger, inexperienced sort of religious people made many Parliament men and ministers overgo themselves. No doubt but much indiscretion appeared, and worse than indiscretion, in the tumultuous petitioners, and much sin was committed in the dishonouring of the king and in the uncivil language against the bishops and liturgy of the Church. But these things came chiefly from the Sectarian, separating spirit which blew the coals among foolish apprentices. And as the Sectaries increased, so the insolence increased. One or two in the House, and five or six ministers that came from Holland, and a few relicts of the Brownists that were settled in the city, did drive on others, and sowed the seeds which afterwards spread over the land." This is striking language from a strong Parliament man, and from one who would talk freely with Cromwell, though he found his theology inadequate. But Baxter never went very far away from the Church. It is one of the greatest blots upon an age of confusion and persecution that so good a man should have been sent to prison by such a judge as Jeffreys; but the act was characteristic of the political, not the religious, animosities of the age. "Thou hast written books enough to load a cart," cried the judge, "and every book as full of sedition as an egg is full of meat." It was thus that the Chief Justice of England could deal with the author of *The Saints' Everlasting Rest.*

Bunyan (1628-88) was in many ways a great contrast to Baxter, for his divinity was unnatural and cramped, and his

Bunyan.

expression of it often bitter and intolerant. But no one has ever excelled him in telling a story. The perils of Christian, the terrors of Apollyon, the humours of Mr. By-ends and Mr. Facing-both-ways, the nobility of Mr. Greatheart, the mysteries of the way, of the visions of fighting souls, of the man with the muck-rake—will never be forgotten by those who read; and the simple pathos and unforced art of the whole picture make *The Pilgrim's Progress* one of the greatest of English books. Bunyan's early teaching was that of the Church, his early training that of military service on the Parliament's side. Bishop Bayly's *Practice of Piety* (see p. 29) was one of the books which drew him to God. But though he went to Church twice a Sunday, he was tormented with sharp doubts, and in the abeyance of Church teaching he found a guide only, and that after long and lonely struggles, in the In-dependent minister who led the worship in St. John's Church in Bedford. From that he became a preacher himself, eloquent with the "fire in his own conscience," and preaching what he "smartingly did feel." For twelve years from 1660 he was a prisoner in Bedford county gaol, the local justices having convicted him, he says, "for an upholder and main-tainer of unlawful conventicles, and for not conforming to the national worship of the Church of England," and sentenced him, as he declares, to a perpetual imprisonment because he refused to conform, a proceeding of very doubtful legality. During the later years of his imprisonment he was allowed to meet with his congregation, and in 1672 he was elected its minister. A few months later he received formal licence to preach, and then a pardon under the great seal. The toleration continued in his case till 1675, when he was again imprisoned.

He now began to write the great work of his life, *The Pilgrim's Progress*. After other books, interesting but not reaching the height of the masterpiece, it was completed in 1684. During all these years the number of those in Bedford who did not conform grew steadily, and the policy of James II., while it freed Bunyan himself from all fear of renewed punishment, helped also to swell the number of his flock. He spoke, indeed, as he wrote, for the people, in their own tongue, with their own homely phrases, but with the dignified, solemn language of the English Bible always at command. And he spoke also to men of every sect and of the Church: his *Book for Boys and Girls*, 1686, contains much in its simplicity that all could accept: the passion of his sincerity in *The Pilgrim's Progress* burst the bounds of his narrow creed, and men forgot, as they still forget, how strangely he limited God's mercy and how sharply he judged some of his brethren whom the old ways still led to Christ. But though it is much wider than Puritanism, for no work of genius can be cabined in a system so confined, yet it is true to say, with Bunyan's ablest editor, that it is "the prose epic of English Puritanism." Its ideals are at first Puritan, just as its dogmas are Puritan; but the spirit of its writer joins the faithful company of all those who have loved God and worked for the souls of men. Englishmen in the Church as well as outside took the book from the first to their hearts.

Great as is the interest which attaches to the names of Baxter and Bunyan, they represent but a small part of the literary activity of their times, and in religious literature churchmen had an easy predominance. Fuller. Probably the most popular writer among churchmen who lived through the days of the Church's disasters was Thomas Fuller (1608-51), the Church historian, a man of wit, whose books sold readily, and by whom—it was his boast—"no stationer ever lost." He was never a Laudian, and he continued to minister throughout the Commonwealth; but he was certainly not a Puritan. He died in 1661, just when the Church could have recognised the merit of his writings, "calling for his pen and ink to the last." Next to him in popularity, and far above him in literary dis-

Jeremy Taylor.

tinction, was Jeremy Taylor (1613-67), whose earlier career, fostered by Laud, was spent in defence of the doctrines and customs of the English Church, but who found preferment at the Restoration in the form of three Irish bishoprics. His successor wrote of him—and the eulogy was accepted without demur—that he had "the good humour of a gentleman, the eloquence of an orator, the fancy of a poet, the acuteness of a schoolman, the profoundness of a philosopher, the wisdom of a chancellor, the sagacity of a prophet, the reason of an angel, and the piety of a saint." The richness of his literary style was the result of the characteristics thus celebrated; and his conversation seems to have been as vivacious as his writing.

A theologian, a preacher, a casuist, a writer of subtle religious appeal, Jeremy Taylor left behind him books such as *Holy Living* and *Holy Dying*, which are true literature as well as true piety. He made himself, with his quaint learning and his ingenious conceits, as much at home when he spoke of marriage as when he consoled the mourner for the dead. Passages of delightful humour mingle with passages of the most serious exhortation, and show that the author combined the holiness of Andrewes with the quaint learning of Sir Thomas Browne. Jeremy Taylor, indeed, mingled in a remarkable degree the literary and religious interests of two generations; and he had, like many of the greatest churchmen of his time, points of contact and intimacy with very different schools of thought. No Laudian surpassed him in piety, no Puritan in the stoutness of his resistance to Roman claims. A man of learning, his work was yet in the best sense popular. No English theologian has ever been at once so famous and so beloved.

But Jeremy Taylor cannot be considered apart from the

The Caroline Divines.

historical school to which he belonged. The Caroline Divines, or the Divines of the Restoration, to whom the title is properly applied, were men of learning

varied and exact. Their age was one when men loved to hear
sermons and even to read theological treatises. An account
of the period, which extended to the death of Queen Anne,
would indeed be imperfect which did not say a word about
the great writers and great preachers who were the glory of
the English Church. Foremost in some respects   Pearson.
stands the close and laborious thinker John Pearson
(1613-86), whose work on the Creed, elaborate and recondite
in its learning, recalls the scholarship of the Elizabethans.
Burnet, with some ill-nature, says that he was a much better
divine than bishop. This could not be said of another
whose learning equally impressed his contemporaries.

No ecclesiastic was more prominent in the last forty
years of the seventeenth century than the handsome and
learned Edward Stillingfleet (1635-99), Bishop of   Stillingfleet.
Worcester. An admirable preacher, to whom Pepys
applies his favourite comparison with the Apostles, he was
also a zealous student and antiquary. His *Origines Sacræ*,
written in the little rectory of Sutton, Bedfordshire, would, says
Bentley, " have been deservedly esteemed a most complete
performance for one of more than twice his age." It attracted
the attention of Bishop Sanderson, and received his warm
approbation. He turned to the support of the English Church
against Rome in a vindication of Laud's controversy with
Fisher, which had been attacked by a Jesuit. A man of
prodigious mental activity, he wrote books on almost every
subject of interest to his day; but it seems, from a petition
among the Stillingfleet MSS., that he was not so assiduous in the
discharge of his parochial duties. A great collector of manuscripts and rare books, he left a magnificent library behind
him, worthy of one whom Burnet described as "the learnedst
man of the age in all respects." He was for many years
prolocutor of the Lower House of the Canterbury Convocation, and was one of the earliest to be made bishop by William
III. Queen Mary, it is said, strongly pressed him for
the primacy, but on the ground of his weak health, and more
probably because of his strength of character, William III. passed
him over. He was constantly consulted by the bishops during
the last years of his life, and was the trusted adviser of Tenison.
An antiquary and constitutional historian of no mean order,

his writings on the Convocation question, on the duties and rights of the parochial clergy, and on the constitutional position of the bishops in the House of Lords, were among the standard works of his day. His last controversy was with Locke, in which he endeavoured to convict the philosopher of Socinianism, with indifferent success. Admired by the learned as a genuine scholar, he was known to the polite world as "the beauty of holiness," and the influence he exerted on each was wholly beneficial. In opinion he sympathised to a great extent with Burnet, and was described, with him, as a "Latitude-man," and in his *Irenicum, or the Unreasonableness of Separation*, he regarded the form of Church government as not essential. Patrick (1626-1707), successively bishop of Chichester and of Ely, a man of deep piety, approximated in *The Friendly Debate* towards the same conclusions, but they were contrary to the general judgment of English churchmen.

The name of Stillingfleet reminds us that the reign of Charles II. was an age of great preachers. One of the most impressive, certainly the most unconventional among them of the day, was Robert South (1634-1716), whose wit was irrepressible and whose earnestness was not to be denied. He was staunchly orthodox, and entirely earnest and self-denying. Sancroft recommended him to James II. for the see of Oxford, but the king had other persons in view. He remained a great and popular preacher to the end of his life; with hesitation he did not become a nonjuror. He was not the man whom busy statesmen, besieged by political claimants, ever care to promote, so that he died a canon of Christ Church, where indeed he had preferred to be. In 1713 the queen had offered to him the bishopric of Rochester. He spoke of the offer in a sarcastic letter to Harley as "gracious and surprising," and added, "having now above these forty years, the best, the ablest, and the most useful part of my age, not been thought fit by my superiors to serve the crown or Church in any other way or station than what I have held hitherto, I cannot but in modesty (and even in respect to them) judge myself unworthy and unfit to serve them in any higher or greater post now, being grown equally superannuated to the active as well as the enjoying part of

South.

life." His reputation survived as a great preacher, a miracle of humour, whose sermons were often punctuated by the laughter of his congregation. But his gifts were also of a more serious and impressive order : he never sank into buffoonery, like some of his imitators, but maintained the dignity and reality of a true minister of Christ.

A greater man, who had wide experience of Church life in East and West—for he had travelled far, and he was chaplain at Smyrna during the latter years of the Protectorate—was Isaac Barrow (1630-77), whom Charles II. made Master of Trinity as "the best scholar in England." His style was strong, comprehensive, fertile, his mental power commanding. But he was never a public man, and the Church, which knew him as a scholar, a preacher, and a controversialist, never brought him forward in the political questions which were prominent in his day. He died at the age of forty-seven, in 1677, saying softly, "I have seen the glories of the world." In him the English Church felt that she had had a link with Catholic learning and the churches over seas. Barrow was the pupil of Hammond and the friend of Tillotson, standing between the Rebellion and the Revolution. Bull (1634-1710), born four years later than Barrow, lived almost to the end of Anne's reign, becoming a bishop only when he was seventy-one. Like Barrow, he helped to make the English Church known throughout Europe. His *Judicium Ecclesiæ Catholicæ* was sent by his friend and pupil Nelson to Bossuet, who submitted it to the Gallican bishops, and desired Nelson "not only to return Dr. Bull his humble thanks, but the unfeigned congratulations of the whole clergy of France, assembled then at St. Germain, for the great service he had done to the Catholic Church, in so well defending her determination of the necessity of believing the divinity of the Son of God." The book was a vindication of the Nicene Creed, historically and theologically, in relation to the controversies of the day and the shallow Deism that was coming into fashion. Of his sermons nothing more fitly can be said than was said by Nelson :

"He had a way of gaining people's hearts and touching their consciences, which bore some resemblance to the apostolical age; and when it shall appear that those bright preachers, who have been ready to throw contempt upon his lordship's performances, can set forth as large a list of persons whom they have converted by their preaching as I could produce of those who owed the change of their lives, under God, to the Christian instruction of this pious prelate, I shall readily own that they are superior to his lordship in the pulpit, though, considering what learned works he published in the cause of religion, and what an eminent pattern he was of true primitive piety, I am not inclined to think that his lordship will, upon the whole of his character, be easily equalled by any one."

Stillingfleet, Barrow, Bull may well be taken as representative clergy of the period.

Tillotson, whose frigid moral essays set the fashion of pulpit oratory for generations after his death, but whose personal kindliness and sincerity endeared him both to high and low, is also typical of a school which had considerable influence. Something has already been said of the Cambridge Platonists. The later "Latitude-men," of whom Wilkins, Bishop of Chester, was another worthy representative, and who approximated closely to the saintly Baxter, a nonconformist in fact not in spirit, had indeed in Tillotson their most striking representative. Thus the Church of England found room for all schools of thought within the limits of her formularies. Two other names may be mentioned rather as peculiar than as representative. The one has received condemnation which is ill deserved. Samuel Parker had none of the vices, or even the time-serving insincerity of Cartwright, though he was almost equally identified with the policy of James II. He had a genuine belief in toleration, an equally genuine belief in the English Church. A "letter sent by Sir Leolyn Jenkins [Principal of Jesus College, Oxford] to the late King James to bring him over to the communion of the Church of England, written by Samuel Parker, D.D." (published 1714), contains much that is characteristic of the writer's sound judgment and evidential of his sincere attachment to the Church, but it is doubly impressive when it is compared with the sane and cogent reasons which the same writer published against the Test Act. Lucid and calm, neither canting with Puritans nor terrified at Romanists, Parker argued with a

The "Latitude-men."

Samuel Parker.

humorous force against requiring from members of the Houses of Parliament an oath of belief or disbelief as to a difficult and controverted point, in which language was everything, and meaning sometimes apparently very little. But while he could put clearly enough the true grounds for removing religious tests from the avenues of public life, he was still insistent on the principles by which the Restoration of the Church had been secured. "The Episcopal society," he wrote, "is the first visible communion of the Christian Church, and a man becomes a member of the Church Catholic by joining in visible communion with the Church Episcopal, for it is impossible to be a member of the Universal Church without being a member of some particular church."

Parker was peculiar in the originality of his opinions at the time in which he lived. Henry Wharton (1664-95) was singular in the extent and accuracy of his labours as a scholar. No words can better summarise his work than those of Bishop Stubbs : " This wonderful man died in 1695, at the age of thirty, having done for the elucidation of English Church history (itself but one of the branches of study in which he was the most eminent scholar of his time) more than any one before or since."   Chaplain to Archbishop Sancroft, but not himself a nonjuror, Henry Wharton, in spite of weak health, amassed an amount of information with regard to early English Church history which every subsequent investigator has spoken of with new enthusiasm and wonder.   He was a devoted student, a shrewd controversialist, a keen antiquary, and all the while a sincere and conscientious priest.   At Chartham, where he lived chiefly after he left Lambeth, he wrote, with some seeming irritation, "all my zeal to the public service must be employed in teaching a few plough-joggers, who look upon what I say to concern them but little," but the familiar complaint of the country parson seems in no way to have diminished his activity or his zeal.

Swift, in his bitter "preface to the B-p of S-r-m's introduction to the third volume of the *History of the Reformation of the Church of England*" (1713), wrote of him as "poor Mr. Henry Wharton, who deserved so much of the Commonwealth of learning, and who gave himself the trouble of detecting some hundreds of the bishop's mistakes."   There was a general feeling that, between strict nonjurors and easy latitudinarians, he had made more enemies than friends; but before long his learning was fully recognised, though not fully rewarded, and his death, says a contemporary, "even foreigners regretted, as it appears in the Act. Erudit., printed at Leipsick, 1696. But if foreigners paid him this compliment, much more did his countrymen, who buried him in a very solemn manner. The king's scholars being ordered to attend his funeral, at which were present the Archbishop of Canterbury, Dr. Tillotson, and other prelates, together with vast numbers of the clergy; and the Quire in Procession sang the Anthems upon this occasion, composed by Mr. Purcel, the Lord Bishop of Rochester performing the burial service."

To Wharton may be added another name of almost equal distinction. Joseph Bingham (1668-1723) was one who, *Bingham.* during the reign of Anne, maintained and advanced the reputation of the Church of England for learning. He was most unjustly censured by the Hebdomadal Board at Oxford in 1695 for a sermon which he, then a fellow of University College, preached at St. Mary's, and after a long controversy he was obliged to resign his fellowship. The rest of his life was passed as a country parson, at Headbournworthy, near Winchester, where he wrote his great work, *Origines Ecclesiasticæ.* This was, for its time, an extraordinarily complete description of the usages of the Early Church, intended, as its writer said, "to give such a methodical account of the antiquities of the Christian Church as others have done of the Greek and Roman and Jewish antiquities, by reducing the ancient customs, usages, and practices of the Church under certain proper heads, whereby the reader may take a view at once of any particular usage or custom of Christians for four or five centuries."

If Wharton be singled out as unique among his contemporaries for the greatness of his work, Bingham's title to fame must not be forgotten The other names that have been selected have each the praise of conspicuous learning. The seven ecclesiastics who have been mentioned,—and they are a small selection indeed from the notable men who have left memorials of their scholarship and piety—might of themselves help to justify the transference to the reigns of the later

Stewarts of the eulogy passed on the English clergy in the reign of Charles I.—" *Clerus Anglicanus stupor mundi.*"

AUTHORITIES. —Burnet, *History of his own Times*, with the various criticisms of it ; Hobbes, *Leviathan ;* Aubrey, *Brief Lives ; An examination of Hobbes's Leviathan*, by Edward Hyde, Earl of Clarendon, 1676 ; *Religion and Policy*, by the same author, 1811 ; the works of Thorndike, Baxter, Jeremy Taylor, Ken, Pearson, South, Barrow, Bull (with Nelson's *Life*) ; lives of Bingham, Wharton, Henry More and others, in the *Dictionary of National Biography ;* Tulloch's *Rational Theology* is interesting in criticism, and Campagnac's *Cambridge Platonists* is useful. *The Pilgrim's Progress* has been edited, with a valuable preface, by C. H. Firth, LL.D.

CHAPTER XVII

THE RELIGIOUS SOCIETIES AND MISSIONARY WORK

THE public work of the Church was disturbed during the reigns of William III. and Anne by unseemly wrangling, yet the moral and spiritual work underwent a great revival. It is difficult to exaggerate the vice of the Restoration age ; and the political immorality of the Revolution was reflected in social life. Burnet speaks of a deep corruption in principle, " a disbelief in revealed religion, and a profane mocking at the Christian faith and the mysteries of it."

Moral and spiritual work.

Some light upon the attitude of the Church towards public morals may be obtained from the famous *Short View of the Immorality and Profaneness of the English Stage*, published in 1698, the work of the learned nonjuring clergyman Jeremy Collier. It cannot, however, be considered to belong strictly to Church history, both from its subject and from the fact that the author stood entirely apart from the general Church life of his day. The book is a powerful attack on the prevalent looseness of the drama, for which, among many small names, the great John Dryden was not a little to blame : he admitted his fault indeed, but added :

Jeremy Collier.

> Perhaps the parson stretched a point too far
> When with our theatre he waged a war,
> He tells you that this very moral age
> Received the first infection from the stage ;
> But sure a banist Court, with lewdness fraught,
> The seeds of open vice, returning, brought.

There can be no doubt that Collier's book did much good ; there is a perceptible improvement in the plays written after it ; and William III., who was unlike his uncles in being private in his immorality, reissued his proclamation of 1692 and directed it against plays of the nature referred to by Collier, using the very words of his book.

Proclamations against vice are futile things.   Happily there were good men who knew that laws were vain without the sanction of public feeling, and under the influence, it appears, of eminent preachers, such as Dr. Horneck and The religious Societies. Mr. Smythies, " Societies " were formed for the cultivation and support of the devotional life.   With plain practical rules of prayer and almsgiving they kept close to the Church of England, and gave themselves to good work. Retiring somewhat into the background in the reign of James II., they still continued to encourage zeal and charity.   They organised special services, strictly observing the vigils and fasts, and being addressed by special preachers.   Compton and Tillotson warmly supported them, and Queen Anne is said to have taken "great satisfaction" in their work.   Horneck was aided by Beveridge, a theologian whose support was a tower of strength.   Bray, famous as an organiser of missionary effort, was another of their leaders, and Woodward, Rector of Poplar, who wrote fully on behalf of their pious designs.

These Societies spread widely in 1710 : it is stated that there were forty-two of the Societies in London and Westminster, and many more in the chief towns of England.   Their Their rapid growth, 1710. work was entirely practical,—charity in every direction, provision for education, for the spiritual needs of prisoners, of soldiers and sailors, and ultimately the support also of foreign missions.   Toulmin, in the *History of Dissenters*, says of their work in London : " They so improved their finances by many collections that they were enabled to remunerate the attendance of many clergymen to read prayers ; these aids to devotions were in a short time afforded at so many different hours and extended to so many places, as to include every hour of the day.   On every Lord's Day there were constant sacraments in many churches, greater numbers attended at prayers and sacraments, and greater appearances of devotion were diffused through the city than had been observed in the memory of man."   The whole literature of the time bears witness to the good work done during the

reigns of William III. and Anne by these excellent Societies;
but, dependent as they were on the action and leadership of
comparatively few individuals, the political changes and the
low moral tone of the early Hanoverians exercised a depressing
effect on them, and they survived in the later eighteenth century
only to inspire John Wesley with the idea, though at last in
a distorted form, of a Society such as his father had strongly
supported and eulogised.

Apart from these purely religious societies stood the
Societies for the Reformation of Manners, established in
1692 to aid the effective carrying out of the orders of the
royal proclamation. Their object was simply to bring vice
to justice. They had among their supporters some of the
best men in England, and as they were conducted almost
entirely by laymen it can hardly be said that they represented
any encroachment by the Church on the province of the
State. But none the less their work, though the testimony to
its success is overwhelming, was one-sided. It is not enough,
though it is necessary, for the law to be a terror to evildoers.
To this the Societies for the Reformation of Manners had
given care. More was needed.

Dr. Thomas Bray, a clergyman who had recently won fame
by a book of *Catechetical Lectures*, set to work to found a
Society with a further aim. He had a genius for religion.
In the holiness and devotion of his personal life, in the
clearness and the far-reaching character of his schemes, there
were few of his contemporaries to equal him. The
The S.P.C.K. main designs of the Society for Promoting Christian
Knowledge, as at first instituted, were to provide missionaries
for "the Plantations," parochial libraries both for England and
abroad, and schools in England "for the education of poor
children in reading and writing, and more especially in the
principles of the Christian religion." The first meeting of the
Society, which consisted of two lawyers, a nobleman, a country
gentleman, and the energetic priest who inspired the foundation, took place on March 8, 1699. The minutes, very carefully kept, of the constant meetings of this little band, show
how eager was their endeavour to advance in every direction
the work of Christ. In their beginnings they met with much
opposition in some parts of the country. The Archdeacon of

Carlisle at his visitation charged against all the Societies "as contrary to the laws both civil and ecclesiastical, and of most pernitious consequence to Church and State, and treated them in very vile terms"; and the Bishop of Exeter (Trelawny) was "utterly averse" to their designs.

But, on the other hand, the new Society was warmly welcomed by pious folk in every county of England, and unions of clergy were founded in several districts. An institution, somewhat after the fashion of the London Societies, was formed in the Northern Dioceses, Carlisle and Durham, in 1687, by which a number of clergy and laity met monthly at Durham to attend the Cathedral services, dine frugally together, and read and discuss papers on "matters of discipline, and more especially about the orders and rules of the Common Prayer-book." A similar Society was founded by Comber in Yorkshire. But the most notable of the bodies now formed was perhaps the Religious Society begun at Epworth on the eve of the Purification 1702 by Samuel Wesley. His reports to the Society in London prove how intimately connected were all the different sides of religious work, which show at this time a renewed energy. Besides constant reference to catechisings in church, to the founding of schools, and to the direct dealing with Romanist and Protestant dissenters, the reports from local sources show constant interest in the increase of communions. Samuel Wesley at Epworth, for example, had no Papists or Presbyterians in his parish, but some Anabaptists and Quakers. He had "set up monthly sacraments but had not above twenty communicants at them," though the population of the whole Isle of Axholme was about 7000. But they were "so extreme ignorant that not one in twenty can say the Lord's Prayer right, not one in thirty the Belief." The revival of daily prayer and catechising, and the setting up of parochial schools, with the inspection of charity schools already existing, were the aims most persistently followed in the earlier years of the work. Again, definite attempts were made to work in the Navy; and gradually the colonial work developed into distinct and aggressive missionary effort. The work of organisations such as these carries us beyond the borders of our own land.

Local religious Societies.

Though the relations of the English Church with the Church in Scotland and Ireland fall outside the field of our survey, the provision made for English settlers in America and India and for direct missionary work claims consideration, because it is an evidence that the Church was really a living and growing body, rising above its own difficulties and dangers to a sense of its responsibilities towards the nations without. Archbishop Laud had been among the first to recognise the responsibility ; and in 1634 a commission was formed to deal with the spiritual affairs of the North American colonies, and an order in Council gave the Bishop of London jurisdiction over English congregations abroad. In 1638 it was planned to send a bishop to Virginia, and after the Restoration Dr. Alexander Murray was designated for the see. But on Clarendon's fall the whole scheme broke down.

The beginnings of missionary work.

Reports from time to time reached the Commissioners of Trades and Plantations. For example, the minutes of the Committee on December 1, 1675, contain a report from Massachusetts in 1673 which states that "the persuasions of the people as to Church government are very different, and those of the better sort being for the Church of England and have the Common Prayer-book in their houses, and will not have their children baptized after any other form."

From this date much more full information of the progress of work among the colonists can be obtained. A number of documents relating to Carolina are in the Shaftesbury Papers (many of them entirely in the writing of John Locke), and are largely concerned with the settlement of Quakers. There are many interesting references to the religious condition of the colonies in these and other papers. In August 1676 we have John Yeo writing to the Archbishop of Canterbury to complain of the deplorable condition of Maryland for lack of an established ministry. There are ten or twelve counties, with a population, he writes, of at least 20,000 souls, and in these are but three ministers of the Church of England—"Though there are others who pretend to be ministers of the Gospel that never had a legal ordination, and sow seeds of division among the people." There are Popish priests and Jesuits, and the Quakers provide for

The West Indies

preachers in their conventicle, but there is no provision for
the ministry of the Church. The archbishop, one is glad to
learn, told the Bishop of London that he thought the design
should be supported by all means; but we do not know the
result.

Among the papers relating to the West Indian Islands,
some of which contain matter enough for the plots of half-a-
dozen romances and tales of adventure, are some curious
minutes relating to religion in St. Kitt's: "First about the
state of religion in those parts and the want of ministers, when
fit proposals can be presented, that the Bishop of London be
discoursed withal to put some better regulation to this great
and shameful neglect. Mem.—Touching the christening of
negroes." The Bishop of London was well disposed to the
work, and, it is interesting to note, would send "able men to
those parts, with assurance of good preferment at their return."
Evidently the English Church rightly honoured and rewarded
missionary work at that period, however little she was able to
undertake it.

Bishop Compton indeed took a keen interest in providing
missionaries, and Charles II. was induced to allow each
minister and schoolmaster £20 for his passage, and
to encourage the building of churches and schools. _{and North America.}
The colonies, however, were still to a great extent
dominated by Puritan influences. For example, between 1677
and 1680 a very pretty quarrel in Boston shows a state of
affairs which recalls England thirty years before. It is asserted
that Christmas was still forbidden to be observed, under severe
punishment, and folk were fined for not going to meeting-house,
and whipped if they did not pay the fines. The "Minutes of
the Lords of Trade and Plantations" show that one of the last
official acts of Archbishop Sheldon was to interest himself in
provision for the spiritual needs of Maryland. But Compton,
Bishop of London, showed especial activity in sending out
ministers, and prohibiting the employment of those who were
not duly ordained—a proceeding which the cupidity of the
planters seems to have led them into. The complaints from
the Leeward Isles in those days seem to have been very similar
to some which reach us in our own time. The Council of St.
Kitt's begs that the next batch of divines sent to them may be

of riper years than the last, and better read in divinity so as to be able to foil the Roman ministers in case of need. It should be noticed, too, that Compton was especially urgent for the baptism of slaves and for their admission to full Christian rights. He seems, too, often to have been defeated by the greed and prejudice of the planters. And religious fanaticism, as in Massachusetts, bitter in sectarian animosities, no less than the general harsh treatment of the Indians, hindered religious work.

A letter from Baltimore to Mr. Gandy, afterwards a non-juring bishop, written by one Joseph Cresbury on January 28, 1714, shows how great were the difficulties which beset churchmen in America. The writer, possibly a nonjuror, speaks of his long absence from "the blessed Sacrament," declares that "the great men of this country are all very Whiggish or else Romans," and thus describes the religious condition of Maryland : "The people of this Province are for the most part very illiterate, there not being one in ten that can write or read, and as ignorant in affairs that concern God and their own souls. Their ignorance and stupidity is in great measure heightened by the debauched wicked lives of their clergy (he who officiates in this parish was about to take a wife here, although he already has one in England ; being told of it, he made answer that she was a long way off, etc.) nothing being so frequent as to see them drunk (when they can get liquor, which is not always to be got here), to hear them swear, talk filthily, and publickly taxed with acting it. I hope God in His infinite mercy will deliver this and all other places, especially my native country, from such workers of wickedness, and send us true orthodox pastors in their rooms."

Much the same, it is to be feared, might be said of the West Indies as of North America. The policy of the English State was not in favour of more than a rarely-disturbed indifference on the part of English churchmen to the needs of their brethren over the seas. As so often in the history of English enterprise abroad, the steps forward came from the enthusiasm of individuals.

A new impetus was given to the work by the energy and enthusiasm of Robert Boyle (1627-91), who for twenty-eight years directed and supported missionary effort among the North American Indians.   John Eliot, the apostle of the Indians, was the hero of the mission, and several **The work of Robert Boyle.** congrègations, after the fashion of the Independents, were formed.   But the provision of church privileges continued scandalously deficient.   Reports from time to time reached the committee which show that both in America and the West Indies pains were taken, under great difficulties, to establish the work.   In 1681 the committee heard that the ministers sent by Compton to the Leeward Islands "had not been so well used as they ought," and commended them to the care of the governors.   In the same year Sir Henry Morgan thus reported from Port Royal (Jamaica) as to the churches established : " In St. Thomas there is a church and **Report from** minister ; in St. David's the like ; both at Port **the West** Royal and so in St. Andrew's ; a church and **Indies, 1681.** minister in St. Katherine's, the like in St. John's ; a church building in St. Dorothy's, but yet no minister ; a minister in Clarendon, and the church building ; in St. Elizabeth's a minister, but no church ; for all parishes on the north side neither church nor minister.   The settlements there are not much above five years' standing, but they improve much, and will provide for their religion as soon as their condition will stand the charge."

In the next year, on October 23, 1682, Sir Thomas Lynch, writing from Jamaica to the Bishop of London, gives a very full account of the ecclesiastical condition of the island, of which the conclusion is that " in **Jamaica,** fine all the parishes must be divided again.   The **1682.** planters' estates I hope will bear it and their piety desires it." He adds, " I know you foresee this and would provide for it betimes, it being easier to guide men into good methods when they have none than to seduce them from wrong methods.   My duty is to keep you informed of this infant church, but this would be better done by a minister or two, were such sober and learned men sent over.   A governor may be overcharged with other business, or negligent, or irreligious."

A letter of Governor Sir Richard Dutton to Sir Leolyn Jenkins from Barbados is worth quoting at length.   It is dated

May 30, 1681.   "Since assuming the government I have

Barbados.   been zealously endeavouring to carry out my instructions.   I began very early to regulate God's House
and worship, which had been but too much neglected by former
governors, which made the people schismatically factious,
and consequently disobedient to authority.   There were very
few persons in most parishes that received the sacrament
once a year, and there are more that never received in their
lives.   This I hope to reform, having ordered the sacrament
to be administered monthly in every parish church, of which
I have already found the effect to be good, not only through the
command but through my own example.   I have also held a
visitation to inquire after the ordinations and presentations of
the clergy and all public schoolmasters, to see that they were
conformable with the discipline of the Church of England,
and that they instructed the children in the Catechism.
These two inquiries have caused great surprise.   One who
pretended himself to be a clergyman, who had been tolerated
by the Government for four and twenty years, who was actually in possession of two livings, administered both the
sacraments, married all that came to him, and was vicious
in the whole course of his life—this man confessed that he
had never been ordained.   Yet though this clergyman be
a man of all these ill circumstances, my predecessor, Sir
Jonathan Atkins, is offended that I should suspend so in-
famous a person, I am sorry that I must so describe him, but
there is so much to his shame that I use the word truly.
And that you may better understand the temper of the
people whom this man had so long influenced—upon my
suspension of him one of the parishes called a vestry and
resolved to steal him off this island, and this in violation of a
fundamental law of the island which provides that all who
intend to leave it must register their names at the secretary's
office, and that captains of ships must give a bond of £1000
that they will receive no passengers that are not so registered.
Yet notwithstanding this, they gave the captain counter-
security to indemnify him (in case his bond were put to suit)
if he would carry this fellow to England, and, moreover,
gave him credit in England for £500, not doubting
but that sum would prevail with any bishop to give him

ordination.   I wrote the whole affair to the Bishop
of London, and I hope he will take care that no such vile
person be admitted to holy orders.   He has married so
many persons the legitimacy of whose children will be
questioned that I am solicited to pass a bill for the confirmation of those marriages to prevent suits at law.   I have
been tedious in my relation of this affair, which I have also
transmitted to the Bishop of London, lest any surprise should
be attempted, and I should be discouraged from the prosecution of such vermin."

A later letter from Sir Jonathan Atkins gives full information as to the ecclesiastical state of Barbados, where the
churches were repaired and Compton had provided able and
orthodox ministers.   There was not one church, says the
retiring governor (who remarks that he had constantly gone
to church himself), which did not constantly observe all the
rites of the Church of England.   In Virginia also the Bishop
of London had provided clergy, and there were some seventy-
six livings, whose value ought to be as much as £80 a year.

The origin of work by English Missionary Societies in
the colonies may be traced to an ordinance of the Long
Parliament of July 27, 1649, establishing a corporation for
promoting the Gospel in New England.   This body was
recognised, or refounded, by a charter of Charles II. in
1662, obtained by the influence of Boyle.   A further development occurred in the reign of Queen Anne.   In the
East Indies too it was largely due to the inspiration
of Boyle that missionary work there also was begun.   The East
Indies.
The magnificent labours of St. Francis Xavier, and
the relentless discipline of the Portuguese governors, had long
before made Goa Christian and raised the gorgeous edifices
and endowed the colleges and schools whose ruins amid
the tropical jungle astonish us to-day.   It seemed strange
that when England acquired from Portugal the district of
Bombay nothing should be done, in Boyle's words, "to bring
those countries some spiritual good things whence we so
frequently bring back temporal ones."   He invited the company to undertake the work, and be "contributors to the
enlarging the pale of the Christian Church."   But little
had yet been done.   In 1678 the foundation stone of

the church of St. Mary at Madras was laid. The president issued stringent regulations against Romanists, whereas in Bombay there was complete toleration.

A few years later public interest in England was aroused. Fell, Bishop of Oxford, writing to Sancroft on June 21, 1681, spoke of the "shame that lay upon us, who had so great opportunities by our commerce in the East, that we had attempted nothing towards the conversion of the natives," and induced the East India Company to take in hand the pecuniary support of the work of conversion. In this he was helped by Robert Boyle and by Burnet. Scholars were to be trained at Oxford, and books printed, and schools were to be established in India. A subscription list was opened, to which many eminent persons contributed, and the work was begun in 1682. Already the company had its own chaplains; and the Levant Company in like manner provided for the spiritual welfare of its officers. The chaplains had before this been instructed, or allowed, to undertake missionary work; but the difficulties were great, and it seems that little if anything had been done. Nor indeed was much achieved after 1681; for in 1695 Bishop Stratford of Chester wrote to Prideaux that the East India Company "can pretend nothing for their neglect and contempt of those poor souls." Prideaux approached Archbishop Tenison on the subject, urging the establishment of schools in each of the three English factories : the charter of 1698 to the new company orders that each factory shall have its chaplain, and that the native servants should be instructed in the Christian religion. Active missionary work was still, owing to the circumstances of the company, restricted within very narrow limits.

It was not until the creation of the Religious Societies spread an enthusiasm for good works that more active and permanent missions were undertaken. In 1696 Dr. Thomas Bray was appointed Commissary for Maryland by the Bishop of London, and in the next year he succeeded in founding a Society for promoting Christian knowledge. In March 1699 Dr. Bray and four others, laymen of eminence, began the work which has grown to such vast proportions. Men of all parties joined in the good work :

The Oxford project, 1681.

Foundation of the S.P.C.K. and the S.P.G.

Bibles and good books were printed and distributed among the poor, and lending libraries were founded in America. Convocation in 1701 supported it as designed for "the promotion of the Christian religion according to the doctrine, discipline, and worship of the Church of England as by law established." A petition was addressed to the king, and the result was the foundation by Royal Charter of the Corporation for propagating the Gospel in foreign parts.

The first meeting of the Society took place at Lambeth on June 27, 1701. It at once began an inquiry into the religious state of the colonies, and, acting on the information received, it undertook to provide a maintenance for orthodox clergy, to minister both to British subjects and to natives, and to collect and distribute charitable gifts for those purposes. In 1710 it was agreed by the Society that preference should be given to the "conversion of heathens and infidels." In North America there was already a settled ministry, though in some colonies, owing to the original constitution, it laboured under great difficulties, as, for example, in New England, where it was only after petition to the king in 1679 that the inhabitants of Boston were allowed to build a chapel, afterwards endowed by William III., for the worship of the Church of England. The Society at once sent ministers, where it could, to districts which needed them. Their letters give the most interesting details of their work, of its need, its dangers, and its blessings. The work in India was not undertaken by the Society till a century later. Here, as well as in America, progress was retarded and the work seriously crippled by the absence of bishops. "It is a dismal thing," said a pamphlet of 1700, "to consider how much the want of a bishop amongst us has retarded the progress of the true religion in America." Among the Dartmouth MSS. is a paper, probably of the year 1700, entitled "The case of his Majesty's subjects, members of the Church of England, in America," which points out the detrimental effects of the want of bishops, and notes Archbishop Tenison's approbation of the scheme, with a promise of £1000. In 1703 and 1709 the scheme was discussed, and in 1712 the Society agreed that it was "very expedient to establish bishops and bishoprics in America." But the project had long to wait.

Work such as this was one illustration of the wide interests

which were characteristic of English development under the
later Stewarts.   Just as the missionary effort received
its initiatory impulse from the revival of personal
religion, and was thus primarily a moral effort, so
also it was greatly aided by the intellectual movement of the
day.   So long as controversy was embittered by dangerous
political combinations it was plain that the thought of reunion
with Rome could not be seriously entertained by English
churchmen.   They were constrained, even the most charitable
of them, to wait, in Archbishop Laud's words, " till Rome is
other than she is."   With the East it was different ; and here
the work of the nonjurors was, later, of considerable importance.   An interesting letter of Sir George Wheler, the
nephew of Dean Grenville and the pupil of Dean Hickes,
records among his experiences in travel in Eastern Europe a
conversation with the Bishop of Salonika, who
questioned him as to the doctrine of the English
Church.   He continues : " Of which, when I had
given him the best account I could, he told me that it was the
same with theirs ; for I informed him that we believe the Holy
Scriptures, the Apostles' Creed, the Nicene, and that of St.
Athanasius ; that our Church was governed by bishops and
archbishops, that our faith was conformable to the primitive
Fathers and the first General Councils until the first five or six
centuries ; and, in fine, that we were not of the Roman Church.
After this I asked him their opinion concerning the Holy
Sacrament, and what they held the bread and wine to be after
consecration.   He answered, the ' Body and Blood of Christ.'
When I asked him how that could be, he gave me this
explication : ' as the sun is in the heaven and yet gives heat
and light to the whole earth, so Christ although in heaven, yet
was in the Sacrament, by His divine power and influence.'
I told him that was what we believed, which was that Christ
was in the Sacrament after a spiritual manner."   This may be
regarded as the beginning of the important correspondence
of twenty years later.

The interest which the nonjurors showed in the Eastern
Church was not confined to that comparatively small body of
men.   The Stillingfleet MSS. contain a letter from Sir
William Trumbull, the British Ambassador at Constantinople,

Marginal notes: Attempts towards reunion: with the Eastern Church,

dated June 10, 1688, which shows what concern was felt for
the wretched state of "the Grecian and Armenian Churches,"
where the patriarchs were constantly changed, at the absolute
will of the viziers, and every new patriarch had to pay £2000.
It is noteworthy that Stillingfleet was one of the Commission
for the revision of the Prayer-book, which proposed the
additional note to the Nicene Creed with a view to the
preservation (or renewal) of Catholic Communion.   The
experience of Frampton, Barrow, and other notable men as
chaplains in the Levant, undoubtedly led them to look with
intelligent sympathy on the work of the Orthodox Church.

A contrast in many respects to the interest felt in England
in the ancient and unaltered Church of the East was the
project of association with the Reformed Calvinistic   with the
Church in Prussia.   In 1706, and again in 1709 and   Reformed
                                                        in Prussia,
1711, Archbishop Tenison entered, though somewhat
tepidly, into a negotiation inaugurated by the King of Prussia,
whose wife was a descendant of James I. of England, with
a view to the introduction of Episcopacy into his country.
There was much dislike of the scheme in England, and it
came to nothing.   Much the same seems to have been the
fate of the tentative suggestion for reunion with the Roman
Church as a whole or with particular churches.   The most
notable step taken during the period was perhaps   with Rome,
the publication by Francis Davenport, or Sta. Clara,
in 1646 of his tractate on the Thirty-nine Articles, dedicated
to Charles I.   This work endeavours to explain the English
articles in a sense not hostile to the dogmatic decisions of the
Church of Rome : notably, for example, it is stated that
"Transubstantiation as defined by the Church is not denied,"
and the interpretation of Article Thirty-one, which has since
been generally held by theologians who have studied the
question, is stated, namely, that the *Sacrificium Missae* is not
condemned but only a commonly received and erroneous
opinion in regard to it.   Sta. Clara became chaplain to Charles
II.'s Queen, Catherine of Braganza, and died in London in
1680 ; but though he was doubtless concerned in the mysterious
negotiations with the Papal Curia in which the Romanist
members of the Cabal took part, he did not accomplish
anything.

The correspondence between Bossuet and Bull, and the formal expression of thanks conveyed by the French bishops,

with the French Church, might be interpretated into something more than the courtesy of learning : but though considerable sympathy was expressed in England for the Gallican liberties as asserted in 1682, no active steps were taken to negotiate for a union of the churches till after the death of Queen Anne.   An informal suggestion for union was, however, made by Charles Leslie.   Of this Burnet spoke with scorn and contempt, an uncharitable piece of insolence on which Swift caustically commented.   It was clear, however, that the time was not ripe for reunion : and this was perhaps even more obvious with regard to the growing bodies of dissenters or nonconformists than with regard to the churches which had preserved the ancient rules of ordination.

None the less it must be remembered that attempts towards union with dissenters were from the Restoration constant and

with English Dissenters. most earnest.   The attitude of the Church seems throughout to have been invitatory : but on the other hand the principles asserted in the preface to the Ordinal were as emphatically reiterated.   Probably the most eager efforts to induce the dissenters to accept the Church's teaching, apart from the various suggestions of a comprehension in different forms, were those which issued in the publication from 1682 to 1685 of a series of pamphlets directed to softening the points of difference.   These dealt in a plain and simple fashion with such points as the lawfulness of forms of prayer in public worship, " a resolution of this case of conscience, whether the Church of England, symbolising so far as it doth with the Church of Rome, makes it unlawful to hold communion with the Church of England," with a defence of the same when it was attacked, the case of infant baptism, the sign of the Cross in baptism, a persuasive to frequent communion, the case of kneeling at the Sacrament, a discourse of profiting by sermons, and " an argument for union taken from the true interest of those dissenters in England who call themselves Protestant."   Some of these were by Edmund Fowler, afterwards Bishop of Gloucester : and the whole series were marked by a strict moderation of tone, and an emphasis on all those points which would naturally attract rather than disunite. But the collection of pamphlets represented the efforts of a party. Hardly more than the last great theological work of the period, Johnson's *The Unbloody Sacrifice* (1714), an impressive attempt to vindicate the English acceptance of the Patristic doctrine of the Eucharist, could it meet with general acceptance in the Church.

It was indeed on a divided body, in spite of its manifest strength, of the holiness of many of the lives which it inspired, and of the awakening of its moral and missionary zeal, that the Hanoverian king looked when he came to receive the inheritance bestowed on him by the English Parliament. But in spite of its divisions, the Church had still behind it the strength of a deep national devotion, and the inspiration of a divine guidance.

Position of the English Church in 1714.

AUTHORITIES.—On the Religious Societies see especially Wordsworth, *Account of the Rise and Progress of the Religious Societies.* *The History of the S.P.C.K.*, 1698-1898, contains the early minutes. On the subject of missions in the colonies and plantations, see especially Birch's *Life of Boyle;* *Calendars of State Papers, America and West Indies;* Treasury Papers : Historical MSS. Commission, *14th Report*, Appendix, part x. ; Tanner MSS.; Rawlinson MSS., including Gandy Papers ; *Fortnightly Review,* May 1896 (an article by Sir W. W. Hunter) ; *Two Hundred Years of the S.P.G.* (C. F. Pascoe, 1901). Dr. F. G. Lee in 1865 republished, with a sketch of the author's life, the *Paraphrastica Expositio* of Sta. Clara.

CHAPTER XVIII

CHURCH LIFE (1660–1714)

THERE is no such great dividing-line in the fifty years that followed the Restoration as in the half century that preceded it. It was the wars that changed England. When they were over, and Church and king had their own again, the clergy soon settled down to their duties, and the external business of the Church went on, with no striking changes or important reforms, till a new era began with the Hanoverian kings.

Position of the Church at the Restoration.

It will be the object of this chapter to collect, from the documents and histories of the time, scattered instances of the social position of the Church and the clergy, of the nature of church customs and usages, and the outward expression of spiritual and devotional life among the laity.

The Restoration period was notoriously an age of great men in the Church. Jeremy Taylor, Pearson, South, Barrow, Stillingfleet, Bull, Burnet, and Henry Wharton, are names which stand for divers and splendid qualities. Something has already been said of them ; and they are a small selection indeed from the notable men who have left memorials of their piety and scholarship.

But it may be that the work of these great men is to be regarded as altogether exceptional. This at least may be argued. In *Ichabod, or the Five Groans of the Church*, 1663, the writer (probably Ken) observed that the children of the Church were discontented, the government complained of, the ordinances neglected, the ministers despised, the peace disturbed, the safety endangered.

Ichabod, 1663.

After a vindication of the discipline and orders of the Church, and a distinct assertion of the Apostolical succession as the foundation, he speaks of the number of young ministers now ordained, often unsettled, rash and inexperienced, some even men expelled from college, many unlearned. Four hundred and twenty-six tradesmen who, "having intruded in former years into the sacred calling of a minister, are now ordained into it," are but part of those who accepted ordination at the Restoration settlement, of whom the whole number is 1342; and their adhesion is due not to the conscience of the Church's principles, but to the prosperity of her cause. And the morals of such men, too, cause scandal, and the simony, the pluralities, the non-residence, and the curates whom the non-resident clergy employ: "I do not know by what law of God or man a clergyman may turn his tithe to private advantage any more than a layman." He calculates that out of 12,000 Church livings, about 3000 are impropriated, and 4165 sinecures or "non-resident" livings. It is clear that the measures of the Parliamentary Committee under the Commonwealth had been ineffectual, and the need for the purchase of impropriations, which Laud and Charles I. had at heart, still remained—and was to remain—pressing.

The poverty of the clergy was notorious. The subject of clerical incomes naturally aroused attention after the disasters of the war. The Dolben Papers contain a list of the clergy of England and their incomes. In 1680 was published a *Book of the Valuations of all the Ecclesiastical Preferments in England and Wales*, estimating their liability to tithes. In 1685 a translation of the Frenchman Simon's book on *Ecclesiastical Revenues* was published in London. The evidence that can be collected shows the life of privation which many of the parish priests must have undergone. The moral as well as the material effects of the Civil War were felt severely, and not less the effects of the relaxed morality of the Restoration.

In Lee's Life of Kettlewell a gloomy account is given of the general standard of clerical performance. The retirement of the nonjurors had led to the appointment of inferior men, who had every temptation to slackness. A notable decrease in the daily services followed, and the weekly celebration of

Y

the holy communion "was now much unfrequented in comparison of what it had been." The cathedral statutes fell into neglect, and preparation for baptism and the holy communion was practically abandoned. Burnet admits that public morals much deteriorated and disbelief in revealed religion spread. "The nation," he writes of the period of the Revolution, "was falling under a general corruption both as to morals and principles"; and Bentley, in his Boyle Lectures, took up the tale against the philosophy of Hobbes as at the root of the evil, declaring that "of this the taverns and coffee-houses, nay, Westminster Hall and the very churches, were full." Thus it would seem that the public morals reflected the decline in the influence of the clergy; but it is hazardous to assert that this was the case.

Undoubtedly the poverty of the clergy remained to the end of the period a serious distress. Swift declares that a reader in a London church would receive £20 a year, a lecturer in a town £60, a chaplain £30, and vails or perquisites; while country incumbents would receive from £20 to £60, and, curates rarely more than £30. Some of these stipends were not low, but the literature of the time shows that the majority of them were thought not to afford a living. From this it might be expected that the clergy were not drawn from a high social class; and indeed, the literature of the period is full of jests at the poor men who took holy orders, and remained in a condition little above that of domestic service. Rising from the *Their social position.* condition wittily satirised in a squib of the time, when the young servitor was glad of anything he could pick up, a humble lad could find his way into the ministry of the Church. "I am a rising lad, mother, and have gott prefarment in college allready, for our sextoun beeing gonn intoo Heryfordshear has left mee his depoty, which is a very good place," the letter begins; and it concludes with believing he shall do very well "if you wull but send me t'other crowne." It was not to be wondered at if some attained no higher dignity than that expressed in Oldham's famous lines :

Diet, an horse, and thirty pounds a year,
Besides th' advantage of his lordship's ear,
The credit of the business and the State,
Are things that in a youngster's sense sounds great.

Little the unexperienced wretch doth know
What slavery he oft must undergo ;
Who though in silken scarf and cassock drest
Wears but a gayer livery at best.
When dinner calls, the implement must wait,
With holy words to consecrate the meat,
But hold it for a favour seldom shown
If he be deign'd the honour to sit down.

From descriptions such as this, from a pamphlet called *The Character of a Whig under several Denominations*, 1700, and from Eachard's *Grounds and Occasions of the Contempt of the Clergy and Religion*, 1670, a famous picture of the social position of the clerical estate under the later Stewarts has been drawn. But it bears small resemblance to the truth. Eachard complains, from the standing-point of a university don, of the ignorance of some of the clergy and the extreme poverty of others ; and as a cause of the latter alleges the " infinite number that are in holy orders," the eagerness and ambition which leads them into the profession, and the ease of procuring men for £25 or £30 a year, and the disproportionate revenues of the bishops. Steele, in the *Tatler* (1710), mocks at the exclusion of the clergy from the later courses of the dinner, and asks what a Roman Catholic priest would think of such treatment ? But all this, and the mirth of the playhouses, was admittedly an exaggeration. Never was the class more respected. Socially, in the later seventeenth century the clergy probably stood higher than ever before that period. Fielding, Fane, Finch, Mountague, Compton, Grenville, Berkeley, Crewe, and Trelawney are among the ancient and honourable names which a contemporary notes among the clergy; and another added, " as for the gentry, there are not many good families in England but either have or have had a clergyman in them." The aspersions on the marriages of the clergy—the statement that their wives were often waiting-maids, or even cast-off mistresses of their patrons—have been disproved by a careful investigation. A sermon of Sprat's in 1678 concludes with a statement which, while eulogising the married state, appears to show that the material condition of the clergy was improving. " As more clergymen were impoverished by the calamities of the late war and oppression of the Church

Eachard's *Grounds of the Contempt of the Clergy*, 1670.

and State than ever in the like space before, so I think it may be said without envy that more clergymen or their heirs than ever in one time before, since they were allowed marriage, have been brought to a plentiful and prosperous condition by his Majesty's, and with him the Church's, most happy restoration "; and the same writer, when Bishop of Rochester, speaks of clerical learning and the clergy's libraries in a manner which implies the sufficiency of each. None the less, the smallness of the revenues of the clergy cannot be denied; even dignitaries like Grenville, who kept up the old hospitality, soon found themselves in difficulties; and it is on that, not on want of learning, breeding, or character, that the real weakness of their position must be allowed to rest. There was no great division between town and country clergy—certainly no greater one than between town and country gentry. Popular feeling was very largely directed by their writings, and their intervention in politics, as in the case of the seven bishops or that of Sacheverell, was often decisive.

The *Clergyman's Vade Mecum*, a work written by John Johnson of Cranbrook, is full of interesting details as to the position, legal, and to some extent social, of the clergy at the close of the seventeenth century. Its success—for it was very frequently reprinted—shows the importance that attached to questions relating to the clerical estate. On the whole, it may be said that the social standing of the clergy, far from declining, advanced during the period under review; and of their influence there are many remarkable instances. Among them may perhaps be noted the extraordinary interest which was aroused by the sermons of the day. The publication of sermons was found lucrative both by preacher and printer. In spite of length—Barrow once preached for three hours and a half on charity before the Lord Mayor; of elaboration—till Tillotson introduced a simpler style; of facetiousness—South's sermons kept his congregation in constant mirth; and of the difficulties of extemporary preaching, which Burnet and others began to encourage, the popularity of sermons increased rather than diminished between the days of Charles I. and Anne. The most remarkable example of this taste is the fact that after Tillotson's death two thousand five hundred guineas were given for the copyright of the two volumes of his discourses, which now would not arouse interest in the most impressionable or the most pious of men.

The substitution of unwritten for written sermons appears to have been due to influences external to the English Church —to the examples of Puritans and Papists. A story of Charles II. and Stillingfleet illustrates the change that was taking place. It is said of the latter that "while chaplain to King Charles, his Majesty asked him 'How it came about that he always read his sermons before him, when he was informed he always preached without books elsewhere?' He told the king that 'the awe of so noble an audience, where he saw nothing that was not greatly superior to him; but chiefly, the seeing before him so great and wise a prince made him afraid to trust himself. . . .' 'But pray,' says Stillingfleet, 'will your Majesty give me leave to ask you a question too? Why you read your speeches when you can have none of the same reasons?' 'Why, truly, doctor,' says the king, 'your question is a very pertinent one, and so will be my answer. I have asked them [the House of Commons] so often and for so much money, that I am ashamed to look them in the face.'" The change made way very gradually; the number of published sermons so late as 1714 shows that it had not even then become general.

With the progress of the change there began to disappear, though gradually, those extraordinary substitutes for the Catholic requiem, the funeral sermons, from which so much of our knowledge of the religious life of the seventeenth century is derived. No endowments were more common at this period than for a yearly sermon on the *obit* of some often quite undistinguished person; and no person of any eminence for position or piety was suffered to be buried without a eulogy, which was then published as a memorial of departed greatness or virtue. A notable sermon of one of the most famous preachers of the day, Dr. Anthony Horneck of the Savoy, on Mrs. Dorothy St. John, fourth daughter of Oliver St. John, preached at St. Martin's-in-the-Fields in 1677, remarks that the office of the preachers "is to convert souls, not to paint them"; but it may well have been thought that the record of genuine piety was a valuable instrument of conversion. It was, indeed, fit and proper that the world should learn of the beauty of a young damsel's life of whom it might be said that "the fruits of the Spirit, which are not seen in others before fifty, appeared in her at eighteen, and the joys of the Holy Ghost, which are not counted *modish* till fourscore, became familiar to her as soon as her reason began to exert itself in action." And no less fit was it that the history of a remarkable conversion like that of the debauched John Wilmot, Earl of Rochester, should be told by those in whose hands God had placed his conversion, "to awaken those who run on to all the excesses of riot." Sermons, indeed, at funerals, as well as the pertinent epitaphs which preached from every church wall, were in the seventeenth century distinct missionary instruments, which the clergy employed in addition to the ordinary weapons of the spiritual warfare.

It may be noticed in this place that the custom during this period was to wear the black gown in the pulpit, Ceremonial though the use of the surplice had been restored of the pulpit. in all the other ministrations of the Church. Strype wrote in 1696: "Yesterday I saw in Low Leighton church that which, to my remembrance, I never did see in a church in England but once, and that is a minister preach in a surplice for Mr. Harrison; whereas other ministers on Feast days do not so much as wear any surplice, he, by way of supererogation, preached in his. The sight did stir up in me more of pity than anger to see the folly of the man; but if he preach in a fool's coat we will go and hear him."

The importance of sermons did not diminish the attention paid to the other agencies by which the religious life was fostered. The Sacraments, fasting, books of devotion, church music, all bore their part, and they were supplemented by the creation of vigorous societies for the cultivation of the devout life. Soon after the Restoration a serious attempt was made by several of the bishops to secure in parish, as well as in cathedral churches, a more frequent celebration of the holy communion.

The number of communicants had clearly diminished since 1640. Frequency of communion had been discouraged by the action of the Puritans when in power. An "Ordinance

of the Lords and Commons assembled in Parliament, together with the rules and directions concerning suspension from the Sacrament of the Lord's Supper" The holy
communion.
(1645), required as conditions of admission to com-
munion assent to statements of doctrine highly disputable,
if not explicitly heretical, and examination by elders in a form
which the letters of Lady Verney show to have been regarded
with disgust and suspicion. The result was natural; and the
custom of frequent communion was never successfully revived.
The first and most obvious result had been the rare administration of the Holy Sacrament. This reformers now set themselves to remedy. The bishops before the war had, it would
appear, combined to desire that "the blessed sacrament of
holy communion be administered in the Church every month
upon the first Sunday, or at least thrice in the year, whereof
Easter to be one." [1] Sancroft's injunctions of 1688 inquire
whether this is carried out. Patrick, when Dean of Peterborough, notes the archbishop's order that there should be a
weekly communion.

Dean Grenville, of Durham, devoted himself persistently for
many years to securing the observance of this rule. In 1683
he recorded a conversation with Fell, Bishop of Oxford, who
agreed with his wish, but advised "the stirring up of some
devout people, ladies or gentlemen, to desire the same from
the dean and chapter, as the best expedient to effect that
good work, saying that the dean and prebends (*sic*) could not
justify the denial thereof; and, besides, it was a very plausible
way for them to steal into their duty without exposing themselves for their past omissions and neglects." He noted at the
same time that Dr. Bury, rector of Exeter College, Oxford,
was "exceedingly positive that it ought to be a constant concomitant of all Feasts as well as the Sunday," etc., and
argued, in writing to Sir William Dugdale, whom he called
"so eminent a champion for our Common Prayer-book," that
the rubric (if it be strictly examined) doth at this very day
suppose daily" communions. He restored weekly communions at Durham; at Ely, Christ Church, and Worcester it
had always been retained; it was reintroduced at Canterbury,
York, at St. Paul's when it was rebuilt, at Gloucester, and

---

[1] Brian Duppa's *Articles of Enquiry*, Chichester, 1638.

apparently at Rochester. It was part of a general revival of interest in Church observances and rubrics. Thus in the royal chapels, when the court was in London, the holy communion was celebrated twice on Sundays, at eight and twelve. The usual hours in the London churches were seven or eight, but at St. Lawrence Jewry, where the vicar was a great-nephew of Nicholas Ferrar, the celebration of holy communion was at six. At St. Dunstan's-in-the-West there was a celebration daily during the octaves of Christmas, Easter, and Whitsuntide. At Easter 1685 Bishop Crewe issued an Injunction to the dean and chapter, and in the October of that year Dr. Grenville wrote to Sancroft, who had formerly been a prebendary of Durham : "Among many other excellent things, my Lord of Durham hath strictly enjoined us to continue the weekly communion with jubilation (fallen into disuse since the death of Bishop Cosin), and to restore sermons on Wednesdays and Fridays in Lent and Advent." The bidding of prayer before the sermon and the weekly communion have continued in Durham cathedral ever since, and the celebration has been "with jubilation," that is, chorally; but, till of late years, this was only done once a month.

Little, if any, change was made in ceremonial. The altar was hung with rich cloths or carpets, of the gifts of which there are many records. It appears from the usage of Sancroft that altar plate was solemnly consecrated to its sacred use. Copes were worn in many of the cathedral churches. The nonjurors, in their careful study of the Prayer-book, were not slow to point out the authority of the ornaments rubric. Gandy wrote that "according to this rubric we are still bound to wear albs and vestments, as have been worn a long time in the Church of God. For the disuse of these ornaments we can attribute it to no other cause than to them that came from Geneva, and, in the beginning of Queen Elizabeth's reign, being set in places of government, suffered every negligent priest to do what him liked, so he would but profess a difference and an opposition in all things (though never so lawful otherwise) against the Church of Rome and the ceremonies therein used." Incense was burnt on solemn occasions ("before the office began," Evelyn

Ceremonial of the altar.

records, on Easter day, 1684, in Whitehall chapel), and censers, judging again by the example of Archbishop Sancroft, appear to have been consecrated; but there seems to be some doubt about the matter, and it is probable that only one of the cathedral churches (Ely) kept up the use of incense during divine service, while in parish churches it was employed from time to time in a confusion that was perhaps hardly recognised between the purposes of fumigation and ceremonial.

Almost universally the Laudian rule as to the position of the altar was accepted at the Restoration. Still, however, in many places the minister came down to give the Sacrament to the people as they knelt in their pews; and Lady Warwick on one occasion speaks as though the holy table was at times moved: "When the minister was going to consecrate the bread and wine, the communion table being a good way from before my pew, he of a sudden drew it till he brought it just before my pew; as he was doing so God was pleased to put this thought into my mind, which much affected me, that as the minister drew the table nearer, so God the Father drew near now to me with an offer of my dear Saviour to take away all my sins."

Frampton's life records as a scandal the case of a parish priest "whose manner was after consecration to carry the holy elements into the reading-desk, and then return and in a most uncanonical manner distribute them to his parishioners." Nelson tells of Bull, that "whenever he officiated at the altar it was exactly agreeable to the rubric, and with the gravity and seriousness of a primitive priest," and that his custom was to offer the elements "upon the holy table, in the first place, in conformity to the practice of the ancient Church, before he began the communion service; and this the rubric after the offertory seemeth to require of all her priests." The revision, in 1662, of the rubric at the end of the communion service clearly points to consideration of two questions: that of desecration by irreverent clergy—a practice which the writings of Cosin and Thorndike show to have formed a convenient weapon for Roman Catholic controversialists; and that of reservation. With regard to the latter there would seem to be no record; but Thorndike's criticism of the Roman practice of reserving in one kind only may perhaps be taken to imply that the English Church reserved in both, and he says (writing in 1670, when the rubrics of 1662 may be concluded to have been understood) :

" And thus far I will particularise as concerning the Eucharist ; that the Church is to endeavour the celebrating of it so frequently that it may be reserved to the next communion. For in the meantime it ought to be so ready for them that pass into the other world that they need not stay for the consecrating of it on purpose for every one. The reason of the necessity of it for all, which hath been delivered, aggravates it very much in danger of death. And the practice of the Church attests it to the utmost. Neither will there be any necessity of giving it in one kind only ; as by some passages of antiquity may be collected, if common reason could deceive in a subject of this nature."

When we pass from the holy communion to holy baptism we find efforts constantly made by members of reforming societies to revive its public use on occasions when the churches were full of worshippers. Bull was very careful to minister it always " on Sundays and holy days, when the greatest number of persons were met together," but the registers show generally that while private baptism in houses was rare, public baptism in church on Sunday was little more common.

Holy baptism.

The penitential system of the Church survived the Civil War without serious alteration. The teaching on the subject is clear and continuous. Heylin, in *The Doctrine and Discipline of the English Church*, 1662, states the accepted view when he writes that the priests " retained their native and original power in the court of conscience by hearing the confession of a sorrowful and afflicted penitent, and giving him the comfort of absolution, a power conferred upon them in their ordination." The *Guide for the Penitent*, attributed to Brian Duppa, contains the advice of particular confession ; and Jeremy Taylor repeated it. So Sparrow wrote, " he that would be sure of pardon, let him seek out a priest and make his humble confession unto him." That this advice was very largely followed the history of the

The penitential system.

period contains abundance of instances to prove.   Morley, Bishop of Winchester, left record of how he acted as " spiritual director and guide " to Anne Hyde, Duchess of York, stating that before every communion " she made a voluntary confession of what she thought she had offended God in, either by omission or commission, professing her sorrow for it, and promising amendment of it, and then kneeling down, she desired and received absolution in the form and words prescribed by our Church."   In the list of "their Majesties' servants in the Chapel Royal at Whitehall," under William and Mary, is included the confessor of the household.   Tenison heard Queen Mary's confession ; Archbishop Sharp was the spiritual director of Queen Anne.   Evelyn records that Jeremy Taylor was his confessor ; Pepys is known to have made his confession to Hickes.   Grenville had Bishop Gunning at one time for his confessor, and himself left elaborate rules for the hearing of confessions.   Lenthall, the Speaker of the Long Parliament, who died in 1662, made his confession to his old friend and chaplain, Ralph Brideoak, then rector of Witney and afterwards Bishop of Chichester.   Seth Ward, Bishop of Salisbury, told Aubrey that "he did the last office of a confessor to his Grace " of Albemarle.   Indeed the instances are too numerous to admit of any doubt as to the frequency of the practice.   And the visitation articles make constant inquiry as to the " priest or minister " of each parish observing strictly the secrecy required by the 113th canon of 1604.   There are also many records of the penances prescribed and enforced.   Many parish churches appear to have benefited, in repair or adornment, by sums of money paid in penance for offences thus estimated by bishops.

Daily services were recognised to be the rule of the Church. In London, daily morning and evening prayers were said in most churches, the congregations being to some   The daily extent provided by the new religious societies.   services. The Life of Frampton shows him as bishop most active in reviving the daily prayer, and familiarising with "the venerable forms of the Church" those who had become "almost strangers to the devotional way of worship in the Church of England." Dean Grenville's Diary notes many places where daily prayer, as well as monthly celebrations, were held ; but it is observed by Nelson in his Life of Bull that when Bull came to Suddington, Gloucestershire, "the Holy Eucharist, the mysterious rite and perfection of Christian worship, was not performed so often as he desired; and yet oftener than is usual in little villages; for he brought it to seven times in the year." Grenville recommended all the clergy of his archdeaconry to observe the rules of George Herbert's country parson "for their direction, in order to the exemplary discharge of their function, having," he added, "always made it mine." His curates frequently resided in his house and pursued their studies under his direction. He was strict in requiring the daily performance of Mattins and Evensong in each of his churches, on working days at six, morning and evening; but on vigils, eves and Saturdays Evensong was at three; and on Wednesday and Friday, and all through Advent and Lent and on the Ember days Mattins was at nine, with a short sermon, not more than a quarter of an hour long. On Sundays and holy day afternoons there was always catechising after the second lessons, and there were sermons on all Sundays and Feasts. The rogation days were always observed by "the perambulation."

The observance of Lent, required by the State as well as the Church, showed some signs of relaxation after the wars.

Lent.

But it was still kept up in many parts of the country, and by devout church folk. One of the first official acts of Juxon as Archbishop of Canterbury was to grant a licence to Secretary Nicholas and his household to eat meat in Lent. The use of the Laudian times was kept up in many parishes, where we find the registers noting exemptions from the rule owing to illness and the order of physicians. As late as 1663 the Corporation of Weymouth ordered the butchers not to "dress, sell, or utter any flesh during the present Lent." Grenville's orders for his own household afford an instance of the observance of private families. Besides Sundays, only on Tuesdays and Thursdays was there "one dish of flesh for those whose necessities require it," and on Mondays, Wednesdays, and Fridays no formal meal was served till after evening prayer, but dispensation was allowed for those who could not eat fish.

How, then, we naturally ask, did the Church's system

affect the general life of the people.   It is both difficult and
rash to generalise.   There is much evidence of a
general low standard.   Books, such as Jeremy Effects on
Collier's famous attack on the contemporary stage, the general
and the "brief lives" of the antiquary Aubrey, or people.
the very private Diary of Pepys, present a painful picture.   But
there is another side.   Never before in English history have
we fuller records, in ordinary society, of the lives of good men
and good women.

Among the holy women of that corrupt age Mary, Countess
of Warwick (1625-78), was conspicuous.   Brought up carefully by a good father, the great Earl of Cork, she Mary,
married for love (which was rare in her days) Countess of
Charles Rich, who became Earl of Warwick, an Warwick.
irritable, gouty husband, whose ill humour sorely taxed her
patience.   Her Diaries note every experience of her religious
life, from her first earnest conversion to God, through years of
sober devotion and daily meditation, till she died, as she had
wished, at her prayers.   Without leaving the world (for she was
constantly in the company of those who were far from sharing
her religious interests, such as the Duchess of Albemarle, the
Duchess of York, young Lord Ranelagh, and the famous Earl
of Rochester) she lived a saintly life, constant in prayer and
meditation, in the daily hearing of the Church's services, and the
monthly reception of the holy communion.   Living her early
married life in a Puritan household, she was one of those
who found the strictness of its discipline helpful, and of
whom, men and women, Sir Philip Warwick wrote in the bad
days of the Restoration, that they "were so regular in their
lives and so exemplary to all (though there were some drinking
Hectors intermixed) that they converted very many ; and had
they kept the same strictness upon his Majesty's return which
they did to make way for his return (to say no more), we had
certainly been in a better state than we are at present."   Lady
Warwick did not desert her religion in spite of the gay attrac-
tions of the new court.   She continued simple and strict in her
personal life, and abounding in charity.   Her religion, like
those of so many of the ladies of her time, was ordered by the
rules of the Church.   The common prayer was said daily in
her household, and fasting days were rigidly observed.   The

Restoration had by no means caused preaching to be less
important.   Lady Warwick's Diary speaks of almost daily
sermons, and she frequently heard Ken, Stillingfleet, Tillotson,
and Compton.   It was so also with her friend Lady Margaret
Maynard, who was commemorated by Ken.

Instances of very deep devotion were by no means rare
in the court of Charles II.   There is no more charming
biography of this age than that which John Evelyn wrote
of Margaret Blagge, one of the maids of honour of Queen
Catherine of Braganza, who died not long after her marriage
to Mr. Godolphin.   "It would become," says Evelyn, "a
steadier hand, and the pen of an angel's wing, to describe
the life of a saint"; and the life which he describes is one
of most singular beauty.   The spiritual history of
this lady, who died when she was only twenty-six,
begins when she was still a young child.   Bishop
Gunning, who confirmed her, "was so surprised at those early
graces he discovered in her, that he thought fit she should be
admitted to the Holy Sacrament when she was hardly eleven
years of age," and her holy life proceeded without any
break or jar.   The account of the origin of her friendship
with Evelyn is written by him with some of the humour for
which the lady herself was renowned : the playfulness of his
description of the office of friendship—"that I may now and
then write to you to cultivate my style, discourse with you to
improve my understanding, read to you to receive your reflections"—delightfully introduces the high and serious thoughts
upon which they habitually conversed.   At court Mistress
Blagge was a brilliant wit, a perfect actress, one of the "con-
stellations of the royal circle."   So soon as she was at liberty
to leave the court she intended, says Evelyn, "a design of
going to Hereford to live by herself under the direction of the
reverend dean of that cathedral, who had long been her
spiritual father," but she was at last prevailed on to marry
Mr. Godolphin, to whom she had long been attached.   She
died soon after giving birth to a son a year later.

Of her religion Evelyn gives many particulars which illustrate the character of the devout life of the time.   "Besides
the monthly communions, she rarely missed a Sunday throughout the whole year wherein she did not receive the Holy Sacra-

Mrs.
Godolphin.

ment, if she were in town and tolerable health ; and I well
know she had those who gave her constant advertisement
where it was celebrated, upon some more solemn Festivals,
besides not seldom on the week days assisting at one
poor creature's or other ; and when sometimes, being in the
country or on a journey, she had not these opportunities, she
made use of a devout meditation upon that sacred mystery
by way of mental communion, so as she was in a continual
state of preparation." The " frequent counsels of her ghostly
father," he says, were assisted by the constant intercourse of
letters, and she kept a book to record her "infirmities," to
"assist her more minute confessions." Very regular in
attendance at divine service, and spending all the time she
could win from her duties at court to visiting the poor and
sick, she was far from being a recluse. " Nothing was more
agreeable than her company wherever she came. Indeed
there was nothing proof against the abundance of her wit and
piety : she made virtue and holiness a cheerful thing, lovely
as herself ; and even in the court, how many of the greatest
there were made to look upon religion as a serious thing, yet
consistent with their post."

And this view of the religion among persons in high
place, indeed, is confirmed by what Roger North records
in the evidence of Dr. John North, the king's clerk of
the closet, who was confessor to many of the court
ladies : " I have heard him say that for the number Ladies of
of persons that resided in the court, a place reputed the court.
a centre of all vice and irreligion, there were as many truly
pious and strictly religious as could be found in any other
resort whatsoever. And he never saw so much fervent
devotion, and such frequent acts of charity as his station gave
him to observe there,"—the lives of Lady Ranelagh (sister
to the Countess of Warwick), Lady Rachel Russell, Lady
Elizabeth Hastings, Lady Margaret Maynard, and Lady
Frances Digby. But while the piety and benevolence of
Christian women has many examples in the period, it would
be a mistake indeed to think that piety was regarded as a
feminine virtue.

Among famous men who lived as Christians should none
was more notable than Robert Boyle, a man "without any

sort of sigularity," yet of unstained honour and absolute
devotion to God, the first governor of the Company
for the Propagation of the Gospel, and the founder
of the Boyle Lectures for the support of the
Christian faith.   His life, ended in 1691, was entirely devoted
to good works, and Addison rightly called him an honour to
his country.   His interests, scientific, theological, literary,
touched the life of the day at many points, and as agreeing
with him in different aspects of his work might be placed
Ashmole the antiquary, Lord Weymouth, the constant friend
of Ken, Sir Thomas Browne, most delightful of the writers of
his age.

Devout laymen.

Among the many laymen of the day whom their contemporaries regarded as eminent for piety and good work, Burnet's
biography enables us to single out Sir Matthew Hale,
a great judge and a saintly man, who, after passing,
with discretion and untainted honour, through the
troubled days of the Commonwealth and Protectorate, held
the office of Lord Chief Baron for eleven years under the
Restoration government, and was then from 1671 Lord Chief
Justice of England.   As a judge he was eminent for his
justice and the care of his judgments; as a Christian for the
devout simplicity of his life and the tolerant earnestness of his
churchmanship.   He was one of those who would willingly
have seen a comprehension of the Presbyterians in the Church
at the time of the Savoy conference, and he was eager in
conference with Wilkins, Bishop of Chester, and with Richard
Baxter, to that end.   The account of his manner of life, of
the worship of his family, of his "extraordinary care to keep
what he did (in private devotion) secret," and of his charities,
is written by Burnet with the genuine enthusiasm for goodness
which was the best feature of his character.   He kept up
some of the medieval customs of charitable hospitality.
Burnet tells that "he usually invited his poor neighbours to
dine with him, and made them sit at table with himself; and
if any of them were sick, so that they could not come, he
would send meat warm to them from his table; and he did
not only relieve the poor in his own parish, but sent supplies
to the neighbouring parishes, as there was occasion for it; and
he treated them all with the tenderness and familiarity that

Sir Matthew Hale, 1609-76.

became one who considered they were of the same nature
with himself, and were reduced to no other necessities but
such as he himself might be brought to."   The friend of
Selden, and, as Burnet says he was, "the great adversary to
Hobbes's errors," Hale was a most earnest believer; and his
influence extended far beyond the ordinary sphere of a
lawyer's life.   The account of his last communion reads like
a passage from the life of a saint of the Middle Ages.   It was a
happy proof of her divine mission that the English Church
could still nurture such lives.

Burnet bears witness to her power also to convert.   Few
books have made more impression on their generation than
*Some Passages of the Life and Death of John, Earl
of Rochester*, written by his own direction on his   *Burnet's Life
of Rochester.*
death-bed, which traces the slow change of the most
dissolute of Charles II.'s courtiers into a penitent.   It is a
most touching tale, and the minuteness of the record shows
the nature of the unbelief with which the Church was then
confronted, and the character of the arguments by which,
before the development of the later philosophy of English
theologians, it was met.

While books such as these had considerable effect, it was
not only by direct attacks on infidelity that churchmen
endeavoured to vindicate their faith.   Dryden's
admirable exposition of his creed as a Protestant of   *Dryden's
Religio Laici.*
the English Church in the *Religio Laici* (1682)
summed up the beliefs, it cannot be doubted, of many a sober
English thinker in relation to Popery, Dissent, and Deism :

> What then remains but, waving each extreme,
> The tides of ignorance and pride to stem ?
> Neither so rich a treasure to forego
> Nor proudly seek beyond our power to know !
> Faith is not built on disquisitions vain ;
> The things we must believe are few and plain ;
> But since men will believe more than they need
> And every man will make himself a creed,
> In doubtful questions 'tis the safest way
> To learn what unsuspected ancients say ;
> For 'tis not likely we should higher soar
> In search of Heaven than all the Church before ;
> Nor can we be deceived, unless we see
> The Scriptures and the Fathers disagree.

If after all they stand suspected, still
(For no man's faith depends upon his will),
'Tis some relief, that points not clearly known
Without much hazard may be let alone ;
And after hearing what our Church can say,
If still our reason runs another way,
That private reason 'tis more just to curb
Than by disputes the public peace disturb.
For points obscure are of small use to learn ;
But common quiet is mankind's concern.

It was not difficult indeed to criticise such a view, especially when it proceeded from such a writer. He came later to taunt the Church with the very freedom of belief which once he had praised, as well as with the alliance with the State which most Englishmen thought her strongest safeguard. "Our adversary knew very well," wrote one of his critics in 1687 [*Notes upon Mr. Dryden's Poems . . . to which are added some Reflections upon " The Hind and Panther,"* London, 1687], "the Church of England to be a body that will never rebel against the king ; therefore in derision he calls her the passive Church. Thanks be to God she is so ; therefore she is the true Church of Christ." The critic then as Dryden formerly, certainly expressed the opinion of many a country squire who helped to support the Church in the days of James II. and after the Revolution. It was not, however, in such men that the true strength of the Church resided. It lay, then as ever, in the mass of quiet, sober, pious people, whose lives were built up on her doctrines and her sacraments, men whose enthusiasm was restrained but fervent, and showed itself on occasion by acts of self-sacrificing devotion, and always by a regular and consistent conduct. There could be no better examples of such men than John Evelyn, the courtier, horticulturist, man of the world, and Izaak Walton, the tradesman and man of letters, the honoured friend and loving biographer of the greatest ecclesiastics of the days before the Restoration.

Further examples of the character of Church life may be found in the development of ecclesiastical music and in the wide circulation of books of devotion.

The Restoration was a great era in Church music. Up to the wars something, at least, of the old pre-Reformation style had survived, and much of the work of the musicians of the Reformation period. The Puritans were never weary of protesting against the organs and the Cathedral service, "so unedifying and offensive." Hacket, speaking before the House of Commons on behalf of deans and chapters, admitted that he had heard that "the service of cathedral churches gives offence to divers for the super-exquisiteness of the music," and that "a great part of it serves rather to tickle the ear than to affect the heart with goodness." At the Restoration the old style had entirely passed away, and, said the writer of *A Short Direction for the Performance of Cathedral Service, published for the Information of such Persons as are ignorant of it and shall be called to officiate in Cathedral or Collegiate Churches where it hath been formerly in use* (Oxford, 1661), the persons and things relating to harmony and order "are not easily rallied after so fatal a rout." The writer, therefore, "put together and published the ordinary and extraordinary parts both for the priest and whole quire. . . . The tunes in four parts to serve only so long till the quires are more learned and musical, and thereby a greater variety used." The revival was fostered by Charles II., who had some knowledge of music and a great affection for the new style of Lulli. The choir of the Chapel Royal at Whitehall became the model for the whole country under Henry Cooke, whose musical education belonged to the days before the war. Pelham Humfrey, John Blow, and Michael Wise were the leaders of the new English sacred music. Henry Purcell, the great master of the school, was only two years old at the Restoration, but nine years later he had composed an ode for the king's birthday. From 1667 to 1695 he wrote a magnificent series of anthems and won the place of the greatest of English musicians. Purcell had, indeed, many followers and imitators, but he had no rivals.

Church music.

It was not, however, without a struggle that musical services, even in cathedrals, became universal. William III.'s Commissioners of 1689 agreed that the chanting of divine service in cathedrals should be laid aside, "that the whole may be rendered intelligible to the common people." Stillingfleet's writings show the nature of the contest that raged on this point. On the one

The controversy concerning instrumental music.

hand, the organs were declared to be "a Levitical service";
on the other, the use of instrumental music at all was taken for
flat Popery.   "The organs" again came into common use with
the Restoration; and cornets and other wind instruments, as
well as fiddles, are heard of at Westminster, Durham, and
the Chapel Royal, St. James's.   An important attempt to win
the dissenters, *Certain Cases Resolved* (2nd edition, 1683),
deals fully and seriously with the question of Church psalmody.
Dodwell's learned treatise, *Of the Lawfulness of Instrumental
Music in Holy Offices* (1698), is a serious vindication of what
was still felt to need defence.   The triumph, indeed, even of
the organ was not assured without the intervention of the
preacher.   Two famous sermons espoused the cause of sacred
music.   One was preached by Towerson at the opening of
a new organ at St. Andrew Undershaft, 1698.   The other
was preached at St. Paul's on November 22, 1699, "being
the anniversary meeting of the Lovers of Musick," by Sherlock,
the Dean.   "Does praise to God," the preacher inquired,
"consist merely in the harmonious melody of voices, and
musical instruments?   Does he praise God best who com-
poses the best anthems, or sings them best?   Or do we think
that we then praise God best when we feel ourselves the most
transported and ravished with excellent musick, performed by
the best voices, the choicest instruments and the greatest
masters?   This is a very easy and a pleasant way of praising
God, if this would carry us to Heaven."

This might seem but an ungracious beginning; but the
good dean speedily explained that his object was merely to
persuade and direct his audience "to turn the delights and
charms of musick into the raptures of devotion, which would
the most effectually silence all the enemies of Church music
and cathedral worship."   Throughout his discourse he took it for
granted that the voices would be accompanied by instruments;
and he treated with something like contempt the objection
that singing as "part of the Mosaical law" was abolished.   "I
see no reason," he said, "why men may not reject vocal prayer
as well as vocal music because they were both used by the
Jews."   And as to further objections to Church music, they were
as good in David's time as now.   But, on the other hand, he
had objections of his own to some of the music of his day, to

"light and airy compositions, which disperse the thoughts and give a gay and frisking motion to the spirits," and to the "needless and endless repetitions," which he observed to have grown very common. Many pertinent criticisms on the duties and character of musicians he added; and his sermon bears witness to the importance which the musical services in the great cathedral church of London had already attained to, and the dangers with which it was beset when he speaks of "very many who resort hither who, especially on the Lord's day, crowd into the church to hear the anthem, and when that is over, to the great disturbance of the worship of God and the scandal of all good Christians, crowd as fast out again." But the attraction of the sermon, the dean was not slow to admit, remained undiminished, for those who departed after the anthem "make room for devouter people, who immediately fill up their places, to attend the instructions of God's Word."

Akin to the question of Church music is that of the metrical psalmody. In 1646 Parliament had substituted for the version of Sternhold and Hopkins that of "Mr. Rous, his Psalms." Rous, whom Clarendon *Metrical psalmody.* disposes of as "an old gentleman of Devonshire, of very mean understanding," was a prominent member of each of the Parliaments of the Interregnum, but his version, except in Scotland, died with him. Sternhold and Hopkins returned with the Restoration, to suffer the sneers of Dryden, and Tate and Brady, authorised by William III. in 1696, soon took not only their place but that of the old book. The use of hymns, in the modern sense of the term, was still to come.

Books of devotion came into a new life with the ordered piety of the later Caroline divines. Bayly and Cosin were followed, if not supplanted, by *The Whole Duty of Man.* This extraordinarily popular book was *Books of devotion.* published in 1657 under the protection of a letter from the saintly Hammond. It sprang almost immediately into popularity. The language used about it in almost every book of the period is laudatory beyond the verge *The Whole* of extravagance; it was placed with the Bible and *Duty of Man,* the Prayer-book as the indispensable requisites of *1657.* the Christian life; it was issued in innumerable editions and followed by innumerable imitations. There can be no better proof than its extraordinary success of the deep-rooted place of the Church in the affections of the people. From first to last it is a plain, sober, orthodox statement of Christian doctrine as the Church held it; it does not turn to right or left, to Geneva or Rome; it is eminently practical, decided, national, without forfeiting its claim to rank among Catholic books of devotion. Dissenters often fell under the power of its fascination; and there must have been very few households in all England from which it was excluded. Its influence can be traced everywhere in literature and life, and there can be no doubt that it was most potent in counteracting the immoral tone of the Restoration court, as well as in confirming the deliberate attachment of Englishmen to the Church. The piquancy of an undiscovered mystery hung, and still hangs, about its authorship. A whole literature exists on the subject without any satisfactory conclusion; and, with a slight preference for the claims of Dorothy Lady Pakington, the question must be suffered to rest unsolved.

Among the many imitations which attained to popularity may be mentioned the *Ladies' Calling*, published at Oxford in 1673. In this rather dull book the duties of a Christian woman are surveyed under the heads of modesty, of meekness, of compassion, of affability, of piety; and advice is given, in a second part, to virgins, to wives, and to widows. The method throughout is that of a sober, wholesome churchmanship, which relies upon regulated habit rather than emotion, but which finds its worship and its devotion centre in the holy eucharist. Its success shows the strength of the reaction against the extravagances of Puritanism, but also marks a distinct step towards the tepid sobriety of the eighteenth century, which came to regard " enthusiasm " as a sin. Very different is the tone of the immortal works of Jeremy Taylor, which at the time of their publication had no such great success—*The Golden Grove, The Marriage Ring, Holy Living and Holy Dying.* Between these extremes of style lie the endless examples of devotional literature associated with the distinguished names of Ken, Sherlock, Comber, Nelson, Patrick Beveridge, Duppa, Samuel Wesley, and many more.

The *Ladies' Calling*, 1673.

A notable exception of originality to the general style is to be found, as might be expected, in the devotional writings of the nonjurors. The most striking of these is the *Devotions in the Ancient Way of Offices, with* Psalms, Hymns and Prayers for Every Day of the Week and Every Holiday in the Year, *reformed by a Person of Quality and Published by George Hickes, D.D.*, the nonjuring Dean of Worcester. This is a work of the greatest liturgical interest, showing an intimate knowledge of ancient sources. It appears to have been compiled by a Roman Catholic; but Hickes carefully revised it, and its devotional standard does not go beyond that of the English Church. It was an attempt to popularise the hours, and three editions show that to a great extent it succeeded; but doubtless its influence did not extend much beyond the nonjurors. It stands apart in the large class of published prayers for families and individuals.

Hickes's Devotions.

It is impossible to close our eyes to the effect of this literature. Books of devotion sold by thousands evidence the hold which the Church had upon the upper classes. Instances of special holiness confirm the impression that the influence was widespread. As might be expected, our chief records, through biographies and funeral sermons, are concerned with the court and the nobility; but there is no reason to suppose that the middle classes were not at least as much influenced by religion as in the preceding period. The age is rich in religious biographies—too rich for a brief survey. Omitting, then, further reference to personal influences and the lives of saintly folk, this sketch may pass on to a very brief notice of the church-building of the period. And for that subject, perhaps, the material assistance which was rendered to the Church in her recovery from poverty and disendowment may fitly be suggested, in this connection, from the State Papers, by the memorandum that Alice, Duchess Dudley, who died at her house near St. Giles's Church, Holborn, January 22, 1668-69, "in her lifetime gave for the augmentation of six vicarages named in county Warwick £20 yearly apiece for ever; also to the same churches, and several others, divers large pieces of plate to be used at the celebration of the sacrament. That she gave

Material gifts to the Church.

to the church of St. Giles the greatest bell in the steeple, and
divers great pieces of massive plate ; paved the chancel with
marble, built the fair blue gate at the entrance to the churchyard, and purchased a fair house of £30 a year value for the
perpetual incumbent. She also gave the hangings for the
choir, which cost £80 : 10s. ; two service books embroidered
in gold £5 ; a velvet altar cloth with gold fringe £60 ; a
cambric cloth to lay over it, with a deep bone lace £4 : 10s. ;
another fine damask cloth £3 ; two cushions for the altar
richly embroidered with gold £10 ; a Turkey carpet to lay
before the altar £6 ; a long screen to sever the chancel from
the church, richly carved and gilt £200 ; a fair organ £100 ;
the organ loft richly wrought and gilt, and a tablet of the 10
Commandments, the Creed, and Lord's Prayer, richly adorned
£80, and £200 for placing out poor apprentices ; £50 to
be distributed to poor people on the day of her funeral ; £5
to each place where her body should rest in its passage from
London to Stoneley in Warwickshire, where she has a noble
monument, erected divers years since, of black and white
marble, which cost above £300 ; also 6d. apiece to every
indigent person meeting her corpse on the road from London
to Stoneley. The rails before the altar curiously carved and
gilt £40. She also gave £100 towards the repair of the
steeple at St. Sepulchre's without Newgate, which was much
defaced by the woeful fire.

"By her will she bequeathed £100 a year for ever for
the redemption of Christian captives out of the hands of the
Turks ; £100 for ever to the poor of the parish of Stoneley
and seven other parishes named ; £400 for the purchase of
lands in augmentation for the maintenance of the poor in the
almshouse near St. Giles Church."

This is a curious picture of the Church customs of the age.
The survivals of such benefactions and arrangements are to
be seen in records, or in visible memorials, within
the walls of many a church to-day. They are
associated very closely with the age *par excellence*
of the country squire. It was an age of conservatism. A
desire to maintain the *status quo* was more than ever
characteristic of the English layman's religion after the restoration of Church and king. And in the country that meant

The power of
the country
squires.

very considerable power for the squire. The position of
comparative independence which Laud would have given
to the country clergy was never recovered after his fall.
Family papers and memoirs all over England show the
laity supreme in parish matters. Characteristic examples
might be quoted from the Verney Papers or from the Diary
of Sir Richard Newdigate. The latter shows the patron of
a living asserting his rights with stubborn ingenuity, having
the books and surplice removed from the church, locking
the doors till his own minister was ready, and concealing
lusty servants in the reading-desk and pulpit to dislodge
possible intruders. Such proceedings naturally led to the
Ecclesiastical Court, where finally the lay interest prevailed.
And the papers of private families do no more than confirm
the admirable sketch of Addison in the 112th number of the
Spectator :

"My friend Sir Roger being a good churchman, has
beautified the inside of his church with several texts of his
own chusing : he has likewise given a handsome pulpit cloth,
and railed in the communion table at his own expence. He
has often told me, that at his coming to his estate he found
(his parishioners) very irregular ; and that in order to make
them kneel and join in the responses, he gave every one of
them a hassock and a Common Prayer Book : and at the
same time employed an itinerant singing master, who goes
about the country for that purpose, to instruct them rightly
in the tunes of the psalms ; upon which they now very much
value themselves, and indeed out-do most of the country
churches that I have ever heard. As Sir Roger is landlord
to the whole congregation, he keeps them in very good order,
and will suffer no body to sleep in it besides himself ; for if
by chance he has been surprised into a short nap at sermon,
upon recovering out of it he stands up and looks about
him, and if he sees any body else nodding, either wakes
them himself, or sends his servant to them. . . . As soon as
the sermon is finished, no body presumes to stir till Sir Roger
is gone out of the church. The knight walks down from his
seat in the chancel between a double row of his tenants, that
stand bowing to him, on each side ; and every now and then
inquires how such an one's wife, or mother, or son, or father

do, whom he does not see in church; which is understood as a secret reprimand to the person that is absent."

The interest of country squires in their parish churches, pushed though it was on occasion to curious extremes, undoubtedly gave great support to the movement for Church restoration, already referred to above (pp. 200-2), which was so marked a feature of the period. From the beginning of Sheldon's primacy the work of rebuilding and reparation all over England was seriously taken in hand. Bishop Turner's letter to his clergy and other memorials, the report of the commission appointed by Bishop Lake of Chichester, and many other visitation charges, show how much work was done. Turner, for example, "having found very many of the churches very sadly dilapidated, or, at least, mightily out of repair, had now (1686) pleasing accounts from many places of the care already taken to repair them." Among the great church builders was Bishop Seth Ward, who at Exeter procured over £25,000 to be spent on his cathedral church, and at Salisbury was as lavish, with results not always happy. The whole history of church restoration is typified by the work done in London, and by the history of Sir Christopher Wren.

The history of the rebuilding of St. Paul's falls entirely within the period under our review. The clearing of the ground began in 1674. In 1675 the first stone was laid. At the end of 1697 the choir was first used for service. It was not till 1710 that the work was finished, based on the magnificent scheme of Wren, which the chapter had considered to be "the most awful and artificial" of all those submitted to their choice. Wren was the nephew of Laud's disciple, the famous Bishop of Ely and Norwich. During his long life (1632-1723) he remained a most sincere, thorough, and devoted churchman. His work was throughout undertaken under a true spiritual as well as artistic inspiration. Like Purcell, he was a man of genius at once original and national, the founder of a school, the characteristic expression of a great age. He applied classical and Italian methods to the special needs of English worship, and on these principles developed a distinct style of his own, dignified, open, solemn, and, above all, fit for common and public worship. Wren's hand may be seen all over England. Fifty-three parish churches in London were built from his designs ; Salisbury, Chichester, and Westminster had their great minsters repaired by him. But the great and characteristic work of his hand was the magnificent cathedral church of St. Paul, a triumphant vindication of his style as the most complete expression ever given to the ideal of Anglican worship as the seventeenth century desired to see it carried out. The history of church building at this important period in English architecture is a subject of special interest. It can only here be mentioned that the Act of Parliament passed in 1710 for the building of fifty-two new churches in London was a fit expression of the widespread national interest. Only twelve churches were actually built. The magnificence of the earlier work, as in St. Paul's, St. James's, Piccadilly, and St. Mary-le-Bow, had set a standard of expense which it was impossible to reach during the wars of William III. and Queen Anne. That the spending of so much money led also to scandals, bickerings, and fraud, was perhaps inevitable ; but the literature of the subject (for example, *Frauds and Abuses at St. Paul's*, and Wren's *Answer*, 1713) is not pleasant reading. The slackness which settled down upon the Church after the death of Queen Anne stayed the work throughout England ; and the era of church restoration ended with the life of the last sovereign of the Stewart house.

Thus, at every point we are brought up, as we close the period of our review, by the sense that a reaction was approaching, induced both by the long strain of the Puritan triumph and by the struggle of the Church to stem the tide which set in against all religious observances and against moral life. As the period draws to its end the political interests, the sharp political contests, tended to engross public attention more and more, and the disturbance of Church life was deep-seated and fraught with future danger.

AUTHORITIES.—Details of the life of the day as it affected the Church may be found in the Diaries of Evelyn and Pepys, in Lady Verney's *Memoirs of the Verney Family*, in Lady Newdigate-Newdegate's *Cavalier and Puritan*, as well as in the State Papers (Domestic) and in many biographies, notably the Lives of Sir Matthew Hale, Wilmot, Earl of Rochester, and Queen Mary, written by Bishop Burnet, with Baxter's note and a sermon preached at the funeral of the Earl of Rochester by the Rev. Mr. Parsons (1774); *Correspondence of Dean Grenville*, vols. xxxvii. and xlvii. of Surtees Society; Tanner MSS., especially vol. xliv.; Rawlinson MSS.; Foxcroft, *Supplement to Burnet* (1902). Among voluminous works on the condition of the clergy, Eachard, *Grounds and Occasions*, 1670; the *Tatler;* Jeremy Collier, *View of the Immorality and Profaneness of the Stage*, 1698; Chamberlayne, *State of Britain*, 1694; Nelson, *Life of Bull*, 1713; these and many more are examined in C. Babington's *Criticism of Macaulay's Character of the Clergy*, 1849; and in this, as in other matters, Dr. Overton's *Life in the English Church*, 1660-1714, is a storehouse of information carefully collected, sifted, and arranged. Recent lives of Mary Rich, Countess of Warwick, by M. Palgrave and C. Fell Smith, already mentioned, contain much of interest. Among other important modern books, which have carefully digested the original authorities, are Abbey and Overton, *The English Church in the Eighteenth Century;* Abbey, *The English Church and its Bishops*, 1700-1800; Perry, *History of the Church of England;* Lecky, *History of England in the Eighteenth Century.*

CHAPTER XIX

THE CHURCH IN WALES, 1625-1715

THE four Welsh dioceses, rightly though they are regarded as forming part of the Church as it has been organised for centuries south of the Tweed, and closely though they are linked to the life of the sees adjacent to them, are yet distinguished from the English sees by racial characteristics, geographical position, and national history. In the seventeenth century this distinction was especially marked, and it has therefore seemed best to treat of the history of the Church in Wales, during the period covered by this book, in a chapter by itself. *Character-istics of the four Welsh dioceses.*

During the period of Reformation the Church in Wales had undergone a process practically amounting to disendowment, owing to the confiscation of the property of the monastic houses, upon which the parishes had cause largely to depend for spiritual ministrations. In the diocese of St. David's, for example, the whole of the tithes enjoyed by the monasteries *Difficulties of the Church in the early seventeenth century. (1) Dissent.* passed away from the Church, and the loss was one which it was impossible to meet. Yet the Reformers had pushed their work among the Welsh people, and Church and State alike had shown much eagerness for the translation of the Bible and of the revised formularies and offices of the English Church into the Welsh language. In 1620 Dr. Parry, Bishop of St. Asaph, with the assistance of several Welsh scholars, brought out a revised translation of the whole Bible in accordance with the authorised version of 1611. Protestant dissent at first made but small progress in Wales. John Parry did his utmost to introduce Puritan principles, but with little or no success. It was not till 1639 that the first chapel was opened in Wales for Protestant dissenters. On the other hand, in North Wales especially, there was long-continued attachment to the Roman obedience. The diocese of St. Asaph was early the resort of pilgrims to the holy well of St. Winifred, and this continued throughout the whole reign of Charles I. In 1632 Bishop John Owen reported that "there hath been this summer more than ordinary concourse of people, and more bold and open practice of superstition," and reminded the Government "that at that well a great part of the powder plot was hatched." A year later he complained that "the number and boldness of some Romish recusants increaseth much in many places"; and in 1636 attention was especially called to the undisguised pilgrimage of Elizabeth, Viscountess Falkland, the mother of the famous Lucius, whereupon Charles ordered her imprisonment. The south of Wales had also given shelter to many Roman emissaries. Dom Leander, Laud's old chamber-fellow, was himself a Welshman, and brought back the Benedictines to his native land. The Jesuit mission had been active, and the presentation of recusants was not infrequent at quarter sessions. With Romanism there grew also, but less actively, dissent. In 1636 it was observed that some preached "against the keeping of all holy days, with divers others as fond or profane opinions," and were threatened with the High Commission in consequence. In the diocese of Llandaff, where in 1633 the Bishop certified that he had not one nonconformist or schismatical minister in his diocese, and that there were but two lecturers, and they licensed preachers, there were in 1636 two notable dissentients, Wroth and Erbury, both of them "in the High Commission for their schismatical proceedings." Wroth was an Anabaptist, and it was he who first formed an independent congregation and opened a conventicle.

The growth of dissent, Romanist and Protestant, was due in a large measure to the unfortunate policy of the English State. The courts of the marches exercised jurisdiction that was alike arbitrary and unfortunate.

(2) Negligent rule.

Much good, thought Archbishop Laud in 1636, might be done in Bangor and the other dioceses, "in a

church way," if it were not "overborne by the proceedings" of
those courts, which interfered with his metropolitical jurisdiction. The appointments to the impoverished sees were
generally only of a temporary nature. Men like Wren, Manwaring, and Laud himself were sent to Wales, and were
intended to regard their sees as stepping-stones, even more
than as training grounds, for what were considered to be more
important positions. The unhappy system of translation was
seen at its worst in Wales, and that notably because it was so
frequently coupled with non-residence. Laud himself, who
held, for his age, so high a view of the obligations of the
episcopal office, affords a conspicuous example of their neglect.
Elected Bishop of St. David's on October 10, 1621, it was
not until the following July that he first entered his distant
and in many parts almost inaccessible diocese. On July
22, 1622, he was present in his cathedral church, and
effectually visited the chapter. He visited the diocese also,
but the whole proceedings took hardly more than a month.
It was not till the year of Charles I.'s accession that he paid a
second visit. He had meanwhile built a private chapel for
his house at Abergwili, near Carmarthen, and on Sunday,
August 28, 1625, the eve of the Decollation of St. John
Baptist, as he noted in his diary with affectionate regard
for his old college, he dedicated it to its sacred use, giving
"rich furniture and costly utensils, and whatsoever else was
necessary or convenient for the service of God." This
beautiful chapel, a characteristic record of the great archbishop's connection with the Welsh Church, was destroyed
by fire in 1903. In 1626 Laud was translated to Bath and
Wells. He seems to have done little for his Welsh diocese
save by careful watching it from without and by charitable
benefactions. Theophilus Feild, who was translated from
Llandaff (to which he had been consecrated in 1619) to St.
David's in 1627, and from St. David's to Hereford in 1635,
suffered, he was persistent in declaring, from the poverty of
each see that he held. He owed his earlier promotion to
Buckingham, and to him he wrote, very soon after he became
Bishop of St. David's, "desiring by his means to be translated
to another bishopric, either Ely or Wells." For reasons he
gave "his poverty, his wife, and six children." While Llandaff

and St. David's thus suffered, and were most frequently held by Englishmen, it appears that Bangor was less unfortunate; and it was also from the Reformation till the accession of George I., when Benjamin Hoadly was appointed, always ruled by Welshmen as bishops. The absence of fit persons of native birth, and not merely the indifference of the English sovereign, seems to have been the cause of this neglect of national claims. As an example it may be noted of Laud that when he was Bishop of St. David's he held only two ordinations; at another ember season there appeared before him only one person, and he was "found to be unfit, upon examination," and was "sent away with an exhortation." The loss of the monastic schools had involved, indeed, a loss of systematic religious instruction. In 1636 it was found that "catechising was quite out of use" in the diocese of Bangor. There need be no wonder that opinions, when the time of militant Puritanism came, were not found to be firmly grounded on Holy Scripture or the order of the Church.

It is not surprising that under these conditions morality was not high. Rhŷs Prichard, a strong Puritan but a conformist, and one whom Laud promoted, has left a (3) Low morality. terrible picture in his *Canwyll y Cymry* of the condition of South Wales at this period. Ignorance and vice are represented as dominant everywhere; drunkenness as common, even amongst the clergy, and with it the smoking of tobacco; and the strict observance of Sunday as practically unknown. Education was far behind that of England, and the bi-lingual difficulty was acutely felt. It was said by a writer in 1651 that he had never seen more than five books printed in Welsh. It was some years before the vernacular translation of the Bible was at all widely spread. It was on such soil that Puritanism, largely of English introduction, spread, slowly at first, but at last with power and enthusiasm.

In South Wales the awakening came through William Wroth, vicar of Llanvaches, near Newport, reported as a schismatic in 1635, the founder of the Independent Church of Llanvaches in 1639. His work, and that of William Erbury and Walter Cradock, received an immense impetus through the political effects of the Civil War.

Throughout the war Wales was predominantly Royalist. The Parliament won its way only by fierce fighting and through frequent defeat.   Disaster culminated in 1648 in the destruction of Fleming's troops and the revolt of South Wales.   Before long the work of conversion, at once political and religious, was taken seriously in hand.   In 1641 a Committee of the House of Commons had made provision for preaching in Wales.   The committees for sequestration set to work to expel the parochial clergy who did not conform to the new rule ; notice, it is said, was publicly given that the only way to propagate the Gospel in Wales was to "sequester all ministers without any exception." Before long, in Baxter's words, Harrison was sent to "put down all the parish ministers in Wales."   The work was largely carried out through the enthusiasm, the bitter persistency and the proselytising zeal of Vavasor Powell.   It was not effected without the keenest strife between the sects, or without political conspiracies, which led in 1651 to the execution of a vehement preacher, Christopher Love of Cardiff, for treason.   But it had the strong arm of Cromwell behind it, and the instrument was a singularly drastic and effective piece of legislation.

Results of the war in Wales.

By the Act passed in 1649 "for the better propagation and preaching of the Gospel in Wales " a committee of seventy-two persons was appointed, which had full power to receive charges against all ecclesiastics, and on the oaths of two witnesses to eject the accused from their benefices or preferments.   It was their duty also to replace those ejected, granting certificates to those who should be presented as fit by a committee of twenty-five ministers, among whom were Presbyterians, Anabaptists, and Independents.   The result was in many cases the absence of any spiritual ministration at all.   The inhabitants of Guilsfield, near Welshpool, made petition to the approvers in 1652 that owing to the sequestration of their vicar for delinquency "they had been without communion, without baptism, visiting the sick, or form of a church, the church door being commonly shut on the Lord's Day, as particularly on Easter Day last and the Sunday following ; that the service of God was much decayed and religion scandalised, and that their

Act for Propagation of Gospel in Wales, 1649.

sacred rights are not only withheld, but invectives published against such as shall minister them to us by ambulating preachers, who tell us their sermons are sufficient for salvation, and recompense enough for the tithes we pay, which are exacted of us with all rigour."

It is unnecessary to give details of the working out of this Act. Ejections for the use of the Prayer-book, for "insufficiency," for scandal, were pressed on, under the control of eager commissioners, of whom Vavasor Powell was the most prominent. Walker sums up the result by saying that, when the work was done, "in a word there were no less than seven hundred parishes in the thirteen counties unsupplied with any ministers." Baxter, from another point of view, and in relation to the execution of Love, states the situation as one in which the Commonwealth became odious to the religious party in the land, "except the sectaries [*i.e.* Independents and Anabaptists], for now the people would not believe that they sought the promoting of the Gospel who killed the ministers for the interest of their faction."

In many parts of England the expense of administering the Act by means of commissioners was enormous, and little indeed of the money that was appropriated ever passed into use for spiritual purposes. In 1651 a petition was presented to the Commons from South Wales in which not only were the Commissioners accused of corruption, but it was declared that the country had "neither the comfort of preaching, nor praying, nor sacraments, nor visiting the sick, nor of any decency of burial." Where reform had been hoped for there was confusion and irreligion worse than before. Welshmen like Henry Vaughan, poet and seer, bewailed the day when arbitrary power was triumphant, personified as "the darksome statesman, hung with weights and woe" :—

> Churches and altars fed him ; perjuries
> Were gnats and flies ;
> It rained about him blood and tears, but he
> Drank them as free.

No wonder that the Restoration was welcomed in Wales as enthusiastically as in England.

The settlement of 1661 found Nonconformity established

in Wales.   The licences granted under the Declaration of Indulgence in 1672 show how largely it had spread. Material condition of the Church at the Restoration. And the Church had undergone material as well as spiritual loss, blows which came to complete the work of the Reformation and lay the burden of permanent poverty on the Welsh clergy.   The Welsh churches suffered severely during the wars, and not least those of cathedral rank.   That of St. Asaph was used by Miller, the postmaster, as a stable, and the font was turned into a trough, and the bishop's throne into a manger.   At St. David's the lead roof was stripped off part of the cathedral church ; Llandaff suffered as severely.   The church of Merthyr Tydfil was made a stable.   It was long before the cathedral churches recovered from the devastation of the wars.   Llandaff, indeed, remained practically in ruins till the nineteenth century.   At the beginning of the eighteenth century Browne Willis printed a report which showed the houses of the prebendaries to be ruinous, and the chapter only to have rebuilt a house where they might meet for their rent audit.   Bishop Davies had given them a small library to replace that which was dispersed during the wars.   "This, sir," said the writer when he concluded his sketch, "is the best account I could procure of the cathedral church of Llandaff, in which, if there were not prayers read every day, and the ecclesiastical courts and offices thereunto belonging constantly held in and kept in the village just by, there would be very small signs of its being the mother church of so wealthy and populous a diocese."   The "choir service" had ceased since 1692.   Cardiff, a mile away, had beautified its church and built a new organ, and it was rumoured that there was a design to remove the episcopal see to that "very elegant town."

But the material decay was happily not reproduced in the work of the church.   The twenty years after the Restoration were marked by a serious effort to provide the Bible and literature of devotion for the Welsh people in their own tongue, as well as schools for the young.   The author of the scheme, Thomas Gouge, did not conform to the church, but his good work was helped by many churchmen.   And the years 1660-1714 saw also the labours of many good bishops.

It was in 1669 that the famous Isaac Barrow was translated from the see of Sodor and Man to that of St. Asaph.

The Welsh Episcopate, 1660-1714. He repaired his cathedral church and his palace, built and endowed almshouses, and did many other charitable works.   He became a devoted Welsh bishop, and when he died he was buried near the west door of the cathedral church, where those who entered should pass over his grave.   On it was inscribed the epitaph which he wrote, " O vos transeuntes in Domum Domini, domum orationis, orate pro conservo vestro ut inveniat misericordiam in die Domini."

Among his successors the first was William Lloyd, who was bishop from 1680 to 1692, an active and enterprising ruler, who endeavoured by conference to win over the dissenters, and who insisted upon the most minute information being furnished to him from every parish in his diocese as to the religious condition of the country.   He issued also, with his clergy, in 1683, a number of orders "for the more decent administration of the holy offices."   He took great pains as to ordination, particularly in supplying the diocese with Welshmen, and at the end of his work at St. Asaph he wrote thus well of the position of the Church.   " For the state of the Church in North Wales I bless God I do not know any reason we have to complain.   I am well assured that in these six counties there are not six persons fewer in the communion of our Church than there were in the beginning of his Majesty's reign.   And for them that are in the Church's communion, who are the generality of our people, I thank God I do not find that they grow worse.   I hope they rather grow better ; and that which is my greatest comfort, I do not know of one scandalous churchman in this diocese."   Lloyd was an eminently practical bishop.   He stood firm in essentials, but in matters where political opinions might reasonably differ he would suffer nothing to disturb his spiritual work.   Thus he was one of the seven bishops, but he was not a Nonjuror.   He retained the respect of those with whose action he did not agree.   Very different was his successor, Edward Jones, translated in 1692 by William III. from Cloyne.   Within five years he was accused by several of his clergy of grievous breaches of discipline and of simony, before the Archbishop of Canterbury.   Burnet says that though the evidence was strong, it was not absolutely certain.

Not till 1700 was the sentence pronounced.   The archbishop ordered that he should be suspended for six months, and, further, till he should give satisfaction.   The case of Thomas Watson, Bishop of St. David's, was similar.   Even he, when he was charged with simony, found defenders.   Burnet declares that he was " passionate, covetous, and false, in the blackest instances, without any one virtue or good quality to support his bad ones," but Browne Willis asserts that the charges of simony were "pretended," and that all the while he was bishop he was "much maligned, and not long after his election intolerably affronted by the rabble."   The same writer describes him as still living, in retirement, in 1717, and says that he "being an opulent man, has disbursed several sums in charity, and on the public, as may be seen in a book entitled *A large summary View of the Articles exhibited against him, and the proofs made thereon, printed in the year* 1702," which declared that the real reason of the attacks made on the bishop was his attempt to enforce residence on the canons of St. David's and some of the parochial clergy.   The case, how- ever, seemed to Tenison to be clear enough, and Watson was deprived on August 3, 1699.   Welsh bishops, however, must not be judged by such scandalous cases.   The life of their dioceses was much apart from that of England : of the good they did English writers knew nothing.   Many lived quiet, estimable lives in their dioceses among their kindred and their clergy.   Others who filled a wider space in men's thoughts had won fame in England, and of these notably William Beveridge and George Bull.

The former was Bishop of St. Asaph from 1704 to 1709, but his real distinction belongs to his earlier life as a scholar and a parish priest.   Pious and indefatigably diligent he appeared even to the critical Denis Gren- ville, who said of him when he was a London clergyman (at St. Peter's, Cornhill) that "the devout practice and order of his church doth exceedingly edify the city, and his congregation in- creases every week."   He was very anxious to forward the work of the religious societies, and to spread their publications in Wales in the language of the people ; but he cannot be said to have left any deep mark on the Welsh Church.   The same is true of George Bull, Bishop of St. David's from 1705 to 1709.

Bishops Beveridge and Bull.

His fame as a scholar and theologian was spread over Europe : his simple and dutiful piety as a parish priest was known to his many eminent and devoted friends.   He was very reluctant to undertake the episcopal office.   Nelson, his biographer, gives reasons which he at least hints were Bull's.   " It is not without reason that persons of the strongest virtue, in the vigour of their days, who best deserve the most honourable employments in the Church, have been most afraid of being advanced to them ; it requireth great firmness of mind not to be dazzled with that honour which adorneth the episcopal throne ; and how difficult it is to be exalted, and not to love the pre-eminence !   The respect and obsequiousness of inferiors insensibly corrupt the mind, and when men are placed above reproof they quickly begin to persuade themselves that they do not stand in need of it."   It was not indeed till he was "earnestly solicited by several of the governors of the Church, which he looked upon as the call of Providence," that the humble and simple-hearted scholar would consent to be consecrated.   He was aged and infirm, but he determined from the first to live entirely in his diocese, and to visit with a thorough oversight.   The visitation, owing to his illness, was conducted for him in 1708 by commissioners, but his charge was an exhortation of extreme impressiveness to the discharge of every clerical duty.   He urged his clergy to become examples to their people of eminent holiness, "which they are obliged to, not only as Christians, but as priests of the living God " ; he dwelt earnestly on the need for audible, distinct, and resonant reading of Divine service, on catechising, on preaching, and on study of the Scriptures ; and "he exhorted to great reverence and solemnity in officiating at the altar, and to the observance of every punctilio, according to the rubrics compiled for that purpose."   In the standard of attainment, spiritual as well as intellectual, which he required from those to be ordained, he set a shining example to the bishops of his see.   Nelson describes with touching eloquence the hours of exhortation, of fasting and prayer, which were spent with, and the exhortations which were given to those upon whom he laid his hands.   He set himself the constant example of obedience by attending the public prayers in church twice a day.   He was eagerly devoted to the work of his diocese,

and short though the time was in which he held office and
great as his infirmities were, he left a memory of encouragement and refreshment to the Church in Wales.   The period
closes, at St. David's, with Adam Ottley, a zealous, earnest, and
active prelate, who set himself to restore the cathedral church,
dilapidated and despoiled.

At Llandaff a curious, and in some ways typical, figure is
that of William Beaw, who held the see from 1679 to his
death in 1706.   He had fought, like Peter Mews, in the Civil
Wars on the king's side.   He was rewarded at last with " a
little bishopric," from which he was always anxious to be
moved to a better," but he remained at Llandaff to the end,
doing his duty with soberness if not diligence.   Under him
it seems clear that the priests ordained to Welsh titles were
almost always of Welsh blood, and that Nonconformity was
neither popular nor strong.

But the Church had not really recovered from the experience of disestablishment and confiscation, or from the effects
of the action of the State.   At the close of the   Conclusion
period the primary charge of Bishop Fleetwood to   of the
the diocese of St. Asaph in 1710 shows the evils   period.
from which the Church was increasingly to suffer to have
already attracted the attention of reformers.   The one was
non-residence, the other neglect of preaching, particularly in
Welsh.   They were not new.   Bishop Morgan in 1666 had
called attention to the same evils.   In spite of Bishop Bull's
earnest advice to the clergy as to the use of Welsh, it became
more and more neglected, with the natural results.   Where so
many of the churches were served by the poorly-paid curates
of non-resident incumbents, it is not surprising that services
were cut down or omitted, and that parochial visitation almost
ceased.   The complaint of decay of preaching was an old one,
perhaps not more common in Wales than in England.   It was
heard often before the wars ; it did not cease during the
Commonwealth or at the Restoration.   It was the same with
the other abuse, non-residence.   William Lucy, Bishop of St.
David's from 1660 to 1683, began, say contemporary authorities, the encouragement or sanction of non-residence among
his cathedral clergy.   "From hence," says Browne Willis,
" came all the calamities of St. David's, under which herculean

labour Bishop Watson sank in extricating and restoring the cathedral church." He, or Bishop Thomas, proposed indeed to remove the see to Carmarthen, near which, at Abergwili, he was himself resident. Happily the protests of the people of Dewisland prevented so disastrous a breach with the famous past.

Thus we have the Church in Wales struggling still after the years of worst stress were over. Though the number of University graduates ordained has been shown to have been declining, the standard of learning among the clergy was not low. During the seventeenth century Wales gave four bishops to English, four to Irish sees, as well as the eighteen Welshmen who became bishops in their own land. But the political influences of the eighteenth century went far to undo much of the good work that had been done in the seventeenth. Here the similarity with England is close ; and, indeed, as we close our survey we are struck by the importance of the ties which bound the Church together in different parts of our island. Unity, the lesson that the Caroline divines never wearied of preaching, was attained in the English Church in a way which under Elizabeth might well have seemed impossible.

AUTHORITIES.—State Papers, Domestic ; Laud, *Works*, especially his diary and reports of his province to the King ; MSS. of the chapter of St. David's, notably the chapter register, the *Collectanea Menevensia* of Canon Payne, and the valuable (eighteenth century) note-books of Archdeacon Yardley ; Prynne, *Canterburie's Doome ;* muniments of the Bishop of St. David's (preserved in 1894, when I inspected them, at Abergwili) ; Browne Willis, *Surveys of the Cathedral Churches :* of *St. David's* (1717), *Llandaff* (1719), *St. Asaph* (1720), *Bangor* (1721); Jones and Freeman, *History and Antiquities of St. David's* (1856) ; Walker, *Memorials, etc. ;* E. J. Newell, *Llandaff ;* W. L. Bevan, *St. David's ;* D. R. Thomas, *St. Asaph* (each in *Diocesan Histories*) ; Nelson, *Life of Bishop Bull ;* on Adam Ottley see the MS. poem of Browne Willis quoted by Jones and Freeman, pp. 334-5 ; *Reliquiæ Baxterianæ*, 1676 ; Prichard, *Canwyll y Cymry*, 1646 ; *Life and Death of Rev. Vavasor Powell*, 1671.

APPENDIX II

KINGS OF ENGLAND	Accession.	ARCHBISHOPS OF CANTERBURY	Accession.	ARCHBISHOPS OF YORK	Accession.
Charles I.	1625	George Abbot .	1610	Tobias Matthew	1606
				George Montaigne .	1628
				Samuel Harsnett .	1628
		William Laud .	1633	Richard Neile .	1632
				John Williams .	1641
(Interregnum) .	1649	(See Vacant from 1645) .		(See Vacant from 1650)	
Charles II.	1660	William Juxon .	1660	Accepted Frewen .	1660
		Gilbert Sheldon .	1663	Richard Sterne .	1664
		William Sancroft .	1677		
James II.	1685			John Dolben .	1683
William III. and Mary II.	1689	John Tillotson	1691	Thomas Lamplugh .	1688
William III. (alone) .	1694	Thomas Tenison	1695	John Sharp .	1691
Anne .	1702				

INDEX